Accuracy and Reliability in Scientific Computing

SOFTWARE • ENVIRONMENTS • TOOLS

The series includes handbooks and software guides as well as monographs
on practical implementation of computational methods, environments, and tools.
The focus is on making recent developments available in a practical format
to researchers and other users of these methods and tools.

Editor-in-Chief

Jack J. Dongarra
University of Tennessee and Oak Ridge National Laboratory

Editorial Board

James W. Demmel, University of California, Berkeley
Dennis Gannon, Indiana University
Eric Grosse, AT&T Bell Laboratories
Ken Kennedy, Rice University
Jorge J. Moré, Argonne National Laboratory

Software, Environments, and Tools

Bo Einarsson, editor, *Accuracy and Reliabilty in Scientific Computing*

Michael W. Berry and Murray Browne, *Understanding Search Engines: Mathematical Modeling and Text Retrieval, Second Edition*

Craig C. Douglas, Gundolf Haase, and Ulrich Langer, *A Tutorial on Elliptic PDE Solvers and Their Parallelization*

Louis Komzsik, *The Lanczos Method: Evolution and Application*

Bard Ermentrout, *Simulating, Analyzing, and Animating Dynamical Systems: A Guide to XPPAUT for Researchers and Students*

V. A. Barker, L. S. Blackford, J. Dongarra, J. Du Croz, S. Hammarling, M. Marinova, J. Waśniewski, and P. Yalamov, *LAPACK95 Users' Guide*

Stefan Goedecker and Adolfy Hoisie, *Performance Optimization of Numerically Intensive Codes*

Zhaojun Bai, James Demmel, Jack Dongarra, Axel Ruhe, and Henk van der Vorst, *Templates for the Solution of Algebraic Eigenvalue Problems: A Practical Guide*

Lloyd N. Trefethen, *Spectral Methods in MATLAB*

E. Anderson, Z. Bai, C. Bischof, S. Blackford, J. Demmel, J. Dongarra, J. Du Croz, A. Greenbaum, S. Hammarling, A. McKenney, and D. Sorensen, *LAPACK Users' Guide, Third Edition*

Michael W. Berry and Murray Browne, *Understanding Search Engines: Mathematical Modeling and Text Retrieval*

Jack J. Dongarra, Iain S. Duff, Danny C. Sorensen, and Henk A. van der Vorst, *Numerical Linear Algebra for High-Performance Computers*

R. B. Lehoucq, D. C. Sorensen, and C. Yang, *ARPACK Users' Guide: Solution of Large-Scale Eigenvalue Problems with Implicitly Restarted Arnoldi Methods*

Randolph E. Bank, *PLTMG: A Software Package for Solving Elliptic Partial Differential Equations, Users' Guide 8.0*

L. S. Blackford, J. Choi, A. Cleary, E. D'Azevedo, J. Demmel, I. Dhillon, J. Dongarra, S. Hammarling, G. Henry, A. Petitet, K. Stanley, D. Walker, and R. C. Whaley, *ScaLAPACK Users' Guide*

Greg Astfalk, editor, *Applications on Advanced Architecture Computers*

Françoise Chaitin-Chatelin and Valérie Frayssé, *Lectures on Finite Precision Computations*

Roger W. Hockney, *The Science of Computer Benchmarking*

Richard Barrett, Michael Berry, Tony F. Chan, James Demmel, June Donato, Jack Dongarra, Victor Eijkhout, Roldan Pozo, Charles Romine, and Henk van der Vorst, *Templates for the Solution of Linear Systems: Building Blocks for Iterative Methods*

E. Anderson, Z. Bai, C. Bischof, J. Demmel, J. Dongarra, J. Du Croz, A. Greenbaum, S. Hammarling, A. McKenney, S. Ostrouchov, and D. Sorensen, *LAPACK Users' Guide, Second Edition*

Jack J. Dongarra, Iain S. Duff, Danny C. Sorensen, and Henk van der Vorst, *Solving Linear Systems on Vector and Shared Memory Computers*

J. J. Dongarra, J. R. Bunch, C. B. Moler, and G. W. Stewart, *Linpack Users' Guide*

Accuracy and Reliability in Scientific Computing

Edited by
Bo Einarsson
Linköping University
Linköping, Sweden

siam.

Society for Industrial and Applied Mathematics
Philadelphia

MATLAB® is a registered trademark of The MathWorks, Inc. For MATLAB® product information, please contact The MathWorks, Inc., 3 Apple Hill Drive, Natick, MA 01760-2098 USA, 508-647-7000, Fax: 508-647-7101, *info@mathworks.com, www.mathworks.com/*

Trademarked names may be used in this book without the inclusion of a trademark symbol. These names are used in an editorial context only; no infringement of trademark is intended.

Library of Congress Cataloging-in-Publication Data

Accuracy and reliability in scientific computing / edited by Bo Einarsson.
        p. cm. — (Software, environments, tools)
    Includes bibliographical references and index.
    ISBN 0-89871-584-9 (pbk.)
    1. Science—Data processing. 2. Reliability (Engineering)—Mathematics. 3. Computer programs—Correctness—Scientific applications. 4. Software productivity—Scientific applications. I. Einarsson, Bo, 1939- II. Series.

Q183.9.A28 2005
502'.85—dc22

                                                                          2005047019

Contents

11   Hardware-assisted Algorithms   241
  Craig C. Douglas, Hans Petter Langtangen

12   Issues in Accurate and Reliable Use of Parallel Computing in
  Numerical Programs   253
  William D. Gropp

13   Software-reliability Engineering of Numerical Systems   265
  Mladen A. Vouk

List of Contributors

Ronald F. Boisvert
*Mathematical and Computational Sciences Division, National Institute of Standards and Technology (NIST), Mail Stop 8910, Gaithersburg, MD 20899, USA,
email:* boisvert@nist.gov

Françoise Chaitin-Chatelin
*Université Toulouse 1 and CERFACS (Centre Européen de Recherche et de Formation Avancée en Calcul Scientifique), 42 av. G. Coriolis, FR-31057 Toulouse Cedex, France,
e-mail:* chatelin@cerfacs.fr

Ronald Cools
*Department of Computer Science, Katholieke Universiteit Leuven, Celestijnenlaan 200A, B-3001 Heverlee, Belgium,
email:* Ronald.Cools@cs.kuleuven.be

Craig C. Douglas
*Center for Computational Sciences, University of Kentucky, Lexington, Kentucky 40506-0045, USA,
email:* douglas@ccs.uky.edu

Kenneth W. Dritz
*Argonne National Laboratory, 9700 South Cass Avenue, Argonne, Illinois 60439, USA,
email:* dritz@anl.gov

Bo Einarsson
*National Supercomputer Centre and the Mathematics Department, Linköpings universitet, SE-581 83 Linköping, Sweden,
email:* boein@nsc.liu.se

Wayne H. Enright
*Department of Computer Science, University of Toronto, Toronto, Canada M5S 3G4,
email:* enright@cs.utoronto.ca

William D. Gropp
*Argonne National Laboratory, 9700 South Cass Avenue, Argonne, Illinois 60439, USA,
email:* gropp@mcs.anl.gov

Sven Hammarling
*The Numerical Algorithms Group Ltd, Wilkinson House, Jordan Hill Road, Oxford OX2 8DR, England,
email:* sven@nag.co.uk

Hans Petter Langtangen
*Institutt for informatikk, Universitetet i Oslo, Box 1072 Blindern, NO-0316 Oslo, and Simula Research Laboratory, NO-1325 Lysaker, Norway,
email:* hpl@simula.no

Roldan Pozo
*Mathematical and Computational Sciences Division, National Institute of Standards and Technology (NIST), Mail Stop 8910, Gaithersburg, MD 20899, USA,
email:* boisvert@nist.gov

Siegfried M. Rump
Institut für Informatik III, Technische Universität Hamburg-Harburg, Schwarzenbergstrasse 95, DE-21071 Hamburg, Germany,
email: rump@tu-harburg.de

Van Snyder
Jet Propulsion Laboratory, 4800 Oak Grove Drive, Mail Stop 183-701, Pasadena, CA 91109, USA,
email: van.snyder@jpl.nasa.gov

Elisabeth Traviesas-Cassan
CERFACS, Toulouse, France. Presently at TRANSICIEL Technologies, FR-31025 Toulouse Cedex, France,
e-mail: ecassan@mail.transiciel.com

Mladen A. Vouk
Department of Computer Science, Box 8206, North Carolina State University, Raleigh, NC 27695, USA,
email: vouk@csc.ncsu.edu

G. William Walster
Sun Microsystems Laboratories, 16 Network Circle, MS UMPK16-160, Menlo Park, CA 94025, USA,
email: bill.walster@sun.com

Brian Wichmann
Retired,
email: Brian.Wichmann@bcs.org.uk

List of Figures

List of Tables

Preface

Much of the software available today is poorly written, inadequate in its facilities, and altogether a number of years behind the most advanced state of the art.
—Professor Maurice V. Wilkes, September 1973.

Scientific software is central to our computerized society. It is used to design airplanes and bridges, to operate manufacturing lines, to control power plants and refineries, to analyze financial derivatives, to map genomes, and to provide the understanding necessary for the diagnosis and treatment of cancer. Because of the high stakes involved, it is essential that the software be accurate and reliable. Unfortunately, developing accurate and reliable scientific software is notoriously difficult, and Maurice Wilkes' assessment of 1973 still rings true today. Not only is scientific software beset with all the well-known problems affecting software development in general, it must cope with the special challenges of numerical computation. Approximations occur at all levels. Continuous functions are replaced by discretized versions. Infinite processes are replaced by finite ones. Real numbers are replaced by finite precision numbers. As a result, errors are built into the mathematical fabric of scientific software which cannot be avoided. At best they can be judiciously managed. The nature of these errors, and how they are propagated, must be understood if the resulting software is to be accurate and reliable. The objective of this book is to investigate the nature of some of these difficulties, and to provide some insight into how to overcome them.

The book is divided into three parts.

1. **Pitfalls in Numerical Computation.**
   We first illustrate some of the difficulties in producing robust and reliable scientific software. Well-known cases of failure by scientific software are reviewed, and the "what" and "why" of numerical computations are considered.

2. **Diagnostic Tools.**
   We next describe tools that can be used to assess the accuracy and reliability of existing scientific applications. Such tools do not necessarily improve results, but they can be used to increase one's confidence in their validity.

3. **Technology for Improving Accuracy and Reliability.**
   We describe a variety of techniques that can be employed to improve the accuracy and reliability of newly developed scientific applications. In particular, we consider the effect of the choice of programming language, underlying hardware, and the parallel

computing environment. We provide a description of interval data types and their application to validated computations.

This book has been produced by the International Federation for Information Processing (IFIP) Working Group 2.5. An arm of the IFIP Technical Committee 2 on Software Practice and Experience, WG 2.5 seeks to improve the quality of numerical computation by promoting the development and availability of sound numerical software. WG 2.5 has been fortunate to be able to assemble a set of contributions from authors with a wealth of experience in the development and assessment of numerical software. The following WG 2.5 members participated in this project: Ronald Boisvert, Françoise Chaitin-Chatelin, Ronald Cools, Craig Douglas, Bo Einarsson, Wayne Enright, Patrick Gaffney, Ian Gladwell, William Gropp, Jim Pool, Siegfried Rump, Brian Smith, Van Snyder, Michael Thuné, Mladen Vouk, and Wolfgang Walter. Additional contributions were made by Kenneth W. Dritz, Sven Hammarling, Hans Petter Langtangen, Roldan Pozo, Elisabeth Traviesas-Cassan, Bill Walster, and Brian Wichmann. The volume was edited by Bo Einarsson.

Several of the contributions have been presented at other venues in somewhat different forms. Chapter 1 was presented at the Workshop on Scientific Computing and the Computational Sciences, May 28–29, 2001, in Amsterdam, The Netherlands. Chapter 5 was presented at the IFIP Working Group 2.5 Meeting, May 26–27, 2001, in Amsterdam, The Netherlands. Four of the chapters—6, 7, 10, and 13—are based on lectures presented at the SIAM Minisymposium on Accuracy and Reliability in Scientific Computing held July 9, 2001, in San Diego, California. Chapter 10 was also presented at the Annual Conference of Japan SIAM at Kyushu-University, Fukuoka, October 7–9, 2001.

The book has an accompanying web http://www.nsc.liu.se/wg25/book/ with updates, codes, links, color versions of some of the illustrations, and additional material.

A problem with references to links on the internet is that, as Diomidis Spinellis has shown in [422], the half-life of a referenced URL is approximately four years from its publication date. The accompanying website will contain updated links.

A number of trademarked products are identified in this book. Java, Java HotSpot, and SUN are trademarks of Sun Microsystems, Inc. Pentium and Itanium are trademarks of Intel. PowerPC is a trademark of IBM. Microsoft Windows is a trademark of Microsoft. Apple is a trademark of Apple Computer, Inc. NAG is a trademark of The Numerical Algorithms Group, Ltd. MATLAB is a trademark of The MathWorks, Inc.

While we expect that developing accurate and reliable scientific software will remain a challenging enterprise for some time to come, we believe that techniques and tools are now beginning to emerge to improve the process. If this volume aids in the recognition of the problems and helps point developers in the direction of solutions, then this volume will have been a success.

Linköping and Gaithersburg, September 15, 2004.

Bo Einarsson, Project Leader

Ronald F. Boisvert, Chair, IFIP Working Group 2.5

Acknowledgment

As editor I wish to thank the contributors and the additional project members for supporting the project through submitting and refereeing the chapters. I am also very grateful to the anonymous reviewers who did a marvelous job, gave constructive criticism and much appreciated comments and suggestions. The final book did benefit quite a lot from their work!

I also thank the National Supercomputer Centre and the Mathematics Department of Linköpings universitet for supporting the project.

Working with SIAM on the publication of this book was a pleasure. Special thanks go to Simon Dickey, Elizabeth Greenspan, Ann Manning Allen, and Linda Thiel, for all their assistance.

Bo Einarsson

Part I

PITFALLS IN NUMERICAL COMPUTATION

Chapter 1

What Can Go Wrong in Scientific Computing?

Bo Einarsson

1.1 Introduction

Numerical software is central to our computerized society. It is used, for example, to design airplanes and bridges, to operate manufacturing lines, to control power plants and refineries, to analyze financial derivatives, to determine genomes, and to provide the understanding necessary for the treatment for cancer. Because of the high stakes involved, it is essential that the software be accurate, reliable, and robust.

A report [385] written for the National Institute of Standards and Technology (NIST) states that software bugs cost the U.S. economy about $ 60 billion each year, and that more than a third of that cost, or $ 22 billion, could be eliminated by improved testing. Note that these figures apply to software in general, not only to scientific software. An article [18] stresses that computer system failures are usually rooted in human error rather than technology. The article gives a few examples: delivery problems at a computer company, radio system outage for air traffic control, delayed financial aid. Many companies are now working on reducing the complexity of testing but are still requiring it to be robust.

The objective of this book is to investigate some of the difficulties related to scientific computing, such as accuracy requirements and rounding, and to provide insight into how to obtain accurate and reliable results.

This chapter serves as an introduction and consists of three sections. In Section 1.2 we discuss some basic problems in numerical computation, like rounding, cancellation, and recursion. In Section 1.3 we discuss implementation of real arithmetic on computers, and in Section 1.4 we discuss some cases where unreliable computations have caused loss of life or property.

1.2 Basic Problems in Numerical Computation

Some illustrative examples are given in this section, but further examples and discussion can be found in Chapter 4.

Two problems in numerical computation are that often the input values are not known exactly, and that some of the calculations cannot be performed exactly. The errors obtained can cooperate in later calculations, causing an error growth, which may be quite large.

Rounding is the cause of an error, while cancellation increases its effect and recursion may cause a build-up of the final error.

1.2.1 Rounding

The calculations are usually performed with a certain fixed number of significant digits, so after each operation the result usually has to be rounded, introducing a rounding error whose modulus in the optimal case is less than or equal to half a unit in the last digit. At the next computation this rounding error has to be taken into account, as well as a new rounding error. The propagation of the rounding error is therefore quite complex.

Example 1.1 (Rounding) Consider the following MATLAB code for advancing from a to b with the step $h = (b - a)/n$.

```
function step(a,b,n)
% step from a to b with n steps
h=(b-a)/n;
x=a;
disp(x)
while x < b,
  x = x + h;
  disp(x)
end
```

We get one step too many with $a = 1$, $b = 2$, and $n = 3$, but the correct number of steps with $b = 1.1$. In the first case because of the rounding downward of $h = 1/3$ after three steps we are almost but not quite at b, and therefore the loop continues. In the second case also b is an inexact number on a binary computer, and the inexact values of x and b happen to compare as wanted. It is advisable to let such a loop work with an integer variable instead of a real variable. If real variables are used it is advisable to replace `while  x  <  b` with `while  x  <  b-h/2`. ∎

The example was run in IEEE 754 double precision, discussed in section 1.3.2. In another precision a different result may be obtained!

1.2.2 Cancellation

Cancellation occurs from the subtraction of two almost equal quantities. Assume $x_1 = 1.243 \pm 0.0005$ and $x_2 = 1.234 \pm 0.0005$. We then obtain $x_1 - x_2 = 0.009 \pm 0.001$, a result where several significant leading digits have been lost, resulting in a large relative error!

Example 1.2 (Quadratic equation) The roots of the equation $ax^2 + bx + c = 0$ are given by the following mathematically, but not numerically, equivalent expressions:

$$x_{1,2}^{\alpha} = \frac{-b \pm \sqrt{b^2 - 4ac}}{2a},$$

$$x_{1,2}^{\beta} = \frac{-2c}{b \pm \sqrt{b^2 - 4ac}}.$$

Using IEEE 754 single precision and $a = 1.0 \cdot 10^{-5}$, $b = 1.0 \cdot 10^3$, and $c = 1.0 \cdot 10^3$ we get $x_1^{\alpha} = -3.0518$, $x_2^{\alpha} = -1.0000 \cdot 10^8$, $x_1^{\beta} = -1.0000$, and $x_2^{\beta} = -3.2768 \cdot 10^7$. We thus get two very different sets of roots for the equation! The reason is that since b^2 is much larger than $4|ac|$ the square root will get a value very close to $|b|$, and when the subtraction of two almost equal values is performed the error in the square root evaluation will dominate. In double precision the value of the square root of $10^6 - 0.04$ is 999.9999799999998, which is very close to $b = 1000$. The two correct roots in this case are one from each set, x_2^{α} and x_1^{β}, for which there is addition of quantities of the same sign, and no cancellation occurs. ■

Example 1.3 (Exponential function) The exponential function e^x can be evaluated using the MacLaurin series expansion. This works reasonably well for $x > 0$ but not for $x < -3$ where the expansion terms a_n will alternate in sign and the modulus of the terms will increase until $n \approx |x|$. Even for moderate values of x the cancellation can be so severe that a negative value of the function is obtained! ■

Using double (or multiple) precision is not the cure for cancellation, but switching to another algorithm may help. In order to avoid cancellation in Example 1.2 we let the sign of b decide which formula to use, and in Example 1.3 we use the relation $e^{-x} = 1/e^x$.

1.2.3 Recursion

A common method in scientific computing is to calculate a new entity based on the previous one, and continuing in that way, either in an iterative process (hopefully converging) or in a recursive process calculating new values all the time. In both cases the errors can accumulate and finally destroy the computation.

Example 1.4 (Differential equation) Let us look at the solution of a first order differential equation $y' = f(x, y)$. A well-known numerical method is the Euler method $y_{n+1} = y_n + h \cdot f(x_n, y_n)$. Two alternatives with smaller truncation errors are the midpoint method $y_{n+1} = y_{n-1} + 2h \cdot f(x_n, y_n)$, which has the obvious disadvantage that it requires two starting points, and the trapezoidal method $y_{n+1} = y_n + \frac{h}{2} \cdot [f(x_n, y_n) + f(x_{n+1}, y_{n+1})]$, which has the obvious disadvantage that it is implicit.

Theoretical analysis shows that the Euler method is stable[1] for small h, and the midpoint method is always unstable, while the trapezoidal method is always stable. Numerical experiments on the test problem $y' = -2y$ with the exact solution $y(x) = e^{-2x}$ confirm that the midpoint method gives a solution which oscillates wildly.[2] ■

---

[1]Stability can be defined such that if the analytic solution tends to zero as the independent variable tends to infinity, then also the numeric solution should tend to zero.

[2]Compare with Figures 4.6 and 4.7 in Chapter 4.

1.2.4 Integer overflow

There is also a problem with integer arithmetic: integer overflow is usually not signaled. This can cause numerical problems, for example, in the calculation of the factorial function "$n!$". Writing the code in a natural way using repeated multiplication on a computer with 32 bit integer arithmetic, the factorials up to 12! are all correctly evaluated, but 13! gets the wrong value and 17! becomes negative. The range of floating-point values is usually larger than the range of integers, but the best solution is usually not to evaluate the factorial function. When evaluating the Taylor formula you instead successively multiply $\frac{(x-a)^n}{n!}$ with $\frac{x-a}{n+1}$ for each n to get the next term, thus avoiding computing the large quantity $n!$. The factorial function overflows at $n = 35$ in IEEE single precision and at $n = 171$ in IEEE double precision.

Multiple integer overflow vulnerabilities in a Microsoft Windows library (before a patch was applied) could have allowed an unauthenticated, remote attacker to execute arbitrary code with system privileges [460].

1.3   Floating-point Arithmetic

During the 1960's almost every computer manufacturer had its own hardware and its own representation of floating-point numbers. Floating-point numbers are used for variables with a wide range of values, so that the value is represented by its sign, its mantissa, represented by a fixed number of leading digits, and one signed integer for the exponent, as in the representation of the mass of the earth $5.972 \cdot 10^{24}$ kg or the mass of an electron $9.10938188 \cdot 10^{-31}$ kg.

An introduction to floating-point arithmetic is given in Section 4.2.

The old and different floating-point representations had some flaws; on one popular computer there existed values $a > 0$ such that $a > 2 \cdot a$. This mathematical impossibility was obtained from the fact that a nonnormalized number (a number with an exponent that is too small to be represented) was automatically normalized to zero at multiplication.[3]

Such an effect can give rise to a problem in a program which tries to avoid division by zero by checking that $a \neq 0$, but still $1/a$ may cause the condition "division by zero."

1.3.1   Initial work on an arithmetic standard

During the 1970's Professor William Kahan of the University of California at Berkeley became interested in defining a floating-point arithmetic standard; see [248]. He managed to assemble a group of scientists, including both academics and industrial representatives (Apple, DEC, Intel, HP, Motorola), under the auspices of the IEEE.[4] The group became known as project 754. Its purpose was to produce the best possible definition of floating-point arithmetic. It is now possible to say that they succeeded; all manufacturers now follow the representation of IEEE 754. Some old systems with other representations are however

---

[3]Consider a decimal system with two digits for the exponent, and three digits for the mantissa, normalized so that the mantissa is not less than 1 but less than 10. Then the smallest positive normalized number is $1.00 \cdot 10^{-99}$ but the smallest positive nonnormalized number is $0.01 \cdot 10^{-99}$.

[4]Institute for Electrical and Electronic Engineers, USA.

still available from Cray, Digital (now HP), and IBM, but all new systems also from these manufacturers follow IEEE 754.

The resulting standard was rather similar to the DEC floating-point arithmetic on the VAX system.[5]

1.3.2 IEEE floating-point representation

The IEEE 754 [226] contains single, extended single, double, and extended double precision. It became an IEEE standard [215] in 1985 and an IEC[6] standard in 1989. There is an excellent discussion in the book [355].

In the following subsections the format for the different precisions are given, but the standard includes much more than these formats. It requires correctly rounded operations (add, subtract, multiply, divide, remainder, and square root) as well as correctly rounded format conversion. There are four rounding modes (round down, round up, round toward zero, and round to nearest), with round to nearest as the default. There are also five exception types (invalid operation, division by zero, overflow, underflow, and inexact) which must be signaled by setting a status flag.

1.3.2.1 IEEE single precision

Single precision is based on the 32 bit word, using 1 bit for the sign s, 8 bits for the biased exponent e, and the remaining 23 bits for the fractional part f of the mantissa. The fact that a normalized number in binary representation must have the integer part of the mantissa equal to 1 is used, and this bit therefore does not have to be stored, which actually increases the accuracy.

There are five cases:

1. $e = 255$ and $f \neq 0$ give an x which is not a number (NaN).
2. $e = 255$ and $f = 0$ give infinity with its sign,
   $x = (-1)^s \cdot \infty$.
3. $1 \leq e \leq 254$, the normal case,
   $x = (-1)^s \cdot (1.f) \cdot 2^{e-127}$.
   Note that the smallest possible exponent gives numbers of the form
   $x = (-1)^s \cdot (1.f) \cdot 2^{-126}$.
4. $e = 0$ and $f \neq 0$, gradual underflow, subnormal numbers,
   $x = (-1)^s \cdot (0.f) \cdot 2^{-126}$.
5. $e = 0$ and $f = 0$, zero with its sign,
   $x = (-1)^s \cdot 0$.

The largest number that can be represented is $(2 - 2^{-23}) \cdot 2^{127} \approx 3.4028 \cdot 10^{38}$, the smallest positive normalized number is $1 \cdot 2^{-126} \approx 1.1755 \cdot 10^{-38}$, and the smallest

---

[5]After 22 successful years, starting 1978 with the VAX 11/780, the VAX platform was phased out. HP will continue to support VAX customers.

[6] The International Electrotechnical Commission handles information about electric, electronic, and electrotechnical international standards and compliance and conformity assessment for electronics.

positive nonnormalized number is $2^{-23} \cdot 2^{-126} = 2^{-149} \approx 1.4013 \cdot 10^{-45}$. The unit roundoff $\mathbf{u} = 2^{-24} \approx 5.9605 \cdot 10^{-8}$ corresponds to about seven decimal digits.

The concept of gradual underflow has been rather difficult for the user community to accept, but it is very useful in that there is no unnecessary loss of information. Without gradual underflow, a positive number less than the smallest permitted one must either be rounded up to the smallest permitted one or replaced with zero, in both cases causing a large relative error.

The NaN can be used to represent (zero/zero), (infinity - infinity), and other quantities that do not have a known value. Note that the computation does not have to stop for overflow, since the infinity NaN can be used until a calculation with it does not give a well-determined value. The sign of zero is useful only in certain cases.

1.3.2.2 IEEE extended single precision

The purpose of extended precision is to make it possible to evaluate subexpressions to full single precision. The details are implementation dependent, but the number of bits in the fractional part f has to be at least 31, and the exponent, which may be biased, has to have at least the range $-1022 \leq exponent \leq 1023$. IEEE double precision satisfies these requirements!

1.3.2.3 IEEE double precision

Double precision is based on two 32 bit words (or one 64 bit word), using 1 bit for the sign s, 11 bits for the biased exponent e, and the remaining 52 bits for the fractional part f of the mantissa. It is very similar to single precision, with an implicit bit for the integer part of the mantissa, a biased exponent, and five cases:

1. $e = 2047$ and $f \neq 0$ give an x which is not a number (NaN).
2. $e = 2047$ and $f = 0$ give infinity with its sign,
   $x = (-1)^s \cdot \infty$.
3. $1 \leq e \leq 2046$, the normal case,
   $x = (-1)^s \cdot (1.f) \cdot 2^{e-1023}$.
   Note that the smallest possible exponent gives numbers of the form
   $x = (-1)^s \cdot (1.f) \cdot 2^{-1022}$.
4. $e = 0$ and $f \neq 0$, gradual underflow, subnormal numbers,
   $x = (-1)^s \cdot (0.f) \cdot 2^{-1022}$.
5. $e = 0$ and $f = 0$, zero with its sign,
   $x = (-1)^s \cdot 0$.

The largest number that can be represented is $(2 - 2^{-52}) \cdot 2^{1023} \approx 1.7977 \cdot 10^{308}$, the smallest positive normalized number is $1 \cdot 2^{-1022} \approx 2.2251 \cdot 10^{-308}$, and the smallest positive nonnormalized number is $2^{-52} \cdot 2^{-1022} = 2^{-1074} \approx 4.9407 \cdot 10^{-324}$. The unit roundoff $\mathbf{u} = 2^{-53} \approx 1.1102 \cdot 10^{-16}$ corresponds to about 16 decimal digits.

The fact that the exponent is wider for double precision is a useful innovation not available, for example, on the IBM System 360.[7] On the DEC VAX/VMS two different double precisions D and G were available: D with the same exponent range as in single precision, and G with a wider exponent range. The choice between the two double precisions was done via a compiler switch at compile time. In addition there was a quadruple precision H.

1.3.2.4   IEEE extended double precision

The purpose of extended double precision is to make it possible to evaluate subexpressions to full double precision. The details are implementation dependent, but the number of bits in the fractional part f has to be at least 63, and the number of bits in the exponent part has to be at least 15.

1.3.3   Future standards

There is also an IEEE Standard for Radix-Independent Floating-Point Arithmetic, ANSI/ IEEE 854 [217]. This is however of less interest here.

Currently double precision is not always sufficient, so quadruple precision is available from many manufacturers. There is no official standard available; most manufacturers generalize the IEEE 754, but some (including SGI) have another convention. SGI quadruple precision is very different from the usual quadruple precision, which has a very large range; with SGI the range is about the same in double and quadruple precision. The reason is that here the quadruple variables are represented as the sum or difference of two doubles, normalized so that the smaller double is ≤ 0.5 units in the last position of the larger. Care must therefore be taken when using quadruple precision.

Packages for multiple precision also exist.

1.4   What Really Went Wrong in Applied Scientific Computing!

We include only examples where numerical problems have occurred, not the more common pure programming errors (bugs). More examples are given in the paper [424] and in the Thomas Huckle web site Collection of Software Bugs [212]. Quite a different view is taken in [4], in which how to get the mathematics and numerics correct is discussed.

1.4.1   Floating-point precision

Floating-point precision has to be sufficiently accurate to handle the task. In this section we give some examples where this has not been the case.

---

[7]IBM System 360 was announced in April 1964 and was a very successful spectrum of compatible computers that continues in an evolutionary form to this day.

Following System 360 was System 370, announced in June, 1970. The line after System 370 continued under different names: 303X (announced in March, 1977), 308X, 3090, 9021, 9121, and the zSeries. These machines all share a common heritage. The floating-point arithmetic is hexadecimal.

1.4.1.1   Patriot missile

A well-known example is the Patriot missile[8] failure [158, 419] with a Scud missile[9] on February 25, 1991, at Dhahran, Saudi Arabia. The Patriot missile was designed, in order to avoid detection, to operate for only a few hours at one location. The velocity of the incoming missile is a floating-point number but the time from the internal clock is an integer, represented by the time in tenths of a second. Before that time is used, the integer number is multiplied with a numerical approximation of 0.1 to 24 bits, causing an error $9.5 \cdot 10^{-8}$ in the conversion factor. The inaccuracy in the position of the target is proportional to the product of the target velocity and the length of time the system has been running. This is a somewhat oversimplified discussion; a more detailed one is given in [419]. With the system up and running for 100 hours and a velocity of the Scud missile of 1676 meters per second, an error of 573 meters is obtained, which is more than sufficient to cause failure of the Patriot and success for the Scud. The Scud missile killed 28 soldiers.

Modified software, which compensated for the inaccurate time calculation, arrived the following day. The potential problem had been identified by the Israelis and reported to the Patriot Project Office on February 11, 1991.

1.4.1.2   The Vancouver Stock Exchange

The Vancouver Stock Exchange (see the references in [154]) in 1982 experienced a problem with its index. The index (with three decimals) was updated (and *truncated*) after *each* transaction. After 22 months it had fallen from the initial value 1000.000 to 524.881, but the correctly evaluated index was 1098.811.

Assuming 2000 transactions a day a simple statistical analysis gives directly that the index will lose one unit per day, since the mean truncation error is 0.0005 per transaction. Assuming 22 working days a month the index would be 516 instead of the actual (but still false) 524.881.

1.4.1.3   Schleswig–Holstein local elections

In the Schleswig–Holstein local elections in 1992, one party got 5.0 % in the printed results (which was correctly rounded to one decimal), but the correct value rounded to two decimals was 4.97 %, and the party did therefore not pass the 5 % threshold for getting into the local parliament, which in turn caused a switch of majority [481]. Similar rules apply not only in German elections. A special rounding algorithm is required at the threshold, truncating all values between 4.9 and 5.0 in Germany, or all values between 3.9 and 4.0 in Sweden!

---

[8]The Patriot is a long-range, all-altitude, all-weather air defense system to counter tactical ballistic missiles, cruise missiles, and advanced aircraft.

Patriot missile systems were deployed by U.S. forces during the First Gulf War. The systems were stationed in Kuwait and destroyed a number of hostile surface-to-surface missiles.

[9]The Scud was first deployed by the Soviets in the mid-1960s. The missile was originally designed to carry a 100 kiloton nuclear warhead or a 2000 pound conventional warhead, with ranges from 100 to 180 miles. Its principal threat was its warhead's potential to hold chemical or biological agents.

The Iraqis modified Scuds for greater range, largely by reducing warhead weight, enlarging their fuel tanks, and burning all of the fuel during the early phase of flight. It has been estimated that 86 Scuds were launched during the First Gulf War.

1.4.1.4   Criminal usages of roundoff

Criminal usages of roundoff have been reported [30], involving many tiny withdrawals from bank accounts. The common practice of rounding to whole units of the currency (for example, to dollars, removing the cents) implies that the cross sums do not exactly agree, which diminishes the chance/risk of detecting the fraud.

1.4.1.5   Euro-conversion

A problem is connected with the European currency Euro, which replaced 12 national currencies from January 1, 2002. Partly due to the strictly defined conversion rules, the roundoff can have a significant impact [162]. A problem is that the conversion factors from old local currencies have six significant decimal digits, thus permitting a varying relative error, and for small amounts the final result is also to be rounded according to local customs to at most two decimals.

1.4.2   Illegal conversion between data types

On June 4, 1996, an unmanned Ariane 5 rocket launched by the European Space Agency exploded forty seconds after its lift-off from Kourou, French Guiana. The Report by the Inquiry Board [292, 413] found that the failure was caused by the conversion of a 64 bit floating-point number to a 16 bit signed integer. The floating-point number was too large to be represented by a 16 bit signed integer (larger than 32767). In fact, this part of the software was required in Ariane 4 but not in Ariane 5!

A somewhat similar problem is illegal mixing of different units of measurement (SI, Imperial, and U.S.). An example is the Mars Climate Orbiter which was lost on entering orbit around Mars on September 23, 1999. The "root cause" of the loss was that a subcontractor failed to obey the specification that SI units should be used and instead used Imperial units in their segment of the ground-based software; see [225]. See also pages 35–38 in the book [440].

1.4.3   Illegal data

A crew member of the USS Yorktown mistakenly entered a zero for a data value in September 1997, which resulted in a division by zero. The error cascaded and eventually shut down the ship's propulsion system. The ship was dead in the water for 2 hours and 45 minutes; see [420, 202].

1.4.4   Inaccurate finite element analysis

On August 23, 1991, the Sleipner A offshore platform collapsed in Gandsfjorden near Stavanger, Norway. The conclusion of the investigation [417] was that the loss was caused by a failure in a cell wall, resulting in a serious crack and a leakage that the pumps could not handle. The wall failed as a result of a combination of a serious usage error in the finite element analysis (using the popular NASTRAN code) and insufficient anchorage of the reinforcement in a critical zone.

The shear stress was underestimated by 47 %, leading to insufficient strength in the design. A more careful finite element analysis after the accident predicted that failure would occur at 62 meters depth; it did occur at 65 meters.

1.4.5   Incomplete analysis

The Millennium Bridge [17, 24, 345] over the Thames in London was closed on June 12, directly after its public opening on June 10, 2000, since it wobbled more than expected. The simulations performed during the design process handled the vertical force (which was all that was required by the British Standards Institution) of a pedestrian at around 2 Hz, but not the horizontal force at about 1 Hz. What happened was that the slight wobbling (within tolerances) due to the wind caused the pedestrians to walk in step (synchronous walking) which made the bridge wobble even more.

On the first day almost 100000 persons walked the bridge. This wobbling problem was actually noted already in 1975 on the Auckland Harbour Road Bridge in New Zealand, when a demonstration walked that bridge, but that incident was never widely published. The wobbling started suddenly when a certain number of persons were walking the Millennium Bridge; in a test 166 persons were required for the problem to appear. The bridge was reopened in 2002, after 37 viscous dampers and 54 tuned mass dampers were installed and all the modifications were carefully tested. The modifications were completely successful.

1.5   Conclusion

The aim of this book is to diminish the risk of future occurrences of incidents like those described in the previous section. The techniques and tools to achieve this goal are now emerging; some of them are presented in parts II and III.

Chapter 2

Assessment of Accuracy and Reliability

Ronald F. Boisvert, Ronald Cools, and Bo Einarsson

One of the principal goals of scientific computing is to provide predictions of the behavior of systems to aid in decision making. Good decisions require good predictions. But how are we to be assured that our predictions are good? Accuracy and reliability are two qualities of good scientific software. Assessing these qualities is one way to provide confidence in the results of simulations. In this chapter we provide some background on the meaning of these terms.[10]

2.1 Models of Scientific Computing

Scientific software is particularly difficult to analyze. One of the main reasons for this is that it is inevitably infused with uncertainty from a wide variety of sources. Much of this uncertainty is the result of approximations. These approximations are made in the context of each of the physical world, the mathematical world, and the computer world.

To make these ideas more concrete, let's consider a scientific software system designed to allow *virtual experiments* to be conducted on some physical system. Here, the scientist hopes to develop a computer program which can be used as a proxy for some real world system to facilitate understanding. The reason for conducting virtual experiments is that developing and running a computer program can be much more cost effective than developing and running a fully instrumented physical experiment (consider a series of crash tests for a car, for example). In other cases performing the physical experiment can be practically impossible—for example, a physical experiment to understand the formation of galaxies! The process of abstracting the physical system to the level of a computer program is illustrated in Figure 2.1. This process occurs in a sequence of steps.

- **From real world to mathematical model**
  A length scale is selected which will allow the determination of the desired results using a reasonable amount of resources, for example, atomic scale (nanometers) or

---

[10]Portions of this chapter were contributed by NIST, and are not subject to copyright in the USA.

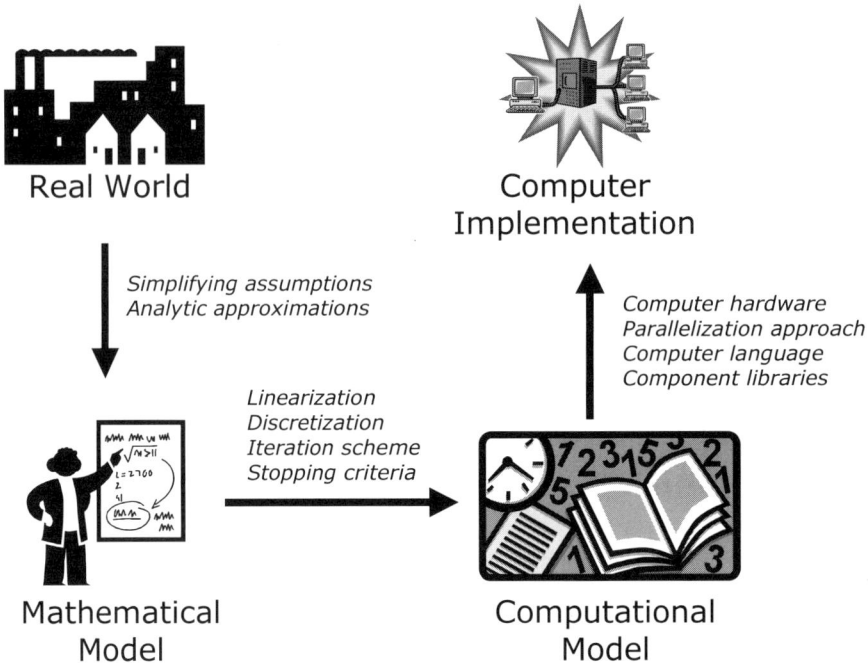

Figure 2.1. *A model of computational modeling.*

macro scale (kilometers). Next, the physical quantities relevant to the study, such as temperature and pressure, are selected (and all other effects implicitly discarded). Then, the physical principles underlying the real world system, such as conservation of energy and mass, lead to mathematical relations, typically partial differential equations (PDEs), that express the mathematical model. Additional mathematical approximations may be introduced to further simplify the model. *Approximations can include* discarded effects and inadequately modeled effects (e.g., discarded terms in equations, linearization).

- **From mathematical model to computational model**
  The equations expressing the mathematical model are typically set in some infinite dimensional space. In order to admit a numerical solution, the problem is transformed to a finite dimensional space by some discretization process. Finite differences and finite elements are examples of discretization methods for PDE models. In such computational models one must select an order of approximation for derivatives. One also introduces a computational grid of some type. It is desirable that the discrete model converges to the continuous model as either the mesh width approaches zero or the order of approximation approaches infinity. In this way, accuracy can be controlled using these parameters of the numerical method. A specification for how to solve the discrete equations must also be provided. If an iterative method is used (which is certainly the case for nonlinear problems), then the solution is obtained only in the limit,

and hence a criterion for stopping the iteration must be specified. *Approximations can include* discretization of domain, truncation of series, linearization, and stopping before convergence.

- **From computational model to computer implementation**
  The computational model and its solution procedure are implemented on a particular computer system. The algorithm may be modified to make use of parallel processing capabilities or to take advantage of the particular memory hierarchy of the device. Many arithmetic operations are performed using floating-point arithmetic. *Approximations can include* floating-point arithmetic and approximation of standard mathematical or special functions (typically via calls to library routines).

2.2 Verification and Validation

If one is to use the results of a computer simulation, then one must have confidence that the answers produced are correct. However, absolute correctness may be an elusive quantity in computer simulation. As we have seen, there will always be uncertainty—uncertainty in the mathematical model, in the computational model, in the computer implementation, and in the input data. A more realistic goal is to carefully characterize this uncertainty. This is the main goal of verification and validation.

- **Code verification**
  This is the process of determining the extent to which the computer implementation corresponds to the computational model. If the latter is expressed as a *specification*, then code verification is the process of determining whether an implementation corresponds to its lowest level algorithmic specification. In particular, we ask whether the specified algorithm has been correctly implemented, not whether it is an effective algorithm.

- **Solution verification**
  This is the process of determining the extent to which the computer implementation corresponds to the mathematical model. Assuming that the code has been verified (i.e., that the algorithm has been correctly implemented), solution verification asks whether the underlying numerical methods correctly produce solutions to the abstract mathematical problem.

- **Validation**
  This is the process of determining the extent to which the computer implementation corresponds to the real world. If solution verification has already been demonstrated, then the validation asks whether the mathematical model is effective in simulating those aspects of the real world system under study.

Of course, neither the mathematical nor the computational model can be expected to be valid in all regions of their own parameter spaces. The validation process must confirm these regions of validity.

Figure 2.2 illustrates how verification and validation are used to quantify the relationship between the various models in the computational science and engineering process. In a

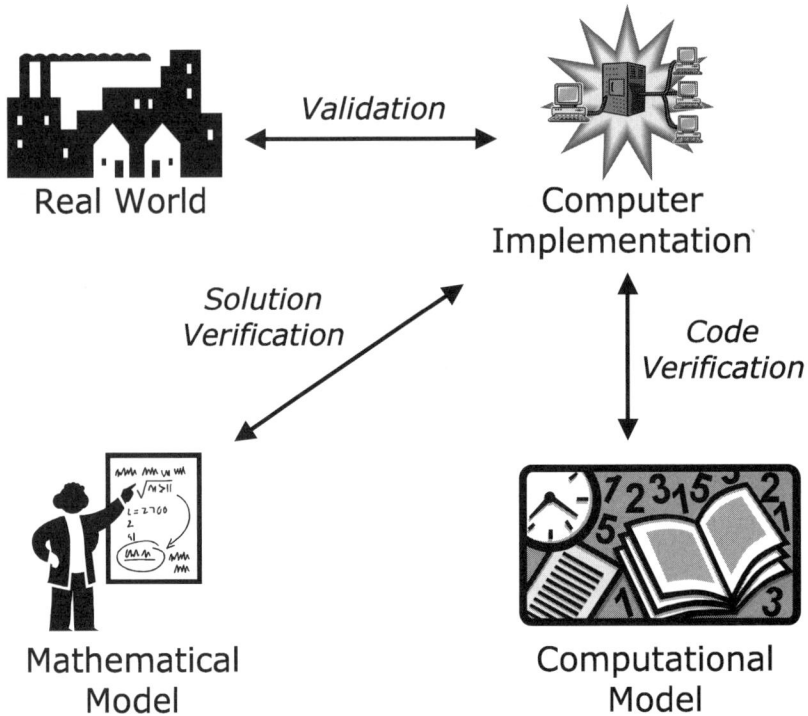

Figure 2.2. *A model of computational validation.*

rough sense, validation is the aim of the application scientist (e.g., the physicist or chemist) who will be using the software to perform virtual experiments. Solution verification is the aim of the numerical analyst. Finally, code verification is the aim of the programmer.

There is now a large literature on the subject of verification and validation. Nevertheless, the words themselves remain somewhat ambiguous, with different authors often assigning slightly different meanings. For software in general, the IEEE adopted the following definitions in 1984 (they were subsequently adopted by various other organizations and communities, such as the ISO[11]).

- Verification: The process of evaluating the products of a software development phase to provide assurance that they meet the requirements defined for them by the previous phase.

- Validation: The process of testing a computer program and evaluating the results to ensure compliance with specific requirements.

These definitions are general in that "requirements" can be given different meaning for different application domains. For computational simulation, the U.S. Defense Modeling

---

[11] International Standards Organization.

and Simulation Office (DMSO) proposed the following definitions (1994), which were subsequently adopted in the context of computational fluid dynamics by the American Institute of Aeronautics and Astronautics [7].

- Verification: The process of determining that a model implementation accurately represents the developer's conceptual description of the model and the solution to the model.

- Validation: The process of determining the degree to which a model is an accurate representation of the real world from the perspective of the intended users of the model.

The DMSO definitions can be regarded as special cases of the IEEE ones, given appropriate interpretations of the word "requirements" in the general definitions. In the DMSO proposal, the verification is with respect to the requirements that the implementation should correctly realize the mathematical model. The DMSO validation is with respect to the requirement that the results generated by the model should be sufficiently in agreement with the real world phenomena of interest, so that they can be used for the intended purpose.

The definitions used in the present book, given in the beginning of this chapter, differ from those of DMSO in that they make a distinction between the computational model and the mathematical model. In our opinion, this distinction is so central in scientific computing that it deserves to be made explicit in the verification and validation processes. The model actually implemented in the computer program is the computational one. Consequently, according to the IEEE definition, validation is about testing that the *computational* model fulfills certain requirements, ultimately those of the DMSO definition of validation. The full validation can then be divided into two levels. The first level of validation (solution verification) will be to demonstrate that the computational model is a sufficiently accurate representation of the mathematical one. The second level of validation is to determine that the mathematical model is sufficiently effective in reproducing properties of the real world.

The book [383] and the more recent paper [349] present extensive reviews of the literature in computational validation, arguing for the separation of the concepts of error and uncertainty in computational simulations. A special issue of *Computing in Science and Engineering* (see [452]) has been devoted to this topic.

2.3 Errors in Software

When we ask whether a program is "correct" we want to know whether it faithfully follows its lowest-level specifications. Code verification is the process by which we establish correctness in this sense. In order to understand the verification process, it is useful to be mindful of the most typical types of errors encountered in scientific software. Scientific software is prone to many of the same problems as software in other areas of application. In this section we consider these. Problems unique to scientific software are considered in Section 2.5.

Chapter 5 of the book [440] introduces a broad classification of bugs organized by the original source of the error, i.e., how the error gets into the program, that the authors Telles and Hsieh call "Classes of Bugs." We summarize them in the following list.

- *Requirement bugs.*
  The specification itself could be inadequate. For example, it could be too vague, missing a critical requirement, or have two requirements in conflict.

- *Implementation bugs.*
  These are the bugs in the logic of the code itself. They include problems like not following the specification, not correctly handling all input cases, missing functionality, problems with the graphic user interface, improper memory management, and coding errors.

- *Process bugs.*
  These are bugs in the runtime environment of the executable program, such as improper versions of dynamic linked libraries or broken databases.

- *Build bugs.*
  These are bugs in the procedure used to build the executable program. For example, a product may be built for a slightly wrong environment.

- *Deployment bugs.*
  These are problems with the automatic updating of installed software.

- *Future planning bugs.*
  These are bugs like the year 2000 problem, where the lifetime of the product was underestimated, or the technical development went faster than expected (e.g., the 640 KiB[12] limit of MS-DOS).

- *Documentation bugs.*
  The software documentation, which should be considered as an important part of the software itself, might be vague, incomplete, or inaccurate. For example, when providing information on a library routine's procedure call it is important to provide not only the meaning of each variable but also its exact type, as well as any possible side effects from the call.

The book [440] also provides a list of common bugs in the implementation of software. We summarize them in the following list.

- *Memory or resource leaks.*
  A memory leak occurs when memory is allocated but not deallocated when it is no longer required. It can cause the memory associated with long-running programs to grow in size to the point that they overwhelm existing memory. Memory leaks can occur in any programming language and are sometimes caused by programming errors.

- *Logic errors.*
  A logic error occurs when a program is syntactically correct but does not perform according to the specification.

- *Coding errors.*
  Coding errors occur when an incorrect list of arguments to a procedure is used, or a part of the intended code is simply missing. Others are more subtle. A classical example of the latter is the Fortran statement DO 25 I = 1.10 which in Fortran 77

---

[12]"Ki" is the IEC standard for the factor $2^{10} = 1024$, corresponding to "k" for the factor 1000, and "B" stands for "byte." See, for example, http://physics.nist.gov/cuu/Units/binary.html.

(and earlier, and also in the obsolescent Fortran 90/95 fixed form) assigns the variable DO25I the value 1.10 instead of creating the intended DO loop, which requires the period to be replaced with a comma.

- *Memory overruns.*
  Computing an index incorrectly can lead to the access of memory locations outside the bounds of an array, with unpredictable results. Such errors are less likely in modern high-level programming languages but may still occur.

- *Loop errors.*
  Common cases are unintended infinite loops, off-by-one loops (i.e., loops executed once too often or not enough), and loops with improper exits.

- *Conditional errors.*
  It is quite easy to make a mistake in the logic of an *if-then-else-endif* construct. A related problem arises in some languages, such as Pascal, that do not require an explicit *endif.*

- *Pointer errors.*
  Pointers may be uninitialized, deleted (but still used), or invalid (pointing to something that has been removed).

- *Allocation errors.*
  Allocation and deallocation of objects must be done according to proper conventions. For example, if you wish to change the size of an allocated array in Fortran, you must first check if it is allocated, then deallocate it (and lose its content), and finally allocate it to its correct size. Attempting to reallocate an existing array will lead to an error condition detected by the runtime system.

- *Multithreaded errors.*
  Programs made up of multiple independent and simultaneously executing threads are subject to many subtle and difficult to reproduce errors sometimes known as race conditions. These occur when two threads try to access or modify the same memory address simultaneously, but correct operation requires a particular order of access.

- *Timing errors.*
  A timing error occurs when two events are designed and implemented to occur at a certain rate or within a certain margin. They are most common in connection with interrupt service routines and are restricted to environments where the clock is important. One symptom is input or output hanging and not resuming.

- *Distributed application errors.*
  Such an error is defined as an error in the interface between two applications in a distributed system.

- *Storage errors.*
  These errors occur when a storage device gets a soft or hard error and is unable to proceed.

- *Integration errors.*
  These occur when two fully tested and validated individual subsystems are combined but do not cooperate as intended when combined.

- *Conversion errors.*
  Data in use by the application might be given in the wrong format (integer, floating

point, ...) or in the wrong units (m, cm, feet, inches, ...). An unanticipated result from a type conversion can also be classified as a conversion error. A problem of this nature occurs in many compiled programming languages by the assignment of $1/2$ to a variable of floating-point type. The rules of integer arithmetic usually state that when two integers are divided there is an integer result. Thus, if the variable A is of a floating-point type, then the statement A = 1/2 will result in an integer zero, converted to a floating-point zero assigned to the variable A, since 1 and 2 are integer constants, and integer division is rounded to zero.

- *Hard-coded lengths or sizes.*
  If sizes of objects like arrays are defined to be of a fixed size, then care must be taken that no problem instance will be permitted a larger size. It is best to avoid such hard-coded sizes, either by using allocatable arrays that yield a correctly sized array at runtime, or by parameterizing object sizes so that they are easily and consistently modified.

- *Version bugs.*
  In this case the functionality of a program unit or a data storage format is changed between two versions, without backward compatibility. In some cases individual version changes may be compatible, but not over several generations of changes.

- *Inappropriate reuse bugs.*
  Program reuse is normally encouraged, both to reduce effort and to capitalize upon the expertize of subdomain specialists. However, old routines that have been carefully tested and validated under certain constraints may cause serious problems if those constraints are not satisfied in a new environment. It is important that high standards of documentation and parameter checking be set for reuse libraries to avoid incompatibilities of this type.

- *Boolean bugs.*
  The authors of [440] note on page 159 that "Boolean algebra has virtually nothing to do with the equivalent English words. When we say 'and', we really mean the Boolean 'or' and vice versa." This leads to misunderstandings among both users and programmers. Similarly, the meaning of "true" and "false" in the code may be unclear.

Looking carefully at the examples of the Patriot missile, section 1.4.1.1, and the Ariane 5 rocket, section 1.4.2, we observe that in addition to the obvious *conversion errors* and *storage errors, inappropriate reuse bugs* were also involved. In each case the failing software was taken from earlier and less advanced hardware equipment, where the software had worked well for many years. They were both well tested, but not in the new environment.

2.4   Precision, Accuracy, and Reliability

Many of the bugs listed in the previous section lead to anomalous behavior that is easy to recognize, i.e., the results are clearly wrong. For example, it is easy to see if the output of a program to sort data is really sorted. In scientific computing things are rarely so clear. Consider a program to compute the roots of a polynomial. Checking the output here seems easy; one can evaluate the function at the computed points. However, the result will seldom be exactly zero. How close to zero does this residual have to be to consider the answer correct? Indeed, for ill-conditioned polynomials the relative sizes of residuals provide a very unreliable measure of accuracy. In other cases, such as the evaluation of a definite integral, there is no such "easy" method.

Verification and validation in scientific computing, then, is not a simple process that gives yes or no as an answer. There are many gradations. The concepts of accuracy and reliability are used to characterize such gradations in the verification and validation of scientific software. In everyday language the words accuracy, reliability, and the related concept of precision are somewhat ambiguous. When used as quality measures they should not be ambiguous. We use the following definitions.

- **Precision** refers to the number of digits used for arithmetic, input, and output.
- **Accuracy** refers to the absolute or relative error of an approximate quantity.
- **Reliability** measures how "often" (as a percentage) the software fails, in the sense that the true error is larger than what is requested.

Accuracy is a measure of the quality of the result. Since achieving a prescribed accuracy is rarely easy in numerical computations, the importance of this component of quality is often underweighted.

We note that determining accuracy requires the comparison to something external (the "exact" answer). Thus, stating the accuracy requires that one specifies what one is comparing against. The "exact" answer may be different for each of the computational model, the mathematical model, and the real world. In this book most of our attention will be on solution verification; hence we will be mostly concerned with comparison to the mathematical model.

To determine accuracy one needs a means of measuring (or estimating) error. Absolute error and relative error are two important such measures. *Absolute error* is the magnitude of the difference between a computed quantity x and its true value x^*, i.e.,

$$|x - x^*|. \tag{2.1}$$

Relative error is the ratio of absolute error to the magnitude of the true value, i.e.,

$$|x - x^*|/|x^*|. \tag{2.2}$$

Relative error provides a method of characterizing the percentage error; when the relative error is less than one, the negative of the $\log_{10}$ of the relative error gives the number of significant decimal digits in the computer solution. Relative error is not so useful a measure as x^* approaches 0; one often switches to absolute error in this case. When the computed solution is a multicomponent quantity, such as a vector, then one replaces the absolute values by an appropriate norm.

The terms precision and accuracy are frequently used inconsistently. Furthermore, the misconception that high precision implies high accuracy is almost universal.

Dahlquist and Björck [108] use the term precision for the accuracy with which the basic arithmetic operations $+$, $-$, $\times$, and $/$ are performed by the underlying hardware. For floating-point operations this is given by the unit roundoff $\mathbf{u}$.[13] But even on that there is no general agreement. One should be specific about the rounding mode used.

---

[13] The unit roundoff $\mathbf{u}$ can roughly be considered as the largest positive floating-point number $\mathbf{u}$, such that $1 + \mathbf{u} = 1$ in computer arithmetic. Because repeated rounding may occur this is not very useful as a strict definition. The formal definition of $\mathbf{u}$ is given by (4.1).

The difference between (traditional) rounding and truncation played an amusing role in the 100 digit challenge posed in [447, 446]. Trefethen did not specify whether digits should be rounded or truncated when he asked for "correct digits." First he announced 18 winners, but he corrected this a few days later to 20. In the interview included in [44] he explains that two teams persuaded him that he had misjudged one of their answers by 1 digit. This was a matter of rounding instead of truncating.

Reliability in scientific software is considered in detail in Chapter 13. **Robustness** is a concept related to reliability that indicates how "gracefully" the software fails *(this is nonquantitative)* and also its sensitivity to small changes in the problem *(this is related to condition numbers)*. A robust program knows when it might have failed and reports that fact.

2.5   Numerical Pitfalls Leading to Anomalous Program Behavior

In this section we illustrate some common pitfalls unique to scientific computing that can lead to the erosion of accuracy and reliability in scientific software. These "numerical bugs" arise from the complex structure of the mathematics underlying the problems being solved and the sometimes fragile nature of the numerical algorithms and floating-point arithmetic necessary to solve them. Such bugs are often subtle and difficult to diagnose. Some of these are described more completely in Chapter 4.

- *Improper treatment of constants with infinite decimal expansions.*
  The coding of constants with infinite decimal expansions, like π, $\sqrt{2}$, or even $1/9$, can have profound effects on the accuracy of a scientific computation. One will never achieve 10 decimal digits of accuracy in a computation in which π is encoded as 3.14159 or $1/9$ is encoded as 0.1111. To obtain high accuracy and portability such constants should, whenever possible, be declared as constants (and thus computed at compile time) or be computed at runtime. In some languages, e.g., MATLAB, π is stored to double precision accuracy and is available by a function call.

  For the constants above we can in Fortran 95 use the working precision wp, with at least 10 significant decimal digits:

  ```
  integer, parameter :: wp = selected_real_kind(10)
  real(kind=wp), parameter :: one = 1.0_wp, two = 2.0_wp,   &
     & four = 4.0_wp,   ninth = 1.0_wp/9.0_wp
  real(kind=wp) :: pi, sqrt2
  pi = four*atan(one)
  sqrt2 = sqrt(two)
  ```

- *Testing on floating-point equality.*
  In scientific computations approximations and roundoff lead to quantities that are rarely exact. So, testing whether a particular variable that is the result of a computation is 0.0 or 1.0 is rarely correct. Instead, one must determine what interval around 0.0 or 1.0 is sufficient to satisfy the criteria at hand and then test for inclusion in that interval. See, e.g., Example 1.1.

- *Inconsistent precision.*
  The IEEE standard for floating-point arithmetic defined in [226] requires the availability of at least two different arithmetic precisions. If you wish to obtain a correct result in the highest precision available, then it is usually imperative that all floating-point variables and constants are in (at least) that precision. If variables and constants of different precisions (i.e., different floating-point types) are mixed in an arithmetic expression, this can result in a loss of accuracy in the result, dropping it to that of the lowest precision involved.

- *Faulty stopping criteria.*
  See, e.g., Example 1.1.

- *Not obviously wrong code.*
  A code can be wrong but it can still work more or less correctly. That is, the code may produce results that are acceptable, though they are somewhat less accurate than expected, or are generated more slowly than expected. This can happen when small errors in the coding of arithmetic expressions are made. For example, if one makes a small mistake in coding a Jacobian in Newton's method for solving nonlinear systems, the program may still converge to the correct solution, but, if it does, it will do so more slowly than the quadratic convergence that one expects of Newton's method.

- *Not recognizing ill-conditioned problems.*
  Problems are ill-conditioned when their solutions are highly sensitive to perturbations in the input data. In other words, small changes in the problem to be solved (such as truncating an input quantity to machine precision) lead to a computational problem whose exact solution is far away from the solution to the original problem. Ill-conditioning is an intrinsic property of the problem which is independent of the method used to solve it. Robust software will recognize ill-conditioned problems and will alert the user. See Sections 4.3 and 4.4 for illuminating examples.

- *Unstable algorithms and regions of instability.*
  A method is unstable when rounding errors are magnified without bound in the solution process. Some methods are stable only for certain ranges of its input data. Robust software will either use stable methods or notify the user when the input is outside the region of guaranteed stability. See section 4.4.2 for examples.

2.6   Methods of Verification and Validation

In this section we summarize some of the techniques that are used in the verification and validation of scientific software. Many of these are well known in the field of software engineering; see [6] and [440], for example. Others are specialized to the unique needs of scientific software; see [383] for a more complete presentation. We emphasize that none of these techniques are foolproof. It is rare that correctness of scientific software can be rigorously demonstrated. Instead, the verification and validation processes provide a series of techniques, each of which serves to increase our confidence that the software is behaving in the desired manner.

2.6.1 Code verification

In code verification we seek to determine how faithfully the software is producing the solution to the computational model, i.e., to its lowest level of specification. In effect, we are asking whether the code correctly implements the specified numerical procedure. Of course, the numerical method may be ineffective in solving the target mathematical problem; that is not the concern at this stage.

Sophisticated software engineering techniques have been developed in recent years to improve and automate the verification process. Such techniques, known as *formal methods*, rely on mathematically rigorous specifications for the expected behavior of software. Given such a specification, one can (a) prove theorems about the projected program's behavior, (b) automatically generate much of the code itself, and/or (c) automatically generate tests for the resulting software system. See [93], for example. Unfortunately, such specifications are quite difficult to write, especially for large systems. In addition, such specifications do not cope well with the uncertainties of floating-point arithmetic. Thus, they have rarely been employed in this context. A notable exception is the formal verification of low-level floating-point arithmetic functions. See, for example, [197, 198]. Gunnels et al. [184] employed formal specifications to automatically generate linear algebra kernels. In our discussion we will concentrate on more traditional code verification techniques. The two general approaches that we will consider are code analysis and testing.

2.6.1.1 Code analysis

Analysis of computer code is an important method of exposing bugs. Software engineers have devised a wealth of techniques and tools for analyzing code.

One effective means of detecting errors is to have the code read and understood by someone else. Many software development organizations use formal *code reviews* to uncover misunderstandings in specifications or errors in logic. These are most effectively done at the component level, i.e., for portions of code that are easier to assimilate by persons other than the developer.

Static code analysis is another important tool. This refers to automated techniques for determining properties of a program by inspection of the code itself. Static analyzers study the flow of control in the code to look for anomalies, such as "dead code" (code that cannot be executed) or infinite loops. They can also study the flow of data, locating variables that are never used, variables used before they are set, variables defined multiple times before their first use, or type mismatches. Each of these are symptoms of more serious logic errors. Tools for static code analysis are now widely available; indeed, many compilers have options that provide such analysis.

Dynamic code analysis refers to techniques that subject a code to fine scrutiny as it is executed. Tools that perform such analysis must first transform the code itself, inserting additional code to track the behavior of control flow or variables. The resulting "instrumented" code is then executed, causing data to be collected as it executes. Analysis of the data can be done either interactively or as a postprocessing phase. Dynamic code analysis can be used to track the number of times that program units are invoked and the time spent in each. Changes in individual variables can be traced. Assertions about the state of the software at any particular point can be inserted and checked at runtime. Interactive code debuggers, as well as code profiling tools, are now widely available to perform these tasks.

2.6.1.2   Software testing

Exercising a code actually performing the task for which it was designed, i.e., testing, is an indispensable component of software verification. Verification testing requires a detailed specification of the expected behavior of the software to all of its potential inputs. Tests are then designed to determine whether this expected behavior is achieved.

Designing test sets can be quite difficult. The tests must span all of the functionality of the code. To the extent possible, they should also exercise all paths through the code. Special attention should be paid to provide inputs that are boundary cases or that trigger error conditions.

Exhaustive testing is rarely practical, however. Statistical design of experiments [45, 317] provides a collection of guiding principles and techniques that comprise a framework for maximizing the amount of useful information resident in a resulting data set, while attending to the practical constraints of minimizing the number of experimental runs. Such techniques have begun to be applied to software testing. Of particular relevance to code verification are orthogonal fractional factorian designs, as well as the covering designs; see [109].

Because of the challenges in developing good test sets, a variety of techniques has been developed to evaluate the test sets themselves. For example, dynamic analysis tools can be used to assess the extent of code coverage provided by tests. *Mutation testing* is another valuable technique. Here, faults are randomly inserted into the code under test. Then the test suite is run, and the ability of the suite to detect the errors is thereby assessed.

Well-designed software is typically composed of a large number of components (e.g., procedures) whose inputs and outputs are limited and easier to characterize than the complete software system. Similarly, one can simplify the software testing process by first testing the behavior of each of the components in turn. This is called *component testing* or *unit testing*. Of course, the interfaces between components are some of the most error-prone parts of software systems. Hence, component testing must be followed by extensive *integration testing*, which verifies that the combined functionality of the components is correct.

Once a software system attains a certain level of stability, changes to the code are inevitably made in order to add new functionality or to fix bugs. Such changes run the risk of introducing new bugs into code that was previously working correctly. Thus, it is important to maintain a battery of tests which extensively exercise all aspects of the system. When changes are applied to the code, then these tests are rerun to provide confidence that all other aspects of the code have not been adversely affected. This is termed *regression testing*. In large active software projects it is common to run regression tests on the current version of the code each night.

Elements of the computing environment itself, such as the operating system, compiler, number of processors, and floating-point hardware, also have an effect on the behavior of software. In some cases faulty system software can lead to erroneous behavior. In other cases errors in the software itself may not be exposed until the environment changes. Thus, it is important to perform exhaustive tests on software in each environment in which it will execute. Regression tests are useful for such testing.

Another useful technique is to enlist a team other than the developers to provide a separate evaluation of the software. The testing team obtains the requirements for the code, inspects it, analyzes it, and develops tests and runs them. Such a team often brings a new perspective which can uncover problems overlooked by the developers. One form of this approach is to enlist prospective users of the software to perform early testing; the alpha and beta releases now common in open source software development are examples of this.

The mathematical software community has established a similar type of evaluation process for reusable components. Since 1975 the *ACM Transactions on Mathematical Software* has used a formal refereeing process to evaluate software which is then published as part of the Collected Algorithms of the ACM [62]. The journal also publishes independent certifications of previously published algorithms.

2.6.2   Sources of test problems for numerical software

Both the code verification and the solution verification steps require the use of test data, or test problems, with which to exercise the software or its components. Such tests are particular instances of the abstract mathematical problem to be solved. Methods for obtaining such data sets are somewhat problem dependent. Nevertheless there are a few general techniques.

2.6.2.1   Analytical solutions

A test problem is most useful if one knows its solution, since it is only then that we can assess the error in the computation with absolute certainty. In many cases there are problems whose analytical solutions are well known that can be used for testing. If the software is to compute something straightforward like definite integrals, then one can test the software by integrating elementary functions. One can also find challenging functions in a table of integrals. In more complex mathematical models, such as those describing fluid flow, analytical solutions may be more difficult to find, although there are often special cases (possibly simple or degenerate) whose solutions are known that can be used. It is sometimes difficult to find such problems that will exercise all aspects of a code, however.

In many cases it is possible to artificially construct any number of problems with known solutions. Consider the case of software for solving Poisson's equation,

$$\frac{\partial^2 u}{\partial x^2} + \frac{\partial^2 u}{\partial y^2} = f(x, y) \qquad (2.3)$$

on the unit square $(0, 1) \times (0, 1)$ subject to Dirichlet boundary conditions (that is, $u(x, y)$ is specified on the boundary). To construct a test problem, first pick any (smooth) function u to use as the solution, for example,

$$u(x, y) = x + \sin(\pi x) \cos(\pi y). \qquad (2.4)$$

Then, put the solution into (2.3), differentiating as necessary to produce a right-hand-side function f, i.e.,

$$f(x, y) = -2\pi^2 \sin(\pi x) \cos(\pi y).$$

Similarly, one can obtain boundary conditions directly from (2.4).

So, we now have the complete specification for a Poisson problem, i.e.,

$$\frac{\partial^2 u}{\partial x^2} + \frac{\partial^2 u}{\partial y^2} = -2\pi^2 \sin(\pi x) \cos(\pi y) \qquad \text{on } (0, 1) \times (0, 1)$$

subject to

$$
\begin{aligned}
u &= 0, & x &= 0, & 0 &< y < 1, \\
u &= 1, & x &= 1, & 0 &< y < 1, \\
u &= x + \sin \pi x, & 0 &< x < 1, & y &= 0, \\
u &= x - \sin \pi x, & 0 &< x < 1, & y &= 1.
\end{aligned}
$$

The solution to this problem is given by (2.4).

Such a procedure can be used to generate test problems for most operator equations, e.g., differential equations, integral equations, and systems of algebraic equations. The method is sometimes known as the *method of manufactured solutions*.

One can argue that the problems generated by this technique are not representative of real problems found in practice. However, if one is simply searching for bugs in the code, i.e., doing verification testing, then this procedure can be used, with care, to generate a wealth of problems that exercise all aspects of a code. For example, in our example of Poisson's equation, the artificiality comes from an unnatural forcing function f. However, the main part of the computation that one is testing is the assembly of a sparse matrix and the solution of the resulting linear system. The structure of this matrix depends only on the form of the differential operator and the boundary conditions, not on the forcing function.

Particularly helpful test problems for verification testing are those for which the underlying numerical method is exact. For example, Simpson's rule for numerical integration is exact when integrating cubic polynomials. Since the only numerical errors for such a problem are roundoff errors, then (provided the underlying method is stable) one should obtain a result whose error is of the same size as the machine precision. Using such problems it is easy to determine whether the underlying coding of the method is incorrect. Many numerical methods for operator equations are exact on spaces of polynomials; in these cases the method of manufactured solutions can be used to generate problems for which the solution should be exact to machine precision.

2.6.2.2 Test set repositories

A number of collections of test problems suitable for code verification and solution verification testing have been developed. These are often put together by communities of researchers interested in numerical methods for particular problem classes. Although the main interest here is the development of a set of standard problems or benchmarks to support the comparison of competing methods, such problems are also useful in verification and validation. Such test problem sets often contain problems whose exact solution is known. However, problems whose analytical solution is not known are sometimes also used. In the latter case test comparisons are typically made with best effort computations from the literature.

Some examples of test data set collections used in the numerical analysis community are provided in Table 2.1. More are available on the accompanying website `http://www.nsc.liu.se/wg25/book/`.

Table 2.1. *Sources of test problems for mathematical software.*

Statistics
`http://www.itl.nist.gov/div898/strd/`
Sparse Linear Algebra [42]
`http://math.nist.gov/MatrixMarket/`
Sparse Linear Algebra
`http://www.cise.ufl.edu/research/sparse/matrices/`
Initial Value ODEs
`http://pitagora.dm.uniba.it/~testset/`
Initial Value ODEs
`http://www.ma.ic.ac.uk/~jcash/IVP_software/readme.php`
Stiff ODEs [186]
`http://www.unige.ch/~hairer/testset/testset.html`
Boundary Value ODEs
`http://www.ma.ic.ac.uk/~jcash/BVP_software/readme.php`
Elliptic PDEs [377]
Multivariate Definite Integrals
`http://www.math.wsu.edu/faculty/genz/software/software.html`
Optimization
`http://plato.la.asu.edu/bench.html`
Optimization [142]
`http://titan.princeton.edu/TestProblems/`
Optimization
`http://www-fp.mcs.anl.gov/otc/Guide/TestProblems/`

2.6.3 Solution verification

In solution verification we try to determine the extent to which the program can be used to solve the abstract mathematical problem that has been posed. Since it is unrealistic to expect an exact solution to be obtained in scientific software, we must be more precise about what we mean here. Most numerical methods have some discretization parameter, such as a characteristic mesh size, h, or the number of terms in a critical approximating series or the number of iterations, n, such that the computed solution approaches the exact solution as $h \to 0$ or $n \to \infty$. A numerical method with this property is termed *convergent*. If a numerical method is convergent, then given a target accuracy, it will be possible to select method parameters (i.e., h or n) such that the code will deliver a solution to the problem with the desired accuracy. (Note that different values of h and n may be needed for different problem instances.) Of course, in practice computing resources such as CPU time, memory, or arithmetic precision may not be available to achieve arbitrarily high accuracy. The solution verification process, then, establishes what levels of numerical convergence can be expected in practice.

2.6.3.1 Convergence testing

Testing numerical convergence is an important part of solution verification. To make our discussion concrete, consider the case of a numerical method with a discretization mesh size h. (Examples include methods for computing integrals or solving differential equations.) *Convergence testing* solves a test problem multiple times with different values of h to verify that some measure e of the norm of the error in the computed solution is approaching zero as h decreases.

Not only can convergence testing be used to demonstrate the validity of the code, it can also be used to uncover errors in the code. Suppose that theory tells us that the norm of the error e behaves as

$$e = ch^p \tag{2.5}$$

for some c independent of h. Such a method is said to have *order of convergence p*. Typically such error behavior is based upon an asymptotic analysis, i.e., the behavior is valid only for sufficiently small h. During the validation process, one can experimentally determine an observed order of convergence $\widehat{p}$ and determine whether the observed value approaches the theoretical value as h gets small, i.e., whether $\widehat{p} \to p$ as $h \to 0$. In particular, given distinct mesh sizes $h_i < h_{i-1}$ leading to computed errors $e_i < e_{i-1}$, respectively, the observed convergence rate can be computed from

$$\widehat{p}_i = \frac{\ln(e_i/e_{i-1})}{\ln(h_i/h_{i-1})}. \tag{2.6}$$

If one computes this value for a sequence of decreasing h_i, one should see $\widehat{p}_i \to p$; if not, then there may be a problem with the code. One instance is with the classical Runge–Kutta method for solving an ODE, which wrongly coded may give $\widehat{p} = 1$ instead of the theoretical $p = 4$. However, this result may also occur because the user's coding of the function defining the ODE has been done in such a way as to make the definition less smooth than is required for the software to function at the higher order. Order of convergence $\widehat{p} = 1$ is often what results. But this error must also be addressed.

It is also possible to estimate the convergence rate in cases where the solution is unknown. If you do not know the exact solution, you may perform three computations using the step lengths h, qh, q^2h and get the results $y(h)$, $y(qh)$, $y(q^2h)$. Now compare with the unknown solution y_0. Using the formula $error = y(h) - y_0 = ch^p$ several times, you form

$$\frac{y(q^2h) - y(qh)}{y(qh) - y(h)} = \frac{c(q^2h)^p - c(qh)^p}{c(qh)^p - c(h)^p} = q^p. \tag{2.7}$$

The value on the far left is a known computed quantity, and the parameter p (or rather $\widehat{p}$) on the far right is now the only unknown and is easy to determine. You can therefore test if your program behaves as theory predicts.

A related testing technique is available when one is solving time-dependent systems of differential equations, such as fluid flow problems. Here one can often find problems with known unique steady-state solutions. One can use such problems to check for convergence to steady state as t gets large. Of course, this does not tell us that correct transient behavior was computed.

It may also be the case that the numerical method in use by the code does not always converge. The method may be stable only for certain combinations of the problem or method parameters. Similarly, approximations used in the method may only be valid for certain inputs. Solution verification testing must also determine regions of convergence for the software. To help determine good tests for determining these, the analyst should be familiar with the theoretical properties of the numerical method in use. Note that good software should be sensitive to these parameters and report failure on its own rather than simply deliver an incorrect result.

Chapter 6 of this volume describes a general-purpose tool, PRECISE, which can be helpful in performing numerical experiments to determine the quality of convergence of numerical software components. There are many other types of diagnostics that can be computed to help in the code verification and solution verification process. Often these rely on particular properties of the given problem domain. Examples of such indicators for the case of initial-value problems for ODEs are provided in Chapter 7.

2.6.3.2   Dynamic analysis methods

In many cases it is possible to develop procedures for estimating errors in computations. For example, the problem may be solved using two different computational meshes, the second a refinement of the first. The difference between the two solutions may then be taken as an estimate of the error for the solution on the coarser mesh. Other procedures use the known form of the theoretical error to develop estimation procedures. Providing an estimate of the error is a very useful feature in mathematical software components, although the error estimate itself must be the subject of verification testing.

Such a posteriori error estimates can be used to improve the functionality of the software itself, of course. For example, error estimates can be used to make a code *self-adaptive*. Given a target error tolerance from the user, the software can solve the problem on a sequence of grids until the error estimate is small enough. In other cases one can use local error estimates to automatically determine where in the computational domain the grid should be refined, or where it can be made coarser. If estimates are good, then the software can make optimal use of resources to solve a given problem. Such adaptive methods have become quite common in computing integrals and in solving differential equations. Adaptive software of this type poses particular difficulties for verification and validation since the adaptivity may hide problems with the implementation of the numerical methods that underlie it.

Another type of dynamic error monitoring is the use of *interval arithmetic*. Here one replaces floating-point numbers with intervals. The width of the interval indicates the uncertainty in the value. All arithmetic operations can be performed using intervals. By using intervals one can automatically track the uncertainty in input quantities through a computation, providing an uncertainty in the result. A variety of tools for computing with intervals is now available. Details on the use of intervals are provided in Chapter 9. When used carefully, intervals can provide the basis for computer-assisted proofs and self-validating numerical methods; see Chapter 10. Such methods can take reliability of numerical software to new levels.

2.6.4 Validation

Validation is the process of determining the extent to which the computer implementation corresponds to the real world system being modeled. This is the most important concern for the scientist who wishes to predict the behavior of a physical system. (For software designed only to solve a class of abstract mathematical problems, validation does not apply.)

In some cases, computational models are useful only for qualitative understanding. In other cases, specific levels of quantitative understanding are desired. For the developer of a multipurpose modeling system, the goal of validation testing is to determine the regions within parameter space in which the model produces acceptable accuracy for its intended purpose. For someone using a modeling system for a particular application, the goal of validation is to characterize the uncertainty of the results. Methods for validation are typically highly problem dependent.

For simulation software, the most meaningful validation procedures involve the comparison with data from real physical systems. However, collecting such real world data is often challenging and sometimes impossible. If the model is computing something simple, like the density of a fluid system, then there may be a wealth of existing benchmark data upon which to draw. But if the simulation output is more complex, such as the flow field around an aircraft wing, then it can be difficult to obtain suitable benchmark data for comparison. Experimental conditions in previously published data may not have been specified in enough detail to be able to specify the mathematical model parameters accurately. In other cases, the exact experimental conditions may be difficult to model. Conversely, experimentalists may not be able to match the somewhat idealized conditions that may be assumed in the mathematical model. Some problem domains are just impossible to realize experimentally; consider long-term climate change!

Even when detailed comparisons of results with real systems are impractical, there are often well-known quantities that can be used as indicators of success, such as the time until a particular event occurs. In most problems a variety of consistency checks is also possible. For example, one can check whether energy or mass is properly conserved, but these measures can also be deceptive if the conservation law is built into the underlying numerical model; i.e., the solution may be nowhere near as accurate as the quantity being conserved. Indeed, it is possible for a solution to be totally incorrect yet a physical quantity to be conserved to high accuracy.

Another technique that can be used in these cases is comparison with other computational models and simulations. Such comparisons are most meaningful when the underlying mathematical model and the numerical solution methods are completely different. A recent development in the area of finite element software is encouraging in this regard. Preprocessing tools are now available that take as input a description of a problem and computational grid and are capable of producing the input for several different finite element solution packages for the given problem. This greatly eases the ability of users to compare results of multiple packages.

Finally, a sound statistical basis can be critical to the success of the validation process. For example, statistical design of experiments [45, 317] is very useful in maximizing the amount of useful information while minimizing the number of experiments. Historically, experiment design has played an important role in the physical sciences and will no doubt play an increasingly important role in validation for the computational sciences. Such techniques are especially important when (a) models have large numbers of input parameters that must be studied, (b) computational experiments require long runs on high-end computers, and/or (c) physical experiments are difficult or expensive to perform.

Statistical techniques originally developed for physical metrology may also have a role here. In such studies, the analysis of measurement errors from all sources (both random and systematic) and their combination into a formal "error budget" are performed in order to develop rigorous estimates of the uncertainties in a measurement [156, 116].

Bayesian inference techniques have also been successfully exploited to develop procedures for quantifying uncertainties in complex computer simulations. Here one develops probability models for distributions of errors from various sources, such as errors in models, input parameters, and numerical solutions to governing equations. By sampling from the relevant probability distributions a series of computer experiments is specified and performed. The Bayesian framework provides systematic methods for updating knowledge of the system based on data from such experiments. See [115] for a description of how this has been applied to problems as wide ranging as flow in porus media and shock wave interactions.

Chapter 3

Approximating Integrals, Estimating Errors, and Giving the Wrong Solution for a Deceptively Easy Problem

Ronald Cools

3.1 Introduction

This is a story about asking the right questions. In the meantime several other problems will be implicitly addressed, and we show that some things are not as obvious as some people expect.

Once upon a time a researcher involved in a large scientific computing project, which as usual used a combination of several basic numerical techniques, ran into a numerical problem. He decided to consult a numerical computation expert only *after* isolating the problem. The expert gave a perfectly good answer for the problem, to the best of his knowledge. The practitioner tried it and discovered that it did not work. In isolating the problem, the practitioner wanted to make it easier for the numerical analyst. He actually made it too easy, leaving out critical information, without knowing that it was critical. In the end he decided to derive his own method and that worked very well. (At least that's what he still believes.) He concluded that he would not consult an "expert" in an area of numerical analysis again soon. This will no doubt sound familiar to some readers. It's even visible if you look at some journals.

A lot can go wrong in a situation as described above. Below we will illustrate some issues using an example that many will find easy to understand but nevertheless contains surprises. The isolated numerical problem is the approximation of an integral. As background information for *you* we say that an optimization problem is hidden behind it. You will see the story both from the practitioner's and the numerical analyst's point of view.

A set of MATLAB [305] m-files comes with this chapter. You can pick it up in the compressed file available in [100].

You should try it before looking at the figures to better understand what goes on.

3.2 The Given Problem

On a nice sunny morning a practitioner enters the office of a numerical analyst with the following problem.

"Consider the function

$$f_\lambda(x) := \frac{0.1}{(x - \lambda)^2 + 0.01}$$

which depends on a parameter $\lambda \in [1, 2]$. I want to compute

$$I[f_\lambda] := \int_1^2 \frac{0.1}{(x - \lambda)^2 + 0.01}\,\mathrm{d}x$$

for several values of λ, not yet available, but all in the range $[1, 2]$." (Ignore that this particular integral can be computed analytically.)

This is part of a bigger problem. The practitioner's original problem is that he wants to know where the function

$$g(\lambda) := 0.01\lambda + \int_1^2 \frac{0.1}{(x - \lambda)^2 + 0.01}\,\mathrm{d}x$$

reaches its maximum in the interval $[1, 2]$. He has a nice routine for optimization available, based on the golden ratio, so he only worries about the integral. He needs something he can easily plug into his optimization routine. This is a deceptively easy problem that can actually be a very difficult problem, partially because of software interfaces. The actual example is not very difficult but is used as an illustration of potential problems.

3.3 The First Correct Answer

Let us investigate, as the numerical analyst does, what $f_\lambda(x)$ looks like for $x \in [1, 2]$, for several values of λ. Is it a smooth function or not?

Figure 3.1 shows $f_\lambda(x)$ for $\lambda = 1 + 0.2s$, $s = 0, \ldots, 5$. (It can be obtained using the MATLAB m-file eng1.m.)

The numerical analyst looks at the integrand, as you just did, and concludes that because $f_\lambda(x)$ is a smooth function on the given interval and for the specified values of the parameter λ, no sophisticated method to approximate the integral is required. A classical Gauss–Legendre quadrature formula is a conventional choice. We denote the result of applying a properly scaled version of the Gauss–Legendre rule with N points to a function f_λ by $Q_N[f_\lambda]$. Any numerical analyst will easily find a routine that applies Gauss–Legendre quadrature to a finite interval.

Such a routine might have a calling interface, such as the MATLAB routine gauleg.m:

```
Usage: int = gauleg (f, a, b, key,...)
  Function gauleg calculates the integral of f in the interval
    [a, b].
```

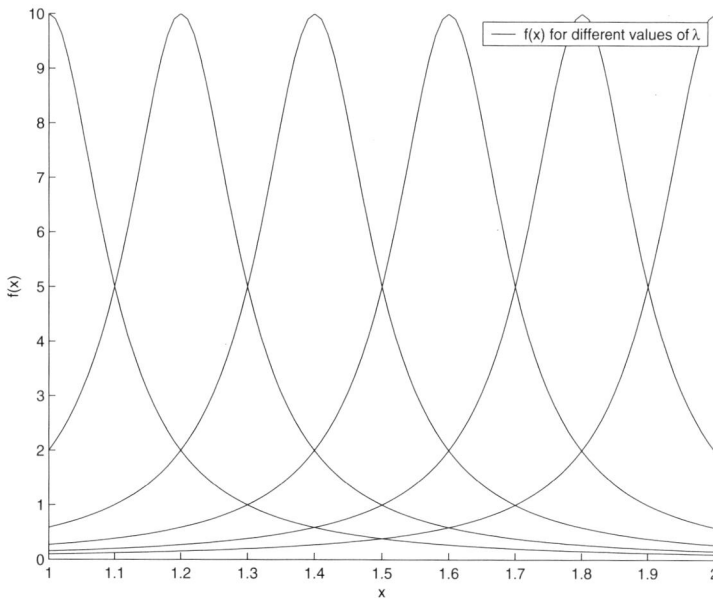

Figure 3.1. $f_\lambda(x)$ *for several values of* λ.

```
Input:
    f: name of the function that must be integrated;
    a, b: boundaries of the integration interval;
    key: integer that determines which Gauss-Legendre formula
        must be used.
        The formula using key points, of degree 2*key - 1 is
            used;
    ...: extra parameters for the integrand function.
Output:
    int: approximation for the integral.
```

With the integrand in the m-file f.m,

```
function value = f(x,lambda)
value = 0.1./((x-lambda).^2+0.01),
```

we compute the integral for fixed λ for a sequence of quadrature rules of increasing accuracy,

```
lambda = 1.2
for key = 5:5:40
    gauleg('f',1,2,key,lambda)
end
```

obtaining the second column of Table 3.1.

Table 3.1. *Some numerical results.*

key = N	$\lambda = 1.2$	$\lambda = 1.3$
5	2.91712527988971	2.47766842145273
10	2.52110630976122	2.71514151485560
15	2.55655278572182	2.68573419810144
20	2.55332314265850	2.67860131191995
25	2.55361396355264	2.67793827052569
30	2.55358791851053	2.67793522992528
35	2.55359023914663	2.67794367597364
40	2.55359003333128	2.67794497275429

3.4   View Behind the Curtain

The exact value of this integral is

$$I[f_\lambda] := \int_1^2 \frac{0.1}{(x-\lambda)^2 + 0.01}\,dx = \mathrm{atan}(-10 + 10\lambda) - \mathrm{atan}(-20 + 10\lambda).$$

This is available in the m-file `exact.m`. The script `eng2.m` combines what we have done so far to plot graphs of the absolute error in the approximations for N-point Gauss–Legendre formulas with $N = 1, 2, \ldots, 40$. Try $\lambda = 1.2$ and 1.3 first, and then try 0.3 by accident!

Figure 3.2 shows the error as a function of the number of points for several values of λ. Discover that for $\lambda < 1$ or $\lambda > 2$ the problem is much easier than for $1 \leq \lambda \leq 2$. Anyway, it appears that relatively few points are needed to obtain significant accuracy.

What this practitioner really wants to know is for what value of λ does

$$g(\lambda) = \frac{\lambda}{100} + \int_1^2 \frac{0.1}{(x-\lambda)^2 + 0.01}\,dx$$

reach its maximum. Observe that the additional term destroys the symmetry of the function. The answer to the above question is $\lambda = 1.503379725865\ldots$.

3.5   A More Convenient Solution

When the practitioner watched the numerical analyst produce the numbers in Table 3.1 he concluded that approximation errors can be estimated by comparing two approximations. If $N_2 > N_1$, one expects that Q_{N_2} is more accurate than Q_{N_1}. So, it's simply a matter of taking the number of points high enough.

The practitioner went back to his office, plugged in the routine the numerical analyst gave to him with a reasonable large number N of points, and discovered to his surprise that his original optimization problem appeared to have more than one (local) maximum. Some results of a search for various values of N in several subintervals $[a, b]$ are listed in Table 3.2. (These can be obtained using the MATLAB m-file `eng3.m`.) So he returned to the

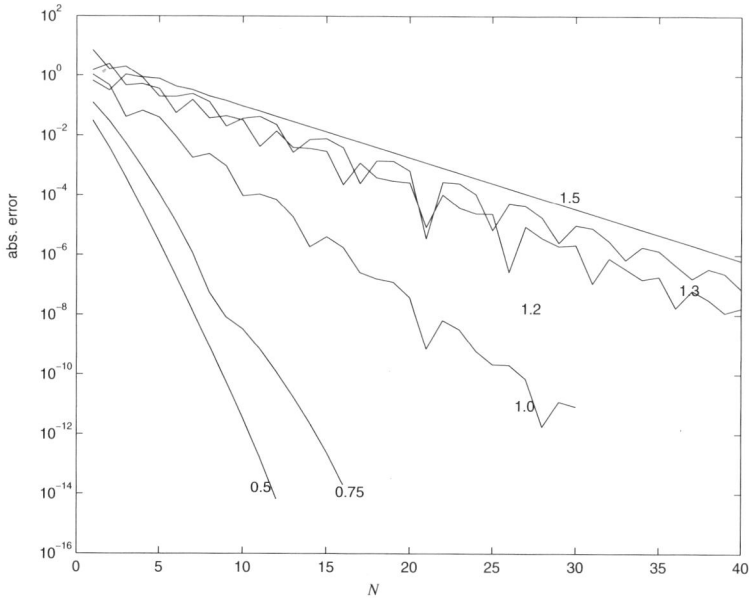

Figure 3.2. *Error as a function of N for* $\lambda = 0.5, 0.75, 1, 1.2, 1.3,$ *and* 1.5.

Table 3.2. *Where the maximum appears to be.*

N	a	b	argmax
10	1.0	1.3	1.2870
10	1.0	1.4	1.4000
10	1.0	1.5	1.4261
10	1.0	1.6	1.4261
10	1.0	2.0	1.5740
15	1.5	2.0	1.5000
15	1.0	2.0	1.5002
20	1.0	1.5	1.4704
20	1.0	1.6	1.4704
20	1.0	1.7	1.5313
20	1.0	2.0	1.5313

numerical analyst and asked him how one can know the accuracy of the approximation and how to choose the required number of quadrature points.

For lack of anything better, in many situations one uses the difference between two approximations $|Q_{N_1}[f_\lambda] - Q_{N_2}[f_\lambda]|$ as an estimate of the error of the *least accurate* approximation, and one expects (assumes) that this is Q_{N_1}, the one using the lowest number of points.

Based on what we have seen before, one can easily offer the following algorithm. Let ε_{abs} be the (absolute) error desired. That is, we want to select the smallest k such that

$|I[f_\lambda] - Q_k[f_\lambda]| < \varepsilon_{abs}$. Here we choose to start with the four-point rule and we skip the odd ones, but that can be changed.

$t := 4; i := 2$
Compute $Q_t[f]$ and $Q_{t+i}[f]$
while $|Q_t[f] - Q_{t+i}[f]| > \varepsilon_{abs}$
    $t := t + i$
    Compute $Q_{t+i}[f]$
end while
Result := $Q_{t+i}[f]$ with estimated error $< |Q_t[f] - Q_{t+i}[f]|$

The practitioner went back to his office, plugged this piece of code in his program, and discovered that things didn't work very well any more. With some frustration he watched the sun go below the horizon, he looked at his watch, and he decided to go home. It was Friday the 13th anyway.

3.6   Estimating Errors: Phase 1

We will now see how unreliable the error estimate of the previous section can be. Let us look at the problem as if the real problem is the approximation of $I[f_\lambda]$. Before proceeding, think a while about how $I[f_\lambda]$ as a function of λ looks like. (That's the easy question.) What does $Q_N[f_\lambda]$ look like? (That's more difficult!)

The MATLAB m-file eng4.m shows you the exact value of $I[f_\lambda]$ as a function of λ and the approximation $Q_N[f_\lambda]$ for your favorite value of N. In Figure 3.3 $I[f_\lambda]$, $Q_4[f_\lambda]$, $Q_6[f_\lambda]$, and $Q_8[f_\lambda]$ are shown.

It's not a surprise that $I[f_\lambda]$ is a very nice function of λ. It's symmetric in the given interval and it doesn't have a large variation.

For many the fact that $Q_N[f_\lambda]$ oscillates around the exact value is a surprise. It shouldn't be. This is a typical phenomenon, similar to that experienced in polynomial approximations of functions. The frequency of the oscillation increases with N. Thus, depending on the value of N we end up with an approximation of the original function that looks different.

This should change our view on using $|Q_{N_1}[f_\lambda] - Q_{N_2}[f_\lambda]|$ as an estimate for the error of $Q_{N_1}[f_\lambda]$, with $N_1 < N_2$. Because $Q_{N_1}[f_\lambda]$ and $Q_{N_2}[f_\lambda]$ are oscillating with different frequencies, they will be identical for several values of λ. At these values of λ, our estimate of the error will be zero. The actual error is not zero at these points. This discussion can be developed to demonstrate that an error estimator based on comparing two such approximations is sometimes unreliable.

With the MATLAB m-file eng5.m you can experiment. You may enter N_1 and N_2. The script generates a figure showing $Q_{N_1}[f_\lambda] - I[f_\lambda]$, $Q_{N_2}[f_\lambda] - I[f_\lambda]$, and $|Q_{N_1}[f_\lambda] - Q_{N_2}[f_\lambda]|$. Because $|Q_{N_1}[f_\lambda] - Q_{N_2}[f_\lambda]|$ is considered an error estimate for the least precise approximation, i.e., Q_{N_1}, we say that this estimator is unreliable if the estimated error is larger than the true error:

$$|Q_{N_1}[f_\lambda] - Q_{N_2}[f_\lambda]| > |Q_{N_1}[f_\lambda] - I[f_\lambda]|.$$

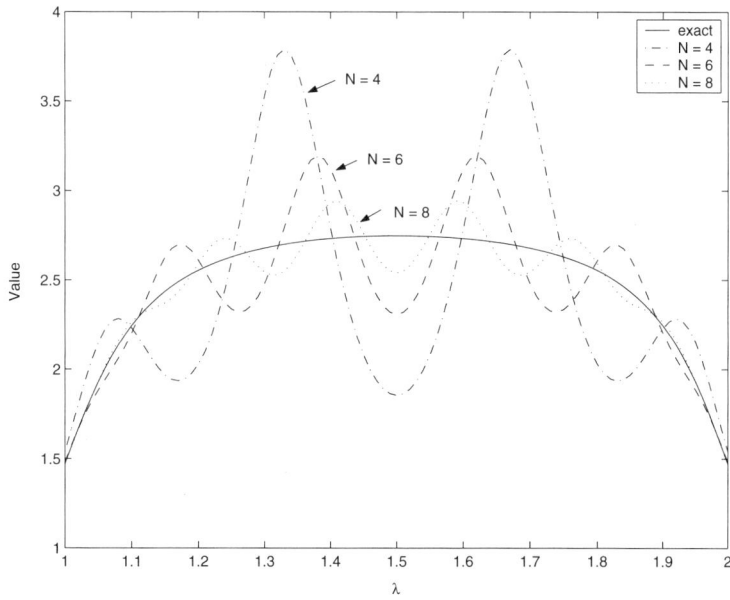

Figure 3.3. $I[f_\lambda]$, $Q_4[f_\lambda]$, $Q_6[f_\lambda]$, $Q_8[f_\lambda]$.

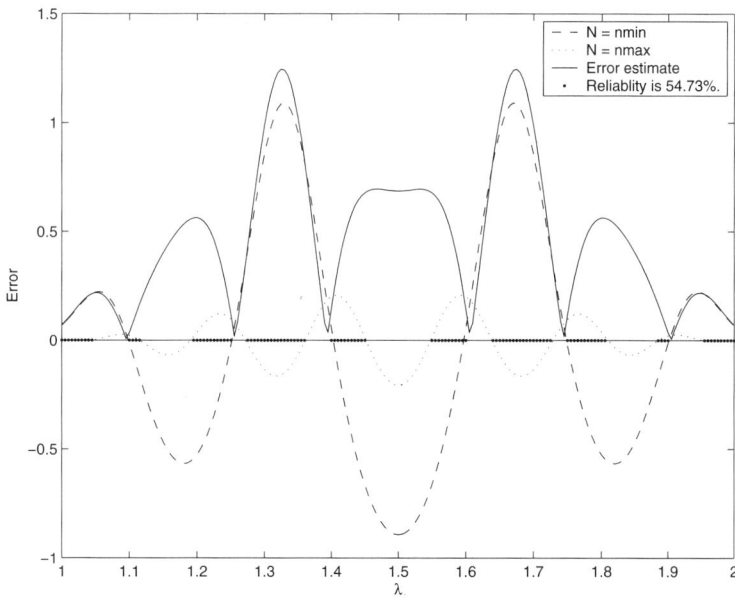

Figure 3.4. *Reliability of the primitive error estimator.*

Whenever this inequality holds, a red dot will appear on the λ-axis. Otherwise a green dot appears.

Take, e.g., $N_1 = 4$ and $N_2 = 8$. What reliability do you expect? The result is shown in Figure 3.4 in black and white (green became dashed, red became dotted, and magenta became solid; green dots appear as thick dots); you obtain a reliability of (only) 55 %.

Please experiment a bit and experience how difficult it is to find a pair of formulas that gives a higher reliability.

It should be clear now that in general, using two approximations in this way to derive an error estimate is not a safe idea.

3.7   Estimating Errors: Phase 2

Although the difference between two approximations tells us something about the error of the least precise approximation, in practice one always presents this error estimate together with the result of the (expected) most accurate rule, i.e., the one that required the most work. Indeed, we spent time to obtain this more accurate result, so why suppress it?

Note that we actually don't know which of the two approximations is the more precise one!

So we return $Q_{N_2}[f_\lambda]$ with error estimate $|Q_{N_1}[f_\lambda] - Q_{N_2}[f_\lambda]|$. Some might say that this returns a pessimistic error estimate. In view of what we have seen before, in practice, however, returning $Q_{N_2}[f_\lambda]$ almost always increases the reliability of this error estimator.

The MATLAB m-file eng6.m is a minor variant of eng5.m implementing what is described above. What do you expect to obtain if you take, e.g., $N_1 = 4$ and $N_2 = 8$? It turns out that the reliability is increased to 96 %. This is still not very high. You can increase the reliability by increasing the difference between N_1 and N_2.

3.8   The More Convenient Solution Revisited

The problem with sending the practitioner away with a routine to evaluate the integral with a Gauss–Legendre rule, as above, is that he must select the number of points N. It's easy, and thus tempting, to make his life easier by offering him a naive automatic integration routine which selects the right value of N to obtain a desired accuracy.

The algorithm given in Section 3.5 returns a result with an estimated error lower than what the user requires. What does the graph of the true error look like as a function of λ? How reliable will the result be?

The algorithm comparing the method of Section 3.5 with the true error is available in the MATLAB m-file eng7.m. Try it with, e.g., a requested accuracy of 0.1, 0.05, or 0.01. The result for 0.05 is given in Figure 3.5.

The result is unreliable if the true error is larger than the requested accuracy. (We could also say that it is unreliable if the real error is larger than the estimated error. That is something different, and stronger!) The unreliability is rather large.

The graph is very irregular. That's because it consists of parts of the graphs of $Q_N[f_\lambda]$ pasted together.

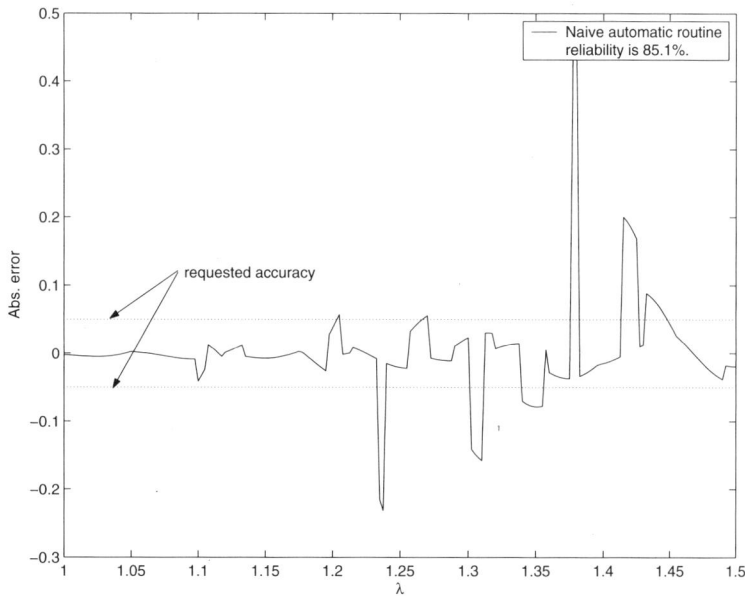

Figure 3.5. *Naive automatic integration with requested error* $= 0.05$.

3.9 Epilogue

Sending the practitioner home with the Gauss–Legendre rule did not make him happy. The nice function $I[f_\lambda]$ was replaced by something oscillating with many local maxima.

It is not a surprise that he was not amused with the naive adaptive routine. It replaced his nice function by something irregular, something that is not appreciated by most optimization software. It is possible to deal with such problems if one is prepared.

So, never give the obvious answer to the short question asked. The first thing to do if someone asks to approximate an integral is ask him why he wants to do that. It is impossible to predict how many questions you will ask before the problem will be solved.

We admit that the example integral was easy and that the problems we showed diminish if more accurate (whatever that means) quadrature rules are used. The problem that a nice convex function is replaced by an oscillating function (if a simple rule is used) or a function with discontinuities (if a more sophisticated algorithm with conditions is used) remains, and that may cause problems elsewhere. The problem was enlarged by considering only Gauss–Legendre rules with an even number of points. Then $Q_N[f_\lambda]$ happens to have a local minimum at the maximum of $I[f_\lambda]$, which is nearby the desired maximum of $g(\lambda)$. That is a consequence of both the symmetry of f_λ and the symmetry of the Gauss–Legendre rule.

One should always be careful if the output of one numerical problem is the input for another numerical problem. As a rule of thumb for the type of problem discussed in this chapter, we suggest that the inaccuracy of the inner problem (the oscillations and irregularities of the quadrature problem) should be below the noise level of the outer problem.

If the relative error of the inner problem is ϵ, one can hope that the relative error of the outer problem is $\sqrt{\epsilon}$. This is an oversimplification of course. There is no easy general solution for this type of problem.

In Table 3.3 we give the value of λ obtained by the standard MATLAB optimization routine fminbnd in combination with the "convenient" quadrature algorithm of Section 3.5 (with $k = 4$ and $i = 1$) and the MATLAB function quad. These numbers can be obtained using the MATLAB m-file eng8.m. They illustrate the rule of thumb given above.

Table 3.3. *Location of maximum by combination of routines.*

Requested quadrature accuracy	Location naive algorithm	Location MATLAB quad
10^{-2}	1.5 4124799532788	1.5 4577759779244
10^{-3}	1.5 0841246619044	1.50 242126547481
10^{-4}	1.50 402381236537	1.503 33850449721
10^{-5}	1.5034 5227748981	1.5033 5986101366
10^{-6}	1.5033 7459447838	1.50338 414175275
10^{-7}	1.50338 334166208	1.50338 248245540
10^{-8}	1.50338 438989809	1.5033 6927399296
exact	1.503379725865	1.503379725865

Finally, we remark that currently we know how to estimate errors in numerical integration rules in a very reliable way. Nevertheless primitive error estimating procedures are still widely used. Even the "new" MATLAB function quadl is far behind the current state of the art in this respect, but that's a different story.

Acknowledgment

The problem that was used here to illustrate several things is borrowed from a very nice paper by Lyness [296]. The presentation of this chapter benefited a lot from discussions with him.

Chapter 4

An Introduction to the Quality of Computed Solutions

Sven Hammarling

4.1 Introduction

This chapter is concerned with the quality of the computed numerical solutions of mathematical problems. For example, suppose we wish to solve the system of linear equations $Ax = b$ using a numerical software package. The package will return a computed solution, say, $\tilde{x}$, and we wish to judge whether or not $\tilde{x}$ is a reasonable solution to the equations. Sadly, all too often software packages return poor, or even incorrect, numerical results and give the user no means by which to judge the quality of the numerical results. In 1971, Leslie Fox commented [148, p. 296]

> "I have little doubt that about 80 per cent of all the results printed from the computer are in error to a much greater extent than the user would believe, ..."

More than thirty years later that paper is still very relevant and worth reading. Another very readable article is Forsythe [144].

The quality of computed solutions is concerned with assessing how good a computed solution is in some appropriate measure. Quality software should implement reliable algorithms and should, if possible, provide measures of solution quality.

In this chapter we give an introduction to ideas that are important in understanding and measuring the quality of computed solutions. In particular we review the ideas of condition, stability, and error analysis and their realization in numerical software. We take as the principal example LAPACK [12], a package for the solution of dense and banded linear algebra problems, but also draw on examples from the NAG Library [332] and elsewhere. The aim is not to show how to perform an error analysis, but to indicate why an understanding of the ideas is important in judging the quality of numerical solutions and to encourage the use of software that returns indicators of the quality of the results. We give simple examples to illustrate some of the ideas that are important when designing reliable numerical software.

Computing machines use floating-point arithmetic for their computation, and so we start with an introduction to floating-point numbers. Floating-point numbers and IEEE arithmetic are also discussed in Chapter 1.

4.2   Floating-point Numbers and IEEE Arithmetic

Floating-point numbers are a subset of the real numbers that can be conveniently represented in the finite word length of a computer without unduly restricting the range of numbers represented. For example, the ANSI/IEEE standard for binary floating-point arithmetic [215] uses 64 bits to represent double precision numbers in the approximate range $10^{\pm 308}$.

A *floating-point number*, x, can be represented in terms of four integers as

$$x = \pm m \cdot b^{e-t},$$

where b is the *base* or *radix*, t is the *precision*, e is the *exponent* with an *exponent range* of $[e_{\min}, e_{\max}]$, and m is the *mantissa* or *significand*, satisfying $0 \le m \le b^t - 1$. If $x \ne 0$ and $m \ge b^{t-1}$, then x is said to be *normalized*. An alternative, equivalent representation of x is

$$x = \pm 0.d_1 d_2 \ldots d_t \cdot b^e$$
$$= \pm \left(\frac{d_1}{b} + \frac{d_2}{b^2} + \cdots + \frac{d_t}{b^t} \right) \cdot b^e,$$

where each digit satisfies $0 \le d_i \le b - 1$. If $d_1 \ne 0$, then we say that x is normalized. If $d_1 = 0$ and $x \ne 0$, then x is said to be *denormalized*. Denormalized numbers between 0 and the smallest normalized number are called *subnormal*. Note that denormalized numbers do not have the full t digits of precision.[14]

The following example, which is not intended to be realistic, illustrates the model.

Example 4.1 (Floating-point numbers)

$$b = 2, \ t = 2, \ e_{\min} = -2, \ e_{\max} = 2.$$

All the normalized numbers have $d_1 = 1$ and either $d_2 = 0$ or $d_2 = 1$; that is, m is one of the two binary integers $m = 10 \ (= 2)$ or $m = 11 \ (= 3)$. Denormalized numbers have $m = 01 \ (= 1)$. Thus the smallest positive normalized number is $2 \cdot 2^{e_{\min}-t} = \frac{1}{8}$ and the largest is $3 \cdot 2^{e_{\max}-t} = 3$. The value $1 \cdot 2^{e_{\min}-t} = \frac{1}{16}$ is the only positive subnormal number in this system. The complete set of nonnegative normalized numbers is

$$0, \frac{1}{8}, \frac{3}{16}, \frac{1}{4}, \frac{3}{8}, \frac{1}{2}, \frac{3}{4}, 1, \frac{3}{2}, 2, 3.$$

The set of nonnegative floating-point numbers is illustrated in Figure 4.1, where the subnormal number is indicated by a dashed line. ∎

Note that floating-point numbers are not equally spaced absolutely, but the relative spacing between numbers is approximately equal. The value

$$\mathbf{u} = \frac{1}{2} \cdot b^{1-t} \tag{4.1}$$

---

[14]Note that for convenience of exposition here, we use a slightly different representation than that of Chapter 1.

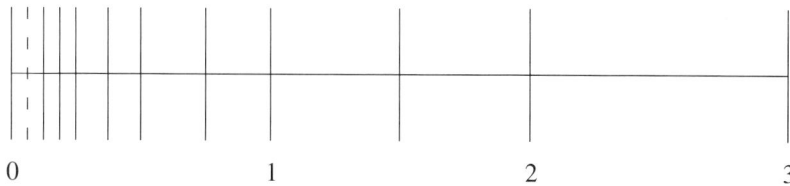

$$b = 2, \ t = 2, \ e_{\min} = -2, \ e_{\max} = 2$$

Figure 4.1. *Floating-point number example.*

is called the *unit roundoff*, or the *relative machine precision,* and is the furthest distance relative to unity between a real number and the nearest floating-point number. In Example 4.1, $\mathbf{u} = \frac{1}{4} = 0.25$ and we can see, for example, that the furthest real number from 1.0 is 1.25 and the furthest real number from 2.0 is 2.5. The quantity $\mathbf{u}$ is fundamental to floating-point error analysis.

The value $\epsilon_M = 2\mathbf{u}$ is called *machine epsilon* or *machine precision* Ψ.

The ANSI/IEEE standard mentioned above (usually referred to as IEEE 754 arithmetic), which of course has $b = 2$ and uses an implicit bit, specifies the following:

- floating-point number formats,

- results of the basic floating-point operations,

- rounding modes,

- signed zero, infinity ($\pm\infty$), and not-a-number (NaN),

- floating-point exceptions and their handling, and

- conversion between formats.

Thankfully, currently almost all machines use IEEE arithmetic. There is also a generic ANSI/IEEE, base independent, standard [217]. The formats supported by the IEEE 754 binary standard are indicated in Table 4.1.

Table 4.1. *IEEE 754 arithmetic formats.*

Format	Precision	Exponent	Approx range	Approx precision
single	24 bits	8 bits	$10^{\pm 38}$	10^{-8}
double	53 bits	11 bits	$10^{\pm 308}$	10^{-16}
extended	$\geq$ 64 bits	$\geq$ 15 bits	$10^{\pm 4932}$	10^{-20}

While the IEEE 754 standard has been an enormous help in standardizing floating-point computation, it should be noted that moving a computation between machines that implement IEEE arithmetic does not guarantee that the computed results will be the same.

Variations can occur due to such things as compiler optimization, use of extended precision registers, and fused multiply-add.

Further discussion of floating-point numbers and IEEE arithmetic can be found in Higham [205] and Overton [355].

The value $\mathbf{u}$ can be obtained from the LAPACK function SLAMCH for single precision arithmetic or DLAMCH for double precision arithmetic and is also returned by the NAG Fortran Library routine X02AJF.[15] It should be noted that on machines that truncate rather than round, ϵ_M is returned in place of $\mathbf{u}$, but such machines are now rare. The MATLAB built-in variable eps returns ϵ_M [305], as does the Fortran 95 numeric enquiry function epsilon [315].

4.3 Why Worry About Computed Solutions?

Chapter 1 gives a number of examples from real applications where numerical problems have occurred. In this section we consider some simple examples of numerical computation that need care in order to obtain reasonable solutions. For clarity of exposition, most of the examples in this and the following sections are illustrated with decimal floating-point (significant figure) arithmetic.

The first example illustrates the problem of damaging subtraction, usually referred to as *cancellation*.

Example 4.2 (Cancellation) Using four figure decimal arithmetic, suppose we wish to compute $s = 1.000 + 1.000 \cdot 10^4 - 1.000 \cdot 10^4$. If we compute in the standard way from left to right we obtain

$$s = 1.000 + 1.000 \cdot 10^4 - 1.000 \cdot 10^4 \Rightarrow 1.000 \cdot 10^4 - 1.000 \cdot 10^4 \Rightarrow 0$$

instead of the correct result of 1.0. Although the cancellation (subtraction) was performed exactly, it lost all the information for the solution. ∎

As Example 4.2 illustrates, the cause of the poor result often happens before the cancellation, and the cancellation is just the final nail in the coffin. In Example 4.2, the damage was done in computing $s = 1.000 + 1.000 \cdot 10^4$, where we lost important information (1.000). It should be said that the subtraction of nearly equal numbers is not always damaging.

Most problems have alternative formulations which are theoretically equivalent, but may computationally yield quite different results. The following example illustrates this in the case of computing sample variances.

Example 4.3 (Sample variance [205, Section 1.9]) The sample variance of a set of n values $x_1, x_2, \dots, x_n$ is defined as

$$s_n^2 = \frac{1}{n-1} \sum_{i=1}^{n} (x_i - \bar{x})^2, \tag{4.2}$$

---

[15] In some ports it actually returns $\mathbf{u} + b^{1-2t}$. See the X02 Chapter introduction [333].

where $\bar{x}$ is the sample mean of the n values

$$\bar{x} = \frac{1}{n} \sum_{i=1}^{n} x_i.$$

An alternative, theoretically equivalent, formula to compute the sample variance which requires only one pass through the data is given by

$$s_n^2 = \frac{1}{n-1} \left(\sum_{i=1}^{n} x_i^2 - \frac{1}{n} \left(\sum_{i=1}^{n} x_i \right)^2 \right). \tag{4.3}$$

If $x^T = \begin{pmatrix} 10000 & 10001 & 10002 \end{pmatrix}$, then using 8 figure arithmetic (4.2) gives $s^2 = 1.0$, the correct answer, but (4.3) gives $s^2 = 0.0$, with a relative error of 1.0. ■

Equation (4.3) can clearly suffer from cancellation, as illustrated in the example. On the other hand, (4.2) always gives good results unless n is very large [205, Problem 1.10]. See also Chan, Golub, and LeVeque [85] for further discussion of the problem of computing sample variances.

Sadly, it is not unknown for software packages and calculators to implement the algorithm of (4.3). For example in Excel 2002 from Microsoft Office XP (and in previous versions of Excel also), the function STDEV computes the standard deviation, s, of the data

$$x^T = \begin{pmatrix} 100000000 & 100000001 & 100000002 \end{pmatrix}$$

as $s = 0$. Considering the pervasive use of Excel and the importance of standard deviation and its use in applications, it is disappointing to realize that (4.3) is used by these versions of Excel.[16] See Cox, Dainton, and Harris [104] for further information, as well as Knüsel [266], McCullough and Wilson [310], and McCullough and Wilson [311]. The spreadsheet from OpenOffice.org version 1.0.2 produces the same result but gives no information on the method used in its help system; on the other hand, the Gnumeric spreadsheet (version 1.0.12) gives the correct result, although again the function description does not describe the method used.

A result that is larger than the largest representable floating-point number is said to *overflow*. For example, in double precision IEEE arithmetic for which the approximate range is $10^{\pm 308}$, if $x = 10^{200}$, then x^2 would overflow. Similarly, x^{-2} is said to *underflow* because it is smaller than the smallest nonzero representable floating-point number.

As with the unit roundoff or machine epsilon discussed in Section 4.2, the overflow and underflow thresholds can be obtained from the LAPACK function S/DLAMCH; from the NAG Fortran Library routines X02ALF and X02AKF, respectively; the MATLAB built-in variables `realmax` and `realmin`; and from the Fortran 95 numeric enquiry functions `huge` and `tiny`.

Care needs to be taken to avoid unnecessary overflow and damaging underflow. The following example illustrates this care in the case of computing the hypotenuse of the right angled triangle shown in Figure 4.2.

---

[16]The algorithm seems to have been replaced in Excel from Office 2003, which now gives the correct answer.

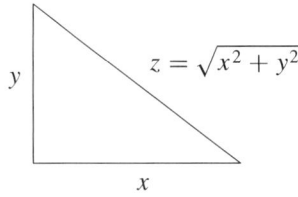

Figure 4.2. *Hypotenuse of a right angled triangle.*

Example 4.4 (Hypotenuse) In Figure 4.2, if x or y is very large there is a danger of overflow, even if z is representable. Assuming that x and y are nonnegative, a safe method of computing z is

$$a = \max(x, y), \quad b = \min(x, y),$$

$$z = \begin{cases} a\sqrt{1 + \left(\frac{b}{a}\right)^2}, & a > 0, \\ 0, & a = 0. \end{cases}$$

This also avoids z being computed as zero if x^2 and y^2 both underflow. We note that [426, p.139 and p.144] actually recommends computing z as

$$z = \begin{cases} s\sqrt{\left(\frac{x}{s}\right)^2 + \left(\frac{y}{s}\right)^2}, & \text{where } s = x + y, \quad s > 0, \\ 0, & s = 0, \end{cases}$$

because this is slightly more accurate on a hexadecimal machine. ∎

We can see that (4.3) of Example 4.3 also has the potential for overflow and underflow and, as well as implementing this formula rather than a more stable version, Excel does not take the necessary care to avoid underflow and overflow. For example, for the values (1.0E200, 1.0E200), STDEV in Excel 2003 from Microsoft Office 2003 returns the mysterious symbol #NUM!, which signifies a numeric exception, in this case overflow, due to the fact that $(10.0^{200})^2$ overflows in IEEE double precision arithmetic. The correct standard deviation is of course 0. Similarly, for the values (0, 1.0E-200, 2.0E-200), STDEV returns the value 0 rather than the correct value of 1.0E-200. OpenOffice.org version 1.0.2 also returns zero for this data and overflows on the previous data. Mimicking Excel is not necessarily a good thing!

The computation of the modulus of a complex number $x = x_r + ix_i$ requires almost the same computation as that in Example 4.4.

Example 4.5 (Modulus of a complex number)

$$|x| = \sqrt{x_r^2 + x_i^2},$$

$$a = \max(|x_r|, |x_i|), \quad b = \min(|x_r|, |x_i|),$$

$$|x| = \begin{cases} a\sqrt{1 + \left(\frac{b}{a}\right)^2}, & a > 0, \\ 0, & a = 0. \end{cases}$$

Again this also avoids $|x|$ being computed as zero if x_r^2 and x_i^2 both underflow. ∎

Another example where care is needed in complex arithmetic is complex division

$$\frac{x}{y} = \frac{x_r + ix_i}{y_r + iy_i} = \frac{(x_r + ix_i)(y_r - iy_i)}{y_r^2 + y_i^2}.$$

Again, some scaling is required to avoid overflow and underflow. See, for example, Smith [421] and Stewart [425]. Algol 60 procedures for the complex operations of modulus, division, and square root are given in Martin and Wilkinson [304] and the NAG Library Chapter, A02, for complex arithmetic has routines based upon those Algol procedures; see, for example, NAG [333]. Occasionally, some aspect of complex floating-point arithmetic is incorrectly implemented; see, for example, [36, Section 7].

Another example, similar to the previous examples, requiring care to avoid overflow and damaging underflow is that of real plane rotations where we need to compute $c = \cos\theta$ and $s = \sin\theta$ such that

$$c = \frac{x}{z}, \quad s = \frac{y}{z}, \quad \text{where } z = \sqrt{x^2 + y^2}$$

or alternatively

$$c = \frac{-x}{z}, \quad s = \frac{-y}{z}.$$

Another convenient way to express the two choices is as

$$c = \frac{\pm 1}{\sqrt{1 + t^2}}, \quad s = ct, \quad \text{where } t \equiv \tan\theta = \frac{x}{y}. \tag{4.4}$$

If G is the *plane rotation matrix*

$$G = \begin{pmatrix} c & s \\ -s & c \end{pmatrix},$$

then, with the choices of (4.4),

$$G\begin{pmatrix} x \\ y \end{pmatrix} = \begin{pmatrix} \pm z \\ 0 \end{pmatrix}.$$

When used in this way for the introduction of zeros the rotation is generally termed a *Givens plane rotation* [164, 170]. Givens himself certainly took care in the computation of c and s. To see an extreme case of the detailed consideration necessary to implement a seemingly simple algorithm, but to be efficient, to preserve as much accuracy as possible throughout the range of floating-point numbers, and to avoid overflow and damaging underflow, see Bindel et al. [33], where the computation of the Givens plane rotation is fully discussed.

Sometimes computed solutions are in some sense reasonable but may not be what the user was expecting. In the next example, the computed solution is close to the exact solution but does not meet a constraint that the user might have expected the solution to meet.

Example 4.6 (Sample mean [206]) Using three-figure floating-point decimal arithmetic,

$$(5.01 + 5.03)/2 \Rightarrow 10.0/2 \Rightarrow 5.00,$$

and we see that the computed value is outside the range of the data, although it is not inaccurate. ∎

Whether or not such a result matters depends upon the application, but it is an issue that needs to be considered when implementing numerical algorithms. For instance, if

$$y = \cos x,$$

then we probably expect the property $|y| \leq 1$ to be preserved computationally, so that a value $|y| > 1$ is never returned. For a monotonic function we may expect monotonicity to be preserved computationally.

In the next section we look at ideas that help our understanding of what constitutes a quality solution.

4.4   Condition, Stability, and Error Analysis

4.4.1   Condition

First we look at the condition of a problem. The *condition* of a problem is concerned with the sensitivity of the problem to perturbations in the data. A problem is ill-conditioned if small changes in the data cause relatively large changes in the solution. Otherwise a problem is well-conditioned. Note that condition is concerned with the sensitivity of the problem and is independent of the method we use to solve the problem. We now give some examples to illustrate somewhat ill-conditioned problems.

Example 4.7 (Cubic equation) Consider the cubic equation

$$x^3 - 21x^2 + 120x - 100 = 0,$$

whose exact roots are $x_1 = 1, x_2 = x_3 = 10$. If we perturb the coefficient of x^3 to give

$$0.99x^3 - 21x^2 + 120x - 100 = 0,$$

the roots become $x_1 \approx 1.000, x_2 \approx 11.17, x_3 \approx 9.041$, so that the changes in the two roots x_2 and x_3 are significantly greater than the change in the coefficient. On the other hand, the roots of the perturbed cubic equation

$$1.01x^3 - 21x^2 + 120x - 100 = 0$$

are $x_1 \approx 1.000, \;\; x_2, x_3 \approx 9.896 \pm 1.044i$, and this time the double root has become a complex conjugate pair with a significant imaginary part.

We can see that the roots x_2 and x_3 are ill-conditioned. Note that we cannot deduce anything about the condition of x_1 just from this data. The three cubic polynomials are plotted in Figure 4.3. ∎

Example 4.8 (Eigenvalue problem) The matrix

$$A = \begin{pmatrix} 10 & 100 & 0 & 0 \\ 0 & 10 & 100 & 0 \\ 0 & 0 & 10 & 100 \\ 0 & 0 & 0 & 10 \end{pmatrix}$$

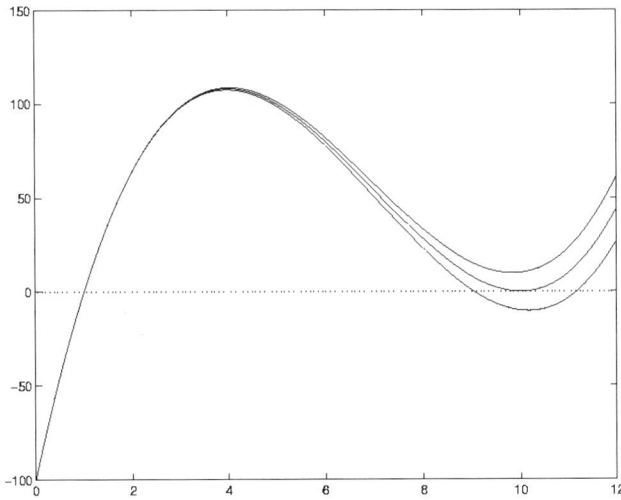

Figure 4.3. *Cubic equation example.*

has eigenvalues $\lambda_1 = \lambda_2 = \lambda_3 = \lambda_4 = 10$, whereas the slightly perturbed matrix

$$B = \begin{pmatrix} 10 & 100 & 0 & 0 \\ 0 & 10 & 100 & 0 \\ 0 & 0 & 10 & 100 \\ 10^{-6} & 0 & 0 & 10 \end{pmatrix}$$

has eigenvalues $\lambda_1 = 11$, $\lambda_2, \lambda_3 = 10 \pm i$, $\lambda_4 = 9$. ■

Example 4.9 (Integral)

$$I = \int_{-10}^{10} \left(ae^x - be^{-x} \right) dx.$$

When $a = b = 1$, $I = 0$, but when $a = 1, b = 1.01$, $I \approx -220$. The function $f(x) = ae^x - be^{-x}$ when $a = b = 1$ is plotted in Figure 4.4. Notice that the vertical scale has a scale factor 10^4, so that a small change in function can make a large change in the area under the curve. ■

Example 4.10 (Linear equations) The equations $Ax = b$ given by

$$\begin{pmatrix} 99 & 98 \\ 100 & 99 \end{pmatrix} \begin{pmatrix} x_1 \\ x_2 \end{pmatrix} = \begin{pmatrix} 197 \\ 199 \end{pmatrix} \tag{4.5}$$

have the solution $x_1 = x_2 = 1$, but the equations

$$\begin{pmatrix} 98.99 & 98 \\ 100 & 99 \end{pmatrix} \begin{pmatrix} x_1 \\ x_2 \end{pmatrix} = \begin{pmatrix} 197 \\ 199 \end{pmatrix}$$

have the solution $x_1 = 100, x_2 = -99$. The two straight lines represented by (4.5) are

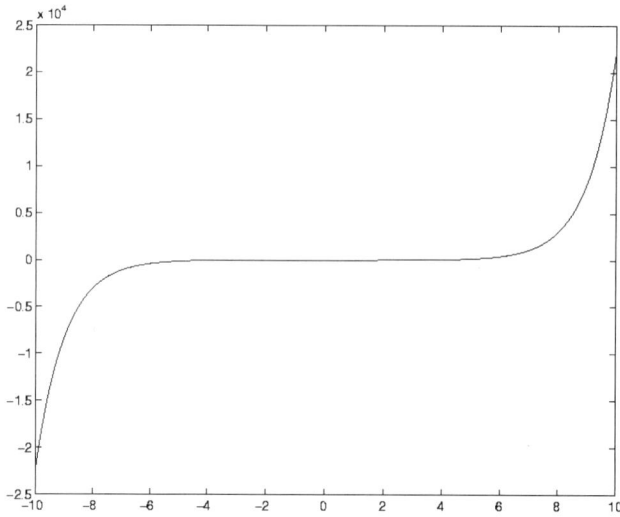

Figure 4.4. *Integral example.*

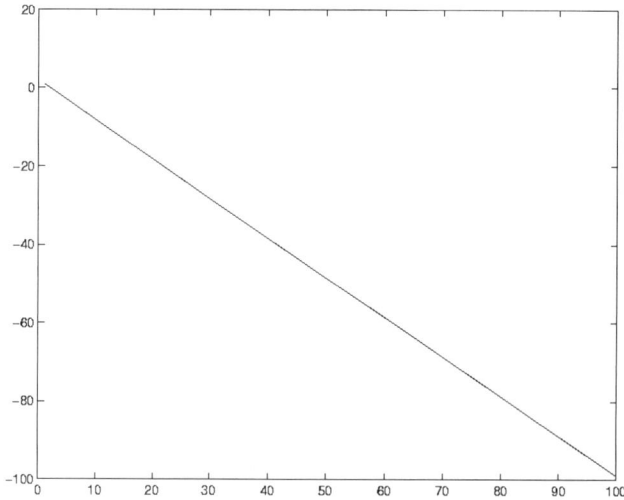

Figure 4.5. *Linear equations example.*

plotted in Figure 4.5, but due to the granularity of the graph we cannot tell the two lines apart. ■

To be able to decide whether or not a problem is ill-conditioned it is clearly desirable to have some measure of the condition of a problem. We show two simple cases where we can obtain such a measure and quote the result for a third example. For the first case we derive the condition number for the evaluation of a function of one variable [205, Section 1.6].

Let $y = f(x)$ with f twice differentiable and $f(x) \neq 0$. Also let $\widehat{y} = f(x + \epsilon)$. Then, using the mean value theorem,

$$\widehat{y} - y = f(x + \epsilon) - f(x)$$
$$= f'(x)\epsilon + \frac{f''(x + \theta\epsilon)}{2!}\epsilon^2, \; \theta \in (0, 1),$$

giving

$$\frac{\widehat{y} - y}{y} = \left(\frac{xf'(x)}{f(x)}\right)\frac{\epsilon}{x} + O\left(\epsilon^2\right).$$

The quantity

$$\kappa(x) = \left|\frac{xf'(x)}{f(x)}\right|$$

is called the *condition number* of f since

$$\left|\frac{\widehat{y} - y}{y}\right| \approx \kappa(x)\left|\frac{\epsilon}{x}\right|.$$

Thus if $\kappa(x)$ is large the problem is ill-conditioned; that is, small perturbations in x can induce large perturbations in the solution y.

Example 4.11 Let $y = f(x) = \cos x$. Then we see that

$$\kappa(x) = |x \tan x|,$$

and, as we might expect, $\cos x$ is most sensitive close to asymptotes of $\tan x$, such as x close to $\pi/2$.[17] If we take $x = 1.57$ and $\epsilon = -0.01$ then we find that

$$\kappa(x)\left|\frac{\epsilon}{x}\right| \approx 12.5577,$$

which is a very good estimate of $|(\widehat{y} - y)/y| = 12.55739\ldots$ ∎

For the second example we consider the condition number of a system of linear equations $Ax = b$. If we let $\widehat{x}$ be the solution of the perturbed equations

$$(A + E)\widehat{x} = b,$$

then

$$A(\widehat{x} - x) = -E\widehat{x}, \text{ so that } \widehat{x} - x = -A^{-1}E\widehat{x},$$

giving

$$\frac{\|\widehat{x} - x\|}{\|\widehat{x}\|} \leq \|A^{-1}\| \cdot \|E\| = \left(\|A\| \cdot \|A^{-1}\|\right) \cdot \frac{\|E\|}{\|A\|}. \tag{4.6}$$

The quantity

$$\kappa(A) = \|A\| \cdot \|A^{-1}\|$$

is called the condition number of A with respect to the solution of the equations $Ax = b$, or the condition number of A with respect to matrix inversion. Since $I = AA^{-1}$, for any norm such that $\|I\| = 1$, we have that $1 \leq \kappa(A)$, with equality possible for the 1, 2, and ∞ norms. If A is singular then $\kappa(A) = \infty$.

---

[17]The given condition number is not valid at $x = \pi/2$, since $\cos \pi/2 = 0$.

Example 4.12 (Condition of matrix) For the matrix of Example 4.10 we have that

$$A = \begin{pmatrix} 99 & 98 \\ 100 & 99 \end{pmatrix}, \ \|A\|_1 = 199$$

and

$$A^{-1} = \begin{pmatrix} 99 & -98 \\ -100 & 99 \end{pmatrix}, \ \|A^{-1}\|_1 = 199,$$

so that

$$\kappa_1(A) = 199^2 \approx 4 \cdot 10^4.$$

Thus we can see that if A is only accurate to about four figures, we cannot guarantee any accuracy in the solution. ∎

The term condition was first introduced by Turing in the context of systems of linear equations [458]. Note that for an orthogonal or unitary matrix Q, $\kappa_2(Q) = 1$.

As a third illustration we quote results for the sensitivity of the root of a polynomial. Consider

$$f(x) = a_n x^n + a_{n-1} x^{n-1} + \cdots + a_1 x + a_0,$$

and let α be a single root of $f(x)$ so that $f(\alpha) = 0$, but $f'(\alpha) \neq 0$. Let $p(x)$ be the perturbed polynomial

$$p(x) = f(x) + \epsilon g(x), \ g(x) = b_n x^n + b_{n-1} x^{n-1} + \cdots + b_1 x + b_0,$$

with root $\widehat{\alpha} = \alpha + \delta$, so that $p(\widehat{\alpha}) = 0$. Then [485, Section 7 of Chapter 2] shows that

$$|\delta| \approx \left| \frac{\epsilon g(\alpha)}{f'(\alpha)} \right|.$$

Wilkinson also shows that if α is a double root then

$$|\delta| \approx \left| \left(-\frac{2\epsilon g(\alpha)}{f''(\alpha)} \right)^{\frac{1}{2}} \right|.$$

Example 4.13 (Condition of cubic) For the root $\alpha = x_1 = 1$ of the cubic equation of Example 4.7, with $g(x) = x^3$ and $\epsilon = -0.01$, we have

$$f'(x) = 3x^2 - 42x + 120$$

so that

$$|\delta| \approx \left| \frac{-0.01 \cdot 1^3}{81} \right| \approx 0.0001,$$

and hence this root is very well-conditioned with respect to perturbations in the coefficient of x^3. On the other hand, for the root $\alpha = 10$, we have

$$f''(x) = 6x - 42,$$

so that

$$|\delta| \approx \left|\left(\frac{-2 \cdot -0.01 \cdot 10^3}{18}\right)^{\frac{1}{2}}\right| \approx 1.054,$$

and this time the perturbation of ϵ produces a rather larger perturbation in the root. Because ϵ is not particularly small the estimate of δ is not particularly accurate, but we do get a good warning of the ill-conditioning. ∎

The book [205, Section 25.4] gives a result for the sensitivity of a root of a general nonlinear equation.

Problems can be ill-conditioned simply because they are poorly scaled, often as the result of a poor choice of measurement units. Some algorithms, or implementations of algorithms, are insensitive to scaling or attempt automatic scaling, but in other cases a good choice of scaling can be important to the success of an algorithm. It is also all too easy to turn a badly scaled problem into a genuinely ill-conditioned problem.

Example 4.14 (Badly scaled matrix) If we let A be the matrix

$$A = \begin{pmatrix} 2 \cdot 10^9 & 10^9 \\ 10^{-9} & 2 \cdot 10^{-9} \end{pmatrix},$$

then $\kappa_2(A) \approx 1.67 \cdot 10^{18}$ and so A is ill-conditioned. However, we can row scale A as

$$B = DA = \begin{pmatrix} 10^{-9} & 0 \\ 0 & 10^9 \end{pmatrix} \begin{pmatrix} 2 \cdot 10^9 & 10^9 \\ 10^{-9} & 2 \cdot 10^{-9} \end{pmatrix} = \begin{pmatrix} 2 & 1 \\ 1 & 2 \end{pmatrix},$$

for which $\kappa_2(B) = 3$, so that B is well-conditioned. On the other hand, if we perform a plane rotation on A with $c = 0.8, s = 0.6$, we get

$$C = GA = \begin{pmatrix} 0.8 & 0.6 \\ -0.6 & 0.8 \end{pmatrix} \begin{pmatrix} 2 \cdot 10^9 & 10^9 \\ 10^{-9} & 2 \cdot 10^{-9} \end{pmatrix}$$

$$= 2 \begin{pmatrix} 8 \cdot 10^8 + 3 \cdot 10^{-10} & 4 \cdot 10^8 + 6 \cdot 10^{-10} \\ -6 \cdot 10^8 + 4 \cdot 10^{-10} & -3 \cdot 10^8 + 8 \cdot 10^{-10} \end{pmatrix}.$$

Since G is orthogonal, $\kappa_2(C) = \kappa_2(A) \approx 1.67 \cdot 10^{18}$, and so C is of course as ill-conditioned as A, but now scaling cannot recover the situation. To see that C is genuinely ill-conditioned, we note that

$$C \approx 2 \cdot 10^8 \begin{pmatrix} 8 & 4 \\ -6 & -3 \end{pmatrix},$$

which is singular. In double precision IEEE arithmetic, this would be the floating-point representation of C. ∎

Many of the LAPACK routines perform scaling or have options to equilibrate the matrix in the case of linear equations [12, Sections 2.4.1 and 4.4.1], [205, Sections 7.3 and 9.8] or to balance in the case of eigenvalue problems [12, Sections 4.8.1.2 and 4.11.1.2].

4.4.2 Stability

The *stability* of a method for solving a problem is concerned with the sensitivity of the method to (rounding) errors in the solution process. A method that guarantees as accurate a solution as the data warrants is said to be stable; otherwise the method is unstable. Stability is concerned with the sensitivity of the method of solution.

An example of an unstable method is that of (4.3) for computing sample variance. We now give two more simple illustrative examples.

Example 4.15 (Quadratic equation) Consider the quadratic equation

$$1.6x^2 - 100.1x + 1.251 = 0.$$

Four significant figure arithmetic when using the standard formula

$$x = \frac{-b \pm \sqrt{b^2 - 4ac}}{2a}$$

gives

$$x_1 = 62.53, \ x_2 = 0.03125.$$

If we use the relationship $x_1 x_2 = c/a$ to compute x_2 from x_1 we instead find that

$$x_2 = 0.01251.$$

The correct solution is $x_1 = 62.55$, $x_2 = 0.0125$. We can see that in using the standard formula to compute the smaller root we have suffered from cancellation, since $\sqrt{b^2 - 4ac}$ is close to $(-b)$. ■

Even a simple problem such as computing the roots of a quadratic equation needs great care. A very nice discussion is to be found in Forsythe [143].

Example 4.16 (Recurrence relation) Consider the computation of y_n defined by

$$y_n = (1/e) \int_0^1 x^n e^x dx, \tag{4.7}$$

where n is a nonnegative integer. We note that, since in the interval $[0, 1]$, $(1/e)e^x$ is bounded by unity, it is easy to show that

$$0 \le y_n \le 1/(n + 1). \tag{4.8}$$

Integrating (4.7) by parts gives

$$y_n = 1 - n y_{n-1}, \ y_0 = 1 - 1/e = 0.63212055882856\ldots, \tag{4.9}$$

and we have a seemingly attractive method for computing y_n for a given value of n. The result of using this forward recurrence relation, with IEEE double precision arithmetic, to compute the values of y_i up to y_{21} is shown in Table 4.2. Bearing in mind the bounds of (4.8), we see that later values are diverging seriously from the correct solution.

Table 4.2. *Forward recurrence for y_n.*

y_0	y_1	y_2	y_3	y_4	y_5	y_6	y_7
0.6321	0.3679	0.2642	0.2073	0.1709	0.1455	0.1268	0.1124
y_8	y_9	y_{10}	y_{11}	y_{12}	y_{13}	y_{14}	y_{15}
0.1009	0.0916	0.0839	0.0774	0.0718	0.0669	0.0627	0.0590
y_{16}	y_{17}	y_{18}	y_{19}	y_{20}	y_{21}		
0.0555	0.0572	-0.0295	1.5596	-30.1924	635.0403		

A simple analysis shows the reason for the instability. Since y_0 cannot be represented exactly, we cannot avoid starting with a slightly perturbed value, $\widehat{y_0}$. So let

$$\widehat{y_0} = y_0 + \epsilon.$$

Then, even if the remaining computations are performed exactly we see that

$$\begin{aligned}
\widehat{y_1} &= 1 - \widehat{y_0} \ = y_1 - \epsilon, \\
\widehat{y_2} &= 1 - 2\widehat{y_1} = y_2 + 2\epsilon, \\
\widehat{y_3} &= 1 - 3\widehat{y_2} = y_3 - 6\epsilon, \\
\widehat{y_4} &= 1 - 4\widehat{y_3} = y_4 + 24\epsilon,
\end{aligned}$$

and a straightforward inductive proof shows that

$$\widehat{y_n} = y_n + (-1)^n n! \epsilon.$$

When $n = 21$, $n! \approx 5.1091 \cdot 10^{19}$. We see clearly that this forward recurrence is an unstable method of computing y_n, since the error grows rapidly as we move forward. ∎

The next example illustrates a stable method of computing y_n.

Example 4.17 (Stable recurrence) Rearranging (4.9) we obtain the backward recurrence

$$y_{n-1} = (1 - y_n)/n.$$

Suppose that we have an approximation, $\widehat{y_{n+m}}$, to y_{n+m} and we let

$$\widehat{y_{n+m}} = y_{n+m} + \epsilon.$$

Then, similarly to the result of Example 4.16, we find that

$$\widehat{y_n} = y_n + \frac{(-1)^{m-n}\epsilon}{(n+m)(n+m-1)\ldots(n+1)},$$

and this time the initial error decays rapidly, rather than grows rapidly as in Example 4.16. If we take an initial guess of $y_{21} = 0$, we see from (4.8) that

$$|\epsilon| \leq 1/21 < 0.05.$$

Using this backward recurrence relation, with IEEE double precision arithmetic, gives the value

$$y_0 = 0.63212055882856,$$

which is correct to all the figures shown. We see that this backward recurrence is stable. ∎

It should also be said that the integral of (4.7) can be evaluated stably without difficulty using a good numerical integration (quadrature) formula, since the function $f(x) = (1/e)x^n e^x$ is nonnegative and monotonic throughout the interval [0, 1].

In the solution of ordinary and partial differential equations (ODEs and PDEs) one form of instability can arise by replacing a differential equation by a difference equation. We first illustrate the problem by the solution of a simple nonlinear equation.

Example 4.18 (Parasitic solution) The equation

$$e^{-x} = 99x \tag{4.10}$$

has a solution close to $x = 0.01$. By expanding e^x as a power series we have that

$$e^{-x} = 1 - x + \frac{x^2}{2!} + \frac{x^3}{3!} + \cdots \approx 1 - x + \frac{x^2}{2!}$$

and hence an approximate solution of (4.10) is a root of the quadratic equation

$$x^2 - 200x + 2 = 0,$$

which has the two roots $x_1 \approx 0.0100005$, $x_2 \approx 199.99$. The second root clearly has nothing to do with the original equation and is called a **parasitic** solution. ∎

In the above example we are unlikely to be fooled by the parasitic solution, since it so clearly does not come close to satisfying (4.10). But in the solution of ODEs or PDEs such bifurcations, due to truncation error, may not be so obvious.

Example 4.19 (Instability for ODEs) For the initial value problem

$$y' = f(x, y), \ y = y_0 \text{ when } x = x_0, \tag{4.11}$$

the midpoint rule, or leap-frog method, for solving the differential equation is given by

$$y_{r+1} = y_{r-1} + 2hf_r, \tag{4.12}$$

where $h = x_i - x_{i-1}$ for all i and $f_r = f(x_r, y_r)$. This method has a truncation error of $O(h^3)$ [224, Section 1.3, Chapter 8].[18] This method requires two starting values, so one starting value must be estimated by some other method. Consider the case where

$$f(x, y) = \alpha y, \ y_0 = 1, \ x_0 = 0,$$

so that the solution of (4.11) is $y = e^{\alpha x}$. Figures 4.6 and 4.7 show the solution obtained by using (4.12) when $h = 0.1$ for the cases $\alpha = 2.5$ and $\alpha = -2.5$, respectively. In each case the value of y_1 is taken as the correct four figure value, $y_1 = 1.284$ when $\alpha = 2.5$ and $y_1 = 0.7788$ when $\alpha = -2.5$. We see that in the first case the numerical solution does a

---

[18]Here it is called the centered method. It is an example of a Nyström method.

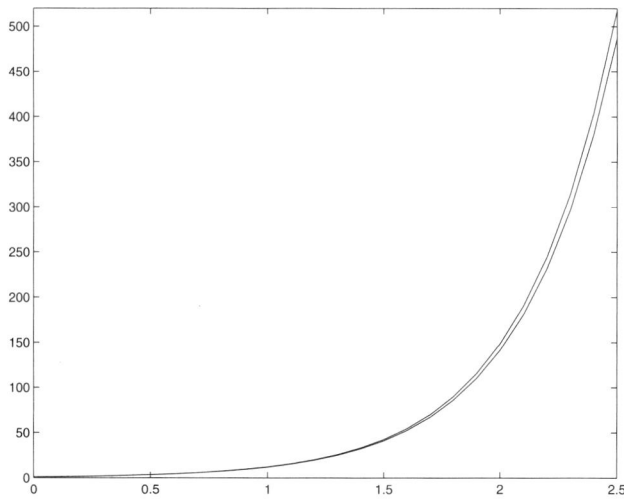

Figure 4.6. *Stable ODE example.*

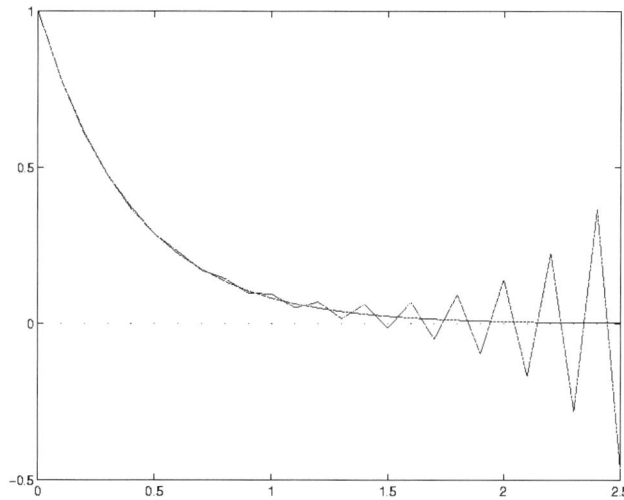

Figure 4.7. *Unstable ODE example.*

good job in following the exact solution, but in the second case oscillation sets in and the numerical solution diverges from the exact solution.   ∎

The reason for the behavior in the above example is that (4.12) has the solution

$$y_r = A \left(\alpha h + \left(1 + \alpha^2 h^2 \right)^{\frac{1}{2}} \right)^r + B \left(\alpha h - \left(1 + \alpha^2 h^2 \right)^{\frac{1}{2}} \right)^r, \qquad (4.13)$$

where A and B are constants that depend on the intial conditions. With the initial conditions $y_0 = 1$, $x_0 = 0$ and $y_1 = e^{\alpha h}$, $x_1 = h$ we find that $A = 1 + O(h^3)$, $B = O(h^3)$. We can see that the first term in (4.13) approximates the exact solution, but the second term is a parasitic solution. When $\alpha > 0$ the exact solution increases and the parasitic solution decays, and so is harmless, but when $\alpha < 0$ the exact solution decays and parasitic solution grows as illustrated in Figure 4.7. An entertaining discussion, in the context of the Milne–Simpson method, of the above phenomenon is given in [3, Chapter 5], a book full of good advice and insight. A more recent book by Acton in the same vein is [4].

4.4.3 Error analysis

Error analysis is concerned with analyzing the cumulative effects of errors. Usually these errors will be rounding or truncation errors. For example, if the polynomial

$$p(x) = p_0 + p_1 x + p_2 x^2 + \cdots + p_n x^n$$

is evaluated at some point $x = \alpha$ using Horner's scheme (nested multiplication) as

$$p(\alpha) = p_0 + \alpha\,(p_1 + \cdots + \alpha\,(p_{n-2} + \alpha\,(p_{n-1} + \alpha p_n))\ldots),$$

we might ask under what conditions, if any, on the coefficients $p_0, p_1, \ldots, p_n$ and α, the solution will, in some sense, be reasonable? To answer the question we need to perform an error analysis.

Error analysis is concerned with establishing whether or not an algorithm is stable for the problem at hand. A *forward error analysis* is concerned with how close the computed solution is to the exact solution. A *backward error analysis* is concerned with how well the computed solution satisfies the problem to be solved. On first acquaintance, that a backward error analysis, as opposed to a forward error analysis, should be of interest often comes as a surprise. The next example illustrates the distinction between backward and forward errors.

Example 4.20 (Linear equations) Let

$$A = \begin{pmatrix} 99 & 98 \\ 100 & 99 \end{pmatrix} \text{ and } b = \begin{pmatrix} 1 \\ 1 \end{pmatrix}.$$

Then the exact solution of the equations $Ax = b$ is given by

$$x = \begin{pmatrix} 1 \\ -1 \end{pmatrix}.$$

Also let $\widehat{x}$ be an approximate solution to the equations and define the **residual** vector r as

$$r = b - A\widehat{x}. \tag{4.14}$$

Of course, for the exact solution $r = 0$ and we might hope that for a solution close to x, r should be small. Consider the approximate solution

$$\widehat{x} = \begin{pmatrix} 2.97 \\ -2.99 \end{pmatrix} \text{ for which } \widehat{x} - x = \begin{pmatrix} 1.97 \\ -1.99 \end{pmatrix},$$

and so $\widehat{x}$ looks to be a rather poor solution. But for this solution we have that

$$r = \begin{pmatrix} -0.01 \\ 0.01 \end{pmatrix},$$

and we have almost solved the original problem. On the other hand, the approximate solution

$$\widehat{x} = \begin{pmatrix} 1.01 \\ -0.99 \end{pmatrix} \text{ for which } \widehat{x} - x = \begin{pmatrix} 0.01 \\ 0.01 \end{pmatrix}$$

gives

$$r = \begin{pmatrix} -1.97 \\ -1.97 \end{pmatrix}$$

and, although $\widehat{x}$ is close to x, it does not solve a problem close to the original problem. ∎

Once we have computed the solution to a system of linear equations $Ax = b$ we can, of course, readily compute the residual of (4.14). If we can find a matrix E such that

$$E\widehat{x} = r, \tag{4.15}$$

then

$$(A + E)\widehat{x} = b$$

and we thus have a measure of the perturbation in A required to make $\widehat{x}$ an exact solution. A particular E that satisfies (4.15) is given by

$$E = \frac{r\widehat{x}^T}{\widehat{x}^T\widehat{x}}.$$

From this equation we have that

$$\|E\|_2 \leq \frac{\|r\|_2\|\widehat{x}\|_2}{\|\widehat{x}\|_2^2} = \frac{\|r\|_2}{\|\widehat{x}\|_2}$$

and from (4.15) we have that

$$\|r\|_2 \leq \|E\|_2\|\widehat{x}\|_2, \text{ so that } \|E\|_2 \geq \frac{\|r\|_2}{\|\widehat{x}\|_2}$$

and hence

$$\|E\|_2 = \frac{\|r\|_2}{\|\widehat{x}\|_2}.$$

Thus, this particular E minimizes $\|E\|_2$. Since $x^Tx = \|x\|_F^2$, it also minimizes E in the Frobenius norm. This gives us an a posteriori bound on the backward error.

Example 4.21 (Perturbation in linear equations) Consider the equations $Ax = b$ of Example 4.20 and the "computed" solution

$$\widehat{x} = \begin{pmatrix} 2.97 \\ -2.99 \end{pmatrix} \text{ for which } r = \begin{pmatrix} -0.01 \\ 0.01 \end{pmatrix}.$$

Then

$$r\widehat{x}^T = \begin{pmatrix} -0.0297 & 0.0299 \\ 0.0297 & -0.0299 \end{pmatrix}, \quad \widehat{x}^T\widehat{x} = 17.761,$$

and

$$E \approx \begin{pmatrix} -0.00167 & 0.00168 \\ 0.00167 & -0.00168 \end{pmatrix}.$$

Note that $\|E\|_F / \|A\|_F \approx 1.695 \cdot 10^{-5}$ and so the computed solution corresponds to a small relative perturbation in A. ∎

From (4.6) we have that

$$\frac{\|\widehat{x} - x\|}{\|\widehat{x}\|} \leq \kappa(A) \frac{\|E\|}{\|A\|}$$

and so, if we know $\kappa(A)$, then an estimate of the backward error allows us to estimate the forward error.

As a general rule, we can say that approximately

$$\boxed{\text{forward error} \leq \text{condition number} \cdot \text{backward error.}}$$

Although the idea of backward error analysis had been introduced by others, it was James Hardy Wilkinson who really developed the theory and application and gave us our understanding of error analysis and stability, particularly in the context of numerical linear algebra. See the classic books Wilkinson [485] and Wilkinson [486]. A typical picture of Wilkinson, cheerfully expounding his ideas, is shown in Figure 4.8. A wonderful modern book that continues the Wilkinson tradition is Higham [205]. The solid foundation for the

Figure 4.8. *James Hardy Wilkinson (1919–1986).*

numerical linear algebra of today relies heavily on the pioneering work of Wilkinson; see also Wilkinson and Reinsch [490].[19]

Wilkinson recognized that error analysis could be tedious and often required great care but was nevertheless essential to our understanding of the stability of algorithms.

"The clear identification of the factors determining the stability of an algorithm soon led to the development of better algorithms. The proper understanding of inverse iteration for eigenvectors and the development of the QR algorithm by Francis are the crowning achievements of this line of research."

"For me, then, the primary purpose of the rounding error analysis was insight" [489, p. 197].

As a second example to illustrate forward and backward errors, we consider the quadratic equation of Example 4.15.

Example 4.22 (Errors in quadratic equation) For the quadratic equation of Example 4.15 we saw that the standard formula gave the roots $x_1 = 62.53$, $x_2 = 0.03125$. Since the correct solution is $x_1 = 62.55$, $x_2 = 0.0125$ the second root has a large forward error. If we form the quadratic $q(x) = 1.6(x - x_1)(x - x_2)$, rounding the answer to four significant figures, we get

$$q(x) = 1.6x^2 - 100.1x + 3.127$$

and the constant term differs significantly from the original value of 1.251, so that there is also a large backward error. The standard method is neither forward nor backward stable. On the other hand, for the computed roots $x_1 = 62.53$, $x_2 = 0.01251$ we get

$$q(x) = 1.6x^2 - 100.1x + 1.252,$$

so this time we have both forward and backward stability. ∎

An example of a computation that is forward stable but not backward stable is that of computing the coefficients of the polynomial

$$p(x) = (x - x_1)(x - x_2) \ldots (x - x_n), \quad x_i > 0.$$

In this case, since the x_i are all of the same sign, no cancellation occurs in computing the coefficients of $p(x)$ and the computed coefficients will be close to the exact coefficients, and thus we have small forward errors. On the other hand, as Example 4.7 illustrates, the roots of polynomials can be sensitive to perturbations in the coefficients, and so the roots of the computed polynomial could differ significantly from $x_1, x_2, \ldots, x_n$.

Example 4.23 (Ill-conditioned polynomial) The polynomial whose roots are $x_i = i, i = 1, 2, \ldots, 20$, is

$$p(x) = x^{20} - 210x^{19} + \cdots + 20!$$

---

[19]Givens's 1954 technical report quoted earlier [164], which was never published in full and must be one of the most often quoted technical reports in numerical analysis, as well as the introduction of Givens plane rotations, describes the use of Sturm sequences for computing eigenvalues of tridiagonal matrices and contains probably the first explicit backward error analysis. Wilkinson, who so successfully developed and expounded the theory and analysis of rounding errors, regarded the a priori error analysis of Givens as "one of the landmarks in the history of the subject" [486, additional notes to Chapter 5].

Suppose that the coefficient of x^{19} is computed as $-(210+2^{-23})$; then we find that $x_{16}, x_{17} \approx 16.73 \pm 2.813i$. Thus a small error in computing a coefficient produced a polynomial with significantly different roots from those of the exact polynomial. This polynomial is discussed in [485, Chapter 2, Section 9] and [487]. See also [488, Section 2].   ∎

4.5 Floating-point Error Analysis

Floating-point error analysis is concerned with the analysis of errors in the presence of floating-point arithmetic. It is concerned with relative errors. We give just a brief introduction to floating-point error analysis in order to illustrate the ideas.

Let x be a real number; then we use the notation $\mathrm{fl}(x)$ to represent the floating-point value of x. The fundamental assumption is that

$$\boxed{\mathrm{fl}\,(x) = x(1 + \epsilon),\ |\epsilon| \le \mathbf{u},}\tag{4.16}$$

where $\mathbf{u}$ is the unit roundoff of (4.1). Of course,

$$\frac{\mathrm{fl}\,(x) - x}{x} = \epsilon.$$

A useful alternative is

$$\mathrm{fl}\,(x) = \frac{x}{1 + \delta},\ |\delta| \le \mathbf{u},\ \text{so that}\ \frac{\mathrm{fl}\,(x) - x}{\mathrm{fl}\,(x)} = \delta.\tag{4.17}$$

Example 4.24 (Floating-point numbers) Consider four figure decimal arithmetic with

$$\mathbf{u} = \frac{1}{2} \cdot 10^{-3} = 5 \cdot 10^{-4}.$$

If $x = \sqrt{7} = 2.645751\ldots$, then $\mathrm{fl}(x) = 2.646$ and

$$\epsilon = \frac{\mathrm{fl}\,(x) - x}{x} \approx 0.94 \cdot 10^{-4}.$$

If $x = 1.000499\ldots$, then $\mathrm{fl}(x) = 1.000$ and

$$\epsilon = \frac{\mathrm{fl}\,(x) - x}{x} \approx -5 \cdot 10^{-4}.$$

If $x = 1000.499\ldots$, then $\mathrm{fl}(x) = 1000$ and again

$$\epsilon = \frac{\mathrm{fl}\,(x) - x}{x} \approx -5 \cdot 10^{-4}.\qquad ∎$$

Bearing in mind (4.16), if x and y are *floating point numbers*, then the standard model of floating-point arithmetic, introduced by Wilkinson [483], is given by

$$\boxed{\begin{array}{c} \mathrm{fl}\,(x \otimes y) = (x \otimes y)(1 + \epsilon),\ |\epsilon| \le \mathbf{u}, \\[2mm] \text{where}\ \otimes \equiv +, -, \cdot, \div. \end{array}}\tag{4.18}$$

It is assumed, of course, that $x \otimes y$ produces a value that is in the range of representable floating-point numbers. Comparable to (4.17), a useful alternative is

$$\mathrm{fl}\,(x \otimes y) = \frac{x \otimes y}{1 + \delta}, \quad |\delta| \leq \mathbf{u}.$$

When we consider a sequence of floating-point operations we frequently obtain products of error terms of the form

$$(1 + \epsilon) = (1 + \epsilon_1)(1 + \epsilon_2) \ldots (1 + \epsilon_r)$$

so that

$$(1 - \mathbf{u})^r \leq 1 + \epsilon \leq (1 + \mathbf{u})^r.$$

If we ignore second order terms then we have the reasonable assumption that[20]

$$|\epsilon| \leq r\mathbf{u}. \tag{4.19}$$

We now give three illustrative examples. In all three examples the x_i are assumed to be floating-point numbers, that is, they are values that are already represented in the computer. This is, of course, a natural assumption to make when we are analyzing the errors in a computation.

Example 4.25 (Product of values) Let $x = x_0 x_1 \ldots x_n$ and $\widetilde{x} = \mathrm{fl}(x)$. Thus we have n products to form, each one introducing an error bounded by $\mathbf{u}$. Hence from (4.18) we get

$$\widetilde{x} = x_0 x_1 (1 + \epsilon_1) x_2 (1 + \epsilon_2) \ldots x_n (1 + \epsilon_n), \quad |\epsilon_i| \leq \mathbf{u}, \tag{4.20}$$

and from (4.19) we see that

$$\widetilde{x} = x(1 + \epsilon), \quad |\epsilon| \leq n\mathbf{u}, \tag{4.21}$$

where

$$1 + \epsilon = (1 + \epsilon_1)(1 + \epsilon_2) \ldots (1 + \epsilon_n).$$

We can see from (4.21) that this computation is forward stable, because the result is close to the exact result, and from (4.20) the computation is also backward stable, because the result is exact for a slightly perturbed problem; that is, the result is exact for the data $x_0, x_1(1 + \epsilon_1), x_2(1 + \epsilon_2), \ldots, x_n(1 + \epsilon_n)$. ∎

Example 4.26 (Sum of values) Let $s = x_1 + x_2 + \cdots + x_n$ and $\widetilde{s} = \mathrm{fl}(s)$. By considering

$$s_r = \mathrm{fl}\,(s_{r-1} + x_r), \quad s_1 = x_1,$$

it is straightforward to show that

$$\widetilde{s} = x_1(1 + \epsilon_1) + x_2(1 + \epsilon_1) + x_3(1 + \epsilon_2) + \cdots + x_n(1 + \epsilon_{n-1})$$
$$= s + (x_1\epsilon_1 + x_2\epsilon_1 + x_2\epsilon_2 + \cdots + x_n\epsilon_{n-1}), \quad |\epsilon_r| \leq (n - r + 1)\mathbf{u}.$$

Here we see that summation is backward stable but is not necessarily forward stable. Example 4.2 gives a case where summation is not forward stable. ∎

---

[20]Those who are uncomfortable with the approximation may prefer to replace the bound $|\epsilon| \leq r\mathbf{u}$ with one of the form $|\epsilon| \leq \gamma_r$, where $\gamma_r = (r\mathbf{u})/(1 - r\mathbf{u})$ and $r\mathbf{u} < 1$ is assumed. See Higham [205, Lemma 3.1].

Note that if the x_i all have the same sign, then summation is forward stable because then

$$|\widetilde{s} - s| \leq (|x_1| + |x_2| + \cdots + |x_n|)n\mathbf{u} = |s|n\mathbf{u}$$

so that

$$\frac{|\widetilde{s} - s|}{|s|} \leq n\mathbf{u}.$$

Example 4.27 (Difference of two squares) Consider the computation

$$z = x^2 - y^2. \tag{4.22}$$

We can, of course, also express z as

$$z = (x + y)(x - y). \tag{4.23}$$

If we compute z from (4.22) we find that

$$\widetilde{z} = \mathrm{fl}\left(x^2 - y^2\right) = x^2(1 + \epsilon_1) - y^2(1 + \epsilon_2)$$
$$= z + (x^2\epsilon_1 - y^2\epsilon_2), \quad \epsilon_1, \epsilon_2 \leq 2\mathbf{u},$$

and so this is backward stable, but not forward stable. On the other hand, if we compute z from (4.23) we find that

$$\widehat{z} = \mathrm{fl}\left((x + y)(x - y)\right) = (x + y)(x - y)(1 + \epsilon)$$
$$= z(1 + \epsilon), \quad \epsilon \leq 3\mathbf{u},$$

and so this is both backward and forward stable. As an example, if we take

$$x = 543.2, \quad y = 543.1, \quad \text{so that} \quad z = 108.63$$

and use four significant figure arithmetic we find that

$$\widetilde{z} = 100, \quad \text{but} \quad \widehat{z} = 108.6.$$

Clearly $\widetilde{z}$ has suffered from cancellation, but $\widehat{z}$ has not. ∎

We now quote some results, without proof, of solving higher level linear algebra problems to illustrate the sort of results that are possible. Principally we consider the solution of the n linear equations

$$Ax = b \tag{4.24}$$

by Gaussian elimination and we assume that the reader is familiar with Gaussian elimination. The kth step of Gaussian elimination can be expressed as

$$A_k = M_k P_k A_{k-1} Q_k, \quad A_0 = A, \tag{4.25}$$

where P_k and Q_k are permutation matrices, one or both of which may be the unit matrix, chosen to implement whatever pivoting strategy is used and M_k is the multiplier matrix chosen to eliminate the elements below the diagonal of the kth column of A_{k-1}. This results in the factorization

$$A = PLUQ,$$

where P and Q are permutation matrices, L is a unit lower triangular matrix, and U is upper triangular. To simplify analysis it is usual to assume that, with hindsight, A has already been permuted so that we can work with $A \Leftarrow P^T A Q^T$. In this case (4.25) becomes

$$A_k = M_k A_{k-1}, \quad A_0 = A,$$

and M_k and A_{k-1} have the form

$$M_k = \begin{pmatrix} I & 0 & 0 \\ 0 & 1 & 0 \\ 0 & -m_k & I \end{pmatrix}, \quad A_{k-1} = \begin{pmatrix} U_{k-1} & u_{k-1} & X_{k-1} \\ 0 & \alpha_{k-1} & b_{k-1}^T \\ 0 & a_{k-1} & \widehat{A}_{k-1} \end{pmatrix}.$$

m_k is chosen to eliminate a_{k-1}, so that

$$a_{k-1} - \alpha_{k-1} m_k = 0, \quad \text{giving } m_k = a_{k-1}/\alpha_{k-1},$$

$\widehat{A}_{k-1}$ is updated as

$$\widetilde{A}_k = \widehat{A}_{k-1} - m_k b_{k-1}^T \equiv \begin{pmatrix} \alpha_k & b_k^T \\ a_k & \widehat{A}_k \end{pmatrix}$$

and

$$A = LU, \quad \text{where } L = M_1^{-1} M_2^{-1} \dots M_{n-1}^{-1}, \quad \text{and } U = A_{n-1}.$$

Since

$$M_k^{-1} = \begin{pmatrix} I & 0 & 0 \\ 0 & 1 & 0 \\ 0 & m_k & I \end{pmatrix}$$

we have that

$$L = \begin{pmatrix} 1 & 0 & \cdots & 0 & 0 \\ m_{21} & 1 & \cdots & 0 & 0 \\ m_{31} & m_{32} & \cdots & 0 & 0 \\ \vdots & \vdots & & \vdots & \vdots \\ m_{n-1,1} & m_{n-1,2} & \cdots & 1 & 0 \\ m_{n1} & m_{n2} & \cdots & m_{n,n-1} & 1 \end{pmatrix}.$$

It can be shown that the computed factors $\widetilde{L}$ and $\widetilde{U}$ satisfy

$$\widetilde{L}\widetilde{U} = A + F,$$

where various bounds on F are possible; for example, for the 1, ∞, or F norms

$$\|F\| \le 3ng\mathbf{u}\|A\|, \quad g = \frac{\max \|\widetilde{A}_k\|}{\|A\|}.$$

g is called the *growth factor*. Similarly it can be shown that the computed solution of (4.24), $\widetilde{x}$, satisfies

$$(A + E)\widetilde{x} = b,$$

where a typical bound is

$$\|E\| \leq 3n^2 g\mathbf{u}\|A\|.$$

We can see that this bound is satisfactory unless g is large, so it is important to choose P or Q, or both, in order to control the size of g. This is essentially the classic result of Wilkinson [484] and [485, Section 25], where the ∞ norm is used and the use of partial pivoting is assumed; see also [205, Theorem 9.5].

The next example gives a simple demonstration of the need for pivoting.

Example 4.28 (The need for pivoting) Consider the matrix

$$A = \begin{pmatrix} 0.001 & 12 \\ 10 & -10 \end{pmatrix}$$

and the use of four significant figure arithmetic. Since this is just a two by two matrix we have that $M_1^{-1} = L$ and $M_1 A = U$. Denoting the computed matrix X by $\widetilde{X}$, we find that

$$L = \widetilde{L} = \begin{pmatrix} 1 & 0 \\ 10000 & 1 \end{pmatrix}, \quad U = \begin{pmatrix} 0.001 & 12 \\ 0 & -120010 \end{pmatrix}, \quad \text{and} \quad \widetilde{U} = \begin{pmatrix} 0.001 & 12 \\ 0 & -120000 \end{pmatrix},$$

which gives

$$U - \widetilde{U} = \begin{pmatrix} 0 & 0 \\ 0 & 10 \end{pmatrix}$$

and

$$F = \widetilde{L}\widetilde{U} - A = \begin{pmatrix} 0 & 0 \\ 0 & 10 \end{pmatrix} = U - \widetilde{U}.$$

Thus while $\|F\|$ is small relative to $\|U\|$, it corresponds to a large relative perturbation in $\|A\|$. On the other hand, if we permute the two rows of A to give

$$\bar{A} = \begin{pmatrix} 10 & -10 \\ 0.001 & 12 \end{pmatrix},$$

we have that

$$L = \widetilde{L} = \begin{pmatrix} 1 & 0 \\ 0.0001 & 1 \end{pmatrix}, \quad U = \begin{pmatrix} 10 & -10 \\ 0 & 12.001 \end{pmatrix}, \quad \text{and} \quad \widetilde{U} = \begin{pmatrix} 10 & -10 \\ 0 & 12.00 \end{pmatrix},$$

which gives

$$U - \widetilde{U} = \begin{pmatrix} 0 & 0 \\ 0 & -0.001 \end{pmatrix}$$

and

$$F = \widetilde{L}\widetilde{U} - A = \begin{pmatrix} 0 & 0 \\ 0 & -0.001 \end{pmatrix} = U - \widetilde{U}.$$

This time $\|F\|$ is small relative to both $\|U\|$ and $\|A\|$. ∎

If we put $m = \max |\widetilde{m}_{ij}|$ then we can show that

$$g \leq (1+m)^{n-1}.$$

Partial pivoting ensures that

$$m \leq 1 \text{ and hence } g \leq 2^{n-1}.$$

Only very special examples get anywhere near this bound, one example due to Wilkinson being matrices of the form

$$A = \begin{pmatrix} 1 & 0 & 0 & \cdots & 0 & 1 \\ -1 & 1 & 0 & \cdots & 0 & 1 \\ -1 & -1 & 1 & \cdots & 0 & 1 \\ \vdots & \vdots & \vdots & & \vdots & \vdots \\ -1 & -1 & -1 & \cdots & 1 & 1 \\ -1 & -1 & -1 & \cdots & -1 & 1 \end{pmatrix} \text{ for which } U = \begin{pmatrix} 1 & 0 & 0 & \cdots & 0 & 1 \\ 0 & 1 & 0 & \cdots & 0 & 2 \\ 0 & 0 & 1 & \cdots & 0 & 4 \\ \vdots & \vdots & \vdots & \vdots & \vdots & \vdots \\ 0 & 0 & 0 & \cdots & 1 & 2^{n-2} \\ 0 & 0 & 0 & \cdots & 0 & 2^{n-1} \end{pmatrix}.$$

Despite such examples, in practice partial pivoting is the method of choice, but careful software should at least include an option to monitor the growth factor.

There are classes of matrices for which pivoting is not needed to control the growth of g [205, Table 9.1]. Perhaps the most important case is that of symmetric positive definite matrices for which it is known a priori that growth cannot occur, and so Gaussian elimination is stable when applied to a system of equations for which the matrix of coefficients is symmetric positive definite.[21]

The choice of pivots is affected by scaling and equilibration, and a poor choice of scaling can lead to a poor choice of pivots. A full discussion on pivoting strategies, equilibration, and scaling, as well as sage advice, can be found in Higham [205].

For methods that use orthogonal transformations we can usually obtain similar error bounds, but without the growth factor since orthogonal transformations preserve the 2 norm and F norm. For example, if we use Householder transformations to perform a QR factorization of A for the solution of the least squares problem $\min_x \|b - Ax\|_2$, where A is an m by n, $m \geq n$ matrix of rank n [169], the computed solution $\tilde{x}$ satisfies

$$\min_x \|(b + f) - (A + E)\tilde{x}\|_2,$$

where f and E satisfy bounds of the form

$$\|f\|_F \leq c_1 mn\mathbf{u}\|b\|_F \quad \|E\|_F \leq c_2 mn\mathbf{u}\|A\|_F$$

and c_1 and c_2 are small integer constants [284, p. 90].

Similarly, for the solution of the eigenvalue problem $Ax = \lambda x$, where A is an n by n matrix, using Housholder transformations to reduce A to upper Hessenberg form, followed by the QR algorithm to further reduce the Hessenberg form to upper triangular Schur form, the computed solution satisfies

$$(A + E)\tilde{x} = \tilde{\lambda}\tilde{x},$$

where

$$\|E\|_F \leq p(n)\mathbf{u}\|A\|_F$$

and $p(n)$ is a modestly growing function of n [486, 12].

---

[21]The variant of Gaussian elimination that is usually used in this case is *Cholesky's method*.

We note that the bounds discussed so far are called *normwise* bounds, but in many cases they can be replaced by *componentwise* bounds which bound the absolute values of the individual elements, and so are rather more satisfactory. For instance, if A is a sparse matrix, we would probably prefer not to have to perturb the elements that are structurally zero. As a simple example, consider the triangular equations

$$Tx = b, \quad T \text{ is } n \text{ by } n \text{ triangular,}$$

and let $\widetilde{x}$ be the solution computed by forward or backward substitution, depending on whether T is lower or upper triangular, respectively. Then it can readily be shown that $\widetilde{x}$ satisfies

$$(T + E)\widetilde{x} = b, \quad \text{with } |e_{ij}| \leq n\mathbf{u}|t_{ij}|,$$

which is a strong componentwise result showing backward stability [205, Theorem 8.5].

Associated with componentwise error bounds are componentwise condition numbers. Once again see [205] for further details and references.

4.6   Posing the Mathematical Problem

In this short section we merely wish to raise awareness of the need to model a problem correctly, without offering any profound solution.

It can be all too easy to transform a well-conditioned problem into an ill-conditioned problem. For instance, in Example 4.16 we transformed the well-conditioned quadrature problem of finding

$$y_n = (1/e) \int_0^1 x^n e^x dx, \quad n \geq 0,$$

into the ill-conditioned problem of finding y_n from the forward recurrence relation

$$y_n = 1 - ny_{n-1}, \quad y_0 = 1 - 1/e.$$

As another example, we noted in section 4.4.3 that polynomials can be very ill-conditioned. It follows that the eigenvalues of a matrix A should most certainly not be computed via the characteristic equation of A. For example, if A is a symmetric matrix with eigenvalues $\lambda_i = i, i = 1, 2, \ldots, 20$, then the characteristic equation of A, $\det(A - \lambda A)$, is very ill-conditioned (see Example 4.23). On the other hand, the eigenvalues of a symmetric matrix are always well-conditioned [486, Section 31, Chapter 2].

The above two examples illustrate the dangers in transforming the mathematical problem. Sometimes it can be poor modeling of the physical problem that gives rise to an ill-conditioned mathematical problem, and so we need to think carefully about the whole modeling process.

We cannot blame software for giving us poor solutions if we provide the wrong problem. We can, of course, hope that the software might provide a measure for the condition of the problem, or some measure of the accuracy of the solution to give us warning of a poorly posed problem.

At the end of section 4.4.1 we also mentioned the desirability of careful choice of measurement units, in order to help avoid the effects of poor scaling.

4.7 Error Bounds and Software

In this section we give examples of reliable software that return information about the quality of the solution. First we look at the freely available software package LAPACK [12], and then at an example of a commercial software library, the NAG Library [332]. The author of this chapter has to declare an interest in both of these software products; he is one of the authors of LAPACK and is a software developer employed by NAG Ltd. Naturally, the examples are chosen because of familiarity with the products and belief in them as quality products, but I have nevertheless tried not to introduce bias.

LAPACK stands for **L**inear **A**lgebra **PACK**age and is a numerical software package for the solution of dense and banded linear algebra problems aimed at PCs, workstations, and high-performance shared memory machines. One of the aims of LAPACK was to make the software efficient on modern machines, while retaining portability, and to this end it makes extensive use of the Basic Linear Algebra Subprograms (BLAS), using block-partitioned algorithms based upon the Level 3 BLAS wherever possible. The BLAS specify the interface for a set of subprograms for common scalar and vector (Level 1), matrix-vector (Level 2), and matrix-matrix operations (Level 3). Their motivation and specification are given in Lawson et al. [285], Dongarra et al. [124], and Dongarra et al. [122], respectively. Information on block-partitioned algorithms and performance of LAPACK can be found in [12, Chapter 3]. See also [170, particularly Section 1.3], and [426, Chapter 2], which also has some nice discussion on computation.

LAPACK has routines for the solution of systems of linear equations, linear least squares problems, eigenvalue and singular value problems, including generalized problems, as well as for the underlying computational components such as matrix factorizations. In addition, a lot of effort was expended in providing condition and error estimates. Quoting from the first paragraph of Chapter 4 ("Accuracy and Stability") of the LAPACK Users' Guide,

> "In addition to providing faster routines than previously available, LAPACK provides more comprehensive and better error bounds. Our goal is to provide error bounds for most quantities computed by LAPACK."

In many cases the routines return the bounds directly; in other cases the Users' Guide gives details of error bounds and provides code fragments to compute those bounds.

As an example, routine DGESVX[22] solves a system of linear equations $AX = B$, where B is a matrix of one or more right-hand sides, using Gaussian elimination with partial pivoting. Part of the interface is

```
SUBROUTINE DGESVX( ..., RCOND, FERR, BERR, WORK, ..., INFO)
```

where the displayed arguments return the following information:

RCOND   -   estimate of reciprocal of condition number, $1/\kappa(A)$,
FERR(j) -   estimated forward error for X_j,
BERR(j) -   componentwise relative backward error for X_j (smallest relative change in any element of A and B_j that makes X_j an exact solution),

---

[22]In the LAPACK naming scheme, D stands for double precision, GE for general matrix, SV for solver, and X for expert driver.

```
WORK(1)    -    reciprocal of pivot growth factor, 1/g,
INFO       -    returns a positive value if the computed triangular factor U is singular
                or nearly singular.
```

Thus DGESVX is returning all the information necessary to judge the quality of the computed solution.

The routine returns an estimate of $1/\kappa(A)$ rather than $\kappa(A)$ to avoid overflow when A is singular, or very ill-conditioned. The argument INFO is the LAPACK warning or error flag and is present in all the LAPACK user callable routines. It returns zero on successful exit, a negative value if an input argument is incorrectly supplied, for example, $n < 0$, and a positive value in the case of failure, or near failure as above. In the above example, INFO returns the value i if $u_{ii} = 0$, in which case no solution is provided since U is exactly singular, but returns the value $n + 1$ if $1/\kappa(A) < \mathbf{u}$, in which case A is singular to working precision. In the latter case a solution is returned, and so INFO $= n + 1$ acts as a warning that the solution may have no correct digits. The routine also has the option to equilibrate the matrix A. See the documentation of the routine for further information, either in the Users' Guide or in the source code available from netlib.[23]

As a second example from LAPACK, routine DGEEVX solves the eigenproblem $Ax = \lambda x$ for the eigenvalues and eigenvectors, $\lambda_i, x_i, i = 1, 2, \ldots, n$, of the n by n matrix A. Optionally, the matrix can be balanced and the left eigenvectors of A can also be computed. Part of the interface is

```
SUBROUTINE DGEEVX( ..., ABNRM, RCONDE, RCONDV, ... )
```

where the displayed arguments return the following information:

```
ABNRM      -    norm of the balanced matrix,
RCONDE(i)  -    reciprocal of the condition number for the ith eigenvalue, s_i,
RCONDV(i)  -    reciprocal of the condition number for the ith eigenvector, sep_i.
```

Following a call to DGEEVX, approximate error bounds for the computed eigenvalues and eigenvectors, say, EERRBD(i) and VERRBD(i), such that

$$|\widetilde{\lambda}_i - \lambda_i| \leq \text{EERRBD}(i),$$
$$\theta(\widetilde{v}_i, v_i) \leq \text{VERRBD}(i),$$

where $\theta(\widetilde{v}_i, v_i)$ is the angle between the computed and true eigenvector, may be returned by the following code fragment, taken from the Users' Guide:

```
EPSMCH = DLAMCH('E')
DO 10 I = 1, N
    EERRBD(I)  =  EPSMCH*ABNRM/RCONDE(I)
    VERRBD(I)  =  EPSMCH*ABNRM/RCONDV(I)
10 CONTINUE
```

These bounds are based upon Table 4.3, extracted from Table 4.5 of the LAPACK Users' Guide, which gives approximate asymptotic error bounds for the nonsymmetric eigenproblem. These bounds assume that the eigenvalues are simple eigenvalues. In addition if the

---

[23]http://www.netlib.org/lapack/index.html

problem is ill-conditioned, these bounds may only hold for extremely small $\|E\|_2$ and so the Users' Guide also provides a table of global error bounds which are not so restrictive on $\|E\|_2$. The tables in the Users' Guide include bounds for clusters of eigenvalues and for invariant subspaces, and these bounds can be estimated using DGEESX in place of DGEEVX. For further details see The LAPACK Users' Guide [12, Chapter 4] and for further information see [170, Chapter 7] and Stewart and Sun [427].

Table 4.3. *Asymptotic error bounds for* $Ax = \lambda x$.

Simple eigenvalue	$\|\widetilde{\lambda}_i - \lambda_i\| \lesssim \|E\|_2/s_i$
Eigenvector	$\theta(\widetilde{v}_i, v_i) \lesssim \|E\|_F/\mathrm{sep}_i$

LAPACK is freely available via netlib,[24] is included in the NAG Fortran 77 Library, and is the basis of the dense linear algebra in the NAG Fortran 90 and C Libraries. Tuned versions of a number of LAPACK routines are included in the NAG Fortran SMP Library. The matrix computations of MATLAB have been based upon LAPACK since Version 6 [305, 204].

We now take an example from the NAG Fortran Library. Routine D01AJF is a general purpose integrator using an adaptive procedure, based on the QUADPACK routine QAGS [361], which performs the integration

$$I = \int_a^b f(x)dx,$$

where $[a, b]$ is a finite interval. Part of the interface to D01AJF is

```
SUBROUTINE D01AJF ( ..., EPSABS, EPSREL, RESULT, ABSERR, ... )
```

where the displayed arguments return the following information:

```
EPSABS  -  the absolute accuracy required,
EPSREL  -  the relative accuracy required,
RESULT  -  the computed approximation to I,
ABSERR  -  an estimate of the absolute error.
```

In normal circumstances ABSERR satisfies

$$|I - \mathrm{RESULT}| \le \mathrm{ABSERR} \le \max(\mathrm{EPSABS}, \mathrm{EPSREL} \cdot |I|).$$

See the NAG Library documentation [333] and Piessens et al. [361] for further details. QUADPACK is freely available from netlib.[25] A Fortran 90 version of QAGS is available from an updated quadrature package, CUBPACK, which is available from netlib. Typically the error estimate for a quadrature routine is obtained at the expense of additional computation with a finer interval, or mesh, or the use of a higher order quadrature formula. See also Chapter 3 of this book for expert information on numerical quadrature.

---

[24] http://www.netlib.org/lapack/index.html
[25] http://www.netlib.org/quadpack/

As a second example from the NAG Library we consider the solution of an ODE. Routine D02PCF integrates

$$y' = f(t, y), \quad \text{given } y(t_0) = y_0,$$

where y is the n element solution vector and t is the independent variable, using a Runge–Kutta method. Following the use of D02PCF, routine D02PZF may be used to compute global error estimates. Part of the interface to D02PZF is

```
SUBROUTINE D02PZF( RMSERR, ERRMAX, TERRMX, ... )
```

where the displayed arguments return the following information:

RMSERR(i)   -   approximate root mean square error for y_i,
ERRMAX   -   maximum approximate true error,
TERRMX   -   first point at which maximum approximate true error occurred.

The assessment of the error is determined at the expense of computing a more accurate solution using a higher order method than that used for the original solution.

The NAG D02P routines are based upon the RKSUITE software by Brankin et al. [49], which is also available from netlib.[26] See also Shampine and Gladwell [406] and Brankin, Gladwell, and Shampine [50]. A Fortran 90 version of RKSUITE is also available[27]; see Brankin and Gladwell [48]. See also Chapter 7 of this book for information on the verification of approximate solutions of ODE solvers.

Many routines in the NAG Library attempt to return information about accuracy. The documentation of the routines includes a section labeled "Accuracy" which, when appropriate, gives further advice or information. For instance, the optimization routines generally quote the optimality conditions that need to be met for the routine to be successful. These routines are cautious, and sometimes return a warning, or error, when it is likely that an optimum point has been found, but not all the optimality conditions have been met. NAG and the authors of the routines feel that this is the best approach for reliability—even if users would sometimes prefer that we were more optimistic!

4.8   Other Approaches

What does one do if the software does not provide suitable estimates for the accuracy of the solution, or the sensitivity of the problem? One approach is to run the problem with perturbed data and compare solutions. Of course, the difficulty with this approach is to know how best to choose perturbations. If a small perturbation does significantly change the solution, then we can be sure that the problem is sensitive, but of course we cannot rely on the converse. If we can trust that the software implements a stable method, then any sensitivity in the solution is due to the problem, but otherwise we cannot be sure whether it is the method or problem that is sensitive.

To help estimate such sensitivity there exists software that uses stochastic methods to give statistical estimates of backward error, or of sensitivity. One such example, PRECISE,

---

[26]http://www.netlib.org/ode/rksuite/
[27]http://www.netlib.org/ode/rksuite/ or http://www.netlib.org/toms/771

is described in Chapter 6 of this book and provides a module for statistical backward error analysis as well as a module for sensitivity analysis. Another example is CADNA[28]; see, for example, Vignes [467].

Another approach to obtaining bounds on the solution is the use of interval arithmetic, in conjunction with interval analysis. Some problems can be successfully solved using interval arithmetic throughout, but for some problems the bounds obtained would be far too pessimistic; however, interval arithmetic can often be applied as an a posteriori tool to obtain realistic bounds. Interval analysis and arithmetic are discussed in Chapters 9 and 10 of this book. We note that there is a nice interval arithmetic toolbox for MATLAB, INTLAB, that is freely available; this is also described in Chapter 10. It should be noted that in general, the aim of interval arithmetic is to return forward error bounds on the solution.

Example 4.29 (Cancellation and interval arithmetic) As a very simple example consider the computation of s in Example 4.2 using four figure interval arithmetic. Bearing in mind that interval arithmetic works with intervals that are guaranteed to contain the exact solution, we find that

$$s = \begin{bmatrix} s1 & s2 \end{bmatrix} = \begin{bmatrix} 1.000 & 1.000 \end{bmatrix} + \begin{bmatrix} 1.000 \cdot 10^4 & 1.000 \cdot 10^4 \end{bmatrix} - \begin{bmatrix} 1.000 \cdot 10^4 & 1.000 \cdot 10^4 \end{bmatrix}$$
$$= \begin{bmatrix} 1.000 \cdot 10^4 & 1.001 \cdot 10^4 \end{bmatrix} - \begin{bmatrix} 1.000 \cdot 10^4 & 1.000 \cdot 10^4 \end{bmatrix}$$
$$= \begin{bmatrix} 0 & 10 \end{bmatrix},$$

so while the result is somewhat pessimistic, it does give due warning of the cancellation. ∎

Finally we comment that one should not be afraid to exert pressure on software developers to provide features that allow one to estimate the sensitivity of the problem and the accuracy of the solution.

4.9 Summary

We have tried to illustrate the niceties of numerical computation and the detail that needs to be considered when turning a numerical algorithm into reliable, robust numerical software. We have also tried to describe and illustrate the ideas that need to be understood to judge the quality of a numerical solution, especially condition, stability, and error analysis, including the distinction between backward and forward errors.

We emphasize that one should most certainly be concerned about the quality of computed solutions and use trustworthy quality software. We cannot just blithely assume that results returned by software packages are correct.

This is not always easy since scientists wish to concentrate on their science, and should not really need to be able to analyze an algorithm to understand whether or not it is a stable method for solving their problem. Hence we emphasize the desirability of software providing proper measures of the quality of the solution.

---

[28]At the time of writing, a free academic version is available from http://www-anp.lip6.fr/cadna/Accueil.php.

We conclude with a quotation:

> "You have been solving these damn problems better than I can pose them."
> Sir Edward Bullard, Director NPL, in a remark to Wilkinson in the mid-1950s. See [488, p. 11].

Software developers should strive to provide solutions that are at least as good as the data deserves.

Chapter 5
Qualitative Computing

Françoise Chaitin-Chatelin and Elisabeth Traviesas-Cassan

5.1 Introduction

Computing is a human activity which is much more ancient than any historical record can tell, as testified by stone or bone tallies found in many prehistorical sites. It is one of the first skills to be taught to small children. However, everyone senses that there is more to computing than the multiplication table.

Why do we compute? What does it mean to compute? To what end? Our technological society wants to compute more and more efficiently. The question of "how to compute" overshadows that of "why compute" in high-technology circles.

And indeed the meaning of the act of computing seems to vanish, while we are gradually surrounded by a digital reality, which tends to shield us from the natural reality. It is vital therefore, more than ever, that we analyze computation through the two questions of **why**, as well as **how**. This can lead the way toward a better understanding of intensive computer simulations in particular and of the dynamics of evolution in general.

These two questions about computation have many different facets which are all interrelated. We refer to them under the global umbrella term of **Qualitative Computing**.

5.2 Numbers as Building Blocks for Computation

Natural integers such as 1, 2, 3, ... are recorded to have emerged in Sumer in the 3rd Millennium BC, where scribes were skilled in basis 60. They used a positional representation and had a special mark for missing digits. However, neither them, nor the Greeks, who were the great computer scientists of the times, had the concept of zero, which is today so evident to us. Why?

5.2.1   Thinking the unthinkable

Zero is not merely a number like any other. It is, before all, a formidable philosophical concept. It takes great courage to pose as an evident truth: "There exists the non existence, and it is called Zero." Aristotle took the risk, then shied away from the logical impossibility. Finally, the leap was taken gradually by various Indian mathematical thinkers, from Brahmagupta (600 A. D.), who conceived of zero, to Bhaskara (1100 A. D.), who showed how to compute with it.

When unleashed and tamed by computation, zero allowed the art of computing, initially developed in India, the Middle East, and Central Asia, to blossom in the Western world. However, algebra, the new Arabic art of computing, was at first met with strong opposition from the abacists, who did not need zero to compute. The new written arithmetic, done with pen and paper, eventually won because it was without rival to balance the checkbooks of the European merchants, while keeping track of all transactions. Once accepted, zero opened the door to the solution of equations, not only linear, but of degree 2, 3, and 4, until a new challenge was met.

5.2.2   Breaking the rule

If the practical notions of debit and credit helped spread the acceptance of *negative* numbers, it was not the case with the new concept $\sqrt{-1}$ created by Cardano to represent one of the two solutions of the equation $x^2 + 1 = 0$. Even with the computing rules enunciated by Bombelli, the strange $\sqrt{-1}$ was met by extremely strong opposition, as testified by the adjective *impossible*, or *imaginary*, which was invariably used to describe it. And the resistance was justified: $\sqrt{-1}$ is not a natural, or real, number, because its square is -1. It is not positive as it should be to qualify; $\sqrt{-1}$ breaks the rule that for any real number $x \neq 0$, its square x^2 is positive. And it took another 300 years before complex numbers became fully accepted. This acceptance was brought about in two steps: first Euler invented the symbol i, and then several scientists used the plane to give it a geometric interpretation. Because a complex number $a + ib$ is in effect *two* dimensional, it has two real components a and b on *two different* axes perpendicular to each other. The first, the real axis, represents the real numbers with positive square. And the second, the *imaginary* axis, represents "alien" numbers, the imaginary numbers with negative square. Therefore a complex number is a *new kind* of number; it is a mix of the two types of numbers, the real and the imaginary types, which are required for the complete solution of equations encountered in classical algebra.

The example of the introduction of 0 and $\sqrt{-1}$ shows clearly the long maturation process required, after their creation, for the use of new concepts which eventually turn out to be essential for our scientific representation of the world. But the story of numbers does not stop with the realization of the complex numbers, if one wants to go beyond classical algebra.

5.2.3   Hypercomputation inductively defined by multiplication

To make a long story short, the complex numbers open the door to more new numbers, the hypercomplex numbers, which are vectors of dimension 2^k, $k \geq 1$, on which a *multiplication* can be defined, in conjunction to the usual vector addition. They form hypercomplex algebras in which the multiplication is defined inductively for $k \geq 1$, from that at the previous level, of dimension 2^{k-1}, by the Dickson doubling process. Two families of such algebras are important for applications:

i) the family of *real* algebras A_k, starting from $A_0 = \mathbb{R}$, the field of real numbers, and

ii) the family of *binary* algebras B_k, starting from $B_0 = \{0, 1\}$, the binary algebra $\mathbb{Z}_2 = \mathbb{Z}/2\mathbb{Z}$ of computation mod 2.

The two families have, in a sense, complementary properties; see [71]. The real algebras express Euclidean geometry; their multiplication is not commutative for $k \geq 2$ and not associative for $k \geq 3$. Difficult and spectacular results in algebraic and differential topology, as well as in Lie groups, rely on the first four algebras A_0 to A_3, which are the four division algebras: the reals $\mathbb{R}$, the complex numbers $A_1 = \mathbb{C}$, the quaternions $A_2 = \mathbb{H}$, and the octonions $A_3 = \mathbb{G}$. See, for example, [22]. Various models of the universe in theoretical Physics also use these algebras, as well as the hexadecanions A_4.

The binary algebras, on the other hand, do not yield a scalar product; their multiplication is associative and commutative for all $k \geq 0$. B_0 is the usual binary algebra (mod 2), and B_1 easily explains the $\sqrt{\text{not}}$ logical gate realized by quantum interference [81]. With an appropriate labeling of the sequences of 0 and 1 of dimension 1, 2, 4, the algebras B_0, B_1, and B_2 are closely related to computation mod 2, 4, and 8, respectively.

What makes hypercomplex numbers so essential in Mathematics and Physics? They allow us to multiply certain vectors that are finite sequences of length 2^k, $k \geq 1$, consisting of ordinary real numbers. Although hypercomplex multiplication becomes noncommutative ($k \geq 2$), nonassociative ($k \geq 3$), and nonisometric ($k \geq 4$), it retains enough structure to allow hypercomplex exponentiation whose unexpected properties explain important phenomena in life's evolution [71] which generalize, in higher dimensions, the classical Euler formula $e^{i\pi} = -1$.

Processing in a similar fashion binary sequences of length 2^k reveals tantalizing connections between Arithmetic, Geometry, and certain fundamental equations, such as the wave equation and the heat equation [72].

Speaking at a more concrete level, multiplication is at the heart of any serious computation, as we are taught by the Newcomb–Borel paradox, to be described now.

5.2.4 The Newcomb–Borel paradox

In 1881, the astronomer Simon Newcomb reported the experimental fact that the significant digits of a number chosen at random from physical data or computation were not uniformly distributed. He stated that, instead, the logarithm of their mantissa is uniformly distributed. In 1909, the mathematician Emile Borel proved that, if one chooses at random a real number between 0 and 1, its decimal digits are almost surely equally distributed.

These two truths, one experimental and the second mathematical, seem at odds [89]. Can they be reconciled? Yes, if we realize that Borel and Newcomb do not see the same numbers. Borel considers the static fixed point representation for $x \in \mathbb{R}^+$

$$x = [x] + \{x\},$$

where $[x]$ is the integer part of x, and $\{x\}$ is the fractional part of x, $0 \leq \{x\} < 1$.

Newcomb, on the contrary, looks at the dynamic floating-point representation in base β for $x \in \mathbb{R}^+$

$$x = \beta^{[\log_\beta x]+1} \beta^{\{\log_\beta x\}-1},$$

which is multiplicative. It is the representation actually used to compute in base β.

The law of Newcomb follows immediately from a theorem by Lévy [288] about the sum mod 1 of identically distributed and independent random variables: $\{\log_\beta x\}$ is uniformly distributed on [0, 1]. The law of Newcomb is ubiquitous in intensive computing. It has found its way to Wall Street and the Internal Revenue Service (to detect frauds).

In any result of a serious computational process involving multiplication or division, the first decimal digit has a 6 times greater chance to be 1 than 9. The Newcomb–Borel paradox is a welcome reminder of the fact that any actual computation creates meaning: the Newcomb law allows us to discriminate between the leading digits, which bear meaning, and the trailing digits, which are uniformly distributed [89].

The Newcomb view (based on $\times$, and the floating-point representation) is very different from Borel's (based on $+$). The paradox suggests the natural hierarchy between operations on numbers which follow from computation in a given basis ($\times$ is dominant over $+$) and creates meaning in the chosen basis.

5.2.5 Effective calculability

It was already clear to the Pythagorean school that numbers have a dual personality: they can be perceived as discrete, as the integers $1, 2, 3, \ldots$, or continuous, as on the number line. This dual character shows up in the axiomatic presentation of the construction of numbers based on addition, in the notion of limit of a Cauchy sequence. One creates the integers by repeatedly adding 1 to the preceding number, starting from 1 (or 0). Then solving $ax = b$ yields the set of rationals $\mathbb{Q}$. The real numbers (resp., complex numbers) are the *closure* of the rational (resp., algebraic) numbers.

Continuity is therefore a limit property, which might be viewed by some, like Borel, as ineffective. Borel repeatedly questioned the usefulness of real numbers for *effective calculation*: he thought that the mind could not process consciously more than a denumerable infinity of steps (as in mathematical induction). And, indeed, the finitist program of Hilbert wanted to exclude from mathematical proof any recourse to a limit process which was not countable. The 1-dimensional version of this program has been shattered by Gödel, Turing, and, most of all, by Chaitin, in a way which allows randomness to invade formal Mathematics, the domain of ultimate rigor [66]. This algorithmic view of randomness (expressed as program size) is used in Theoretical Computer Science to expose the limit of Turing computability with numbers which are 1-dimensional.

Does it mean that any finitist program is doomed to failure, as many have argued in the aftermath of Gödel's incompleteness result for Arithmetic? To better understand the issues at stake, let us look at another finitist program, the Greeks' program, which was more flexible than Turing's in a subtle but essential way. They allowed all operations that could be realized with ruler and compass. This means, broadly speaking and in modern vocabulary, that they allowed quadratic numbers (i.e., numbers that are solutions of equations of degree 2 with integer coefficients). When they could not produce an exact rational solution, they worked with rational approximations of irrational numbers. They clearly realized that the world could not be captured with rational numbers only. The profoundity of their program, the Greek miracle, was that they had a working compromise, by means of Geometry in 2 and 3 dimensions and of successive approximations, between what they conceived of computing and what they could actually compute. Time only adds to the shining perfection of Archimedes' method to approximate the transcendental number π.

It becomes clear that the main difference between Turing and the Greeks is in terms of the dimension of the numbers they allow in their computing game. In both cases, the procedure is algorithmic. But Turing numbers are 1-dimensional; they are discrete points on the number line. Whereas the Greeks' numbers are 2-dimensional; their variety of quadratic numbers cannot be represented on a line, but in a plane. And we know that certain problems apparently stated on 1-dimensional numbers can be solved only by a call to 2-dimensional numbers. The most famous example is the d'Alembert–Gauss theorem of Algebra: any polynomial of odd degree with real coefficients has at least one real solution. It cannot be proved without an appeal to continuity, elegantly resolved by going complex. This is the first instance of the "topological thorn" planted in the "flesh" of algebra. The phenomenon is intimately connected with the notion of connectivity, which is sensitive to the topological dimension.

Remarkably, at the time that the Austrian logician Gödel discovered the incompleteness of Arithmetic (1931), the Polish logician Tarski had already shown the completeness of elementary 2-dimensional Geometry (1930) [438]. In other words, incompleteness can exist with 1-dimensional numbers but not with 2-dimensional numbers! It is worth commenting that the *negative* result of Gödel attracted much more attention than the *positive* result of Tarski. The greater generality of Gödel's result overshadowed the constructive power of Tarski's own result. This is still true today, despite the fact that Tarski's result is at the foundation of Computer Algebra, one of the success stories of Computer Science!

In summary, the problem for computation is not in the limit (potential versus actual infinity). It is in the **number of dimensions** of the building blocks used for computation. And as Dickson showed, once you allow two dimensions instead of one, you might as well allow any number 2^k for dimension: you construct inductively all hypercomplex numbers!

It is interesting to remark that Turing's dimensional limitation was bypassed, at least in theory, in the 1980's by the emergence of **Quantum Computing**, a theory of computability based on 2-dimensional numbers to represent the probability amplitudes of Quantum Mechanics. Quantum Computing can be seen as the computer age version of the Greeks' program [81]. It remains to be seen if this intensively researched topic can be turned into a practical tool.

5.3 Exact Versus Inexact Computing

5.3.1 What is calculation?

Calculation is a transformation of information from the implicit to the explicit. For example, to solve an equation $f(x) = g$, where f and g are known, is to find the solution x. The implicit solution x becomes explicit in the form $x = f^{-1}(g)$. This operation can seldom be performed exactly. As an example, only polynomial equations in one variable of degree less than 5 are explicitly solvable with radicals. So one very quickly faces the need for approximation techniques, which is the domain of mathematical analysis.

But suppose we know how to compute $x = f^{-1}(g)$ exactly; a new and equally important question arises. Is the exact solution always pertinent to understanding the visible world around us, a world of phenomena perceived with limited accuracy?

The fool says yes (exact is always better than approximate), but the wise realizes that in certain phenomena of very unstable evolution, the exact solution of the model can be so unstable that it is not realized in the physical world, because its window of stability is below the threshold necessary for us to see it.

5.3.2   Exact and inexact computing

It is very important to keep in mind that the challenge of calculation is expressed by the two questions "how" and "why," as we maintained in the introduction.

The answer to the question of "how" appears easy: it suffices in principle to use an **algorithm**, a mechanical procedure, which after a finite number of steps delivers a solution. However, it cannot be that simple in practice: everyone has experienced the frustration created by a bad algorithm!

One of the difficulties of "how to design a good algorithm" is that the designer should have a clear view of the type of understanding that is expected from running the algorithm. He should know "Why compute?" There are two very different types of world for which insight can be sought:

  i) a type of world where accuracy is **unlimited**, as exemplified by Mathematics, or

  ii) a type of world where accuracy of the available data is **intrinsically limited**, as in the phenomenological world of Natural Sciences (Physics, Biology, etc.).

To refer conveniently to the act of computing in one of these two types of world, we shall speak of *exact* versus *inexact computing*.

5.3.3   Computer arithmetic

Implicitly, theoretical mathematical analysis applies to a world of type i) where abstract notions such as convergence to 0, exact arithmetic, and equality have a meaning. This is why certain numerical methods that are proved convergent in mathematics fail miserably on a computer: they ignore the issue of algorithmic reliability required by the limited precision of computer arithmetic. The basic principles to address such a question, with a strong emphasis on "why," are given in [75], where the key notion of an **optimally reliable** algorithm is developed.

In a nutshell, an algorithm which is optimally reliable shields the user from the possibly negative consequences of the limited precision of computer arithmetic.

> Expert numerical software developers make the necessarily finite precision
> of computer arithmetic become transparent with respect to the effect
> of the limited accuracy available for the data.

More on reliable algorithms and the toolbox PRECISE to test the quality of reliable software on a computer can be found in Chapter 6, on pages 95–108.

If an optimally reliable algorithm is used, then computer arithmetic is never to be blamed for unexpected behavior. On the contrary, it is an asset in the sense that it can reveal a computational difficulty, but it cannot create it.

The bad reputation of computer arithmetic is largely undeserved. It may not be the best of all possible arithmetics for exact computing (like for Mathematics), but it is, for essential reasons, without rival for inexact computing (that is for experimental sciences). It allows computer simulations to capture aspects of the phenomenological reality that exact computation would miss, especially in the area of chaotic evolution.

Despite its powerful practical implications for science and technology, this fact is far from appreciated, even by software developers. So strong is the appeal of **exact** computing, even in a world of limits.

5.3.4   Singularities in exact and inexact computing

Singularity and regularity are mathematical notions that give technical content to the idea of abrupt change: a property that was present disappears suddenly in certain conditions, or a new property emerges. Singularities are, in some sense, exceptional with respect to the background, which is regular.

In many areas of classical mathematics, singularities can be ignored because they are not generic [395]; they form a set whose interior is empty. Does this extend to inexact computing?

Not at all. Let us look at the simple example of a matrix A. The singular points of the resolvent map $z \to (A - zI)^{-1}$ are the eigenvalues of A. They form the *spectrum* of A, a nongeneric finite set of points in $\mathbb{C}$ of *measure zero*.

Now let us assume that we cannot distinguish between the given matrix A and any matrix of the form $A + \Delta A$, for ΔA such that $\| \Delta A \| \le \alpha$, where α denotes the level of uncertainty of the data. Therefore any z in $\mathbb{C}$ that is an eigenvalue of $A + \Delta A$, but not of A, will nevertheless be interpreted as an eigenvalue of A. The spectrum of A, denoted $\sigma(A)$, in exact computing becomes, in inexact computing, the *pseudospectrum* of A (relative to the level α), that is,

$$\{z \text{ eigenvalue of } A + \Delta A \text{ for any } \Delta A \text{ such that } \| \Delta A \| \le \alpha\},$$

which is a closed set of *positive* Lebesgue measure in $\mathbb{C}$, and *generic* [75].

The classical theory of singularities does not apply in inexact computing, because pseudosingularities form a generic set. As a consequence, singularities cannot be ignored. Their influence can be enormous. Chapter 11 in [75] provides illuminating examples of this phenomenon. See also the website "Gateway to Pseudospectra" in [135].

5.3.5   Homotopic deviation

Considering a nearby matrix $A' = A + \Delta A$ to analyze the properties of A is one of the favorite devices in the numerical analyst's toolbox. And it can go a long way toward a useful description of the local neighborhood of A, for $\| \Delta A \|$ small enough [75, 87, 88, 90]. This amounts to explaining a computation on A by the *local* topology in the variety of matrices around A.

If one is to take the consequences of limited accuracy seriously, however, one should not rule out the possibility of nonlocal effects in which ΔA is not small in a metric sense. In other words, how can we weaken the constraint of perturbation theory, which is expressed by "$\| \Delta A \|$ small enough"?

One possibility is by means of **homotopic deviation**. In addition to A, let there be given a deviation matrix E. We introduce a complex parameter t to define the homotopic family of matrices $A(t) = A + tE$, such that $A(0) = A$. The family realizes a homotopic deviation of A, associated with E.

A linear problem, such as solving a set of n linear equations in n unknowns, is regular whenever the matrix of the system is regular, that is, invertible. Associated with a matrix A, there are two dual classes of problems: the regular (resp., singular) problems, which are associated with the matrix $A - zI$ for $z \in \mathbb{C}$, whenever it is invertible (resp., singular). We denote by $\rho(A)$ the spectral radius of A, that is, $\rho(A) = \max(|\lambda|, \lambda \in \sigma(A))$.

Solving linear systems with the matrix $A - zI$ of full rank is the regular problem associated with A, while the eigenproblem for A is the associated singular problem. We address the general question: is it possible to relate the singular/regular problems posed on $A(t) = A + tE$ to the ones posed on A with no assumption on E? The answer turns out to be remarkably simple. This is possible by analyzing the factorization,

$$A + tE - zI = (I + tE(A - zI)^{-1})(A - zI),$$

where $z \in \mathbb{C}$ is not an eigenvalue of A, that is, $z \in \mathbb{C} \backslash \sigma(A)$. Let μ_z denote an eigenvalue of $F_z = -E(A - zI)^{-1}$ for $z \notin \sigma(A)$. The point $z \notin \sigma(A)$ is an eigenvalue of $A + tE$ if and only if there exists an eigenvalue $\mu_z \neq 0$ of F_z such that $t\mu_z = 1$.

Any z in $\mathbb{C}$ that is not an eigenvalue of A can be interpreted as an eigenvalue of at least one matrix $A + tE$, as long as $0 < \rho(F_z) < \infty$. This is not possible if $\rho(F_z) = 0$, because all $\mu_z = 0$, and t is not defined. In parallel to this interpretation, any z such that $0 < \rho(F_z) < \infty$ can be interpreted as a regular point: $A + tE - zI$ is invertible for any t such that $t \neq 1/\mu_z$.

The *two* interpretations (z an eigenvalue of $A + tE$, versus $A + tE - zI$ invertible) *hold in parallel for any z in $\mathbb{C} \backslash \sigma(A)$ such that $\rho(F_z) > 0$.*

Definition 5.1. *A point $z \in \mathbb{C} \backslash \sigma(A)$ such that $\rho(E(A - zI)^{-1}) = 0$ is a* **critical point** *associated with (A, E). We denote by $K(A, E)$ the set of critical points for (A, E), and write $\Sigma(A, E) = \sigma(A) \bigcup K(A, E)$.*

This definition follows from the fact that such a z is a singular point for the map $z \to \rho(F_z)$ (see [65] and paragraph 5.3.6 below). Do critical points exist, that is, can $K(A, E)$ be nonempty? We know that

$$\lim_{|z| \to \infty} \rho(F_z) = 0.$$

Do there exist points z at finite distance such that $\rho(F_z) = 0$? If E is rank 1, such that $E^2 \neq 0$, the answer is yes in general. There exist at most $n - 1$ points in $\mathbb{C}$ such that $F_z^2 = 0$; hence $\rho(F_z) = 0$ [83, 68]. What is the meaning of such critical points from the point of view of computation when rank $E = 1$, $E^2 \neq 0$? If $\zeta \in K(A, E)$, then ζ cannot be interpreted as an eigenvalue of $A + tE$. There is only *one* possible interpretation: $A + tE - \zeta I$ is a regular (invertible) matrix for which we know a *finite* representation, valid for any t (recall that F_ζ is nilpotent: $F_\zeta^2 = 0$):

$$(I - tF_\zeta)^{-1} = I + tF_\zeta \qquad \text{and}$$
$$(A + tE - \zeta I)^{-1} = (A - \zeta I)^{-1}(I + tF_\zeta) = R(t, \zeta).$$

The analyticity domain (with respect to t) in $\mathbb{C}$ of $R(t, z)$, which is $\{t; \; | t | \rho(F_z) < 1\}$ for z in $\mathbb{C}\backslash\sigma(A)$ but not in $K(A, E)$, becomes *all of* $\mathbb{C}$ when z is a critical point. The convergence in t is not conditional on z; z and t are independent. This is a nonlocal effect that depends on the algebraic structure of E (rank $E = 1$) and not on a metric condition on $\|E\|$. Moreover, the eigenvalues of $A(t)$ which remain at finite distance when $| t | \rightarrow \infty$ converge to the critical points in $K(A, E)$, which are not in $\sigma(A)$ (see [68]).

The above discussion can be summarized by looking at the properties of the resolvent matrix $R(t, z) = (A + tE - zI)^{-1}$ as a function of the two complex parameters t and z. Three properties are of interest: existence or nonexistence (singularity), and, if existence, analyticity in t for a given z.

The choice of one property induces a specific relationship between z and t, which is listed in Table 5.1. In this table, μ_z denotes any eigenvalue of $F_z = -E(A - zI)^{-1}$ that is not 0, and $\rho_z = \rho(F_z)$.

Table 5.1. *Properties of $R(t, z)$ as a function of t and z.*

Singularity = nonexistence	Yes	i) $t = 0$ and $z \in \sigma(A)$ ii) $t = \frac{1}{\mu_z}$, $\mu_z \neq 0$, and $z \in \mathbb{C}\backslash\Sigma(A, E)$
	No	$z \in K(A, E)$

Existence	Yes	$t \neq \frac{1}{\mu_z}$, $\mu_z \neq 0$, and $z \in \mathbb{C}\backslash\sigma(A)$
	No	$t = 0$ and $z \in \sigma(A)$
Analyticity	Yes	i) asymptotic : $| t | < \frac{1}{\rho_z}$ and $z \in \mathbb{C}\backslash\Sigma(A, E)$ ii) polynomial : $t \in \mathbb{C}$ and $z \in K(A, E)$
	No	$t = 0$ and $z \in \sigma(A)$

Table 5.1 shows clearly that the nature of the coupling between t and z changes with our point of view. The change can be smooth or abrupt, and this has computational consequences. The "why" rules the "how."

5.3.6 The map $\varphi : z \to \rho(F_z)$

The map $\varphi : z \to \rho(F_z)$ will provide a useful graphical tool to analyze homotopic deviation. The role of φ comes from the fundamental property that it is a **subharmonic** function of z. A subharmonic function is the analogue, for a function of two real variables, of a convex function in one real variable. The level curves $z \to \rho(F_z) = constant$ are closed curves that enclose eigenvalues of A (maximal value $\rho = +\infty$) or local minima of ρ with values ≥ 0. There are two values for which the map φ has special properties, namely, the value ∞ and the value 0.

a) The value $\rho = \infty$: there exist n points in $\mathbb{C}$, the n eigenvalues of A such that $(A - zI)^{-1}$ does not exist, and therefore $\rho(E(A - zI)^{-1}) = +\infty$ for any matrix E. The spectrum of A is the set of singular points of $z \to (A - zI)^{-1}$. It also belongs to the set of singular points of φ, because ρ is not defined at any eigenvalue of A, for an arbitrary E. At such points in $\mathbb{C}$, the value of rank$(A - zI)$ jumps from n to a value $\leq n - 1$.

b) The value $\rho = 0$: we know that $\rho \to 0$ as $|z| \to \infty$. The critical points at finite distance that satisfy $\rho = 0$ also belong to the set of singular points of φ. At such points, there is a qualitative change in the behavior of the Neumann series. It jumps from an asymptotic representation (an infinite number of nonzero terms) to a finite one (for example, two nonzero terms when rank $E = 1$).

This shows that globally the properties of $A + tE$ can be affected not only by the eigenvalues of A, but also by the critical points of (A, E) when they exist. The singular points of φ (where ρ takes the value 0 or $+\infty$) consist of both the eigenvalues of A and the critical points of (A, E).

In exact computing, these singular points have zero measure and their influence is almost surely nonexistent. However this cannot be true any longer in inexact computing. And the phenomenon is clearly visible if one considers the computed map $\widetilde{\varphi} : z \to \widetilde{\rho}(E(A - zI)^{-1})$. This amounts to taking machine precision ψ as the relative level of uncertainty of the data. The maps φ and $\widetilde{\varphi}$ do not describe the same reality. The map φ expresses the view of homotopic deviation in exact arithmetic, whereas the computed map $\widetilde{\varphi}$ expresses the view in finite precision ψ. The two views differ in the region of $\sigma(A)$ in a way that is well understood, thanks to the notion of pseudospectrum. They also differ in the region of $K(A, E)$ in a way that has been uncovered only recently [83].

In both cases, the effect of inexact computing is to replace the set of singularities of measure 0 by a set of positive measure. In the case of $\sigma(A)$, this is usually viewed as negative because this decreases the domain where $A + tE - zI$ is invertible. But, in the case of $K(A, E)$ nonempty, this has definitely a positive flavor: on a region of *positive* measure around the critical set $K(A, E)$, the convergence is **better than predicted** because the computational process is essentially finite rather than asymptotic. The role of finite precision on the singular points of φ is twofold:

i) In the pseudospectrum region around $\sigma(A)$, it makes the eigenvalues of A appear *closer* than they are in exact arithmetic (this is a *local* effect, $|t|$ small).

ii) In the pseudocritical region around $K(A, E)$, it makes the eigenvalues of A appear *farther apart* than they are (this is a *nonlocal* effect, $|t|$ large). Or said differently, it makes the solution of linear systems on a computer easier than predicted by mathematics: the computation is essentially a finite process.

For a general E, the set $K(A, E)$ can be empty. But we know that if E is of rank 1, $E^2 \neq 0$, then $K(A, E)$ consists of at most $n - 1$ points in $\mathbb{C}$. And the question asked at the beginning of paragraph 5.3.5 has been answered in the following way by homotopic deviation: the introduction of the parameter t has allowed us to replace the metric condition "$\| E \|$ small enough" by the algebraic structure condition "E of rank 1." Meanwhile, this has complemented the set of n eigenvalues $\sigma(A)$ by the set of at most $n - 1$ critical points $K(A, E)$. In the neighborhood of these points finite precision creates **computational opportunities** by providing better convergence than predicted: the computational process is finite rather than asymptotic.

Our exposition of homotopic deviation theory has focused so far on the very particular case where E is of rank 1 and nondefective ($E^2 \neq 0$), due to its extreme simplicity. The complete theory of homotopic deviation studies the general dynamics of the coupling $t \rightarrow A(t) = A + tE$, where $t \in \mathbb{C}$, and E is a deviation matrix of rank $\leq n$. A comprehensive treatment is given in [68, 70, 73] depending on whether 0 is an eigenvalue of E or not. When $0 \in \sigma(E)$, one has to distinguish whether 0 is semisimple or defective. In the latter case, the sophisticated perturbation theory of Lidskii plays an essential role [324].

A quadratic eigenproblem in computational acoustics is treated in [84]. It consists of the wave equation with a partially impeding boundary condition. The homotopy parameter is the complex admittance, that is, the inverse of the impedance.

5.3.7   Graphical illustration

We illustrate the map φ (or rather φ^{-1}) on the following example. We call **One**(n) the matrix A of order n that is the companion matrix associated with the polynomial

$$p_n(z) = \sum_{i=0}^{n} z^i = z^n + p_{n-1}(z), \ n \geq 1.$$

The eigenvalues of A are the roots of $p_n(z) = 0$, that is, the n roots of $z^{n+1} = 1$ that are distinct from 1.

We choose the deviation matrix E such that $A + E$ is the companion matrix associated with z^n. That is, we set $E = ee_n^T$, with $e = (1, \ldots, 1)^T$, and e_n is the nth canonical vector in $\mathbb{C}^n$. The eigenvalues of $A(t) = A + tE$ are the roots of $p_n(z, t) = z^n + tp_{n-1}(z)$.

E is of rank 1. The critical points of (A, E) are the roots of $p_{n-1}(z) = 0$. Therefore the n eigenvalues and the $n - 1$ critical points are the roots of 1 of order $n + 1$ and n, respectively, each different from 1. They are intertwined on the unit circle $|z| = 1$.

For $n = 8$, Figure 5.1 displays the map $\varphi^{-1} : z \rightarrow 1/\rho(E(A - zI)^{-1})$ (in logarithmic scale) in three dimensions. The bold curve is the unit circle $|z| = \rho = 1$.

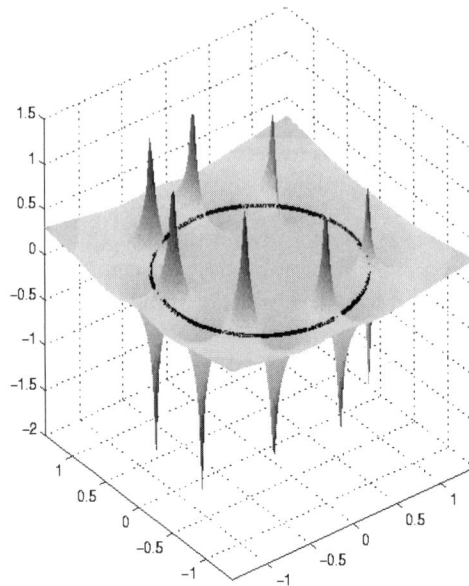

Figure 5.1. *The map $\varphi^{-1} : z \to 1/\rho(E(A - zI)^{-1})$ for the matrix One ($n = 8$) in three dimensions. The alternating peaks and sinks are clearly visible.*

Figure 5.1 indicates that a small variation in z near the unit circle induces a drastic change in $\rho(F_z)$, from extremely small to extremely large values. This global knowledge allows a better control of the quality of the algorithmic resolution as t varies, by knowing in advance that, of the n eigenvalues $\lambda(t)$ of $A(t)$, $n - 1$ converge, as $|t| \to \infty$, to the roots of $p_{n-1}(z) = 0$, and that one escapes to ∞.

5.4   Numerical Software

As we already pointed out in the previous section, the design and use of good numerical software intended to provide insight on a particular question of experimental sciences is best analyzed with the conceptual tools of inexact computing. Most important amongst them is the method called **backward error analysis**, which emerged in the 1950's and 1960's, mainly under the influence of Wilkinson. The basic idea has the ideal beauty of simplicity: just consider any computed solution (any output of computer simulations) as the exact solution of a nearby problem. The curious reader should also look at Chapter 6, pages 95–108, which presents a complementary viewpoint on backward error analysis: it gives guidelines on how to realize such an analysis in practice.

5.4.1   Local error analysis in finite precision computations

One of the most important features of backward error analysis is that it allows us to factor out in the error bound the contribution of the algorithm (the backward error) from the contribution of the problem (the condition number). In this subsection we consider only perturbations due to roundoff, which is the situation originally considered in [164] and [483].

Let us suppose that the problem to be solved is $Ax = b$. A computed solution $\widetilde{x}$ is interpreted as the solution of a nearby problem of the same form, that is,

$$(A + \Delta A)\widetilde{x} = b + \Delta b. \tag{5.1}$$

In general, ΔA and Δb are not unique and are not known. However, in this simple case, there are formulae to compute $\min(\|\Delta A\|, \|\Delta b\|)$, which is the backward error associated with $\widetilde{x}$. Subtleties of the perturbations ΔA, Δb are discussed at length in [75]; see also Chapter 6.

Therefore a local error analysis can be carried out by means of the first order bound

forward error $\leq$ condition number $\times$ backward error

whenever the problem to be solved is *regular*, where the backward error results from roundoff only.

This approach can be easily related to the homotopic deviation presented in the previous section. If we choose to allow perturbation only in A, and not in b, then equation (5.1) becomes $(A + \Delta A)\widetilde{x} = b$, where ΔA is a perturbation matrix that is *unknown*; we have access only to the metric quantity $\min \|\Delta A\|$ which represents the normwise backward error resulting from roundoff. Because there is a condition on $\|\Delta A\|$, we call ΔA a *perturbation* of A. And, as said previously, we reserve the term *deviation* for E without metric constraint.

Therefore, finite precision computations can be analyzed in the framework of homotopic deviation where the deviation matrix is unknown, with an arbitrary or prescribed structure (preserving sparsity, for example).

The same remark extends readily to computation with uncertain data, leading to the notion of uncertain computing. The relationship between inexact and uncertain computing is analyzed in [70].

5.4.2   Homotopic deviation versus normwise perturbation

It is interesting to compare the homotopic deviation theory of Section 5.3 to the more traditional approach of *normwise perturbation theory* [75]. In particular, the normwise point of view leads to the notion of the **normwise pseudospectrum** of a matrix A of level α [75, Chapter 11] which is defined for any $\alpha > 0$ as

$$\{z \in \mathbb{C}, z \text{ is an eigenvalue of } A + \Delta A \text{ for all } \Delta A \text{ such that } \|\Delta A\| \leq \alpha\}$$
$$= \{z \in \mathbb{C}; \|(A - zI)^{-1}\| \geq 1/\alpha\}.$$

The map $\gamma : z \to \|(A - zI)^{-1}\|$ defined on $\mathbb{C} \setminus \sigma(A)$ is also subharmonic. However, the properties of a norm exclude the possibility of critical points.

Let us compare the maps φ and γ in the following example.

Example 5.2 We call **Venice** the companion matrix B associated with the polynomial

$$p(z) = (z - 1)^3 (z - 3)^4 (z - 7)$$
$$= z^8 - 22z^7 + 198z^6 - 958z^5 + 2728z^4 - 4674z^3 + 4698z^2 - 2538z + 567,$$

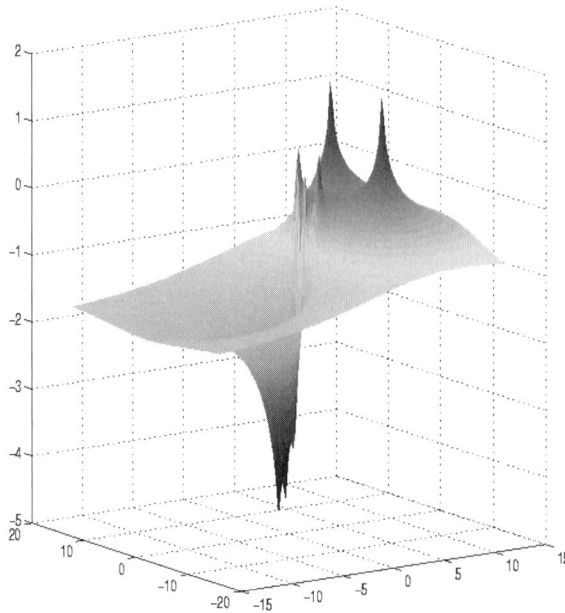

Figure 5.2. *Map* $\varphi : z \rightarrow \rho(E(A - zI)^{-1})$, $A = B - E$, *with* B = *Venice and* E *is rank 1.*

and we consider the rank 1 perturbation $E = ee_8^T$ with $e = (1, \ldots, 1)^T$ and $e_8 = (0, \ldots, 0, 1)^T$.

We set $A = B - E$: it is the companion matrix associated with the polynomial $q(z) = p(z) + r(z)$, with $r(z) = \sum_{i=0}^{7} z^i$. The 7 zeros of $r(z) = 0$ on the unit circle are the critical points of (A, E). Figures 5.2 and 5.3 display, respectively, the maps $\varphi : z \rightarrow \rho(E(A - zI)^{-1})$ and $\gamma : z \rightarrow \left\| (A - zI)^{-1} \right\|$.

The critical zone for φ is clearly visible in Figure 5.2: there is a very sharp sink which resolves in 7 points on the unit circle $|z| = 1$, $\rho = 0$. Interestingly, the map γ in Figure 5.3 displays also a local minimum in the same region of the complex plane. From the definition of a norm, it follows that the exact value of this minimum is necessarily positive. Its computed value is, indeed, larger than 1. A detailed analysis of Venice can be found in [83]. ∎

5.4.3 Application to Krylov-type methods

It was realized during the 1990's that Krylov-type methods exhibit a **remarkable robustness** under large perturbations. As a result, inner-outer iterations, where the outer iteration is of Krylov type, can accept *inexact* inner iterations with almost no degradation of the global convergence [80].

A convincing explanation of this wonderful robustness can be given by means of homotopic deviation theory applied to the incomplete Arnoldi algorithm, where the deviation

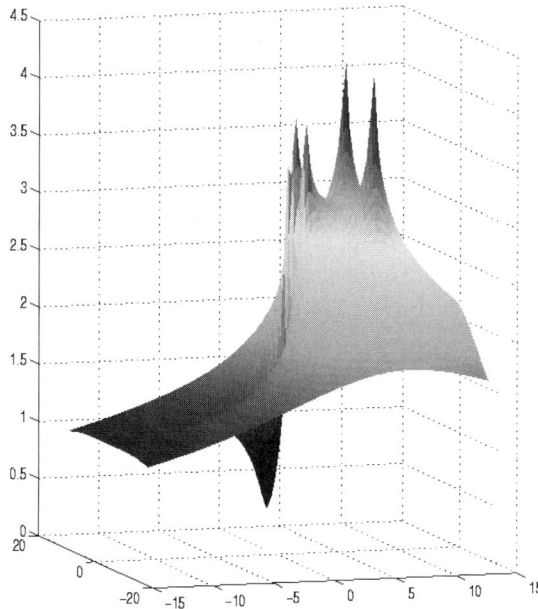

Figure 5.3. *Map* $\gamma : z \rightarrow \|(A - zI)^{-1}\|$, $A = B - E$, *with B = Venice.*

matrix E is rank 1 and *defective* ($E^2 = 0$). A simplified version of Lidskii's theory applies which gives a purely algebraic justification based on the structure of E [69, 73].

5.5 The Lévy Law of Large Numbers for Computation

The law of large numbers, which assesses the activity of measurements (in data collection and its interpretation), is given by the *Laplace–Gauss normal distribution*: the average (arithmetic mean) of a large number of random variables has a normal distribution.

Because this law is so ubiquitous in experimental sciences, it has been assumed that it also rules computation. And indeed, this can be the case in very specific situations such as fixed point computation, but **not in general**, when floating point is the rule.

We already indicated that the Newcomb–Borel paradox means that the *Lévy uniform distribution* is at work in floating-point computation (in a given base) and induces the dominant role of multiplication over addition. The Lévy law is concerned with the limit distribution of the sum mod 1 of N independent random variables with a common law as $N \rightarrow \infty$ [288]: the limit distribution is uniform.

In floating-point computation, it applies to the logarithms of the mantissa. Another important domain of application of the Lévy law is clearly the multiplication of complex numbers in the trigonometric form of Euler: the arguments add mod 2π; therefore they are uniformly distributed in $[0, 2\pi[$. This fact accounts for some of the differences, in Mathematics, between analysis in real or complex variables. It has important consequences in Fourier analysis.

Another way to reflect upon these phenomena is to realize that there are major differences, from the point of view of computation, between working with numbers of dimension 1 (which are scalars) or with numbers of higher dimension (dim > 1).

We mentioned this fact when discussing the two finitist programs of Hilbert and of the Greeks.

At that point, the *topological* notion of connectivity arose. Later, when presenting homotopic deviation, we encountered the *algebraic* notion of a nilpotent matrix (all the eigenvalues are zero but the matrix itself is nonzero), which enables a generically nonpolynomial computation to become polynomial at critical points.

These are two prominent aspects (topology and algebra) under which the dimensional quality of numbers manifests itself most naturally in computation.

5.6 Summary

We have analyzed two basic principles which underlie scientific computing. The first principle is the dominant role of multiplication/division in any nonlinear floating-point computation in a given base. This entails a nonuniform distribution for the leading digit: it is more likely to be 1 in a typical result. As a consequence, the law of large numbers which applies in general to scientific computing is the Lévy law. The domain of validity of the normal law of large numbers is reduced to particular calculations, such as linear fixed point computation.

However, there exists a natural way to define inductively the multiplication of any two vectors of size 2^k, $k \geq 0$, leading to algebras of hypercomplex numbers. Hypercomplex exponentiation uncovers new properties beyond Euler's formula ($1 + e^{i\pi} = 0$), with application for life's evolution by synthesis.

The second principle is the role of backward analysis to understand the consequences of uncertainty in the data and/or roundoff, which are always present in experimental sciences. The traditional normwise approach for backward analysis has been complemented by Homotopic Deviation theory, which studies the coupling $A + tE$ when the coupling parameter t ranges over $\mathbb{C}$. This allows us to capture nonlocal effects ($\mid t \mid$ large, $\mid t \mid \to \infty$) which are out of reach by a classical normwise approach. This results in a purely algebraic justification of successful heuristics for Krylov-type methods (such as restart, inexact matrix-vector product, and preconditioning).

All technical reports from the CERFACS Parallel Algorithms Project are available online from http://www.cerfacs.fr/algor/reports/.

Part II

DIAGNOSTIC TOOLS

Chapter 6

PRECISE and the Quality of Reliable Numerical Software

Françoise Chaitin-Chatelin and Elisabeth Traviesas-Cassan

6.1 Introduction

It is well known that a computation becomes unstable (and in particular computer results differ significantly from exact ones) in the neighborhood of a singularity. And a singularity is not generic: the perturbations generated by finite-precision arithmetic are such that one almost always solves a regular problem. However, the properties of computations are ruled by the underlying singularity, and the distance to the mathematical singularity, as viewed by the computer, is an essential parameter in interpreting the computation.

We present an overview of the toolbox PRECISE (**PR**ecision **E**stimation and **C**ontrol **In** **S**cientific and **E**ngineering computing) designed to assess the quality of numerical software in industrial environments, as well as for research purposes. PRECISE is a set of tools to perform numerical experiments exploring the robustness of computational schemes. Designed for developers and users of numerical software, it provides a means for studying the reliability and stability properties of both numerical algorithms and mathematical problems. Using PRECISE, one can determine the quality of computed solutions with respect to a choice of algorithm, finite-precision arithmetic, data imprecision, or any other uncertainties. When used with a backward stable algorithm, one may investigate instabilities in the physical or mathematical problem itself, particularly near singularities. Conversely, when used with well-understood mathematical problems, one can study the reliability of a numerical algorithm and its implementation.

An important aspect of PRECISE is that it is based on the analysis of *computed* results, that is, those that are actually obtained by a computer implementation of a numerical algorithm applied to a specific problem. As such, a PRECISE analysis is complementary to the standard a priori error bounds usually obtained for numerical algorithms. Moreover, since a priori error bounds are generally overestimates of worse-case error and often assume error-free implementations, the results obtained by PRECISE may be viewed as more

95

pertinent to the problem at hand. For those who have ever obtained a numerical result and then wondered "Is it correct?" PRECISE is designed to address the inherent subtleties of this question.

Like any tool PRECISE requires both knowledge and experience for its effective use. For this purpose, Section 6.3 is included to provide background material on the ideas behind PRECISE. It gives an elementary introduction to the concepts necessary for experiments in numerical stability and reliability; references to the ample literature in this field are provided to allow further investigations into specific areas. For researchers already familiar with this type of numerical analysis, this section should serve as a reminder and reference during the use of the PRECISE modules.

6.2   Reliability of Algorithms

We first introduce the very important notion of "**machine precision**," which is equal to $\Psi = 1^+ - 1$, where 1^+ is the successor of 1 in the computer's arithmetic.

In the rigorous theory of *computability in finite precision* presented in [75, Chapter 1], it is essential to *prove* that there exists a limit (equal to the exact solution) to the computation in finite precision as the parameter Ψ tends to 0. This corresponds to a mantissa of increasing length for the computer representation of numbers. In practice, this is, of course, impossible: such a goal can be achieved by mathematical analysis only. The classical way to realize this is to analyze the first-order propagation of a particular type of error in an algorithm, namely, the roundoff errors resulting from the finite-precision arithmetic of the computer. This leads to the notion of *numerical stability with respect to roundoff*, or, in short, *numerical stability*, as it came to be called after Wilkinson, Bauer, Dahlquist, and Björck, to name a few authorities.

However, this historical terminology is very unfortunate for two important reasons:

1. It conflicts with the earlier mathematical notion of numerical stability (in exact arithmetic) for a numerical method to approximate integral or differential equations.

2. No notion of "stability" (in the mathematical sense) is involved. Instead, this is a notion of *consistency of order 1* in the parameter Ψ.

This explains why we have abandoned such misleading terms to replace them by the notion of **arithmetical reliability**; see [75, pp. 20–23].

In what follows, we assume that the algorithms under study have been *proven* reliable with respect to machine precision. They are assumed to be arithmetically reliable.

6.3   Backward Error Analysis

Backward error analysis was introduced by Givens in the late 1950's and developed by Wilkinson in the 1960's to analyze the quality of algorithmic computations in a world of limited accuracy. It is the tool of choice to address the question of the quantification of the arithmetic quality of an algorithm, in order to assess the choice of this algorithm to solve a problem on a given computer. It is therefore an important method for devising **recommender systems** [372, 371, 82]. Below, all quantities overlined by a tilde represent computed versions of their exact counterparts.

The essence of backward error analysis is to set the exact and the finite precision computations in a common framework by means of the following trick, that we call the **Wilkinson principle**:

> Consider the computed solution $\widetilde{x}$ as the exact solution of a nearby problem.

This almost trivial idea turns out to be much more powerful than it looks:

i) It allows us to hide the details of the computer arithmetic: the errors made during the course of the computation are interpreted in terms of equivalent perturbations in the given problem, and the computed quantities are *exact* for the perturbed problem.

ii) One advantage is that rounding errors are placed on the same footing as errors in the original data, and the effect of uncertainty in the data must usually be considered in any case.

iii) It enables us to draw on powerful tools, such as derivatives and perturbation theory.

iv) It allows us to factor out in the error bound the contribution of the algorithm from the contribution of the problem.

v) Finally, it allows us great flexibility in the sensitivity analysis by providing a large choice of perturbations to the data of the problem.

Such an error analysis is referred to as backward error analysis because the errors are *reflected back* into the original problem. One essential ingredient is the **backward error** that we now define in a sketchy presentation. All the necessary details can be found in [75], in particular, in Chapter 5 on "Arithmetic Quality of Reliable Algorithms."

Let $\widetilde{x} = \widetilde{G}(y) = \widetilde{g}(z)$ be the computed solution for the problem (P) $F(x) = y$ by means of the finite algorithm G, that is, $x = G(y) = g(z)$. The backward error measures the minimal distance of (P) to the set of perturbed problems that are solved exactly by $\widetilde{x}$. Such a notion requires us to specify the admissible perturbations of (P), that is, the class (τ) of admissible perturbations Δz of the data z (a subset of F, y which defines (P)) in a space Z and the norm $\| . \|_Z$ on Z.

Definition 6.1. The *backward error* at $\widetilde{x}$ associated with (τ) is defined by

$$B(\widetilde{x}) = \inf \left(\|\Delta z\|_Z ; \ \Delta z \in (\tau) \text{ and } g(z + \Delta z) = \widetilde{x} \right),$$

assuming that the set $\mathcal{E} = \{\Delta z \in (\tau); \ g(z + \Delta z) = \widetilde{x}\}$ is nonempty.

The backward error at $\widetilde{x}$ gives the minimal size of the perturbation Δz of the data z when Δz varies in the set $\mathcal{E}$. If the class (τ) of perturbations of Δz is a good model for the perturbations actually generated by the computer arithmetic, then $B(\widetilde{x})$ gives the minimal size of perturbation of the data that is equivalent to computation in finite precision.

6.3.1   Consequence of limited accuracy of data

Although the notion of backward error is mainly used by software developers and scientists to assess the quality of computer simulations, it has a broader scope. It should not be seen as just a method restricted to the analysis of the effects of roundoff due to the limited precision of the computer arithmetic. In fact, it is a way to analyze the impact of limited accuracy of the data on a solution whether or not it is computed in exact arithmetic. Indeed it is clear in Definition 6.1 that $\tilde{x}$ does not need to be the computed solution. It can be any potential solution of a nearby problem that is indistinguishable from the original problem because of the limited accuracy of the data.

Therefore, backward error analysis is an essential tool to assess the solution of any problem in experimental sciences where no data are exact (Physics, Biology, etc.). It is only in Mathematics, where accuracy is unlimited, that alternate routes can be taken, such as computer algebra.

6.3.2   Quality of reliable software

The arithmetic quality of a reliable algorithm/numerical method is related to the size of the backward error, which should be as small as possible compared to the level of accuracy of the data. The best one can do by running an algorithm on a computer is to introduce no more uncertainty than the unavoidable one that results from introducing the data in the computer. The level of this unavoidable uncertainty is that of machine precision Ψ. Indeed the reliability of an algorithm is equivalent to the fact that the backward error $B(\tilde{x})$ is of order 1 in Ψ at regular points. But, the algorithm is of poor quality when the smallest constant C such that $B(\tilde{x}) \leq C\Psi$ is too large.

Definition 6.2. The *quality index* of a reliable algorithm at $\tilde{x}$ is defined by

$$J(\tilde{x}) = \frac{B(\tilde{x})}{\Psi}.$$

By definition, $J(\tilde{x}) \geq 1$. The best quality corresponds to $J = 1$, and poor quality to J significantly larger than 1.

Definition 6.3. A reliable algorithm is said to be *optimal* when $J \approx 1$.

In the numerical software literature, the property of an algorithm that we have just defined as **optimal reliability** is referred to as **backward stability**, after [483]. Here we have changed the conventional terminology once more in order to avoid another conflict with the classical concept of stability in Mathematics and Physics. The term "optimal reliability" clearly conveys the notion that the quality of the computed solution is as good as can be achieved by the finite-precision arithmetic.

When the data are known with a relative accuracy of the order of η (i.e., $\|\Delta A\| \sim \eta \|A\|$, for instance), then the backward error should be compared to η; this is important when η is significantly larger than machine precision. Such a situation is frequent in most applications outside mathematics: for instance, uncertainty in physical measurements leads to inaccurate data. The accuracy of the computed solution may decrease accordingly: it cannot be smaller than η.

How should we stop iterative algorithms which, in exact mathematics, yield the solution after an infinite number of steps? In this case again, backward error is the answer: it provides a reliable stopping criterion that no forward error can match [16, 23, 75, 309].

In numerical software, the essence of backward analysis is to set the exact and computed problems in a common framework of perturbation theory in order to derive, for *regular* problems, an estimate of the error in the computed solution, that is, the forward error, via the first order bound

$$\textbf{forward error} \ \leq \ \textbf{condition number} \ \times \ \textbf{backward error}, \qquad (6.1)$$

where the condition number quantifies the stability of the problem (P). How accurate this error estimate is depends on the ability of the model for the perturbations (data, metrics, structure), chosen to derive the condition number and the backward error, to represent accurately the perturbations actually created by the implemented algorithm when run on a given computer [75].

6.4   Finite Precision Computations at a Glance

The following three criteria are crucial for assessing the validity of numerical software. They are listed below in the strict order in which they have to be considered.

A. **Computability in finite precision**

numerical stability with respect to roundoff $\Leftrightarrow$ arithmetical reliability
$\Rightarrow$ computability in finite precision

B. **Quality of reliable software**

backward error $\sim C(\text{data}) \times$ machine precision
backward stability $\Leftrightarrow$ optimal reliability $\Leftrightarrow C(\text{data}) \approx 1$

C. **Robustness under perturbations**

behavior of the constant $C(\text{data})$ under perturbations on the data

The reader is referred to [75] for a comprehensive presentation of these three criteria. Criterion A requires a rigorous mathematical analysis [205], whereas the two criteria B and C are on the borderline between theory and practice, as is evidenced by the $\approx$ sign in criterion B. The last two criteria are the "raison d'être" for the toolbox PRECISE that we proceed to describe.

6.5   What Is PRECISE?

PRECISE is a set of tools provided to help the user set up computer experiments to explore the impact of finite precision, as well as other types of prescribed perturbations of the data, on the quality of convergence of numerical methods. Because **stability** is at the heart of the phenomena under study—mathematical as well as numerical stabilities—PRECISE allows one to experiment with stability by a straightforward **randomization** of selected data and then lets the computer produce a sample of perturbed solutions and associated residuals or a sample of perturbed spectra.

The idea of using random perturbations on a selection of data, or parameters, to obtain information on the stability of dynamical processes is very natural and very old. It has been used extensively in Physics and technology. But it has not gained popularity in numerical analysis, nor in numerical software. However, the idea has often been recommended by the best specialists, as illustrated by the following quotation taken from [108]:

"In larger computational problems, the relations between input data and output data are so complicated that it is difficult to directly apply the general formulas for the propagation of error. One should then investigate the sensitivity of the output data for errors in the input data by means of an *experimental perturbational calculation:* one performs the calculations many times with perturbed input data and studies the relation between the changes (perturbations) in the input data and the changes in the output data."

This quotation serves as an excellent introduction to PRECISE, which provides an experimental environment for the engineer or the software developer to test the robustness of a numerical method or of an algorithm with respect to finite precision and data uncertainty. It allows us to perform a complete statistical backward error analysis on a numerical method or an algorithm to solve a general nonlinear problem of the form $F(x) = y$ (notably matrix or polynomial equations) at regular points or in the neighborhood of algebraic singularities. It provides an estimate of the distance to the nearest singularity viewed by the computer, as well as of the order of this singularity. It can also help us to perform a sensitivity analysis by means of graphical displays of samples of perturbed solutions.

PRECISE offers the following facilities [75, 309]:

- **Module 1**: a module for statistical backward error analysis providing a statistical estimation for:

    - condition numbers at regular and singular points, for the algorithm/method and the problem,

    - backward errors,

    - reliability and quality indexes,

    - distances to singularity, or dangerous borders,

    - order of Hölder-singularities.

- **Module 2**: a module for sensitivity analysis providing graphical displays of:

    - perturbed spectra,

    - spectral portraits and pseudospectra for matrices, and matrix pencils,

    - sensitivity portraits and sets of pseudozeros for polynomials,

    - divergence portraits for iterations depending on a parameter.

The backward error is closely linked to the type of perturbations allowed in the data of the problem to be solved. Most discussions of backward error are written in terms of perturbations of the size of the machine precision Ψ, since these must always be considered with any numerical algorithm. Similarly, the backward stability (i.e., optimal reliability) of an algorithm is often expressed strictly in terms of machine precision.

However, it is important to keep in mind for the use of PRECISE that if an algorithm is indeed backward stable, it will be stable for a range of perturbation sizes and not only for those close to the machine precision. Thus, one may examine numerical stability (i.e., reliability) by intentionally introducing, in a controlled way, perturbations to a problem and observing the resulting outcomes. One may observe how different types of perturbations affect the results and can lead to the discovery of sensitive or unreliable features in the solution. In cases where the perturbations reveal no instabilities, then the analysis provides the user with further evidence of the fact that the computed solution can be considered accurate, stable, or reliable, i.e., a "good" solution.

Interestingly, different types of perturbations can produce markedly different behavior for the same algorithm applied to the same problem. It is not only a question of the size of the perturbations; the manner in which they are applied to the problem under study can affect the outcomes. The term *perturbation model* is used to describe the set of perturbations that are chosen to produce the computed results. It is important to keep in mind that the quantitative measures of reliability and sensitivity are defined only with respect to a specific perturbation model. In other words, the values for backward error and condition numbers differ according to each perturbation model. There is an infinite variety of perturbation models that can be applied to any problem.

Behind the use of all the PRECISE software is the use of structured perturbations to the numerical data. The notion behind a perturbation model is to mimic the effects of finite-precision arithmetic or data uncertainty to the point of producing observable, quantifiable behavior. It is most interesting to observe the behavior over a range of meaningful perturbation sizes and observe if the behavior remains consistent over the entire range. If instabilities are found, then this reveals much about the numerical problem; if not, this provides strong evidence of numerical reliability.

The basic items that compose a perturbation model are the range of perturbation sizes, the type of metric for the data, the choice of data items to be perturbed, and the type of perturbations to be performed. Each of these items is explained below.

6.5.1 Perturbation values

In general, a wide range of perturbation values should be used, spanning at least a few orders of magnitude. For data obtained from experimental measurements or truncated approximations, the perturbation range should include the order of the data uncertainty; we need to know if there is a qualitative change in the results for perturbations of this size.

For the same reason, perturbations of the same order of magnitude as the unit roundoff $\mathbf{u} = \frac{1}{2}\Psi$ are also frequently used. For computers implementing IEEE 754 [215] floating-point arithmetic, the values for the unit roundoff $\mathbf{u}$ are shown in Table 6.1. An example range of perturbation values, therefore, might be ten values taken uniformly from the range $[2^{-54}, 2^{-10}]$. The magnitude of the perturbation values is closely related to the type of perturbations applied to the data, which are discussed below.

Table 6.1. *Unit roundoff* **u** *for IEEE 754 standard floating-point arithmetic.*

Single precision	$\mathbf{u} = 2^{-24} \approx 5.96 \times 10^{-8}$
Double precision	$\mathbf{u} = 2^{-53} \approx 1.11 \times 10^{-16}$

6.5.2 Perturbation types

For numerical linear algebra algorithms, the two most common types of perturbation models involve either normwise or componentwise perturbations. As the name implies, in a normwise model the data components of (P) are perturbed by values $\| F \|$ and $\| y \|$, which correspond to the magnitude of the data with respect to the chosen metric.

In a componentwise model the data components are perturbed according to each component's individual value, $| F |$ and $| y |$, which correspond to the modulus of the values of the data. As an example, consider the case of studying a linear system $Ax = b$ with perturbations of size t. A normwise perturbation model would produce a set of perturbed systems of the form $(A + \Delta A)x = (b + \Delta b)$, where the perturbation matrices satisfy

$$\| \Delta A \| \leq t \| A \|,$$
$$\| \Delta b \| \leq t \| b \|,$$

while in a componentwise perturbation model, the inequalities defining the perturbations are given by

$$| \Delta A | \leq t | A |,$$
$$| \Delta b | \leq t | b |,$$

where the modulus inequalities are understood to be satisfied for each component. The componentwise model is seen to preserve the structure of the data; in particular, for sparse matrices the sparsity pattern is maintained by the componentwise perturbations, but not for normwise perturbations.

These distinctions were originally developed because of the type of theoretical analysis performed for certain algorithms. Inspection of the above inequalities shows that a normwise analysis is based on more of a global treatment of the problem than a componentwise analysis. As such, analytical error bounds obtained through a normwise analysis may be more pessimistic in some cases than those obtained from a componentwise analysis; this is the case, for example, in the solution of linear systems by Gaussian elimination.

For the purposes of PRECISE, however, these distinctions are not so critical. One powerful aspect of PRECISE is that any type of perturbation model can be used to search for meaningful results; there is no restriction in this regard. It is useful, therefore, to generalize the inequalities defining the perturbation types. The normwise perturbations must satisfy

$$\| \Delta A \| \leq t\alpha,$$
$$\| \Delta b \| \leq t\beta$$

for some quantities $\alpha \geq 0$ and $\beta \geq 0$, which can be adjusted according to the perturbation model. For instance, values of $\alpha \approx \| A \|$ and $\beta = 0$ indicate the same normwise perturbation on the matrix A as before, but no perturbations on the right-hand-side b. Another example might be $\alpha = 1$ and $\beta = 1$, specifying perturbations that are fixed in size for both A and b. Any combination of values for α and β gives a valid perturbation model for a study by PRECISE, except of course the combination $\alpha = 0$ and $\beta = 0$.

Similarly, the componentwise perturbations are generalized by the inequalities

$$| \Delta A | \leq tE,$$
$$| \Delta b | \leq tf,$$

where E is any matrix of the same order as A and f is a vector of the same size as b, with both E and f having nonnegative components. For problems involving sparse matrices, both E and f are usually specified to have the same structural properties as A and b, respectively.

6.5.3 Data metrics

This choice pertains to the choice of norm used to measure distances in the data space. For instance, in linear algebra contexts commonly used norms are the 2 norm, the 1 norm, the ∞ norm, or in some cases, the Frobenius norm. In Module 1, a metric is required to determine the estimators for the backward error. This choice is problem dependent and depends also on the goals of the user. For normwise perturbation models, this choice obviously affects the magnitude of the perturbations to the components. To perform an error analysis, a suitable choice is often the ∞ norm, which gives a good upper bound on error quantities and, in addition, is inexpensive to compute, particularly when the data are distributed in a multiprocessor environment.

6.5.4 Data to be perturbed

One has the flexibility to perturb all or just a subset of the data components in the problem. For example, when studying a linear system $Ax = b$, one can perturb only the matrix A, only the right-hand-side b, or both A and b. One might also choose to perturb only a few elements of A, for instance, those that correspond to certain critical unknown variables. One usually starts with a simple approach, such as perturbing all the data elements, and then trying other combinations for comparison.

6.5.5 Choosing a perturbation model

While there are infinite possibilities for choosing a perturbation model, there are some clear guidelines to follow to make the choice quite straightforward. When performing a stability analysis, most often, a series of perturbation models will be used to gain deeper insight into the numerical behavior of the problem and its solution. Therefore, one may start with almost any model and then refine the choice according to the phenomena that are observed. The choices are always problem dependent, but the following general principles can be used to guide the analysis.

Initially, one usually starts with a wide range of perturbation sizes that includes the machine precision or any level of data uncertainty. For example, if the numerical procedure calls for a parameter to define the error tolerance of the approximate solution, then the perturbation range should include this value. A special case of this situation is the specification of the stopping criterion for iterative solvers; for example, if the iterations are stopped using a criterion of 10^{-k}, then the perturbation interval should bracket this value. While the range of perturbation values can initially be quite large, the actual number of perturbation sizes taken from the range does not have to be large. Five to ten perturbation sizes taken from the range $[\xi^{-k_{\min}}, \xi^{-k_{\max}}]$ should suffice for initial tests. As values for the stability indicators are observed, one may increase the number of perturbations taken form the range, and also adjust the values of $k_{\min}$ and $k_{\max}$ accordingly. Note that the user is free to specify any value for ξ, but a value of $\xi = 2$ allows a fine sampling of the interval range.

The choices of perturbation types, data metrics, and the data to be perturbed are all problem dependent. If the numerical algorithm under study is known to exhibit certain behavior for a particular type of perturbation, then this most certainly should be used in a stability analysis. On the other hand, if no theoretical behavior is predicted, then the user is free to make these choices based on other criteria. Notably, the manner in which the numerical procedure is implemented can be used to guide the choice for an initial perturbation model. In other words, the model that is most conveniently implemented may be used first. See also Section 6.6 for a discussion on implementation issues concerning perturbation models.

Finally, after an initial perturbation model has been selected and the results interpreted, the choice of subsequent perturbation models will depend on the observed results. There are in general three categories of behavior that might be observed. If the results show no evidence of numerical instability, then this provides corroborative evidence of the reliability of the numerical procedure. In this case, one might apply more rigorous tests to the problem in the hope that the same positive results can be obtained. The more tests that are applied with positive outcomes, the stronger the validation of the numerical procedure. For this situation, the user is free to change the perturbation model in any number of ways, for instance, by changing the perturbation sizes, the perturbation type, or the data metric. The process can continue in this way until the user is confident of the results.

The second category of results involves the situation when instabilities are observed. Thus, the subsequent perturbation models should be designed to investigate this condition. If instabilities are observed, further insight can be gained by using the same perturbation sizes and changing the type of perturbation or by limiting the data that are being perturbed. In such cases, it is not uncommon for different perturbation models to produce remarkably different behavior in the numerical problem; the results are not contradictory, but provide a more complete characterization of the numerical properties of the problem under study.

It can happen that the indicators may be inconclusive for some perturbation values. This can either be the result of an ill-chosen perturbation model or an actual problem in the numerical procedure. In this case, the range of perturbation values should be changed to determine if the indicators reveal different results. Different perturbation types or data metrics may also be used. If a number of perturbation models are attempted without conclusive results, then most likely some anomaly in the numerical procedure is present. For example, a numerical procedure that returns a constant error value for a certain range of perturbation values would exhibit this behavior. Thus, in such cases, the numerical procedure requires a more thorough inspection to determine the cause.

6.6 Implementation Issues

A backward error analysis requires a small amount of programming effort.

- The first task is to implement the perturbation model, including the iteration to produce samples of perturbed solutions for each perturbation size.

- A second task involves processing the samples to calculate the statistical indicators. This processing may be done simultaneously while the data are generated, or the samples may be written to a file and the indicators calculated in a separate phase.

- A final task is to visualize the stability indicators once they have been calculated. This task depends on the type of graphical software available.

These issues are examined in what follows. For examples of completed implementations of backward error analysis routines using popular software libraries, see [75, 309]. A general discussion of perturbation models was given in Section 6.5. Here, some practical concerns when implementing a perturbation model are discussed. One should also be aware of these issues when deciding what perturbation model(s) to apply for a study with PRECISE; the choice of perturbation model may depend on how it is to be implemented.

The main idea is to use perturbation sizes t taken from a range of values $[\xi^{-k_{\max}}, \xi^{-k_{\min}}]$. For each perturbation size, a number of samples of perturbed solutions will be produced. A starting point is to decide how to specify the perturbation values. Since in general a wide range of values is required that spans several orders of magnitude, a simple method is to specify the lower and upper exponents of the range. That is, using some base value such as $\xi = 2$, for instance, one need only specify the range $[\xi^{-k_{\max}}, \xi^{-k_{\min}}]$ by providing $k_{\min}$ and $k_{\max}$. Any base value ξ can be used. However, the particular choices of $\xi = 10$ or $\xi = 2$ are usually the most convenient; the former value allows perturbations of corresponding decimal digits in the data components, while the latter value corresponds to bitwise perturbations of the data. To store the perturbation values in an array, a counter k can be incremented from $k_{\min}$ to $k_{\max}$ to produce a uniform sample of perturbation values t. In a distributed parallel environment, each processor can perform this operation without communication, as long as $k_{\min}$ and $k_{\max}$ are constants known to all processors. Note that the particular order in which the perturbation sizes are used to produce indicators is usually not important; they can be increasing or decreasing in size during the indicator calculations as long as the correct order is presented during their visualization.

A number of samples will be generated for each perturbation size t. The number of samples does not need to be large; usually between 5 and 15 samples give very satisfactory results [75]. The number of samples should remain constant for all the different perturbation values taken from the perturbation range.

A random number generator is also required. All the routines in PRECISE use the routine named RANDOM, which can be modified according to system requirements (see Section 3.3 in [309]). If perturbations are to be produced on distributed data in a parallel environment, care should be taken to ensure the sequences of pseudorandom numbers on each processor are independent; this can be achieved by using different seeds on each processor.

Another issue concerns perturbations of real or complex data. When randomly perturbing a real data value x by a perturbation of size t, the result is either $x + t$ or $x - t$, each having equal probability. However, when randomly perturbing a complex data value, care should be taken since random number generators usually produce only real random (or, more precisely, pseudorandom) numbers. To perturb a complex data value z by a perturbation size t, let r represent a random number between 0 and 1; then a valid perturbation is given by $z + w$, where $w = te^{i2\pi r}$.

In some cases, the perturbations may need to be adjusted to suit a particular data metric. For example, when performing a normwise analysis on matrices, care should be taken to ensure that the inequalities defining normwise perturbations are satisfied as equalities. The type of norm used may require additional scaling of the perturbation values. In particular, using the $\| \cdot \|_\infty$ matrix norm, the perturbation of each component should be scaled according to the number of nonzero row elements. This is particularly important for large, sparse matrices, where one usually chooses to perturb only the nonzero elements since algorithms for these problems are designed specifically to manipulate only these elements.

A diagram of the general procedure for producing the sample data is given in Table 6.2. First, the numerical problem under study is solved without introducing user-defined perturbations. Following this, an iteration is required, where a number of samples of perturbed problems are solved for each perturbation size. For each perturbed solution $\widetilde{x}$ obtained, both $\widetilde{x}$ and the value obtained by the reverse mapping $F(\widetilde{x})$ are required for the analysis. Note that in general $F(\widetilde{x})$ differs from $\widetilde{F}(\widetilde{x})$, and only the former quantity is needed. For example, if the problem under study is a linear system $Ax = b$ and the perturbed problem $\widetilde{A}\widetilde{x} = \widetilde{b}$ is solved, then the quantities used for the analysis are $\widetilde{x}$ and $A\widetilde{x}$.

Table 6.2. *General scheme for generating data for a backward error analysis. The data are indicated by arrows ($\Longrightarrow$). Note that after each perturbed solution $\widetilde{x}$ is obtained, the unperturbed mapping F (not $\widetilde{F}$) is used to generate the image $F(\widetilde{x})$.*

$$\boxed{\text{solve } F(x) = y} \quad \Longrightarrow \quad x, F(x)$$

for each perturbation size t:
    for each sample:

$$\boxed{\text{perturbed problem } \widetilde{F}(x) = \widetilde{y}}$$

$$\boxed{\text{solve } \widetilde{F}(\widetilde{x}) = \widetilde{y}} \quad \Longrightarrow \widetilde{x}, F(\widetilde{x})$$

For most applications, it should be quite straightforward to place the numerical solver in an iterative procedure as shown in Table 6.2. In general, the iteration requires a separate copy of all the input data for the problem to be saved so that it will be available for each subsequent perturbed problem. If this is not feasible due to memory constraints, then the initial data for the problem may be reloaded from disk files for each perturbation. While this can be time-consuming, the issue of efficiency is not the primary concern during a backward error analysis. If the numerical solver has been designed to work in a parallel environment, we should ensure that the processors are synchronized throughout the iteration.

The example software discussed in [309] can be used to generate perturbations for most types of problems. In those examples, routines to produce perturbations on vectors can be used for matrices as well. Modifications to these routines to produce more complicated perturbation models can be easily performed. In addition, other perturbation techniques are possible for special cases. For instance, since iterative algorithms for large, sparse matrices usually access the matrix data only through matrix-vector multiplications, it may be worthwhile to perturb only the vector resulting from the matrix-vector product. As explained above, any approach to producing perturbations can produce valid results in the context of PRECISE.

6.7   Industrial Use of PRECISE

PRECISE has been used intensively, since 1988, in several industrial environments (IBM-France, Thomson-CSF, and CERFACS) to test various *laws of computation* that emerge from invariant patterns of behavior for computations in finite precision (see [75]). It has also been used, more classically, to assess the numerical quality of computations in industrial problems such as

-   the flutter phenomenon for Aerospatiale [47, 166],

-   an aeroelasticity problem for ONERA (Division Hélicoptères) [29, 46],

-   electromagnetic guided waves for Thomson-CSF [46],

-   the reliability of an orbitography software for CNES [78, 76, 151, 174, 175],

-   fluid dynamics and electromagnetism at CERFACS [150, 153, 445],

-   ambiguity resolution in GPS (the Jason project) for CNES [74],

-   astrophysics for Observatoire Midi-Pyrénées and Politechnico Milano.

The PRECISE code was a vital part of the HPCN (High Performance Computing and Networking) European project PINEAPL (1996–1998) to produce a general purpose library of parallel numerical software suitable for a wide range of computationally intensive industrial applications and to port several application codes that use this library to parallel computers. The industrial consortium led by NAG included British Aerospace, CERFACS, LCR Thomson-CSF, CPS (Napoli, Italy), the Danish Hydraulic Institute (Denmark), IBM SEMEA, the University of Manchester (UK), Math-Tech, and Piaggio (Italy).

The toolbox PRECISE for MATLAB given in the Annex of [75] was translated into Fortran to allow large and realistic problems to be handled and was used to **test each item of numerical software produced during the project**. The Fortran toolbox is now available as freeware from CERFACS at `http://www.cerfacs.fr/algor/Softs/PRECISE/precise.html` [309].

Between July 2000 and May 2002 a total of 86 MATLAB and Fortran PRECISE codes have been downloaded from this web site by users from Argentina, China, England, France, Greece, Ireland, Morocco, Russia, Spain, and the U.S.A.

6.8   PRECISE in Academic Research

In parallel to its use in various industrial environments, PRECISE has been used to test many conjectures about computer simulations in the neighborhood of singularities. Such conjectures range from the influence of nonnormality on iterative processes [77, 79] and on eigenvalues [29, 67, 47, 166] to the assessment of computation near algebraic singularities. The computation of a Jordan form has been a point of special focus [222, 79].

We conclude by stating that PRECISE has proved an extremely versatile tool to test algorithmic behavior on the computer as illustrated by the following example. The spectral norm $\|A^{-1}\|_2$ for a very large matrix A can be computed using the Lanczos algorithm on A^*A, with inversion. Such an algorithm requires the solution of linear systems of the kind $A^*Ax = b$.

Extensive experimentations with PRECISE led to the discovery of the theoretical formulae for the the condition number and the backward error for such linear systems where only A is perturbed. This study is of importance in designing a reliable code for computing the spectral portrait of a matrix [152, 309]. **So PRECISE helped design itself.** For more, the interested reader is referred to the Qualitative Computing Group web pages at http://www.cerfacs.fr/algor/Qualitative/Qualitative.html.

6.9   Conclusion

The toolbox PRECISE (**PR**ecision **E**stimation and **C**ontrol **I**n **S**cientific and **E**ngineering computing) is not intended to be yet another software tool for automatic control of roundoff error propagation. It is as much a matter of personal taste as of performance that should guide the user's choice among the available methods and software for automatic control of accuracy.

We view PRECISE as an aid in investigating difficult cases, such as computations in the neighborhood of a singularity, or computations in the presence of high nonnormality, to gain better insight on the underlying mathematical instability.

In particular, PRECISE helps greatly in the many cases where there do not yet exist any closed form formulae for the backward error or the condition number. The better understanding of the problem provided by PRECISE allows in turn a better use of current software for error control. We foresee tools such as PRECISE to be more in demand as our technological society relies more exclusively on numerical simulation, in areas where the human safety is central, such as civil engineering or biotechnologies.

Chapter 7

Tools for the Verification of Approximate Solutions to Differential Equations

Wayne H. Enright

7.1 Introduction

Scientific computation is often carried out in general purpose problem-solving environments (PSEs), such as MATLAB or MAPLE, or in application-specific PSEs, such as those associated with large-scale, high-performance simulations. When practitioners work in these environments it is essential that they have access to state-of-the-art numerical software and tools to visualize approximate solutions produced by such software. It is equally essential (although not yet standard practice) to have available tools that can be used to verify (or validate) that the approximate solution is consistent with the true solution of the underlying mathematical model. In this chapter we will identify a suite of tools that has been developed to address this need for the case where the underlying model is a system of ordinary differential equations (ODEs).

The resulting suite of tools can be used to improve the practitioner's confidence in the results and are suitable for use with any numerical method. In developing and implementing these tools we have assumed that the approximate solution is provided as a piecewise polynomial on an arbitrary mesh. The tools perform such tasks as measuring the size of the associated defect, estimating the global error, estimating the condition number, and checking that a different method generates a consistent approximate solution.

7.1.1 Motivation and overview

In the last decade there has been a significant change in the way scientific computing is undertaken. Software developers must become aware of this change if their software is ever going to be widely used and have an impact. Applications often require data compression, interactive data viewing (or data mining), and remote visualization, and involve the distributed collaboration of experts.

A PSE is often how students are first exposed to scientific computing. It is also the environment where scientists and engineers formulate and investigate approximate solutions to their problems. We focus on this environment, but the tools we develop and the observations we make are also applicable in any environment where large-scale simulations are investigated.

In the next section we identify various aspects of a PSE that affect how numerical software can be implemented and used effectively. We then justify and develop four "verification tools" for use with standard ODE solvers. In the fourth section we present the application of these tools to two typical simulations and show how the tools we have developed can give insight into and understanding of the quality of an approximate solution. We conclude with a discussion of current and future extensions of this work.

7.2   Characteristics of a PSE

Although the basic problem we consider is to approximate the continuous solution $y(x)$ of an ODE on a specified interval of interest $[a, b]$, most numerical methods partition the interval $[a, b]$ into a discrete set of mesh points $a = x_0 < x_1 < \cdots x_N = b$ and provide approximate solution values, $y_i \approx y(x_i)$, only for these mesh points. In a PSE the focus is on visualizing and investigating various aspects of approximate solutions. Visualization generally involves graphical representation of a "subset" of the results. It can involve the use of color, texture, lighting, animation, and sound. Although stringent accuracy is rarely necessary, some off-mesh accuracy is frequently required. It is essential that the tools and packages that are provided in a PSE be easy to understand and use. The interface and documentation must be simple and structured in a hierarchical fashion. (Information should be hidden unless necessary to define the problem.) In this environment ease of use is as important as efficiency.

A consequence of these observations is that software that is used in PSEs should satisfy some extra design requirements. For example, robustness is as important as reliability. In particular, it is acceptable for the software to fail, as long as it does so gracefully and early. It is also important to adopt a standard interpretation of error control, and a standard program interface (calling sequence) for methods that perform the same or similar tasks. Similarly, options and additional parameters (if required) should be specified in the same way for all methods. This includes mesh-constraints, initial guess of the solution, specification of partial derivatives, and accuracy specification. It is also important to adopt a standard representation of an approximate solution. (For example, in the case of solving systems of ODEs one can choose to represent an approximate solution by a vector of piecewise polynomials.)

An effective PSE must provide tools to do the following:

1. Formulate a mathematical model of the problem.

2. Approximate the solution of the mathematical problem.

3. Visualize an approximate solution.

4. Verify that an approximate solution is consistent with the mathematical model and the requested accuracy.

5. Verify that the mathematical model is well-posed. (That is, quantify the underlying inherent conditioning.)

Of these requirements, the first three are satisfied in virtually all PSEs for most classes of problems, while the latter two requirements are often not satisfied. The verification tools that do address these latter requirements are generally designed to be used for particular problem classes but they are a very important part of computer simulations. In the next section we will develop and justify a collection of such tools for use when solving ODE problems in a PSE. We will use the MATLAB PSE [305] and in particular the numerical method, ode45, to illustrate the details and trade-offs one faces when introducing and using these tools. For a good introduction to MATLAB and its use in scientific computation see [204], and for details and guidance in formulating and visualizing mathematical models in MATLAB involving systems of ODEs see [407].

7.3   Verification Tools for Use with an ODE Solver

If the underlying numerical method provides a continuous approximation to the solution (over the domain of interest) then generic tools for the verification of an approximate solution and the estimation of the mathematical conditioning can be developed. Examples of such tools that would be useful and which we have implemented include those based on assessing the magnitude of the defect (or residual) of the approximate solution; estimating the global error by solving the same problem with a more stringent accuracy request or with a different method; and estimating the global error by determining the exact error associated with the approximate solution of a "nearby problem" using the same method.

The key assumption we make of the methods that generate the approximate solutions is that, when applied to the initial value problem (IVP)

$$y' = f(x, y), \ y(a) = y_0, \ \text{on} \ [a, b],$$

with a specified accuracy TOL, the numerical method M generates a piecewise polynomial $z_{TOL}(x)$, defined for $x \in [a, b]$ and satisfying

$$\|z_{TOL}(x) - y(x)\| \leq K_M TOL.$$

This assumption is satisfied by most state-of-the-art ODE software and certainly by the built-in numerical methods of MATLAB [408]. Note that K_M can depend on the method and the problem and can be interpreted as the "numerical condition number" associated with method M.

The restrictions we imposed on the tools we produced include the following:

1. They must be easy to use. If possible the calling sequence should be the same as that used to generate the approximate solution, with no more information required.

2. The "cost" associated with applying the tool should not be much greater than that involved in generating the approximate solution (or visualizing it).

3. The calling sequence should be the same for any method to which it is applied. The tool may require some knowledge of the method, but this information is transparent to the user. Some of the tools can be independent of the method.

The four verification tools we have implemented for ODEs in MATLAB are as follows:

Check 1: A consistency check based on solving the problem with a more stringent value for TOL and returning the difference between the two approximations as a piecewise polynomial. That is, we compute

$$E_{TOL}(x) = z_{TOL}(x) - z_{TOL1}(x),$$

where $TOL1 < TOL$. The "cost" of computing this quantity will depend on the order of the method and the value of $TOL1$ but will generally be no more than double the cost of generating $z_{TOL}(x)$.

Check 2: A consistency check based on solving the problem with an alternative method, $\underline{M}$. The piecewise polynomial returned by this routine is

$$\widetilde{E}_{TOL}(x) = z_{TOL}(x) - \widetilde{z}_{TOL}(x),$$

where $\widetilde{z}_{TOL}(x)$ is the approximate solution associated with $\underline{M}$. (Note that this check is most credible if the method $\underline{M}$ is very different from M. For example, in our implementation of this tool we use a variable-order Adams method when assessing a Runge–Kutta method from MATLAB.)

Check 3: A check that computes the defect,

$$D_{TOL}(x) = z'_{TOL}(x) - f(x, z_{TOL}(x)).$$

Note that although $D_{TOL}(x)$ is not a piecewise polynomial, it is a function that can be evaluated at any point in $[a, b]$.

Check 4: A consistency check based on the idea of [502], where we determine a piecewise polynomial,

$$EST_{TOL}(x) = z_{TOL}(x) - w_{TOL}(x),$$

where $w_{TOL}(x)$ is the approximate solution produced by method M (applied to the perturbed IVP, $z' = f(x, z) + D_{TOL}(x)$) on the same mesh that was used to determine $z_{TOL}(x)$.

For each of the vector-valued functions returned by Check 1, Check 2, and Check 4, we can interpret its max value for $x \in [a, b]$ to be a measure of the maximum global error. Therefore, a crude indicator of the numerical condition number is the ratio of this max value to TOL. Similarly, for Check 3, the maximum magnitude of the components of $D_{TOL}(x)/TOL$ can be considered an indication of the contribution of the numerical method to the overall numerical conditioning of the problem (it does not reflect the underlying mathematical conditioning of the problem).

7.4   Two Examples of Use of These Tools

A predator-prey relationship can be modeled by the well-known IVP

$$y'_1 = y_1 - 0.1y_1y_2 + 0.02x,$$
$$y'_2 = -y_2 + 0.02y_1y_2 + 0.008x,$$

with

$$y_1(0) = 30, \quad y_2(0) = 20, \quad \text{and } x \in [0, 100],$$

where $y_1(x)$ represents the "prey" population at time x and $y_2(x)$ represents the "predator" population at time x. The solution can then be visualized as a standard x/y solution plot or by a "phase portrait" plot.

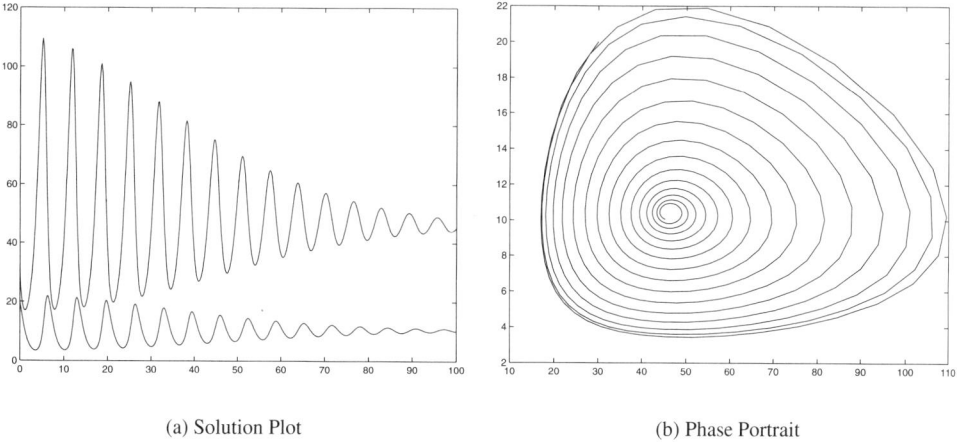

(a) Solution Plot   (b) Phase Portrait

Figure 7.1. *Approximate solution produced by ode45 for predator-prey problem.*

A second example is the well-known Lorenz problem, which arises in the study of dynamical systems and is known to have solutions that are potentially poorly conditioned. We will consider the IVP

$$y_1' = 10(y_2 - y_1),$$

$$y_2' = y_1(28 - y_3) - y_2,$$

$$y_3' = y_1 y_2 - \frac{8}{3} y_3,$$

with

$$y_1(0) = 15, \quad y_2(0) = 15, \quad y_3(0) = 36, \quad \text{and } x \in [0, 20].$$

Using ode45 to investigate solutions of these problems allows us to illustrate the ability of our tools to detect potential conditioning difficulties. Figures 7.1–7.2 show visualizations of numerical solutions to these problems determined by ode45, and Tables 7.1–7.4 and Figures 7.3–7.11 report the results of applying our verification tools to a selection of numerical solutions computed by ode45.

In the tables, whenever a maximum value is reported it has been determined numerically by sampling over 500 equally spaced points in the interval of integration. In these

(a) Solution Plot

(b) Phase Portrait

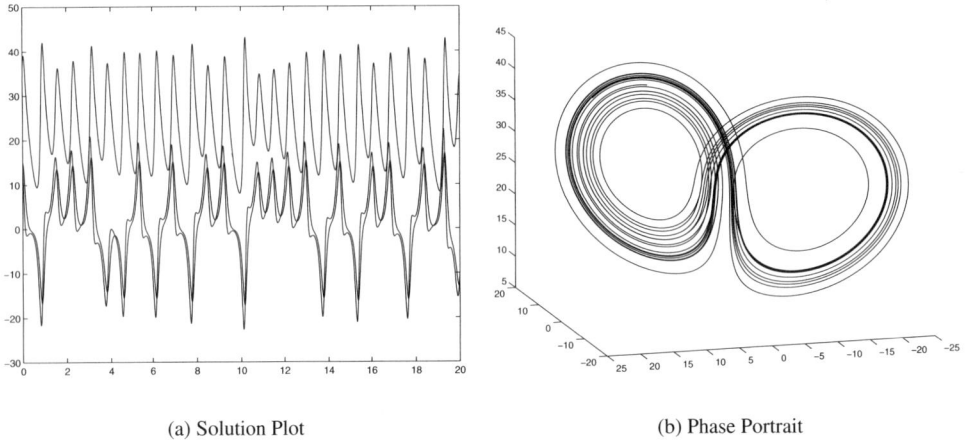

Figure 7.2. *Approximate solution produced by ode45 for Lorenz problem.*

Table 7.1. *Check 1 results for ode45.*

$RTOL$	$max\|E(x)\|_R$	CoNum	NST1	NST2
10^{-3}	$.16 \cdot 10^{-1}$	15.8	98	232
	$.26 \cdot 10^{-1}$	26.2		
10^{-5}	$.31 \cdot 10^{-4}$	3.1	232	582
	$.38 \cdot 10^{-4}$	3.8		
10^{-7}	$.23 \cdot 10^{-6}$	2.3	582	1461
	$.22 \cdot 10^{-6}$	2.2		

(a) Predator-Prey Problem

TOL	$max\|E(x)\|_R$	CoNum	NST1	NST2
10^{-6}	$.35 \cdot 10^{2}$	$.35 \cdot 10^{8}$	1086	2754
	$.21 \cdot 10^{3}$	$.21 \cdot 10^{9}$		
	$.31 \cdot 10^{1}$	$.31 \cdot 10^{7}$		
10^{-8}	$.85 \cdot 10^{2}$	$.85 \cdot 10^{10}$	2754	6914
	$.23 \cdot 10^{2}$	$.23 \cdot 10^{10}$		
	$.64 \cdot 10^{0}$	$.64 \cdot 10^{8}$		
10^{-10}	$.23 \cdot 10^{0}$	$.23 \cdot 10^{10}$	6914	17358
	$.63 \cdot 10^{-1}$	$.63 \cdot 10^{9}$		
	$.13 \cdot 10^{-1}$	$.13 \cdot 10^{9}$		

(b) Lorenz Problem

tables we report the number of steps required by ode45 to generate the numerical solution, NST1, and the number of extra steps, NST2, required by the respective tool. (This latter count quantifies the cost of applying the tool relative to that of generating the approximate solution.) For Check 1, Check 2, and Check 4, results also include the indicator of the numerical condition number, CoNum. Similarly, for Check 3 we include the indicator of the contribution of the method to the numerical conditioning, NCon.

The method ode45 allows one to specify a mixed relative and absolute error tolerance by setting $ATOL$ and $RTOL$, respectively. For the predator-prey problem, as Figure 7.1 shows, the components of the solution remain bounded and positive and a pure relative error

Table 7.2. *Check 2 results for ode45.*

$RTOL$	$max\|\tilde{E}(x)\|_R$	CoNum	NST1	NST2
10^{-3}	$.20 \cdot 10^{-1}$	19.5	98	271
	$.28 \cdot 10^{-1}$	28.5		
10^{-5}	$.11 \cdot 10^{-3}$	10.6	232	515
	$.12 \cdot 10^{-3}$	12.1		
10^{-7}	$.91 \cdot 10^{-6}$	9.1	582	772
	$.12 \cdot 10^{-5}$	12.0		

TOL	$max\|\tilde{E}(x)\|_R$	CoNum	NST1	NST2
10^{-6}	$.64 \cdot 10^{2}$	$.64 \cdot 10^{8}$	1086	1530
	$.25 \cdot 10^{4}$	$.25 \cdot 10^{10}$		
	$.13 \cdot 10^{1}$	$.13 \cdot 10^{7}$		
10^{-8}	$.42 \cdot 10^{3}$	$.42 \cdot 10^{11}$	2754	2291
	$.17 \cdot 10^{2}$	$.17 \cdot 10^{10}$		
	$.13 \cdot 10^{1}$	$.13 \cdot 10^{9}$		
10^{-10}	$.18 \cdot 10^{0}$	$.18 \cdot 10^{10}$	6914	3141
	$.52 \cdot 10^{-1}$	$.52 \cdot 10^{9}$		
	$.11 \cdot 10^{-1}$	$.11 \cdot 10^{9}$		

(a) Predator-Prey Problem   (b) Lorenz Problem

Table 7.3. *Check 3 results for ode45.*

$RTOL$	$max\|D(x)\|_R$	NCon	$max\|D2(x)\|_R$	NCon2	NST1
10^{-3}	$.13 \cdot 10^{1}$	17.4	$.12 \cdot 10^{1}$	15.5	98
	$.44 \cdot 10^{1}$	16.6	$.14 \cdot 10^{1}$	17.3	
10^{-5}	$.18 \cdot 10^{0}$	18.8	$.19 \cdot 10^{-1}$	6.5	232
	$.42 \cdot 10^{-1}$	15.0	$.38 \cdot 10^{-2}$	6.8	
10^{-7}	$.24 \cdot 10^{-3}$	69.8	$.16 \cdot 10^{-4}$	2.4	582
	$.42 \cdot 10^{-3}$	60.0	$.44 \cdot 10^{-4}$	2.4	

TOL	$max\|D(x)\|_R$	NCon	$max\|D2(x)\|_R$	NCon2	NST1
10^{-6}	$.63 \cdot 10^{-3}$	9.8	$.20 \cdot 10^{-3}$	1.6	1086
	$.75 \cdot 10^{-3}$	18.0	$.70 \cdot 10^{-4}$	1.6	
	$.82 \cdot 10^{-3}$	13.0	$.12 \cdot 10^{-3}$	1.0	
10^{-8}	$.19 \cdot 10^{-4}$	16.0	$.15 \cdot 10^{-5}$	1.1	2754
	$.77 \cdot 10^{-4}$	26.0	$.11 \cdot 10^{-6}$	1.7	
	$.37 \cdot 10^{-4}$	39.0	$.24 \cdot 10^{-5}$	.82	
10^{-10}	$.65 \cdot 10^{-7}$	40.0	$.13 \cdot 10^{-7}$	1.1	6914
	$.67 \cdot 10^{-6}$	59.0	$.99 \cdot 10^{-8}$	1.4	
	$.11 \cdot 10^{-4}$	87.0	$.87 \cdot 10^{-7}$	.84	

(a) Predator-Prey Problem   (b) Lorenz Problem

control is appropriate. We have chosen to use a range of $RTOL = TOL$ values that would be typical in a PSE (10^{-3}, 10^{-5}, and 10^{-7}). In cases where we report a norm of a vector (as one of the statistics) we tabulate for each component of the vector the magnitude of that component relative to the magnitude of the corresponding solution component. That is, we report a measure of the componentwise relative error. For the Lorenz problem, as Figure 7.2 shows, $y_1(x)$ and $y_2(x)$ oscillate around zero while $y_3(x)$ remains positive. A mixed relative/absolute error control is appropriate in this case and we have used $RTOL = ATOL = TOL$ with a range of values (10^{-6}, 10^{-8}, and 10^{-10}).

In visualizing the results of the verification tools (that is, the respective piecewise polynomials or function) for the Lorenz problem (where exponential growth in the global error as a function of the length of the integration interval is to be expected) we found that standard plots were not particularly helpful. We found it more meaningful to present plots

Table 7.4. *Check 4 results for ode45.*

$RTOL$	$max\|EST(x)\|_R$	CoNum	NST1
10^{-3}	$.34 \cdot 10^{-1}$	33.7	98
	$.18 \cdot 10^{-1}$	18.2	
10^{-5}	$.25 \cdot 10^{-4}$	2.5	232
	$.26 \cdot 10^{-4}$	2.6	
10^{-7}	$.24 \cdot 10^{-6}$	2.4	582
	$.22 \cdot 10^{-6}$	2.2	

TOL	$max\|EST(x)\|_R$	CoNum	NST1
10^{-6}	$.27 \cdot 10^3$	$.27 \cdot 10^9$	1086
	$.24 \cdot 10^2$	$.24 \cdot 10^8$	
	$.35 \cdot 10^1$	$.35 \cdot 10^7$	
10^{-8}	$.51 \cdot 10^1$	$.51 \cdot 10^9$	2754
	$.41 \cdot 10^2$	$.41 \cdot 10^{10}$	
	$.28 \cdot 10^1$	$.28 \cdot 10^9$	
10^{-10}	$.17 \cdot 10^0$	$.17 \cdot 10^{10}$	6914
	$.62 \cdot 10^{-1}$	$.62 \cdot 10^9$	
	$.14 \cdot 10^{-1}$	$.14 \cdot 10^9$	

(a) Predator-Prey Problem   (b) Lorenz Problem

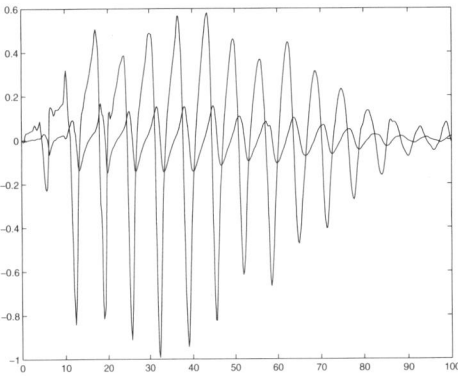

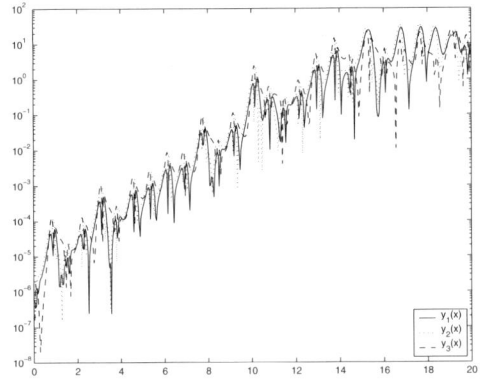

(a) Predator-Prey Problem, $TOL = 10^{-3}$ (b) Lorenz Problem, $TOL = 10^{-6}$

Figure 7.3. $E_{TOL}(x)$ *for ode45.*

of the logarithm of the magnitude of the respective global error estimate for each component of the approximate solution, and this is what is presented in Figures 7.3–7.11.

From these results one observes a consistent estimate of the condition number for each of the relevant tools (Check 1, Check 2, and Check 4) at each tolerance. This condition number estimate can be seen to be exponential in the length of the interval of integration. That is, if the interval were $[0, T]$, then the condition number estimate for each component roughly satisfies

$$CoNum \approx 10^{0.45T}.$$

This observation can be used to help decide when a higher order method should be used

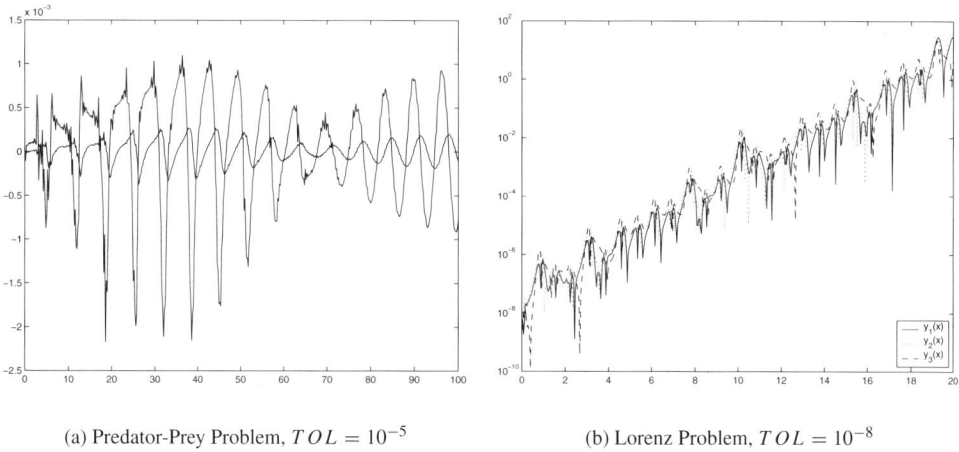

(a) Predator-Prey Problem, $TOL = 10^{-5}$ (b) Lorenz Problem, $TOL = 10^{-8}$

Figure 7.4. $E_{TOL}(x)$ *for ode45.*

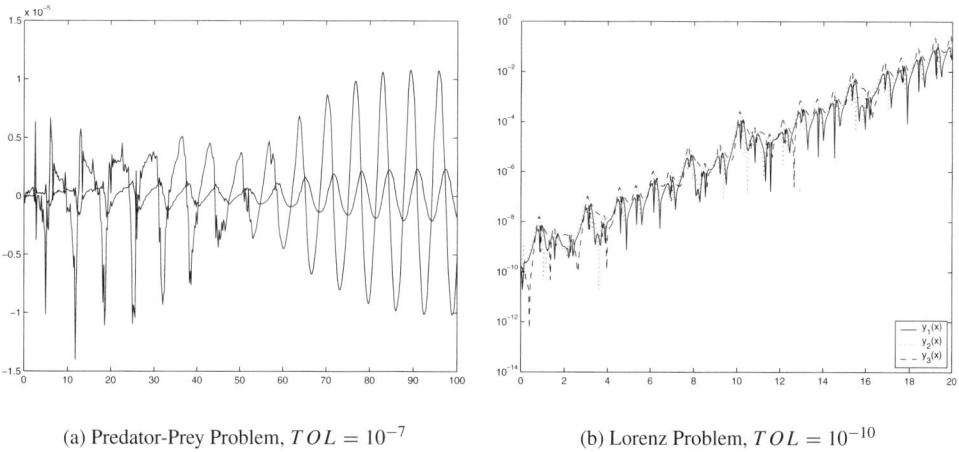

(a) Predator-Prey Problem, $TOL = 10^{-7}$ (b) Lorenz Problem, $TOL = 10^{-10}$

Figure 7.5. $E_{TOL}(x)$ *for ode45.*

(because of the need for stringent values of TOL) and when higher precision (such as quadruple precision) would be necessary in a computation.

Table 7.3 and Figures 7.9–7.11 reveal that the size of the defect and the associated potential contribution to the overall mathematical conditioning are both greater than would be expected, especially at the more stringent values of TOL. The reason for this is that the piecewise polynomial returned by ode45 has a corresponding defect that is only $O(h^4)$ rather than the $O(h^5)$ accuracy associated with the underlying method. It is well known that a piecewise polynomial with an $O(h^5)$ defect is available for any fifth order numerical method (see, for example, [137]). We have derived such a generic interpolant at a cost of

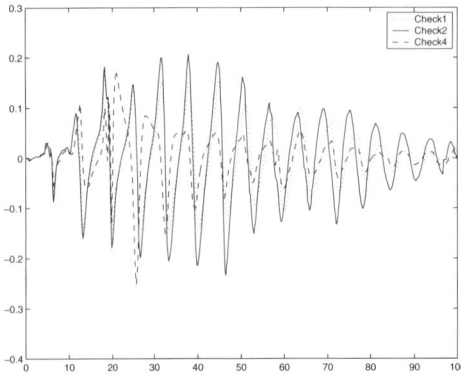

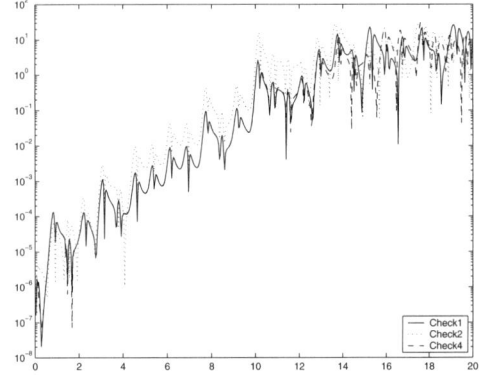

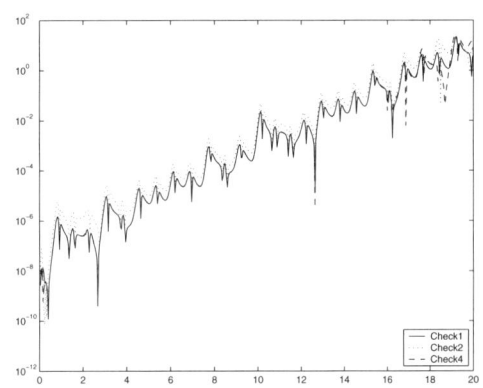

(a) $y_2(x)$ of Predator-Prey Problem, $TOL = 10^{-3}$ (b) $y_3(x)$ of Lorenz Problem, $TOL = 10^{-6}$

Figure 7.6. *Check 1, Check 2, and Check 4 results for ode45.*

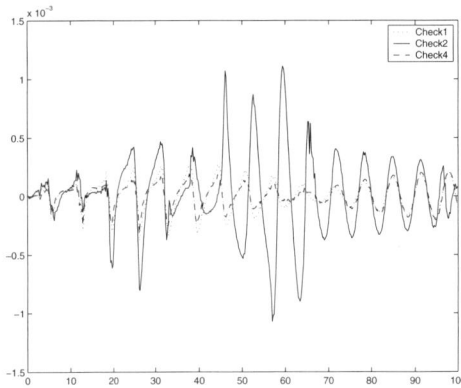

(a) $y_2(x)$ of Predator-Prey Problem, $TOL = 10^{-5}$ (b) $y_3(x)$ of Lorenz Problem, $TOL = 10^{-8}$

Figure 7.7. *Check 1, Check 2, and Check 4 results for ode45.*

two extra derivative evaluations per step, and the resulting piecewise polynomial, $\bar{z}_{TOL}(x)$, has an associated defect, $D2(x)$. Table 7.3 reports the maximum magnitude of this defect and the corresponding indicator of the numerical contribution to the overall mathematical conditioning, NCon2.

The numerical experience reported here for ode45 on these two problems is typical of our experience with other problems. The tests show, as one would expect from the definitions, that Check 2 gives a less accurate estimate of the magnitude of the global error than that provided by the more expensive verification tools, Check 1 and Check 3. On the other hand, all the tools give a consistent confirmation when the results are reliable. In

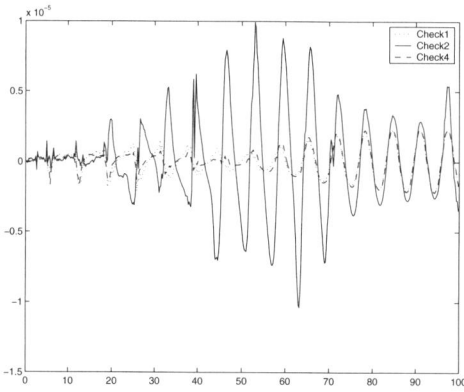

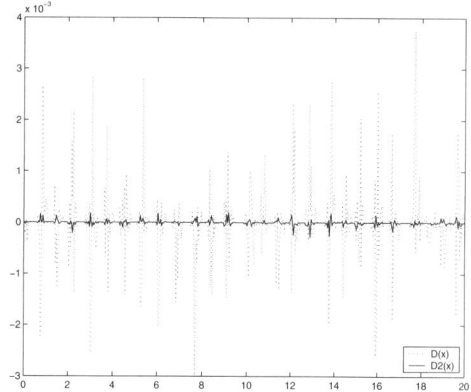

(a) $y_2(x)$ of Predator-Prey Problem, $TOL = 10^{-7}$ (b) $y_3(x)$ of Lorenz Problem, $TOL = 10^{-10}$

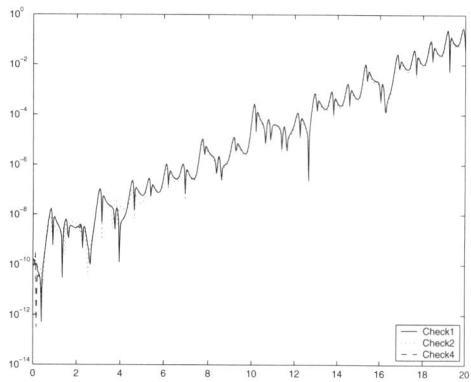

Figure 7.8. *Check 1, Check 2, and Check 4 results for ode45.*

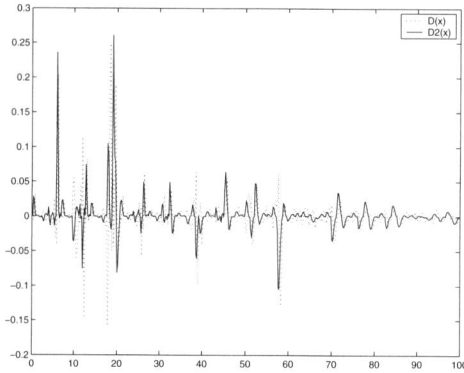

(a) $y_2(x)$ of Predator-Prey Problem, $TOL = 10^{-3}$ (b) $y_3(x)$ of Lorenz Problem, $TOL = 10^{-6}$

Figure 7.9. *Check 3 results for ode45.*

particular, they allow one to have confidence in the quality of solution, and they all indicate that the predator-prey problem is well-conditioned over the specified range of TOL values and that the Lorenz problem is poorly conditioned (but that accurate approximate solutions are possible as long as appropriate values of TOL are specified).

7.5   Discussion and Future Extensions

We implemented these verification tools as standard MATLAB functions and demonstrated that they can be used in an effective way to quantify the quality of an approximate solution.

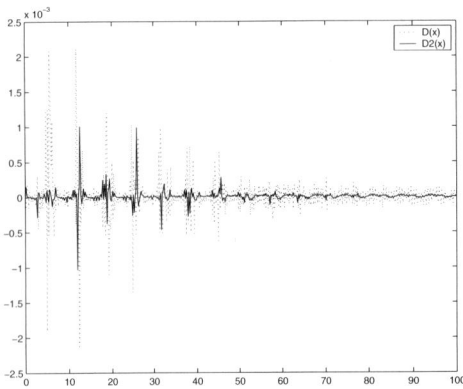

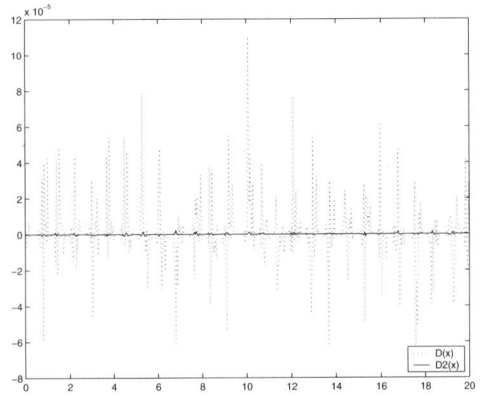

(a) $y_2(x)$ of Predator-Prey Problem, $TOL = 10^{-5}$ (b) $y_3(x)$ of Lorenz Problem, $TOL = 10^{-8}$

Figure 7.10. *Check 3 results for ode45.*

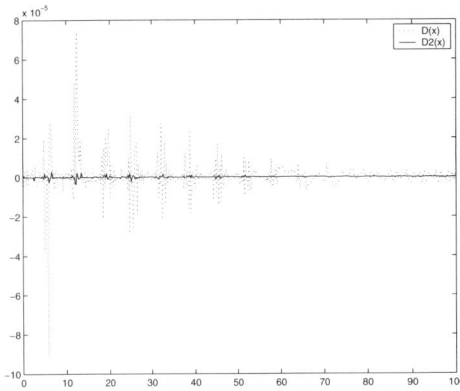

(a) $y_2(x)$ of Predator-Prey Problem, $TOL = 10^{-7}$ (b) $y_3(x)$ of Lorenz Problem, $TOL = 10^{-10}$

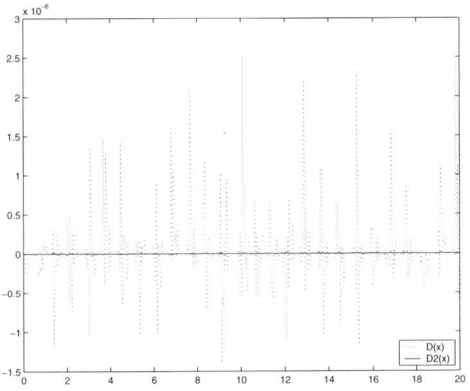

Figure 7.11. *Check 3 results for ode45.*

These tools could have options that would be specified in a straightforward way that is identical to (or at least consistent with) the way options are set when using the ODE methods of MATLAB. Possible options include the number of sample points used to "visualize" or display the function associated with each verification tool (we have used a default value of 500); the reference alternative method to use in Check 2 (we have used the method ode113 as the default); and the stringent value to use for $TOL1$ in Check 2 (we have used $TOL/100$ as the default value). Such options could be changed from their respective default values in the same way that the default options are now changed for the different ODE methods of MATLAB.

We are currently developing tools similar to those introduced here for use on other problem classes in the MATLAB PSE. In particular, we are experimenting with preliminary versions of similar tools for use with boundary value problems and differential delay problems. We are also considering the design of such a tool for classes of two-dimensional and three-dimensional partial differential equations (PDEs). For PDEs the costs involved in generating and visualizing the approximate solution are much greater than that for ODEs, and the complexity and cost of each verification tool will also be greater.

Part III

TECHNOLOGY FOR IMPROVING ACCURACY AND RELIABILITY

Chapter 8

General Methods for Implementing Reliable and Correct Software

Bo Einarsson

The simplest and quickest way for a knowledgeable user to get accurate and reliable results is to use a standard package built in to a problem-solving environment (PSE), such as Maple, Mathematica, or MATLAB.[29] Such environments have good data visualization facilities, which enables the problem area to be explored in depth.

In some cases, the PSE route may not be appropriate, for instance, because the resulting code needs to be integrated into another system, there is a need to produce a specialized solution, very high performance is required, or there is a need for the code to be in a specific language.

If you wish to program yourself it is advisable to use a programming language with some built-in security, like Ada 95, Fortran 95, or Java. Such languages protect the programmer against many mistakes and therefore enable a reliable solution to be developed quickly. In contrast, C provides very little protection, although its mathematical library now contains a few new functions, for example, `log1p(x)=log(1+x)` and `expm1(x)=exp(x)-1`, with the purpose of avoiding common cases of cancellation. FORTRAN 77 cannot be recommended since it lacks the convenience of the current Fortran standard.

An article which stresses the importance of type-safe languages is [492]; although that article is slanted toward security, much of its content also applies to accuracy and reliability.

While spreadsheets are often very convenient for producing a quick solution to some simple problems, they cannot be recommended due to the inherent difficulties in maintaining such code. Also, specific systems like Excel lack a detailed semantic description necessary to ensure that software will always produce the desired result.

For good accuracy and reliability it is also advisable to use high-quality software like BLAS and LAPACK, routines from TOMS or `netlib`, or one of the commercial libraries IMSL or NAG.

The control of the accuracy of a computation is a difficult area which can be the key

---

[29]There are also open-source systems which could be useful in some contexts.

to an effective solution for some problems. The accuracy may be improved by simply using higher precision, provided that the environment supports such higher precision. The use of a multiple-precision package is also a possibility. Similarly, further improvement is obtained with almost exact arithmetic [272] (inner products delivering the exact result before the final rounding) or interval arithmetic [273], but interval methods are mainly used as diagnostic tools. See also the book [242].

In order to obtain accurate and reliable scientific computing it is certainly not only important to observe all the numerical properties that may be important, but even more that all the rules of programming in general are observed. There exists an international journal devoted to reliable mathematical computations based on finite representations and guaranteed accuracy, *Reliable Computing*, from Kluwer Academic Publishers, ISSN 1385-3139. Two relatively old but still most readable reports on software reliability and quality are [39] and [110]. Data flow analysis, which can be applied to improve software reliability, is described in, for example, [145].

The importance of teaching testing has been stressed recently in an article by Terry Shepard, Margaret Lamb, and Dianne Kelley in [410].

A most interesting book on errors in scientific software is the one by Les Hatton, *Safer C: Developing Software for High-integrity and Safety-critical Systems* [200]. Chapter 6 of that book contains a comparison with other languages; Section 6.3 on comparing C with C++ is most interesting. He concludes, "the author's experience in implementing safety-related systems in C++, although limited, suggests that very considerable restrictions are currently necessary to promote a safe style."

Debugging is given full treatment in the book *The Science of DEBUGGING* [440]. The book [336] *Managing Software Quality* discusses cost and budget limitations, schedule due dates, and other systems engineering constraints which influence the degree to which software development and maintenance can achieve maximum quality.

Present-day compilers do much more than compile the program. They check that the formal rules of the language are followed, signal usage of language extensions (if allowed at all), and indicate variables that may not have been assigned a value and variables whose values have never been used. In addition, runtime checks may be performed; for example, the Fortran standard does not require a processor dynamically to check the validity of indices, but most compilers have that feature as an option. The article [14] on comparing Fortran compilers discusses diagnostic capabilities of compilers and how they can be used to detect different possible errors.

It is important to study the compiler warnings and any additional information, perhaps available as options, very carefully. Data-Flow Analysis is a valuable tool; both static and dynamic versions exist. Debuggers can also be used for the analysis of a working program.

We now discuss the properties of some important programming languages: Ada, C, C++, Fortran, Java, and Python.

Further information will be available on the accompanying website `http://www.nsc.liu.se/wg25/book/`.

8.1   Ada

Brian Wichmann and Kenneth W. Dritz

8.1.1   Introduction and language features

This introduction to Ada emphasizes the numerical features of the language and applies most strongly to numerically intensive applications.[']

The Ada language [228], based on Pascal, has a "readable" syntax that uses reserved words. Identifiers, like reserved words, are case insensitive. By convention, reserved words are written in lower case, but numerous styles for capitalization within identifiers are exhibited by individual authors. Ada programs are free-format, but a particular formatting is used consistently in the standard and in textbooks.

A distinguishing feature of Ada is the *package*, which provides a mechanism for collecting related entities, such as types, variables, and the operations on them. Packages, like subprograms, have a specification and a body. These two parts can be compiled separately, allowing substantial implementation detail to be hidden within the body. Interface errors can therefore be detected at compile time, which is often not the case in other languages. Details of a type declared in a package can also be hidden by making the type *private*. Packages and private types play a major role in the creation of abstractions and in information hiding, thus helping to ensure reliable and robust applications.

Subprogram parameters can have a default value, which can be used to increase the generality of a subprogram without burdening the user with excessive detail. This feature supports *reusability*, which enhances the reliability of a program by reducing the number of its parts that have to be designed, written, and tested, thereby lowering the chance for error.

A subprogram or a package can be made *generic* and given *generic parameters*, introducing a further level of parameterization and providing another means to achieve reusability. Such parameterization can include types, as well as values needed to characterize types within an application. A generic unit must be explicitly instantiated to obtain an ordinary (nongeneric) package or subprogram for use within a program. Generic instantiation binds actual types, values, names, and so forth to the generic parameters. This powerful feature is not just text substitution, nor should it be confused with the compilation of the generic unit; it is an action that occurs logically at runtime.

The Ada standard [228] defines the semantics of the running program in great detail. This includes the behavior of a program when a precondition needed for the successful execution of a statement or evaluation of an expression is not satisfied. For instance, if an array index is not within the bounds of an array, then an *exception* is raised. Without using low-level features of the language, it is not possible for an Ada program to "run wild."

An Ada program can have more than one thread of control via *tasking*. This facility is not considered in detail here. Tasking is a major area of research in programming, both numerical and nonnumerical. Suffice it to say that the techniques being developed to exploit parallel computation on multiprocessors, which usually involve extralingual means to express, partition, and otherwise harness the concurrent parts of an application, can be practiced in Ada without going outside the language itself. They are therefore highly portable, given Ada implementations on suitable multiprocessors. Programs using Ada's tasking features also run, without change, on uniprocessors, though without speedup (of course).

Speaking of portability, Ada programs are typically highly portable since the language is widely implemented with standardized semantics. Ada encourages the view that the program should be able to run in any appropriate environment. There are natural limitations to this; for instance, if a program uses the library package for accessing command-line parameters, then, since considerable freedoms are permitted to implementations of that package, it is clear that the program will almost surely not be portable to an environment that primarily supports embedded applications. In many cases, suitable use of *attributes* allows programs to adapt to their execution environment. In general, attributes are expressions that query particular characteristics of a type, a variable, or other object, or the environment, though some have another purpose. Such self-adaptation to the environment represents an essential kind of portability. As an example, the most appropriate action might depend on whether or not an exception is raised on floating-point overflow:

```
if Float'Machine_Overflows then
    ...
else
    ...
end if;
```

Note that this example appears to evaluate an attribute dynamically during execution, exhibiting a programming style quite different from the usual textual preprocessing practiced in C to adapt programs to their environment. The potential inefficiency of the runtime evaluation is not an issue in Ada, however; compilers are free to evaluate expressions at compile time if their runtime values can be reliably predicted, and they are also free to remove "dead code" that can never be reached. Ada compilers uniformly do a good job of such compile-time optimization.

The Ada language includes object-oriented features; they were added in the 1995 revision of the Ada standard, making Ada the first object-oriented language to be defined by an ISO standard. These features are not used in the standard mathematical libraries, nor typically in the numerically intensive parts of applications (though they may be used to decompose and structure parts of any application, including numerically intensive applications), and hence, for simplicity, we ignore them here, except to say that, like Java, Ada excludes multiple inheritance.

The language contains several Annexes. Two are part of the core language and must therefore be supported by all implementations; six are Specialized Needs Annexes, which implementations may or may not support. Serious numerical programming requires the use of the Numerics Annex, one of the Specialized Needs Annexes, and the use of the *strict* mode defined in that Annex (to ensure tight bounds on the accuracy of floating-point operations, for example). Fortunately, the compilers of most, if not all, Ada vendors implement the Numerics Annex. Here we assume the use of this Annex and the strict mode. (In the strict mode, an implementation cannot perform a floating-point division by instead using multiplication by the reciprocal; if it did, it would not satisfy the accuracy requirements.)

8.1.2   The libraries

The libraries in Ada are defined by specifications in the core language. The actual implementation can be written in Ada and often is. The use of generics and default parameters allows for substantial generality, which is fully exploited in, say, the input-output library.

The standard library is hierarchical with the root package, `Standard`, visible implicitly. The entire hierarchy is as follows, with library units that must be provided by every implementation of Ada marked by an asterisk:

```
Standard (*)
   Ada (*)
      Asynchronous_Task_Control
      Calendar (*)
      Characters (*)
         Handling (*)
         Latin_1 (*)
      Command_Line (*)
      Decimal
      Direct_IO (*)
      Dynamic_Priorities
      Exceptions (*)
      Finalization (*)
      Interrupts
         Names
      IO_Exceptions (*)
      Numerics (*)
         Complex_Elementary_Functions
         Complex_Types
         Discrete_Random (*)
         Elementary_Functions (*)
         Float_Random (*)
         Generic_Complex_Elementary_Functions
         Generic_Complex_Types
         Generic_Elementary_Functions (*)
      Real_Time
      Sequential_IO (*)
      Storage_IO (*)
      Streams (*)
         Stream_IO (*)
      Strings (*)
         Bounded (*)
         Fixed (*)
         Maps (*)
            Constants (*)
         Unbounded (*)
         Wide_Bounded (*)
         Wide_Fixed (*)
         Wide_Maps (*)
            Wide_Constants (*)
         Wide_Unbounded (*)
      Synchronous_Task_Control
      Tags (*)
      Task_Attributes
```

```
      Task_Identification
      Text_IO (*)
         Complex_IO
         Editing
         Text_Streams (*)
      Unchecked_Conversion (*)
      Unchecked_Deallocation (*)
      Wide_Text_IO (*)
         Complex_IO
         Editing
         Text_Streams (*)
   Interfaces (*)
      C (*)
         Pointers (*)
         Strings (*)
      COBOL (*)
      Fortran (*)
   System (*)
      Address_To_Access_Conversion (*)
      Machine_Code (*)
      RPC
      Storage_Elements (*)
      Storage_Pools (*)
```

The purpose of this list is to illustrate the functionality available (either on a required or an optional basis) in the predefined library. Optional functionality is defined in one Specialized Needs Annex or another. Ada implementations are not required to support any particular Special Needs Annex, but if they do, then they must provide all the functionality defined by that annex. As indicated, some of the children of `Ada.Numerics` (one of the Specialized Needs Annexes) are required for all implementations; the remaining children of `Ada.Numerics` are required only for those implementations supporting the Numerics Annex (see section 8.1.3). Not shown are several children of `Ada.Numerics` that are nongeneric equivalents to the predefined floating-point types other than `Float`; they have the names `Long_Elementary_Functions`, `Short_Complex_Types`, `Long_Complex_Types`, `Long_Long_Complex_Elementary_Functions`, etc.

8.1.3 The Numerics Annex

The Numerics Annex is required for serious numerical computation, and it should be supported in those environments where such computation is likely to be performed. This ensures good accuracy of the operations and functions provided.

The package `Ada.Numerics` merely defines two constants, but it has generic and nongeneric child packages for the elementary functions, etc., as listed in the previous section. Its specification is as follows:

```
package Ada.Numerics is
   pragma Pure(Numerics);
   Argument_Error : exception;
```

```
Pi :  constant :=
   3.14159_26535_89793_23846_26433_83279_50288_41971_69399_37511;
e :  constant :=
   2.71828_18284_59045_23536_02874_71352_66249_77572_47093_69996;
end Ada.Numerics;
```

The pragma informs the compiler that there is no change in state when the package is elaborated,[30] thus permitting some optimizations. The declaration of the exception allows the user to provide a single exception handler for erroneous calls of the functions provided by instantiations of the generic child packages (such as the square root of a negative value); that is, all such instantiations share this one exception instead of defining independent exceptions. Note that the declarations of the two constants are effectively named literals and can therefore be used in any real expression (both single and double precision, or even fixed point, say).

Now consider the following excerpt from the elementary functions package in its generic form:

```
generic
    type Float_Type is digits <>;
package Ada.Numerics.Generic_Elementary_Functions is

pragma Pure(Generic_Elementary_Functions);
function Sqrt (X: Float_Type'Base) return Float_Type'Base;
function Log (X: Float_Type'Base) return Float_Type'Base;
function Log (X, Base :  Float_Type'Base) return Float_Type'Base;
function Exp (X: Float_Type'Base) return Float_Type'Base;
function "**" (Left, Right :  Float_Type'Base) return Float_Type'Base;
function Sin (X: Float_Type'Base) return Float_Type'Base;
function Sin (X, Cycle :  Float_Type'Base) return Float_Type'Base;
...
```

The use of `Float_Type'Base` is to ensure that any instantiation with a subtype (having a constraint, say, just positive values) does not then force range checking on the implementation of each of the functions; it also ensures that the same constraint, even when correct for the arguments, does not apply to the result, which could be mathematically incorrect. Note that there are two `Log` functions—an example of overloading in Ada. This allows for the generality of an arbitrary base while providing a convenient default for natural logarithms. (Note that an alternate specification would have sufficed: a single `Log` function, with arbitrary base, and with a default value for the `Base` parameter. With either specification, the user obtains natural logarithms by writing, e.g., `Log(X)`. However, numerical analysts know that the best implementations of the natural logarithm function require a specially tailored argument reduction step, necessitating a separate function implementation.) Similar considerations apply to the `Sin` function.

The exponentiation operation can be invoked using the conventional infix notation, which is distinct from the predefined exponentiation operation whose right argument is an integer. Hence there should be no confusion between X**3, which is equivalent to X*X*X, and X**3.0, which invokes the operation defined in the above package and yields an approximation to the value of $\exp(3.0 * \log(X))$, with error bounds specified if the strict

---

[30]Elaboration is the action performed at runtime when a declaration, or the specification or body of a program unit, is encountered.

mode applies. Of course, the right operand of the exponentiation operation will typically not have an integral value.

Further packages are available for the complex type and for vectors and matrices [230]. For machines having special fast machine instructions for vectors, one would expect the implementation of these packages to exploit the machine's capabilities.

8.1.4   Other issues

The consideration here of a number of key issues allows the characteristics of Ada to be contrasted with those of other languages.

Understanding a program. Ada was specifically designed for writing large systems. Managing such systems is always a challenge, especially if reliability is a major concern. The Ada package concept helps, but when it comes to the millions of lines typical of some defense systems, other technical measures are also needed.

However software is written, maintenance and enhancement require a detailed understanding that is often difficult to obtain. The compiler, in some sense, has the necessary understanding in order to produce the machine code. There is a secondary standard for Ada that provides a means for the information collected during compilation to be preserved as a data structure. The Ada Semantic Interface Specification (ASIS) [227] provides a means for an analysis of a program in ways that are barely possible otherwise. No other language seems to have this capability.

High- and low-level code. Ada is a broad-spectrum language. One can use Ada in a conventional procedural style or in a higher-level object-oriented or functional style. In contrast, one can perform much machine-level processing by using explicit low-level features of the language. For instance, if a device produces input in which several values are packed into a word, then this can be handled directly in Ada using a feature to specify the layout of a record.

Some care is needed to ensure high portability in numeric codes. For instance, the type `Long_Float` will not exist on an implementation that has only one floating type, since this will be `Float`.

It is informative to compare Java with Ada on these issues. Naturally, Java excludes such low-level features needed to lay out a record in order to have a very high level of portability. In Ada, one has this option—very high-level portability is possible. Code written in a portable Ada style can even be compiled into J-code![31]

General storage management. Like most modern languages, Ada (implicitly) uses stack storage. In addition, the runtime system must support dynamic storage for objects whose size can vary, as well as storage for multiple tasks, which can come and go in an arbitrary order.

If storage is allocated for objects of a variable size, then that storage will be recovered once the scope of the corresponding type declaration is exited. Given an application

---

[31]The Java High-Order Language defined by Sun is intended to compile to an executable bytecode, sometimes called J-code.

that requires a general (nonstack) storage scheme for some type (say, sparse matrices) but in which exit from the scope of the type is not possible, then one can write one's own storage scheme—the snag being that this uses low-level features of the language, potentially compromising portability. Alternatively, it may be sufficient (especially with modern paging systems) not to recover storage, in which case portability is easy to achieve. (In C terms, `malloc` is safe, but `free` is not, since a dangling pointer could result.)

In principle, the Ada language allows compilers to recover storage automatically. However, compilers do not do this, since it conflicts with hard real-time performance constraints, which are important for many applications. Also, since Ada has explicit (but safe) pointers, recovery is technically more demanding than with Java.

High-integrity software. In the revision of the language in 1995, it was recognized that Ada was being used for many critical applications, like railway signaling. Providing the necessary high assurance is not easy. On the other hand, if Ada coding is restricted to those features that can be easily analyzed, then aspects like strong typing can facilitate techniques like formal proof of program correctness. Reasoning along these lines led to the Ada Safety and Security Annex and the development of a guide to the use of Ada in high-integrity systems [232]. Ada is the only language to have such internationally accepted guidance. Of course, such high-integrity systems invariably include numerical computations.

Full support for IEEE 754. This standard, usually referred to as the IEEE floating-point standard [215, 226], provides extensive functionality in a complete implementation. The Ada language itself does not *require* support for IEEE 754 (unlike Java). Instead, Ada systems using IEEE 754 are *able* to exploit most features of that standard.

For instance, if `'Machine_Overflows` is `False`, then operations that would otherwise raise `Constraint_Error` can produce an infinite value as required by IEEE 754. On the other hand, Ada does not provide literals for infinite values or NaNs. (This is not a serious impediment, since, if needed, they can be generated dynamically, once, during "program initialization.")

In Ada, numeric expressions can come in three flavors: those that *must* be evaluated at compile time (such as those involving only numeric literals); those that *may* be evaluated at compile time as a consequence of some optimization; and those that *cannot* be evaluated at compile time and therefore must be evaluated at runtime. If one's aim is to obtain the same result, bit for bit, on all systems, then the very small differences in the evaluation of these expressions can cause problems. Although the evaluation must be at least as accurate as that of the floating-point type, implementations are allowed to evaluate with more accuracy, hence giving rise to differences in the rounding errors between implementations. Unlike Java, Ada does not therefore support portability to the level of rounding errors.

Ada is designed so that substantial optimization is possible. This usually involves discrete expressions, but to exclude real expressions would be unnatural. In consequence, the multiply-and-add instructions on some machines can be exploited by an Ada compiler, unlike the situation of the strictly conforming Java system.

For those Ada implementations for which `'Signed_Zeros` is `True` (likely to be those systems supporting IEEE 754), various requirements are made to facilitate the use of that feature:

- The sign is preserved in a literal (or static expression).
- The standard gives implementation advice on complex addition and several other complex operations and functions.
- The standard requires that the appropriate sign of zero be delivered for the cyclic standard functions.
- If a value underflows to zero, it has the proper sign.
- When a number composed from a fraction and exponent using the `'Compose` function yields a result of zero, the zero has the sign of the fraction. (Such a result may be produced by an underflow, or by a zero fraction.) Similar considerations apply to related functions.
- The standard provides a `Copy_Sign` function, which can be used, among other purposes, to transfer the sign of a zero value to some other (typically nonzero) value, or to impose a particular sign on a zero value.
- The sign of zero is preserved on input.

For full details of the above, see [223, 228].

One can see from the above that a significant attempt has been made to accommodate IEEE 754. However, Ada does not support the following:

- Control over rounding.
- Signaling NaNs.
- Use of the exact mode.

Alternative arithmetics. Ada provides an infix notation for functions; for an example of its use, see the exponentiation function "`**`" on page 131. By overloading the predefined infix operations with new function definitions, it is possible for the user to write packages that provide interval arithmetic or arbitrary length arithmetic without resorting to nested function calls. Even so, such packages are tedious to write, since, for user convenience, many operations and type conversions need to be provided. For instance, the operations on the type `Complex`, as defined in the Numerics Annex, include 60 functions. However, the result of using the infix notation makes the calls very readable.

Efficiency. In some cases, the efficiency of numerical codes is vital. It may be possible to gain speed by the use of the *relaxed* mode—the alternative to the strict mode. In the relaxed mode, the implementation is free to generate any available fast machine instructions that do not meet the accuracy requirements of the strict mode; for example, it is permitted to use multiplication by the reciprocal instead of floating-point division. Similarly, speed can be gained by suppressing the checks necessary to raise exceptions (as required by default in Ada) when such checks are not provided "for free" by the hardware and must therefore be implemented in software (at some cost in runtime). Clearly, careful examination of the application (to determine what approximations are acceptable) and perhaps defensive programming (for example, screening of data in initialization steps to support assertions that exceptions cannot logically occur subsequently in computationally more expensive inner loops) should be undertaken before using these options. Getting "the wrong result fast" is not the Ada way!

As an example of an optimization issue, the vector and matrix packages have functions that can return a value of variable size. Depending on the compiler, using such functions may have a significant overhead compared with the equivalent using procedures.

Efficiency can also sometimes be increased by judicious use of compile-time options. Alternatively, it may be that efficient and effective code already exists, typically in Fortran. In this case, the optimal Ada solution may be to use `Interfaces.Fortran` to call the Fortran routine from the Ada program, in conjunction with

```
pragma Convention(Fortran,...)
```

as a means of informing the Ada compiler to store matrices passed to the Fortran routine in Fortran's column-major order; without the pragma, such matrices will be copied from the row-major form in which Ada normally stores matrices into a column-major temporary before being passed, and copied back after the return.

Any comparison of Ada with a language or system that does not support runtime checks unfairly brands Ada as inefficient. When the Ada language feature of discrete ranges is used properly, simple optimizations implemented by most Ada compilers will remove most, if not all, subscript-range checking. On the other hand, Ada code obtained by literally converting a program from another language typically does not use discrete ranges, thus making it much more difficult for the compiler to produce code competitive with that obtained by translating to C instead. Given well-written Ada code, there are many cases in which the best Ada compilers will produce machine code superior to that generated by C.

Fixed point. This introduction to Ada has concentrated on the use of conventional floating-point arithmetic, since most numerical computation is undertaken with floating point, supported by special hardware. However, many embedded microprocessors do not have floating-point hardware, and emulating floating point would be inefficient. Consequently, Ada has very powerful fixed-point facilities in which the scaling and accuracy are part of the type system. The scaling can be chosen to reflect the units of the input data from (say) a sensor. The scaling is not limited to powers of two and even includes a facility to handle decimal values consistent with commercial financial practice. The authors know of no other major mainstream language, except for Cobol, that offers this capability.

8.1.5 Conclusions

There is no universal solution to the problem of numerical programming. However, Ada provides almost all that could be expected of a conventional, compiled programming language. Java provides stricter portability than Ada, while having much in common, but for an Ada view of Java, see [160].

8.2   C

Craig C. Douglas and Hans Petter Langtangen

8.2.1   Introduction

C [231] is a language that originated at Bell Labs in the 1970's as the language to program the UNIX operating system in [257]. Since UNIX in the 1970's came with source code, the language was learned and used by many students who took computer science courses.

The early C compilers are now referred to as either Kernighan and Ritchie or K&R C compilers, but tended to be slightly different due to individual interpretations, additions, or missing features. Many C compilers today still support K&R C through a compiler switch.

C was standardized in 1989 as ANSI C [13]. A very nice history of C up through the standardization was published in [380] and is reproduced on the Web by permission of the ACM.

C is very popular. In fact, Borland reported that it sold more than 4 million licensed copies of version 5 of its C/C++ compiler (this includes paid-for updates). Due to a subsequent takeover of Borland, this figure was actually confirmed.

Many students have learned basic C programming with respect to numerical coding using *Numerical Recipes in C* [367]. The book is now available in its entirety on the Web. The programs in the book are not known for high performance, nor robustness, but provide in one place a very large collection of solution routines that give a beginner a good start at solving numerical problems.

C has also led to a number of variations and new languages that are widely used today, including C++, Java, and to a degree C#.

8.2.2   Language features

C delivers a number of nice features:

- *Multitasking, Multithreading, and Shared Memory Segments*
  Using the `fork` system call,[32] multiple tasks can be created—either separate tasks or light weight ones. Communication between tasks can be done easily using shared memory. Writing an overlapped I/O and computation package is easily accomplished using this technique.

- *Type Checking*
  A programmer has to type cast an object in order to use it as something it is not declared to be (leading to all sorts of neat programming, but data type crimes). Robustness and reliability are not supported with C's type checking.

- *Scope of Variables*
  Variables can be either local to a routine or global to all. Any variable declared in a

---

[32]Available in Unix and also on Windows with Posix compliant libraries.

routine is local and only accessible in that routine. Any variable declared outside of a
routine is global. Great care must be given to global variable names in order to avoid
conflicts at link time.

- *Dynamic Memory Management*
  C (using `malloc` and `free`) provides a completely user controlled set of library
  calls for dynamic object creation and destruction. Many programs do not check to
  see if `malloc` succeeds. Many bugs are caused by calling `free` more than once for
  memory allocated by `malloc` or using an invalid memory address. Memory leaks
  are common by not calling `free` once objects are no longer needed. See section
  8.2.7 for more details.

- *Standardized Preprocessor*
  Macros, spaghetti coding, parameter-based compilation of code segments, etc. are all
  portably and reliably supported. The C preprocessor has been used in clever ways to
  extend many languages, including text processing systems (e.g., LATEX).

- *Standardized Libraries*
  Libraries are accessed in C through the `#include` preprocessor directive and header
  files in the `/usr/include` directory hierarchy and at runtime through (dynamically
  linked) already compiled libraries. Declarations of subprograms and global constants
  are thus provided in files that are processed as if they are part of the source code. Literally hundreds of standard header files are in the standard `/usr/include` directory
  and subdirectories, not all of which are part of standard C, however.

- *Math Libraries*
  C supports a mathematical library similar to what FORTRAN 77 supports. Functions
  like $\sin(x)$ or $\exp(x)$ produce `double` results for the sine and e^x functions. The
  arguments are `double` valued since call by value is used (see section 8.2.4 for more
  details on numerical oddities).

- *Variable Length Argument Lists to Functions*
  Functions can optionally be written to accept a variable number of arguments. A
  reliable mechanism is provided so that only the provided arguments are used.

- *I/O*
  An alternative to Fortran's format statements that is powerful, easy to use, and self-
  implementable in C is part of the `stdio` library. Formatted output uses the library
  function `printf` and formatted input uses `scanf`. There are variations for standard
  input and output, error output, file access, and using memory variables as the source
  or target of I/O. Both `printf` and `scanf` support variable length argument lists.

- *Access to System Calls*
  The system libraries in UNIX became a de facto standard for C programmers on all
  other operating systems that C has been ported to. This led to the POSIX standard
  for which many operating systems now are accredited.

- *User Defined Data Structures and Types*
  This is one of C's most powerful features that is trivially learned and is used extensively. Object-oriented features can be achieved somewhat using `typedef` and macros to emulate simple C++ classes (cf. sections 8.2.8 and 8.3.9).

- *Array Edge Methodology to Access Array Parts and Elements*
  C allows several ways of accessing all or part of arrays. The methodology turned out to be a significant contribution to compiler optimization for many languages. See section 8.2.6 for more details.

- *Address/Pointer Arithmetic*
  This allows almost assembler-like coding in a higher-level language. Whether or not it is readable is another story. No effort is made to check if a pointer is pointing to a legitimate memory location, however.

- *Assertions*
  This is a macro package to discover logic versus implementation errors at runtime. See section 8.2.3 for more details.

C does not provide the following features:

- *Array Bounds Checking*
  There are clever (mostly commercial) packages that add this to C. When checking is added to C, robustness improves at the standard expense that is seen in languages like Java and Ada.

- *Classes and Inheritance*
  Classes can be simulated using data structures and very careful programming. After all, early versions of C++ (the CFRONT program) produced C code for compilation. Inheritance is much harder to do in C in a readable form, but it can be done. However, classes and inheritance is beyond the programming abilities of all but a tiny number of C programmers.

- *Operator Overloading*
  What you see is what it really is. C is not like C++ or APL, which are, in a sense, write-only languages that are difficult to tell easily what standard operators really are doing on a random line of code. For example, in a user defined C++ matrix class, the operator $+$ can be defined to add two matrices or it can be defined to be the pseudo-inverse multiplied by the object on the right. Both make sense mathematically, but a reader must know which was defined to really understand a line of code that reads, "$M + N$." In C, the $+$ operator means addition.

8.2.3   Standardized preprocessor, error handling, and debugging

C was one of the first languages to allow both user defined data types and a well-defined, integrated preprocessor. The preprocessor originally was a separate program, however, and has been routinely used by other applications and languages.

Some vendors have erroneously left out a separate preprocessor from their proprietary C compiler. This leads to a wave of user complaints and normally leads to the addition of a separate preprocessor. It is quite common to find the GNU C preprocessor on systems where the rest of the compiler is not installed.

The preprocessor has been so popular that on the UNIX and UNIX-like systems, the file extension .F is associated with passing the file first through the C preprocessor, then the Fortran compiler, whereas the file extension .f is associated only with the Fortran compiler (note the file extension case sensitivity).

The output of a preprocessor rarely resembles the source code input. Extra lines and spacing are common. This makes using source code debuggers difficult. Specially formatted directives keep track of the original source lines so that debuggers can be given enough information to provide a user with the correct source code line(s) at runtime.

Standard directives are provided for defining (#define), undefining (#undef), including other files (#include), and if-then and if-then-else (#if, #then, #else, and #elif), There are variations of the if, such as if defined (#ifdef) and also if undefined (#ifundef). Arguments can be concatenated with other symbols and arguments in standard C using the ## operator.

Related to the preprocessor is a sophisticated assertion package which is used with (#include <assert.h>). By setting assertions, program correctness (see [177]) can be guaranteed in a simple, routine by routine manner. Global program correctness is beyond the scope of this package, however. All manners of logic versus implementation errors can be quickly discovered at runtime using this package.

8.2.4   Numerical oddities and math libraries

C still suffers to a degree in that what precision you get on one machine may not be exactly the same on the next. This is rapidly going away as an issue due the almost uniform acceptance of IEEE 754 arithmetic. However, there is a potential in the future that it can come back to haunt programmers.

Floating-point numbers are represented as

- double: typically assumed to be 64 bits,

- float: typically assumed to be 32 bits.

Note that there is no built-in complex data type in C.[33]

Programmers used to get an unpleasant experience on Cray supercomputers since both float and double had twice as many bits as above. Since 128 bits were supported through software emulation, a Cray could be converted into (slowed down to) a VAX just by using double instead of float. Eventually a compiler switch was added to do what was finally tolerated by programmers (both as 64 bits).

Any floating-point calculation by default results in a double, whether or not it is wanted or appropriate to the calculation. This feature leads to unexpected roundoff properties when single precision arithmetic is expected.

All floating numbers put on the stack to pass as call-by-value arguments are converted to double. Hence, even though a variable can be declared as float in the calling program, the resulting variable in the subprogram header must be declared double. Only using call-by-reference results in a float in the subprogram.

---

[33]Type complex has been added in [231] but is not widely implemented.

In essence, C assumes that double precision is what all calculations are wanted in and provides it independent of the programmer's wishes. This feature irritates some theoretical numerical analysts but does not seem to bother computational scientists.

C has catered well to the group of numerically intensive programmers who want results and assume that the reliability and accuracy are just *good enough* and do not want to know the details.

8.2.5   Calling Fortran libraries

Libraries like Lapack, the BLAS, ATLAS, and most other known libraries are accessible easily from C. If the library is written in Fortran, there can be a naming problem due to how compilers handle program name translation. The four most common translations (or name mangling as the C++ community added to compiler terminology) of Fortran names are as follows:

- Add one underscore after the name, which is in lower case.

- Add two underscores after the name, which is in lower case.

- Convert the name to all upper case, no underscores.

- Convert the name to all lower case, no underscores.

By far the most common Fortran naming convention on UNIX or UNIX-like systems is the first translation rule.

Some compilers have a mechanism to define that a called program is in a particular language and the resulting translated name and calling sequence are correctly generated. This feature is not standard in C and is definitely not portable.

Due to no standard name translation in compilers (which the standards committees for all languages should define precisely), calling other language programs from C is best done using macros and conditional compilation (see section 8.2.3).

An interesting bug in the early Intel Math Library for Linux was that the library was written in C and its Fortran interface assumed that the underscores should go before the name, not after. Hence, Fortran could not call the Pentium nor Itanium tuned BLAS or Lapack whereas C and C++ could.

8.2.6   Array layouts

The order of indices in C is the reverse of Fortran. While Fortran always allocates an array as one large memory block and standard C requires it, there have been C compilers with compiler options that allow for a different memory layout that enhances cache memory reuse (see the last paragraph of this section).

Consider an example of a two-dimensional array in C:

```
double A[4][5];
```

The array A has 4 rows and 5 columns, corresponding to the Fortran array $A(5,4)$.

C is 0 based, not 1 based. So $A[0][0]$ is the same as the Fortran $A(1,1)$. C programmers cannot access $A[4][5]$ since it is out of bounds. The correct construction for accessing the last element is $A[3][4]$. The difference between 0 and 1 based languages is irritating to programmers who use both systems routinely and has led to numerous bugs that have to be found and fixed. It is a primary reason why C programmers do not use Fortran, no matter how many new features similar to C are introduced in new versions of Fortran.

C uses *edge arrays* to access array data. This technique is now a standard compiler optimization trick used even in some Fortran compilers. $A[2][3]$ points to the element in A in row 2, column 3 (assuming C's 0 based notation). $A[2]$ points to the first element in row 2 and is a perfectly valid C construct to use while programming. $*A[2]$ is equivalent to $A[2][0]$ and is also a valid C construct.

A few C compilers have options to allow array memory to be laid out in a cache memory aware manner. Hence, A is not one block of memory in our example, but each row is allocated separately with memory padding in order to avoid cache thrashing problems. This requires a significant change in how machine language code is generated by a C compiler.

8.2.7   Dynamic data and pointers

C has supported dynamic memory, pointers, and pointer arithmetic from its first origins. These features are essential in writing an operating system. They were quickly cited as an example of the superiority of C over early versions of Fortran and any version of either Pascal or Modula. Clearly pointers are useful since both Cray and Digital Equipment Corporation (DEC) added both pointers and dynamic memory allocation to their Fortran compilers. A fault of the GNU FORTRAN 77 compiler is that it never allowed an easy mechanism to add dynamic memory allocation to it (as most vendors provided in slightly incompatible forms).

No built-in methods exist to provide safety from pointer errors, pointer over- or underruns, reuse of freed memory, or freeing memory multiple times. The number of bugs related to these deficiencies in C is an uncountable number.

There is no garbage collector. Finding memory leaks requires auxiliary software that is not part of C's standard libraries. A small collection of companies have made fortunes providing memory safe (or tracing) software that can actually be implemented by a good programmer in a few hours.

8.2.8   Data structures

C allows quite general user defined data types and structures. A structure is a block of data encapsulating one or many different datums. There are no serious restrictions on the datums as long as each is already a defined data type or a pointer to a data type. Once a structure is defined, using the `typedef` key word, a data type is defined that can be conveniently used in declarations later.

Many types of data represent a set of objects (e.g., fruit could be a set of apples, oranges, and kiwis). Using the `enum` key word, a set can be defined with named data (e.g., the fruits). The named data are given small integer values by the compiler which are used in generating code without the developer having to worry about the actual values.

Combining the `struct`, `typedef`, and `enum` definition methods with the macro preprocessor, a surprising amount of object-based programming (see section 8.3.9) can be done in C easily. While operator overloading, inheritance, and conveniently hiding local data and functions either cannot be done or is very difficult to do robustly, many C programs can be written in a style similar to C++ codes for enhanced maintenance and reliability.

8.2.9   Performance issues

Many years ago, C was noted as a language that produced machine language code significantly slower than an equivalent numerically intensive code written in Fortran. This is no longer really true for several reasons:

- Most vendors' compilers now use the same back end no matter what language's front end is used by a programmer. Optimizations now work equally well for multiple languages. Vendors are unwilling to spend money on multiple, uniquely programmed compilers, nor should they for efficiency reasons.

- Fortran has added a number of features over the years that are similar to features in C and C++. What caused C and C++ programs to not optimize well now cause Fortran programs to not optimize well.

- C has matured as a language and programmers have learned many of the same tricks that only Fortran programmers once seemed to use.

8.3   C++

Craig C. Douglas and Hans Petter Langtangen

8.3.1   Introduction

C++ [429] was created by Bjarne Stroustrup at Bell Labs at the beginning of the 1980's so that he would never again have to add linked list functionality to a new data structure while programming in C. In hindsight, it is surprising how one irritating, missing feature in a language like C can lead to an entire new language.

C++ extended C with object-oriented programming support, with much of the inspiration coming from the Simula67 programming language. During the 1990's the language was extended significantly and standardized by an ANSI committee [233]. Despite the standardization efforts, C++ compilers still differ in their support of the standard, and only a subset of the standard can be used if portability is an important issue.

C++ quickly attracted a lot of attention. In particular, lots of C programmers converted to C++. In the early 1990's, C++ was a very widespread and popular language, but mainly for nonnumerical applications. Through the last decade the language has attracted significant interest also for numerical applications, as the initial inferior performance compared to FORTRAN 77 has decreased, because of advances in compiler technology and better knowledge of how to use C++ constructs carefully in scientific computing contexts.

There are literally hundreds (thousands?) of books teaching different groups how to program in C++. Two of note to the computational science community are [253, 499]. The former is a first course in numerical analysis but assumes that all problems will be solved on a parallel computer using MPI. The latter is a more traditional book for engineers and scientists. The software developed in both books is readily available.

8.3.2   Basic language features

C is a subset of C++ so (almost) all features of C are available in C++. However, certain C constructs are not recommended or are replaced by alternative C++ constructs. Macros, assertions, and `printf`-formatting are three examples. However, this is subject to debate and personal taste.

- *Type Checking*
  C++ applies the same type checking as C; i.e., all variables must be declared with a specific type, and this type cannot change during execution. Types include both the built-in fundamental types (`int`, `char*`, etc.) as well as user defined types in terms of classes. The use of `void*` (no type) is highly discouraged in C++.

- *Scope of Variables*
  Variables declared in a function are local to that function and are deleted upon return. Global variables can be defined, but it is considered better in C++ to use static variables in a class (i.e., a global variable in a class namespace) instead. Variables defined inside a block, e.g., in a for-loop, are local to that block and deleted when the leaving the block. Nested declarations of utility variables (e.g., a counter `i`) leads to very hard to find errors in assignment statements (unless the compiler issues warnings about shadowed variables).

  C++ supports namespaces. The name and extent of namespaces are defined by the programmer. There is support for working with a default namespace and thereby avoiding the namespace prefix.

- *Standard Preprocessor*
  C++ compilers call up a C preprocessor in the same way as a C compiler does (currently the preprocessor is sometimes not a stand-alone `cpp` program, but a part of the C++ compiler). The preprocessor is mainly used for conditional compiling and including header files. C++ has constructs (especially `inline` functions and constant variables) to reduce the need for macros.

- *Standardized Libraries*
  The standard C library can be called from C++, but many parts of the standard C library have been improved and extended for C++. Two important examples are string operations and input/output functionality. C++ comes with the Standard Template Library, known as STL, which offers many common data structures and associated algorithms. The types of data structures in STL include vector, list, and hash (map).

- *Built-in Numerical Types*
  C++ has (of course) the same types as C: `double`, `float`, and `int`. In addition, there is a `complex` type where the real and imaginary parts can be of any other numerical type.

- *User Defined Data Structures and Types*
  New types are created by writing classes. A special feature of C++ is the potential speed of the code even if classes are utilized to a large degree. Using the `inline` key word causes small functions to be compiled without the function call, assuming

that the C++ compiler follows the request (which is considered advisory only). See section 8.3.10.

- *Array Structures*
  The basic array structures in C++ are the same as in C. However, STL offers a general vector type (`vector`) and a special vector type for numerical computing (`valarray`). Unfortunately, there are no standard class implementations for higher-dimensional arrays, although there are many third-party array libraries, both commercial and free (some examples are [43, 117, 112, 350, 414, 444, 463]).

- *Array Bounds Checking*
  There is no built-in array bounds checking in plain C/C++ arrays, but array classes in C++ libraries sometimes have a compilation mode (macro definition) that turns on array bounds checking.

- *Address/Pointer Arithmetic*
  C++ contains C's pointer functionality. In addition, C++ offers *references*, which are implemented in terms of pointers, but without arithmetics and assignment (i.e., a reference cannot change). C++ programmers tend to prefer references instead of pointers, especially in function and class interfaces.

- *Dynamic Memory Management*
  C++ employs basically the same tools as C for dynamic memory management, but the operators `new` and `delete` are used instead of C's `malloc` and `free`. When an object is declared as a standard variable, e.g., `MyClass x` in a function, `x` is destroyed when it goes out of scope at the end of the function. If `x` is created by `new`, as in `MyClass x = *new MyClass()`, the programmer is responsible for deallocating the object. Memory management is as error-prone as in C and represents perhaps the biggest obstacle for creating reliable code.

- *Constant Data Structures*
  C++ has a keyword `const` for indicating that a variable should be constant. If the variable holds a user defined object, `const` means that only `const` member functions of the object can be called. The `const` member functions do not alter the state of the object. In this way it is possible to build large libraries with a consistent use of constant data structures; the compiler will check that any variable (or function argument) declared as `const` is not altered. Compared to C and Fortran, one can use `const` to protect arrays from being changed.

- *I/O and Formatting*
  C++ may use the I/O facilities of C, but it is more common to apply the improved C++-specific I/O tools, represented by the `iostream` hierarchy of classes. The authors of this section think formatting with `iostream` is tedious and lengthy compared to the `printf` family of functions and recommend the `stdio` C++ class instead.

- *Access to System Calls*
  C++ applies C's *system* function to run other applications or operating system commands.

- *Multitasking, Multithreading, and Shared Memory Segments*
  The support for process management tasks consists of the corresponding C tools, but often a class-based interface, which is more convenient to use, can be found. For example, see [61].

- *Error Handling*
  C++ has support for exceptions, and this is now the standard way of handling errors. However, exceptions were added in the 1990's and it took some time before all major compilers supported exceptions in a portable way, so there are many C++ libraries around that handle errors in a more manual way (C `assert` calls, library-specific class hierarchies, or functions for error treatment).

- *Classes and Inheritance*
  Both single and multiple inheritance are allowed in C++ classes.

- *Operator Overloading*
  All operators in the C++ language can be defined by the user. Overloaded operators in combination with templates make it difficult to realize what an operation like `a+=b` actually means, since the exact type of neither `a` nor `b` is known and therefore the associated `operator+=` function is unknown. Sometimes uncommon operators are overloaded to achieve what the programmer thinks is a nice syntax, e.g., `^A` to indicate the transpose of a matrix `A`. Confusion due to overloaded operators represents potential decreased reliability and sometimes gives C++ a bad reputation as a write-only language like APL.

- *Compilation and Linking*
  C++ programs are compiled and linked similarly to C and Fortran code. It is therefore easy to call up C and Fortran functions. However, such functions must be prototyped in a special environment to notify the C++ compiler about their existence and their signatures.

8.3.3 Special features

- *Compatibility with C*
  Given the large amount of reliable C code that has been developed over the last three decades, a great strength of C++ is its ability to easily integrate with C. This also means that C++ can be used for procedural-oriented programming, i.e., just as a better and safer C, without employing the potential overhead of classes.

- *Templates*
  Contrary to other strongly typed languages, such as Fortran, C, and Java, C++ can parameterize a type in terms of templates. A single function can in this way work for many different types of arguments. A class can parameterize, via templates, the type of internal data structures and the type of member function arguments. Templates provide some of the flexibility found in dynamically typed languages, like Python and Perl (a variable cannot change its type, however). Until recently, templates have been implemented differently by different compiler vendors, a fact that has contributed to portability problems with template-based code. Many portable C++ libraries therefore

use other methods (macros, automatic code generation) to offer code that works with many types.

Templates also represent a kind of programmer-controlled compiler. This has led to *template metaprogramming*, or *expression templates*, which enable C++ libraries to perform optimizations that otherwise are in the hands of a compiler [463]. The technique has been used to create very flexible software, yet with a very high performance for numerical computing [464]. However, expression templates are challenging to implement and debug, and might therefore provide a source of decreased software reliability.

- *Inline Functions*
  The great advantage of C++ over C is classes, where data structures can be accessed through convenient functions. Especially for numerical computations, function calls imply unacceptable overhead. To solve this problem, C++ has a keyword `inline` to mark inline functions, i.e., functions whose bodies should be copied into the calling code. This should eliminate the overhead of function calls and still keep the flexibility and convenience of class interfaces. Unfortunately, the `inline` keyword is only a suggestion to the compiler, and it is up to the compiler to decide whether to make the function inline or not. Nested inline function calls have (at least until recently) been hard for most compilers to unroll. The result is often that the code is full of functions specified as inline, but the compiled code still has calls to some of these inline functions. This is crucial for array classes with overloaded subscripting operators calling up other inline functions.

- *Public/Nonpublic Access*
  C++ has three keywords for controlling access to data and functions in classes: `public` (access for all), `protected` (access for subclasses), and `private` (no external access). In theory, this allows for a compiler to guarantee that the code outside a class does not alter data structures in the class. In practice, such reliability is not achieved automatically: the programmer must use these keywords (along with `const`) in a careful way to implement the desired degree of reliability.

  Extension of software libraries or coupling to other libraries occasionally requires access to certain nonpublic parts of an interface, a fact that sometimes leads to ugly workarounds or declaring nonpublic parts as public. Possible access of nonpublic parts in exceptional cases, by a careful programmer, would then be advantageous.

8.3.4   Error handling and debugging

The C++ programmer must apply the same tools as the C programmer for debugging code. The only difference is that the C++ programmer has exceptions at his disposal. This does not directly enhance debugging, in comparison with `assert` and plain tests, but libraries are easier to use for application codes if errors are handled as exceptions. We refer to the "C" section for further information about debugging support and techniques.

8.3.5 Math libraries

The standard math library in C (math.h) is also used from C++. In addition, C++ has a complex type with associated numerical functions. No additional *standard* libraries aid mathematical computations.

However, there is now a wide range of numerical libraries written in C++. The Web site [347] represents one overview with many links to numerical C++ software. At present, there are many contributions, but there is little tendency to standardizing interfaces (in special disciplines, like linear systems solution, attempts to standardize interfaces have been made [448]).

8.3.6 Array layouts

The plain C++ arrays have the same layout as in C, and we refer to the "C" section for details. Array classes in C++ are normally implemented in terms of plain C/C++ arrays, at least when we speak of dense arrays.

8.3.7 Dynamic data

Dynamic memory management basically follows the ideas and tools of C. However, with C++ classes programmers tend to build more complicated dynamic data structures than what is encouraged by the C language. Tracking the life-time of objects and deleting them at the right time and place is challenging. Memory leaks, dangling pointers, and unexpected segmentation faults are therefore common in C++ code.

Fortunately, C++ classes make it possible to build memory management tools with high reliability. Most large libraries have, for example, a "smart pointer" class. Usually, such a class contains a pointer, plus some extra data for keeping track of objects being pointed to. Smart pointers mostly use reference counting to check whether an object is no longer in use. In that case, the smart pointer deletes the object. This solves to a large degree most of the memory management problems in C and C++ and provides the same memory management reliability as experienced in Java and Python. With overloaded operators, smart pointers may look and (seemingly) behave like ordinary pointers.

8.3.8 User defined data structures

User defined data structures are created in terms of classes. C++ classes are more flexible than Java classes (e.g., C++ has overload operators), but less dynamic than those in Python (e.g., C++ needs a fixed interface at compile time).

Since C++ is strongly typed, a particular class can only work with a set of predefined classes, and this is checked by the compiler. Given two objects, their interaction is only possible if the programmer has explicitly notified the compiler about their potential interaction. This is often taken as a basic ingredient of reliable software. Unfortunately, objects are often cast to other types, thus reducing the compiler's ability to check that types really match according to the declarations.

8.3.9   Programming styles

C++ is a flexible programming language with full support for traditional procedural programming, object-oriented programming, and generic programming (template programming). Most C++ programs utilize user defined data structures (i.e., classes) to a high degree. There are typically three programming styles associated with classes:

- object-based programming: mostly stand-alone classes,

- object-oriented programming: classes collected in hierarchies, mainly accessed through virtual function calls,

- generic programming: separation of algorithms and data, with data types parameterized by templates.

Object-based programming is the supported style in Fortran 90. Java programming is solely object-oriented, while scripting languages like Python are mostly used in a generic programming style.

8.3.10   Performance issues

C++ was constructed to have the flexibility of object-oriented languages, yet with the speed of C. This is in theory fulfilled, but the practical realization of the performance potential might be hard for nonexperts. Unfortunately, C++ equips the programmer with many easy to use (even encouraged, no less) tools for reducing the performance. To obtain implementations with good performance the programmer needs to know the language well and have considerable experience.

When it comes to numerical code, C++ has traditionally been somewhat slower than FORTRAN 77 code. After Fortran 90 started to gain widespread use, experience showed that both Fortran 90 and C++ were normally slower than either FORTRAN 77 or C. Such a potential performance loss is typical when a language gets too many new features with too much flexibility.

The efficiency of C++ has improved over the years, partly due to better understanding of how to use the language [234] and partly due to better compilers. There is much experience and evidence that C++ codes can compete with FORTRAN 77 code with respect to speed [15] and in some cases the flexibility of C++ makes it possible to beat FORTRAN 77 [464, 463]. Today, most compiler vendors apply the optimization techniques to a common object code, implying that C++ and FORTRAN 77 should be equally fast if exactly the same programming technique is used. Usually this means that the programming technique must be FORTRAN 77-style array processing, i.e., for loops over plain C++ array structures. Application of sophisticated data structures with many small objects may decrease performance significantly. Nevertheless, more flexible but less efficient data structures may lead to faster problem solving, so there is always a trade-off between computer and human efficiency.

The potentially high performance of C++ together with the support for classes and templates constitutes a powerful tool for a wide range of application areas, including numerical computing. Given sufficient experience, knowledge of the many technical details of the language, and careful programming, C++ may lead to more reliable and flexible code than what is obtained with C and Fortran, yet with (almost) the same performance.

C++'s reliability and safety in programming is still debatable. Hatton [200] documents safety issues with respect to programming in C instead. On the other hand, in [189] a safe C++ toolbox for reliable computing is developed and documented.

8.4 Fortran

Van Snyder

8.4.1 Introduction

Fortran was developed at IBM in the mid-1950's, by John Backus and his colleagues, for the purpose of scientific and technical computing. The name was an acronym for FORmula TRANslation. One of their criteria for success was that programs written in Fortran would not be much slower or larger than programs written in "machine language."

Fortran became successful, and remains successful, because it met Backus's original criteria, and because using Fortran reduces labor costs and increases reliability.

8.4.2 History of Fortran

The original Fortran was twice revised by IBM, being called FORTRAN II and FORTRAN IV. It was then standardized by the American Standards Association (ASA) in 1966 as X3.9, and again by the American National Standards Institute (ANSI), the successor to ASA, in 1978. This revision was known as FORTRAN 77. A major revision, commonly known as Fortran 90, was published in 1991 by the Organization for International Standardization (ISO). Fortran 90 provided substantially better support for modern software engineering practices than had FORTRAN 77. A minor revision, commonly known as Fortran 95 [229], was published in 1997. Two minor additions to the 1997 standard have been published, in the form of Type 2 Technical Reports [376] and [97]. A draft of a substantial revision of the 1997 standard was completed in August 2003; publication by ISO was in November 2004. This revision will be commonly known as Fortran 2003.

Almost all compilers now support Fortran 95, so we will emphasize this version here. Although Fortran 95 is a substantially more powerful language than FORTRAN 77 (some might even say unrecognizably different), the goals of efficient usage of computing resources, and compatibility with FORTRAN 77, have been maintained and satisfied.

8.4.3 Major features of Fortran 95

The distinguishing characteristic of Fortran is that it provides important features specifically intended for numeric computation, designed in such a way as to allow processors to produce programs that are portable and maintainable and that use computing resources efficiently.

- Fortran 90 introduced the concept of a *parameterized type*, and a number called a *kind type parameter* that indicates which range, precision, or representation is to be used for an object of the type. Inquiry functions can be used to get the kind type parameter corresponding to characteristics of the object, such as range or precision. If one is careful to use a named constant, perhaps with a value gotten by reference to an inquiry function, instead of a literal constant for the kind parameter, one can change a program unit from one precision to another with one local change instead of changing the declaration of every variable, as would be required in FORTRAN 77, C, or C++. FORTRAN 77 provided for a *length parameter* for objects of character type, which specifies the number of characters in a scalar character object, or each element of an array character object.

- At least two precisions of floating-point numbers, called *real* numbers, are distinguished by their kind type parameters.

- The processor offers built-in complex numbers and complex arithmetic, for real numbers of every kind.

- Arrays of up to seven dimensions. Dimensions of arrays can have fixed bounds or bounds that are determined as the program executes. The variable-size feature makes it possible to write general-purpose linear algebra software. Procedure arguments that are arrays include dimension bounds information, which allows for runtime bounds checking, and bounds determination without using additional arguments.

  Automatic arrays are arrays that have dimension extents determined when the program executes, but that are not procedure dummy arguments. These are especially useful for intermediate results. In FORTRAN 77 it was common practice for a procedure that needed space for intermediate results to be given the space by the calling procedure. In Fortran 90, this is no longer necessary.

- Expressions that operate on whole arrays or array sections. This allows for clear expression of many array operations without the use of loops.

- Numerous built-in procedures—115 altogether in Fortran 95—including square root, exponential, logarithm, trigonometric, and inverse trigonometric functions, for both real and complex numbers, inquiry about the arithmetic, operations on arrays, etc. A technical report [376] has amended Fortran 95 to include access to features of the IEEE floating-point standard.

Fortran also incorporates features to support good software engineering practices, which reduces the long-term ownership cost of software.

- The most important feature added in Fortran 90 to support modern software engineering practices is the *module*. Modules are a powerful tool to collect related procedures, type definitions, variables, and named constants. These entities can be shared with other program units (or not), according to PUBLIC and PRIVATE declarations in the module.

- Although FORTRAN 77 provided only the block-IF and DO control structures, Fortran 95 provides a complete complement of modern control structures, which usually allows one to eliminate use of GO TO statements.

- In FORTRAN 77, it was the programmer's responsibility to ensure that a procedure was referenced with actual arguments that had the same type as their corresponding dummy arguments. Deliberate abuse was always considered a poor practice, but FORTRAN 77 provided no built-in mechanisms to detect accidents. An important addition in Fortran 90 was the explicit procedure interface. If a procedure has an explicit interface, a Fortran 95 processor is required to check that actual arguments and corresponding dummy arguments have identical type, kind, and number of dimensions.

- Generic interfaces allow procedures that operate on data that have different type or kind to be collected together and given a common name or operator symbol, or used to define assignment. This allows a program to be written in a more abstract form. If carefully done, this makes it easier to understand a program.

- Structured data objects are useful to organize data in any but the simplest programs. The type of a structured data object is called a *derived type*.

- Two mechanisms for storage allocation, deallocation, and dynamic data structures. The POINTER is type safe but is otherwise quite general. Pointers include information about array bounds and strides. Arithmetic operations on pointers per se are not permitted, and the addresses of objects cannot be determined. This prevents numerous errors that could otherwise arise from the use of pointers. Declared objects that are the targets of pointers must be explicitly specified to have the target attribute. This allows optimizers to make more advantageous assumptions concerning register usage; even so, using pointers still sabotages several optimizations. ALLOCATABLE variables have semantics that restrict their generality but allow more possibilities for optimization and reduce risks of memory leaks.

- Optional procedure arguments and procedure arguments identified by name instead of position provide for easy usage of "library" software and allow extension of existing software without affecting existing usage.

8.4.4   Features of Fortran 2003

Fortran 2003 is a major revision. The two technical reports [376] and [97] that amended Fortran 95 are included in Fortran 2003. Numerous features that are not directly important to numerical software are not mentioned here.

- 45 new built-in procedures, including those for access to features of the IEEE floating-point standard.

- Substantial new capabilities for derived types:

  – In the same way that Fortran 95 provides for a kind parameter for every intrinsic type, and a length parameter for character type, derived types in Fortran 2003 can have kind and length parameters. In the same way as for intrinsic types, kind type parameters must be constants and can be used for generic procedure resolution, while length parameters need not be fixed but cannot be used for generic resolution.

  – Procedures can be bound to types, so that the procedure is always accessible from every scoping unit that contains an object of the type. A type-bound procedure is referenced using the same syntax as for a data component, or by way of a type-bound operator or assignment. If the object is polymorphic (two paragraphs below), the invoked procedure is the one associated with its dynamic type.

– The most commonly used variety of derived types is *extensible*. The extension type is a new derived type that has all of the components and type-bound procedures of the extensible type, and any desired additional ones. Type-bound procedures of the extensible type can be overridden in the extension type.

– *Polymorphic* data objects can have, during execution, any type that is an extension of their declared type. The dynamic type of a pointer or allocatable object is determined when it is allocated. The dynamic type of a pointer object is determined by its target. The dynamic type of a dummy argument is determined by its associated actual argument.

These new features provide a powerful object-oriented programming facility.

• Extensive facilities to interoperate with the C programming language.

• Specification and initialization expressions can now access essentially all of the intrinsic functions.

• *Finalization* is a process that can be applied to objects of derived type, to make sure they cease to exist correctly. This is especially useful in releasing memory for pointer components.

• Procedure pointers—especially ones that are components of derived types—are useful to specify user-provided code to a "library" procedure.

• The array constructor syntax includes provision to specify the data type of the elements.

• A PROTECTED attribute allows access to a variable in a module, while prohibiting changes to it except from within procedures in the same module.

• User defined derived-type input/output procedures allow for input and output according to the user's needs. This also allows for input and output of derived-type objects that have pointer components. There are numerous other input/output enhancements.

In Fortran 2003 it is possible to implement abstractions for arithmetics not provided by the standard, such as extended precision, polynomials, intervals, and Taylor series, while maintaining reasonable efficiency and not "leaking memory."

A complete summary of additions to Fortran in 2003 can be found at `ftp://ftp.nag.co.uk/sc22wg5/N1551-N1600/N1579.pdf` or `ftp://ftp.nag.co.uk/sc22wg5/N1551-N1600/N1579.ps.gz`.

The complete Final Committee Draft of Fortran 2003 can be found at `http://www.nag.co.uk/sc22wg5/`.

The new Standard was published on November 18, 2004, as ISO/IEC 1539-1:2004.

8.4.5 Beyond Fortran 2003

Technical report ISO/IEC TR 19767:2005, which was published on March 1, 2005, provides a new program unit, a *submodule*. This provides for substructuring a module, and allows to divide a procedure into separately compiled interface and body, in the same way as can be done in Modula-2 and Ada. This breaks "compilation cascades," which cause irritating delays during development, but more importantly can cause substantial recertification expense in large programs.

8.4.6 Conclusion

Throughout the history of Fortran, new features have been introduced to improve its ability to express solutions to scientific and technical problems, while maintaining compatibility with previous standards. Care has been taken in its development to continue to allow producing programs that use computing resources efficiently. As new methods of program expression and software engineering are developed, tried in other languages, and found to reduce labor costs for development and maintenance, the best features of those methods are incorporated into Fortran, so long as doing so does not compromise users' investments in existing software, or the ability of processors to produce programs that use computing resources efficiently.

8.5   Java

Ronald F. Boisvert and **Roldan Pozo**[34]

8.5.1   Introduction

The Java programming language and environment have become extremely popular since their introduction in the mid-1990's. Indeed, some claim that the number of Java programmers will soon exceed those who use C/C++. Java was not designed for numerical computing, and few scientific applications exist in pure Java as of this writing. Nevertheless, Java has a number of features that make it quite desirable if one's goal is the development of highly reliable software. Among these are the portability provided by the Java Virtual Machine (JVM) and language features that promote safety. In addition, Java provides an object-oriented development framework, a network-aware environment, and access to a rich base of system utilities that make the development of complete applications quite convenient. Such features make it an attractive alternative to Fortran, C, or C++ for the development of scientific applications.

   Our goal here is to provide some guidance to non-Java programmers as to whether Java might be appropriate for scientific applications. We will discuss some of Java's features which promote safety, reliability, and portability, and then briefly address the biggest

---

[34]This section is a contribution of NIST, and is thus not subject to copyright in the USA.

   A number of trademarked products are identified in this section. The identification of commercial products in this paper is done for informational purposes only. Such identification does not represent recommendation or endorsement by NIST.

concern of most scientific users: performance. We conclude with a short discussion of some deficiencies of Java in the context of scientific computing.

8.5.2   Language features

While Java's first applications were related to the development of embedded systems, the language itself is a general-purpose programming language [172]. Its syntax is very similar to C/C++. It is object-oriented like C++, although it is a much simpler language. For example, in Java everything except a small set of primitive types is an object; conventional constructs like C `structs` have been eliminated.

It is widely believed that the simplicity of the Java language leads to an ease in constructing software which, itself, leads to software with fewer errors. Unfortunately, there has yet to be a definitive study which establishes this. We are aware of only one published work on this topic [360]. While it was a very limited experiment,[35] the conclusion was that programming in C++ resulted in three times as many bugs as in a comparable Java program.

The features that Java eliminates from C/C++ that have been accused of leading to programmer error and unintended behavior at runtime include the following.

- *Address/Pointer Arithmetic*
  While there are pointer variables in Java one cannot perform arithmetic operations on them. One cannot determine the address of objects or primitive variables in Java. As a result, many types of vulnerabilities associated with undisciplined or malicious use of pointers and addresses are avoided.

- *malloc/free*
  In Java there is no explicit deallocation of memory. One creates an object with a `New` statement and the runtime system decides when the associated memory can be deallocated (i.e., when nothing is pointing to it). The Java runtime system uses a garbage collector to manage memory on behalf of the user. This eliminates the very common problem of memory leaks in C/C++ programs.

- *goto Statements*
  It has long been known that goto statements are not necessary in programming languages, and most people agree that their undisciplined use leads to inscrutable code. Nevertheless, most languages still include goto statements, and their use persists. Java does not have a goto statement.

- *Multiple Inheritance*
  The concept of inheritance is fundamental to object-oriented languages. This remains the case in Java. C++ allows classes to be descendants of two or more different parent classes. This multiple inheritance leads to very complex code dependencies that can result in unintended behavior. In Java, a class can have only one parent, greatly simplifying class hierarchies.

Java adds to the mix a number of features, only partially supported in Fortran/C/C++, that promote safety and reliability of software. Among these are the following.

---

[35]A single experienced programmer implemented two systems of comparable size, each requiring three months of work, using a formal process to record information about work time, software defects, and bugs.

- *Type Checking*
  Arguments passed to procedures in FORTRAN 77 and Kernighan and Ritchie C are not
  checked to determine whether they match the types expected by the procedure. While
  this is used as a "feature" by some programmers, argument mismatches are the cause of
  much unintended behavior in numerical software. Java, like Fortran 90 and Standard
  C/C++, is a strongly typed language. The Java runtime system is required to check
  variables passed as arguments to verify that they are of the correct type. This catches
  many programmer errors during software development, leading to more reliable code.

- *Runtime Array Bounds Checks*
  Another common programmer error is indexing an array outside its boundaries. The
  Java specification requires that all index variables be verified for legality before they
  are used. This protects both the programmer and the system which is running the
  software.

- *Applet Security Model*
  Java introduces the notion of an *applet*, a special type of Java application that can be
  downloaded over the network to execute in the local environment. Of course, down-
  loading executables poses significant security risks. Because of this, Java applets
  execute in a special restricted environment (a "sandbox"). Many system calls are
  prohibited, including those providing access to local files. These restrictions, along
  with the additional safety that comes from features such as array bounds checking,
  work to ensure that applets can be safely executed.

- *Exception Handling*
  Java, like C++, supplies a uniform method of handling all exceptional conditions,
  such as out-of-bounds array references or attempting to access an object through a
  null pointer. Programmers can write code to "catch" exceptions and handle them
  as they see fit. Programmers can also extend system defined exceptions with those
  of their own. When error handling is a natural part of the language, programmers
  need not invent ad hoc error handling facilities. Such ad hoc facilities may conflict
  when multiple external packages are utilized in a given application. The use of Java
  exception handling avoids this.

8.5.3   Portability in the Java environment

Portability is itself an aspect of reliability. One hopes to get similar behavior from an
application regardless of the hardware on which it executes. The sensitivity of numerical
computations to the details of floating-point arithmetic make cross-platform reliability a
very difficult issue to deal with in scientific applications.

Java's high level of portability is a result of the Java Virtual Machine (JVM) [291].
The JVM is a simple stack-oriented machine with a well-defined instruction set. Floating-
point operations are based on the IEEE 754 standard [355]. In order to run a Java program
one needs an emulator for the JVM; this is provided as a part of each Java implementation.
Java programs are compiled into a sequence of instructions, called bytecodes, for the JVM.
The compiled Java class files are then device-independent object files which can execute in
any Java environment.

One of the goals of Java is to support programs that behave exactly the same regardless of what hardware/software environment in which they execute. The JVM is the key contributor to this. Another is the strict semantics of the Java language itself. More than other languages, Java regulates how compilers map language constructs to object code (bytecodes in this case). In many cases it is possible to get exact cross-platform reproducibility of results with Java to an extent impossible with other languages.

Another feature of Java which enhances portability of applications is the wealth of standard class libraries for various types of utility operations, or for particular types of applications. Portability of applications in other languages is impeded because many of these facilities are not universally available, or are provided in a different way on different platforms. In Java, libraries for developing graphical user interfaces (GUIs) are standardized, for example, allowing one to develop GUIs that are portable between Unix, Windows, and Apple platforms. Libraries for two-dimensional and three-dimensional graphics are available. Classes for manipulating network sockets are standardized. Threads are included as an integral part of the language to support concurrent programming.

The portability provided by the JVM and standardized class libraries admits the possibility of dynamic network distribution of software components. Such a distribution system would greatly simplify the maintenance of scientific applications.

8.5.4   Performance challenges

Java programs have a reputation of being highly inefficient. Indeed, many of the features that promote reliability, safety, and portability add overhead to Java's runtime processing. Early experience with Java certainly verified this impression for many. Java systems are steadily improving in their performance, however, and today there are Java systems that rival (and sometimes exceed) the performance of Fortran or C code. This is an issue which is critical in the selection of a scientific computing language. In this section we will touch on some of the main issues regarding the performance of Java.

One of the main characteristics of Java performance has been its high variability [41, 60]. This is partly due to the fact that Java is a relatively young programming language and many routes to its optimizations have barely begun to be explored. Nevertheless, it is certain that the Java environment is much more complex that that of traditional programming languages like Fortran or C [254]. For example, in Java one must cope with two levels of compilation. First, a Java compiler converts source code to Java bytecodes. Then, perhaps using a different Java system on a computer of different manufacture, the bytecodes are "executed" by a JVM simulator. Each step employs separate layers of abstraction and hence provides further opportunities for inefficiencies to creep in.

The earliest JVMs simply interpreted bytecodes, leading to horribly inefficient execution. Today almost all JVMs employ some kind of *just-in-time* (JIT) compilation strategy; i.e., the bytecodes are compiled into native machine code as a runtime preprocessing step. Various strategies have been proposed for reducing the effect of the preprocessing phase for JIT compilers, the most notable being Sun's HotSpot JVM. HotSpot begins by interpreting bytecodes, while generating an execution profile. When it discovers portions of the code that are heavily executed, it compiles just those parts into machine code. Using this strategy, compilation overhead is expended only where it is likely to pay off. At the other end of the spectrum are Java native compilers, which translate Java directly into machine code. While such compilers have demonstrated fairly high levels of performance, they sacrifice the portability provided by Java bytecodes, one of the main reasons for using Java in the first place.

The issues that make obtaining high performance in Java a challenge for compiler writers include the following.

- *Array Bounds Checking*
  Java mandates that all references to array elements outside of declared bounds generate a runtime exception. Array bounds checks can lead to very inefficient code, though the reported effects vary widely [322, 378]. A variety of optimizations exists to allow compilers to minimize the overhead of bound checking, and these are finding their way into Java environments. Such checks can, for example, be overlapped with other computation on modern processors with multiple functional units. Checks can be removed completely if the fact that no exceptions will occur can be deduced at compile time. Unfortunately, such theorem-prover approaches are sometimes too time-consuming for a dynamic compilation environment. Even if such deductions are impossible at compile time, code versioning can remove many checks. Here, code for a given loop both with and without checks is generated. At runtime a logic test is performed to determine whether an exception will occur. If no exception will occur, the code without checks is executed.

- *Strict Exception Semantics*
  Java requires that exceptions are thrown precisely, i.e., at the point corresponding to the Java source code at which they occur. This requirement places severe restrictions on the compile-time optimization of Java code. For example, it prevents rearranging the order of execution of statements across points where exceptions might occur. This makes optimizing of array bounds checks a challenge.

- *Floating-point Semantics*
  Floating-point numbers in Java (`float` and `double` variables) adhere to the IEEE 754 standard for *single* and *double* precision numbers. Each floating-point operation in Java must, in general, produce numbers in this format. This presents a problem on some architectures (such as Intel's X86, the basis of the Pentium) which has registers based on the optional IEEE 754 *single extended* and *double extended* formats. The extended formats provide additional bits in both the fractional part and the exponent. Naive adherence to the requirements of Java on such machines led to the practice of storing the result of each floating-point operation to memory to properly round it down and to cause an exception if the exponent was out of range. As you might expect, such practices lead to very severe performance penalties for compute-intensive codes (as much as 10-fold in some cases).

  With the release of Java 1.2, a slight loosening of this requirement suggested by [244] of [243] was introduced which removed this performance penalty. Technically, in Java's default floating-point mode, anonymous variables, i.e., temporaries introduced by the compiler, may have extended exponents. Since Pentium processors have a control bit which automatically rounds the fractional part of results to single and double precision, only the extended exponent length is at issue. Allowing temporary variables to have larger exponent ranges permits them to stay in registers, removing a significant part of the performance penalty. At the same time, this loosens the implicit requirement that all executions of Java bytecode produce the exact same result on all JVMs, though not by much.[36] Java programmers who need universal reproducibility may use the `strictfp` modifier on classes and methods to obtain the Java's original strict floating-point semantics.

- *Elementary Functions*
  A related issue is the definition of elementary functions, such as `sin` and `exp`. The original strict definition of these functions was operational; i.e., it required implementations to reproduce the results `fdlibm`, the freely available C `libm` software developed by Sun. This had several problems. First, while `fdlibm` was widely acknowledged as good software, it did not produce the correctly rounded version of the exact result. Thus, it required results be forever inaccurate, even in the face of improved algorithms. Second, it was largely ignored. This definition was subsequently replaced by one suggested by the Java Numerics Working Group, which allowed any result within one unit in the last place (ulp) of the correctly rounded result (0.5 ulp is optimal). Although this again relaxed Java's requirement for exact reproducibility, it admitted highly efficient machine-specific implementations of the elementary functions. A new standard Java class library *StrictMath*, which does produce the same results on all platforms, is now available for users who require exact reproducibility.

- *Floating Multiply-add Instructions*
  Another roadblock to high levels of floating-point performance in Java is the implicit prohibition of the use of floating multiply-add instructions (FMAs). FMAs compute $\alpha x + y$ as a single instruction (i.e., with a single round). Java's semantics require two rounds, which is less accurate but reproducible on all architectures. This can lead to as much as a 50 % performance penalty in the inner loops of linear algebra computations on processors, such as the PowerPC and the Itanium, on which FMAs are available. This issue has yet to be resolved for Java.

8.5.5   Performance results

In spite of the challenges facing Java system designers, the performance of Java systems for scientific applications, as tracked in a variety of benchmarks and studies, has been steadily increasing [60, 399, 378]. One benchmark useful for tracking Java peak performance is [399]. Scimark includes five kernel benchmarks: fast Fourier transform (FFT), dense LU matrix factorization, Jacobi SOR matrix iteration, sparse matrix multiply, and Monte Carlo quadrature. The benchmark comes in two versions, one whose problems fit into most caches, and one whose problems do not. A version of each component is also provided in C. The in-cache benchmark is distributed from the Scimark Web page as a Java applet; clicking on the URL will download the benchmark, run the applet, and allow one to upload the results back to an NIST database. Results are reported in megaflops; both individual components and an average of the five components are reported. The results are continuously updated on the Scimark Web page; as of this writing some 1500 results have been submitted. The range of reported results is impressive: from 0.03 Mflops (on a Winbook running Netscape

---

[36]Operations which overflow on one processor might complete successfully on another.

in 1999) to 404 Mflops (on a 2.8 GHz Pentium IV running Linux 2.5.52 and an IBM 1.4.0 JVM in 2003).

One thing immediately evident from Scimark results is the steady improvement of performance over time due to better Java compilation systems and JVMs. Figure 8.1 illustrates this by showing increasing performance of the Scimark benchmark over time on a 333 MHz Sun Ultra 10 system using successive releases of a particular Java system.

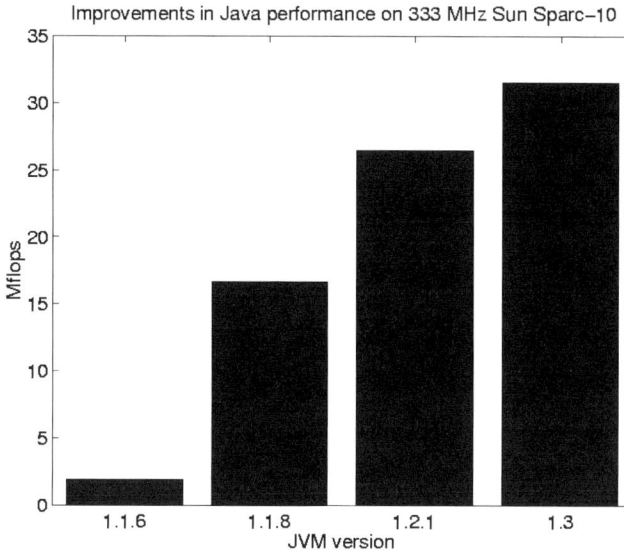

Figure 8.1. *Java Scimark performance on a 333 MHz Sun Ultra 10 system using successive releases of the JVM.*

Much variability of Java performance across platforms has also been reported, however. JVMs for PC-based systems have been seen to outperform their counterparts running on traditional Unix workstations and servers [41]. This may seem counterintuitive; however, it may simply reflect the fact that developers of Java for PC-based systems have been more aggressive in producing efficient Java implementations than their counterparts on traditional high-performance workstations. Since a variety of JVMs are available for most platforms, we also see variability in Java performance on a single processor.

Recently we compared the performance of Scimark on two separate C/C++ environments and three separate Java environments on a 500 MHz Pentium III system running Microsoft Windows. The Java applications ran at 46, 55, and 58 Mflops, while the C applications ran at 40 and 42 Mflops. (High levels of optimization were enabled for the C compilers.) Remarkably, the applications written in Java outperformed those written in C on this platform. Figure 8.2 shows the performance of the Scimark component benchmarks on this platform for the best Java and C environments from these tests.

While the relative performance of C and Java shown here is far from universal, it does illustrate that much more attention has been directed in recent years to optimizing Java

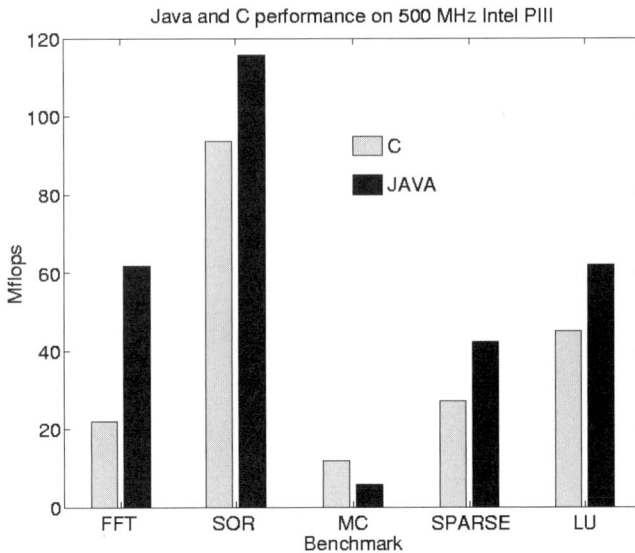

Figure 8.2. *Performance of Scimark component benchmarks in C and Java on a 500 MHz Pentium III system.*

performance on PC platforms than to optimizing C performance. In many real scientific applications Java performance is typically 50 % of that of optimized Fortran or C [378].

8.5.6   Other difficulties encountered in scientific programming in Java

While the performance of Java is steadily improving, there are a number of additional difficulties that one encounters when attempting to use Java for large-scale scientific and engineering computations. Some of these are outlined below.

- *Lack of Complex Data Type*
  There is no complex data type in Java as there is in Fortran. Since Java is an object-oriented language, this should, in principle, present no problem. One simply defines a complex class and develops a set of methods which operate on objects in that class to implement the basic arithmetic operations. For Java, a straightforward approach like this leads to performance disaster [494]. Complex numbers implemented in this way are subject to substantial overhead, and paying this overhead for each arithmetic operation leads to extremely inefficient code. Also, each operation creates a temporary object, and the accumulation of huge numbers of small objects can lead to repeated calls to the garbage collector. Finally, code based upon such a class would be very unpleasant to write and to read. For example, a simple operation such as

$$a = b+c*d;$$

would be expressed as either

```
a.assign(Complex.sum(b,Complex.product(c,d))
```

or

```
a.assign(b.plus(c.times(d)))
```

Efficient manipulation of complex numbers requires that the programmer manage real and complex parts separately, a burden that is both inconvenient and error-prone.

- *Difficulty in Implementing Alternate Arithmetics*
  The same difficulties as noted above for complex arithmetic exist in the implementation of any alternate arithmetics in Java, such as interval or multiprecision arithmetic. The problem stems from the fact that no lightweight aggregation facilities, like C `structs`, are available. In addition, no facilities for operator overloading are available to make arithmetic on alternate datatypes look natural. The absence of lightweight objects and operator overloading contribute significantly to the simplicity of the language, a feature that is central to Java's design philosophy, and hence it is unlikely that they will be added.

A much more feasible approach is the development of language preprocessors admitting specialized datatypes of interest to the scientific computing community. If such preprocessors would emit pure Java, then all the advantages of Java would be preserved, while providing an environment much more conducive to the development of scientific applications. The feasibility of such preprocessors for complex arithmetic has been demonstrated [185].

- *Lack of True Multidimensional Arrays*
  The performance of scientific applications is often dependent upon linear algebra operations, such as the matrix multiplication, or the solution to linear systems, which lie at the core of the computation. As a result, highly optimized linear algebra libraries have been developed to provide the best performance possible for these fundamental operations. Effective management of the flow of data through the memory hierarchy is key to obtaining high performance on modern architectures. Doing this requires a careful coordination of data and how it is laid out in memory and the order of processing in a given algorithm. Fortran provides a complete specification of how multidimensional arrays are linearized for storage, thus providing the algorithm designer with a good indication of how such arrays may be laid out in memory.

Java does not support multidimensional arrays. Instead, Java provides arrays of one-dimensional arrays, as in C. Rows of these simulated multidimensional arrays need not be contiguous in memory. Indeed, there is no guarantee in Java that adjacent elements of a one-dimensional array are contiguous! These facts make developing highly efficient and portable Java linear algebra kernels somewhat problematic. All kernels in the Scimark benchmark use native Java arrays, with fairly satisfactory performance, however. Nevertheless, there has been considerable interest in developing Java language extensions or specialized class libraries for efficient manipulation of multidimensional arrays [323].

- *32-bit Addressing*
  Indexes to Java arrays are limited to 32-bit integers, implying that one-dimensional arrays longer than 2,147,483,647 are not possible. While this is quite large, the size of routine numerical computations is also growing quite fast. While new 64-bit computer architectures support much larger address spaces, Java programs are unable to take advantage of them.

- *Lack of a Legacy of Mathematical Software Packages*
  Since Java remains a relatively new language, it suffers from the lack of an existing base of available mathematical software components to aid in the development of applications. In addition, since the numerical analysis community remains wedded to Fortran, and to some extent C and C++, new packages that demonstrate state-of-the-art methods are not finding their way to Java. While it is possible to invoke components from other languages from the Java environment, this removes the advantages of portability provided by pure Java. Some Java class libraries for fundamental mathematical operations have begun to emerge, but progress has been slow. A list of known Java class libraries for numerical computing is maintained on the Java Numerics Web page at NIST [244].

8.5.7   Summary

Java has a number of features which naturally lead to more reliable software. These, along with Java's universal availability, make it a strong candidate for general-purpose scientific and engineering applications. However, these advantages come at a cost. While Java's raw performance can exceed that of optimized C in some cases, it still lags behind optimized C and Fortran on many platforms. Also, since it was not designed with scientific applications in mind, and there is not yet a strong legacy of scientific codes in Java, programmers face a number of inconveniences in practical code development. Nevertheless, Java may be a reasonable candidate, especially when portability and reproducibility are extremely important.

8.6   Python

Craig C. Douglas and Hans Petter Langtangen

8.6.1   Introduction

Python [369] was originally created by Guido van Rossum in the late 1980's, when he was working at the CWI in Amsterdam. The language design borrows ideas from Modula, C, and ABC. It was created because the distributed operating system Amoeba that van Rossum was helping to create needed a general-purpose scripting language [465].

Python soon attracted interest among computational scientists as a replacement for Unix shell scripts to glue applications and automate numerical experiments. In the mid-1990's, a group of people wrote the Numerical Python extension (see [348]) that offered efficient array processing of the nature found in MATLAB. Scientific computing with Python normally implies heavy use of the Numerical Python extension.

Along with the growth of e-commerce and the need for dynamic Web sites at the end of the 1990's, a boost in the use of and interest in scripting languages arose. Among such languages, Perl attracted by far the greatest attention. However, Python's popularity grew quickly since it delivered basically the same functionality as Perl but tended to be easier to maintain and use in large projects. The many built-in consistency checks in Python also provided high reliability and thereby fast and safe development.

During the last 20 years, MATLAB has become the scripting language of choice in the scientific computing workplace. It is used for prototyping codes as well as general purpose computing. MATLAB's market has shifted from primarily academia to many other fields that generate quite significant revenue as well as intellectually interesting research areas for the The MathWorks to tackle.

Python and its extensions (particularly Numerical Python) are easily combined with tools allowing smooth integration with existing Fortran, C, and C++ libraries. Hence, Python may well be the basis for interesting, freely available replacements for MATLAB in the near future.

Like MATLAB, Python puts a premium on saving people time, not saving computers time. However, its extensibility allows saving time for both under the right conditions.

8.6.2 Basic language features

The Python interpreter is implemented in C, a fact that made it natural and easy to support many of C's features. In addition, Python incorporates most of the operating system interaction provided by Unix shells, as well as programming with user defined objects along the lines of C++ and Java.

- *Type Checking*
  A variable in Python may contain any type so there is, seemingly, no type checking. However, at runtime the interpreter will often detect if the type of a variable is incompatible with the current operation on it. Most of the type inconsistencies detected by compilers in type-safe languages (such as C, C++, Fortran, and Java) are therefore found by the interpreter at runtime in the case of dynamically typed languages like Python.

- *Scope of Variables*
  Variables declared in a function are local to that function and are automatically deleted upon return. Variables in the main program are considered global; they can be looked up in functions, but not modified, unless they are explicitly declared as *global* in the function. Class variables and functions must be prefixed by the name of the class object. Similarly, variables and functions in a module are prefixed by the name of the module (there is a way to avoid this prefix, if desired). Classes and modules thus provide convenient name spaces.

- *Standard Preprocessor*
  There is no associated preprocessor. The need for a preprocessor is less than in C and C++ since conditional compilation is not an issue; no files need to be included and the code is interpreted so the efficiency gain of macros (inline functions) is less

important. If the convenience of macros for writing compact and readable code is wanted, the m4 tool is an option.

- *Standardized Libraries*
  Python has a huge *standard* library, much larger than what programmers are used to in C, C++, and Fortran. There are also a large number of modules and packages available on the Internet [462]. It seems that the Python community, to a large extent, avoids producing multiple, competing modules for doing a certain task, thereby achieving a kind of implicit standardization of third-party modules. Many of these modules find their way into the core Python distribution over time.

- *Built-in Numerical Types*
  Python has a floating-point number type (`float`) corresponding to `double` in C and an integer type corresponding to C's `int`. There is also a double precision complex type and also arbitrary length integers. Single precision is not available in pure Python, but the Numerical Python extension offers arrays with different type of precision, including 16-bit integers and 32-bit floating-point numbers.

- *User-Defined Data Structures and Types*
  Python offers the class concept to define new types and tailored data structures. The class concept is more flexible and dynamic than what is found in C++ and Java. A simple combination of built-in list and hash types may yield tailored data structures without writing new classes.

- *Array Structures*
  Plain Python has a list structure, which is internally implemented in terms of C vectors. The list structure can be nested and thus used for multidimensional arrays. However, the flexibility of lists makes such structures computationally inefficient. Numerical Python has a multidimensional array type, which should always be used for numerical computing. The base index of all Python array-like structures is zero. Actually it does not make much sense in simulating an arbitrary base index because negative indices in Python have a special and rather useful meaning: a[-1] is the last element, a[-2] is the second last element, and so on.

  Python, like most scripting languages, has an efficient implementation of hash structures, called dictionaries in Python terminology, which occasionally constitute a convenient replacement for lists or arrays. The key in Python dictionaries is not limited to a string. It can be almost any object as long as the object cannot be modified.

- *Array Bounds Checking*
  Indices out of bounds are immediately detected in both plain Python lists and Numerical Python arrays.

- *Address/Pointer Arithmetic*
  Python has no pointer or reference type and cannot perform pointer arithmetics.

- *Dynamic Memory Management*
  Data in Python can be created on the fly when needed. The garbage collection system automatically deallocates data structures that are no longer in use.

- *Constant Data Structures*
  There is no keyword in Python to specify that a data structure cannot be modified. However, Python distinguishes clearly between *mutable* and *immutable* types. Mutable types allow in-place modifications, while with an immutable type any changes result in a new variable; i.e., the contents of the original variable are preserved. Lists, dictionaries, arrays, and user defined objects are mutable, while tuples ("constant lists"), strings, and numbers are immutable. The bottom line, in a scientific computing setting, is that the most common data structures (arrays and user defined objects) allow in-place modifications, and there is no way to prevent this.

- *I/O and Formatting*
  All the file types known from C are available in Python, i.e., sequential ASCII and binary files for reading, writing, and appending. Direct file access as in C is also offered. A built-in `xdr` module allows writing and reading binary files in a platform-independent way using the XDR library.

  Format control is achieved by a syntax borrowed from C's `printf` family of functions.

- *Access to System Calls*
  The *system* call known from C is also available in Python. This is the preferred way to launch other applications from Python programs. If input or output to/from such applications is desired, a pipe version of the system call can be used.

- *Multitasking, Multithreading, and Shared Memory Segments*
  Most of Unix and Windows process management is supported by Python, often in a cross-platform fashion. The multitasking of C is mirrored, while multithreading is based on Unix threads (like pthreads) with a Java-inspired programming interface on top.

- *Error Handling*
  Errors occurring at runtime are reported in terms of exceptions (as in Java and C++). Exceptions that are not explicitly handled lead to termination of execution and a report of the error.

- *Classes and Inheritance*
  Python supports classes with both single and multiple inheritance. With the recent introduction of Python 2.2, the resolution of method calls in cases of multiple inheritance has been revised in a manner that is not entirely backward compatible. Hence, older code may require modification to maintain correctness. As with any feature revision that is not backward compatible, this can lead to reliability problems with old scripts (so-called dusty decks) that no one remembers writing.

- *Operator Overloading*
  Python classes can define the call operator, the four arithmetic operators, the power operator, output operators, indexing and slicing operators, comparison operators, Boolean evaluation of an object, conversion (to `float`, `int`, `complex`) operators, and in-place arithmetic operators (`+=`, `*=`, etc.). Compared with C++, Python lacks only the assignment operator (but it is partly present in terms of *properties*; see the

"User Defined Data Structures" section). The combination of dynamically typed data and overloaded operators makes it difficult to predict, by just looking at the code, what an expression like a*b really means.

- *Compilation and Linking*
  Python programs are compiled to bytecode and then interpreted, much in the same way as Java programs. However, the compilation to bytecode is not explicit; one just runs the program. From a programmer's point of view, it appears that Python programs are neither compiled nor linked. The benefit is a fast edit-and-run debugging and development process.

8.6.3 Special features

- *Clean Syntax*
  A striking and attractive feature of Python is its clean syntax. There are no special characters as in Perl, a semicolon does not need to end a statement (unless there are multiple statements on a line), there are no curly braces, and indentation is required(!).

- *Keyword Arguments*
  Besides standard (positional) arguments, Python functions may take keyword arguments. Such arguments consist of a keyword (argument name) and a default value:

  ```
  plot(data, xrange=[0,10], xlabel='t')
  ```

  The hypothetical function plot has one required (positional) argument data, while the rest are optional keyword arguments. In the sample call we specify two keyword arguments, and plot may have lots of other keyword arguments for fine-tuning a plot (title, tickmarks, linetype, etc.). Keyword arguments simplify usage and contribute to documenting the function interface.

- *Generation of Code at Runtime*
  Python, like many other scripting languages, enables generation of code at runtime. Any code segment can be represented as a string and executed. This makes it possible to let parts of the code depend on input data.

- *Cross-Platform OS Interface*
  Another special feature of scripting languages, Python included, is a rich set of platform-independent functions for performing operating system commands like removing files and directories, getting the size and age of files, listing files, recursive traversal of directory trees, and launching other applications, just to mention a few typical tasks.

- *Properties*
  Direct access of class attributes may imply a function call, typically through "get/set" functions, as in C#.

- *Extensions in C, C++, and Fortran*
  Python was initially designed to be extended with new functionality written in C. The support for C programming actually implies convenient combination with C++ and

Fortran as well. For scientific computing this means that Python can be extended with efficient computational modules implemented in C, C++, or Fortran. Numerical Python is an example of such a module and is already a standardized extension [348].

8.6.4   Error handling and debugging

Perhaps the most important feature for reliable programming in Python is the comprehensive system for error handling. Errors are issued as exceptions, and the Python libraries perform extensive runtime checking and raise exceptions when inconsistencies are detected. Such exceptions can be handled explicitly in the calling code, and appropriate remedies can be implemented. If the calling code does not handle a raised exception, the program terminates with a printout of the exception type and the call stack with references to source code lines. In practice this means that a Python program aborts with an instructive error message as soon as a detectable error has occurred. Such errors include wrong use of a variable (inconsistent type, for instance), opening of nonexisting files, list indices out of bounds, and look up of nonexisting hash keys.

Exceptions are organized in a class hierarchy. Any programmer can define his or her own exceptions, and raise and handle these when needed. In many occasions reuse of the wide range of built-in exceptions is sufficient.

Debugging and code development become fast and safe in Python due to the built-in consistency checks and the fact that the program can be quickly edited and immediately run without any time-consuming compilation and linking process.

8.6.5   Math libraries

The standard math library of C and Fortran is mirrored in Python (i.e., the C functions defined in C's header file `math.h` are offered in the Python module *math*, to be precise). There is a counterpart of complex functions to be used with Python's `complex` type. Beyond that, the Numerical Python extension offers a standard array manipulation and computing library.

There is a software package [398] containing lots of useful functionality for scientific computing: automatic differentiation, integration, vector and tensor analysis, handling of Fortran and netCDF files, conversion of physical units, simple statistics, and some visualization tools.

A current initiative, [400], tries to offer an extended numerical library for Python, much like the NAG and IMSL Fortran libraries. Most of SciPy's numerical functionality is based on Netlib packages written in FORTRAN 77. For example, SciPy offers interfaces to (the Atlas version of) BLAS, LAPACK, FFTPACK, ODEPACK (for numerical solution of ordinary differential equations), MINPACK (for optimization), SuperLU (for sparse Gaussian elimination), and others.

Making a Python interface to a Fortran package is quite easy with the aid of F2PY [138]. This tool reads the Fortran files and automatically generates an interface (wrapper) code such that the Fortran functions can be called directly from Python programs. Fortran arrays are mapped to Numerical Python arrays and vice versa. Despite different layouts of Fortran and Numerical Python arrays, F2PY handles the differences transparently (at a cost of array copying when strictly needed). A very nice feature of F2PY is that the

Python interface is very Pythonic; i.e., arrays are transferred without explicit arguments for their sizes, work arrays (needed in many Fortran libraries) may be automatically allocated and hidden in the wrapper code, and functions called from the Fortran libraries may be implemented in Python. In other words, the calling Python program is not affected by the very different programming style of Fortran.

SWIG [433] is a tool for automatically generating wrapper code for C and C++ functions such that these can be called from Python. Unfortunately, SWIG has no explicit support for mapping Numerical Python arrays to C/C++ arrays. This means that interfacing scientific computing libraries written in C or C++, which make heavy use of arrays, is not as easy as interfacing Fortran packages with F2PY. Numerical Python arrays also do not have multiple pointers and are hence not compatible with multidimensional C/C++ arrays built with, e.g., double- and triple-edge pointers (see the "Array layouts" section for more details).

It should be mentioned that one can, of course, write wrapper code manually and thereby generate tailored interfaces to numerical libraries in C/C++ and Fortran.

There is a Web source [462] trying to collect all freely available third-party Python modules. Here one can find many ready-made interfaces to classical Fortran and C packages for scientific computing and visualization. Hence, when programmers have used F2PY or SWIG to generate an interface to some numerical Fortran or C/C++ library, or when the library is written entirely in Python, the code is often available from the Vaults of Parnassus.

8.6.6   Array layouts

When discussing arrays in Python, we limit the attention to Numerical Python arrays, hereafter called NumPy arrays. A NumPy array is, as seen from C, a struct with a `char*` pointer to a memory segment containing the data plus a set of variables holding the dimensions of the array. The array data are stored as in C and C++, i.e., row by row. There are no pointers to the beginning of each row, as in C and C++. This may cause some trouble when sending NumPy arrays to Fortran or C/C++ functions.

Fortran arrays apply a column-by-column storage scheme. That is, a NumPy array must be transposed before being sent to a Fortran function. The NumPy array data are then fully compatible with a Fortran array.

C functions requiring multidimensional arrays often apply multiple pointers (see section 8.2.6). For example, if a C function has a two-dimensional array as argument, the argument type is often a double pointer like `double **A`. NumPy arrays do not contain such a double pointer; only the pointer to the whole data segment in memory, `&A[0][0]`, is available. This fact makes communication with such C code cumbersome as the wrapper code may need to allocate extra row pointers before calling the C function expecting a double pointer.

C++ functions taking array arguments employ either plain C/C++ arrays (pointers) or array objects defined in some library. In the latter case, some conversion between a NumPy array and the library's array classes is needed. Unfortunately, different C++ libraries tend to use different array classes. The amount of work required to write the conversion depends on the differences in the layout of the NumPy array and the C++ array class.

As soon as proper wrapper code is established between NumPy arrays and the actual array type used in C or C++ code, the data transfer is normally efficient: a pointer to the array data is transferred, plus occasionally some extra data (dimensions, row pointers, or similar data).

8.6.7 Dynamic data

The most convenient feature of Python, as seen from a Fortran, C, and C++ programmer's point of view, might well be the handling of dynamic data. There is no need to free memory as this is the responsibility of the built-in garbage collector. All communication of data is done via references (actually C pointers with reference counting in the underlying implementation). Hence, data are created when needed and passed around without any concern for inefficient copying or dangling pointers. In other words, the programmer can forget thinking about memory handling, a fact that makes programming very convenient and reliable.

The only concern with automatic memory management is the possible overhead, especially with respect to temporary arrays that are created without explicit control of the programmer. Simple tests with intensive large-scale computations in Numerical Python show that the garbage collector is capable of removing large temporary arrays quickly and avoiding growth in memory usage. The user can also to some extent force deallocation in the sense that variables can be deleted with the `del` keyword.

8.6.8 User defined data structures

A Python class can be used to implement a user defined data structure, as in C++ and Java. However, the convenient programming with nested, heterogeneous list and hash structures in Python greatly reduces the need to create a new class in order to store some compound data.

The classes in Python are more dynamic than those in C++ and Java. For example, one can add or remove class data (variables and functions) at runtime. This allows for building user defined data structures according to input data.

The contents of a class are visible to any programmer. That is, all variables and functions are public. Nonpublic entries are indicated by prefixing the names with an underscore, but this is just a programming convention and not a technical means for eliminating modifications from a user code. Names prefixed with two underscores are mangled in a special way so direct access is protected, but the name-mangling scheme is known (and simple) so there is actually no technical obstacle with respect to accessing any part of a class.

With Python 2.2 a new feature, called *properties*, was added. Properties allow variable assignment and look-up (using the = operator) to be associated with functions. Think of the statement `a.m=2`, where the integer 2 is stored in the variable m in an object a. Having declared m as a property, the assignment `a.m=2` actually implies a function call, say, `a.set_m(2)`, which controls what actually happens in the assignment. Similarly, a variable look-up, say, `b=a.m`, may imply a function call `b=a.get_m()`. When defining a property, one can define a get function, a set function, and a delete function (for deleting the underlying variable). Omitting the set function makes assignment impossible. In this way, properties can be used to limit the access to certain data.

The dynamic behavior of Python classes and the minor technical support for protecting the class interfaces may be considered as features reducing the reliability of programming, because the user may accidentally modify the state of the data structures. Python's property construction improves the situation to some extent. One might say that the protection of class interfaces, as known from C++ and Java, is traded in favor of more programming convenience and dynamic behavior.

8.6.9   Programming styles

Python supports traditional procedural programming, object-oriented programming, and generic programming (also known as template programming in C++). The latter technique is supported by the fact that variables are not constrained to be of a specific type. Hence, a function written with one class of argument types in mind may well be applied to other types (as a template function in C++). Python also offers elements from function programming (e.g., lambda functions, reduce and filter operations).

Some developers claim that the lack of strong typing in scripting languages reduces software reliability. The main reason is that a function may be applied to data, reliable structures it was not intended for. Object-oriented programming ensures that only an object of a type registered in a class hierarchy can be accepted in a function. In a nutshell, object-oriented programming limits the applications of functions, while lack of strong typing extends the possible use of functions. Very often, programmers need more flexibility than what object-oriented programming offers and therefore cast objects to some base class. Sometimes such casting throws away the benefits of strong typing. For example, in Java the need for flexibility may imply a cast to `Object`, while in C, a similar cast to `void*` is often performed for flexibility. In both cases, the type information (and checking) is lost.

8.6.10   Performance issues

Python has numerous features that contribute to a more reliable code development than what is achieved in compiled languages like Fortran, C, C++, and Java. Since the reliability is closely related to extensive consistency checking at runtime, the cost is naturally speed. Computational scientists are traditionally very concerned about any trade of speed, almost regardless of the gain. Despite the fundamental importance of performance in numerical computing, we want to point out two facts that make Python relevant also in a scientific computing context: (i) Python may be fast enough, and (ii) slow code may be migrated to C, C++, or Fortran.

Regarding (i), much work of computational scientists does not require large amounts of CPU time on modern laptop or desktop computers. If the response time of a certain operation in a Python code is just a few seconds, it may not be serious that the same operation executes in milliseconds in Fortran or C/C++.

Loops over large array structures constitute the main area where Python code is really slow. For example, filling a 1100×1100 array with function values takes 200 times longer in pure Python, with two nested loops, than in Fortran 77, C, or (plain) C++. A mathematical formula given as string can be evaluated like a function call at runtime (as in MATLAB). With the grid point values given in terms of a string formula, the Python code ran about 700 times slower than Python.

With Numerical Python and vectorized expressions (such as those needed for speed in MATLAB), the Python code runs only two times slower than Fortran 77, *even when the expression for the grid point values is given as a string* instead of a Python function (the string is evaluated once in a vector operation so the evaluation overhead is negligible). In contrast to MATLAB, Python functions for scalar arguments will often work without modifications even for array arguments, a feature that simplifies vectorization.

If the two nested loops in the pure Python code are migrated to a Fortran, C, or C++ function, and the grid point values are computed one by one by a callback to a Python function, the resulting program requires about 140 times the CPU time of the FORTRAN 77 code. In other words, callbacks from Fortran to Python are very expensive (but also very convenient). Therefore, callbacks should be vectorized such that the Python function operates on the whole array at once. Migrating the loops from Python to Fortran, C, or C++ code and computing the grid point values in a function in the compiled language (no Python callback) can be done without any measureable overhead in this test case.

According to our experience, the differences between the speed of Python and the speed of MATLAB are rather small in this test problem, provided that one compares similar programming styles (native loops, vectorization, or migration of loops to compiled code).

Chapter 9

The Use and Implementation of Interval Data Types

G. William Walster

9.1 Introduction

The use and implementation of interval data types are examined. In particular, innovations are described and justified that support intrinsic interval data types in Sun Microsystem's Sun™ ONE Studio Fortran 95 compiler and C++ class library.[37] Implications for future Fortran and other language extensions are described.

The chapter elaborates topics that naturally arise when implementing intrinsic support for interval data types in Fortran and C++ compilers. The topics are noteworthy for a number of reasons:

- Each is the result of designing complete, flexible, fast, and user-friendly compiler support of interval data types.

- Some are new to computer language design.

- Some lead directly to new results in real and interval analysis.

- Some logically lead to computer language extensions.

For readers unfamiliar with interval arithmetic and analysis, a brief introduction is provided.

9.2 Intervals and Interval Arithmetic

In "The dawning" Ramon Moore [321] describes the genesis of his idea to use computers to perform arithmetic on intervals that are both closed and bounded. The date was 1957. The place: Lockheed Missiles and Space Company Inc. in Sunnyvale, California. *Interval*

Analysis [318] traces the idea of computing numerical bounds to Archimedes, but Moore was the first to recognize both the power of interval analysis (as contrasted with real analysis of points) and the practical utility of implementing interval arithmetic on digital computers. A brief history of early interval research and computing can be found in [194].

The paper [501] deals with arithmetic on sets of values and thus is an early precursor of interval arithmetic. Several people independently had the idea of bounding rounding errors by computing with intervals; see, e.g., [130, 432, 479, 480, 486]. However, interval mathematics and analysis can be said to have begun with the appearance of R. E. Moore's book *Interval Analysis* in 1966. Moore's work transformed this simple idea into a viable tool for error analysis. In addition to treating rounding errors, Moore extended the use of interval analysis to bound the effect of errors from all sources, including approximation errors and errors in data.

9.2.1   Intervals

The book [318] defines interval arithmetic for rational functions composed of finite sequences of the four basic arithmetic operations on closed and bounded intervals of real numbers. Moore and most others since then have defined interval arithmetic in terms of arithmetic on real numbers. Therefore, corresponding to the situation with real numbers, operations on intervals with extended (including infinite) endpoints and division by intervals containing zero were not defined. Originally, neither was raising an interval to an integer power. Since the original formulation, the integer and real power functions have been given interval extensions, but only for intervals contained within a function's natural domain of definition. The sets of real values that interval operations are defined to contain are described as follows:

Let $[a, b]$ denote a real, closed, bounded interval constant. That is, for example,

$$[a, b] = \{x \in \mathbb{R} \mid a \leq x \leq b\}, \tag{9.1}$$

where $\mathbb{R}$ denotes the set of finite real numbers $\{x \mid -\infty < x < +\infty\}$.

9.2.2   Interval arithmetic

If $\bullet \in \{+, -, \times, \div\}$ denotes one of the four basic arithmetic operations, then arithmetic operations on a pair of intervals, $[a, b]$ and $[c, d]$, must produce a new interval, say, $[e, f]$, such that

$$[e, f] \supseteq \{x \bullet y \mid x \in [a, b] \text{ and } y \in [c, d]\}, \tag{9.2}$$

where $d < 0$ or $0 < c$ in the case of division, because division by zero is not defined for real numbers. The right-hand side of (9.2) defines the sets of values that must be contained in interval arithmetic operations on finite real intervals. While computing narrow intervals is desirable, the only *requirement* is containment. The right-hand side of (9.2) is the set of values that the operation $[a, b] \bullet [c, d]$ must contain. The term *containment set* is used to refer to this set of values. The relation in (9.2) is referred to as the *containment constraint* of interval arithmetic.

Arithmetic operation monotonicity makes possible the following rules for computing endpoints of finite interval arithmetic operations from their endpoints:

$$[a, b] + [c, d] = [a + c, b + d], \tag{9.3a}$$

$$[a, b] - [c, d] = [a - d, b - c], \tag{9.3b}$$

$$[a, b] \times [c, d] = [\min (a \times c, a \times d, b \times c, b \times d), \tag{9.3c}$$
$$\max (a \times c, a \times d, b \times c, b \times d)], \text{ and}$$

$$[a, b] \div [c, d] = [\min (a \div c, a \div d, b \div c, b \div d), \tag{9.3d}$$
$$\max (a \div c, a \div d, b \div c, b \div d)],$$

where, to exclude division by intervals containing zero, $d < 0$ or $0 < c$. Directed rounding is used to guarantee containment when interval operations are implemented using IEEE 754 floating-point arithmetic. See [477] and [215].

9.3 Interval Arithmetic Utility

With the above brief introduction, the utility of computing with intervals is now described. First the logical consequences and implications of fallible data are described. Then the connection to interval arithmetic is made.

9.3.1 Fallible measures

Except when counting objects, almost all measurements contain uncertainty. The most accurate (to about 10 decimal digits), frequently used, measured physical constants are documented by the National Institute of Standards and Technology in [346]. The implication is that almost all measured continuous inputs to any computation should be intervals to bound the consequences of input uncertainty.

The following example illustrates the fact that useful intervals need not have narrow width. Suppose one wants to calculate how long it will take to double a sum of money if invested at an annual interest rate (compounded monthly) in the interval [3, 6] %. The minimum value in months is the interval [11 $yr.$ 7 $mo.$, 23 $yr.$ 2 $mo.$].

Alternatively, to illustrate that the interval evaluation of an expression does *not* always increase interval result width, evaluate the expression in (9.4) over the short interval [2.716, 2.718]:

$$f(x) = \frac{\ln (x)}{x}. \tag{9.4}$$

The answer is [0.3678793, 0.3678795]. A simple convention (see [475, 397, 431] and section 9.4.2.3) can be used to display numbers accurate to ± 1 unit in the last digit (uld) printed. For example, denote the interval $X = 2.717$ (which represents the interval [2.716, 2.718]). Then the value of $f(X)$ is 0.3678794 (which represents the interval [0.3678793, 0.3678795]), clearly showing *decreased* interval width in $f(X)$ compared to the width of X.

The familiar "$x \pm \varepsilon$" notation is convenient to *represent* fallible values; however, using this notation to *compute* is cumbersome. Using assumed statistical distributions to represent input uncertainty is even more difficult, cumbersome, and risky unless interval bounds are included in the development. Steady progress using intervals to solve this problem continues to be made; see [31]. If input uncertainty and finite precision arithmetic errors are simultaneously considered, the complexity of nonlinear expression error analysis quickly becomes overwhelming. Rigorous error analysis of even modestly small algorithms is so labor-intensive that in practice it is almost never performed. At the same time, there is an ever-increasing requirement to use computers for mission-critical computations in which errors must be bounded because their consequences can be catastrophic; see [245].

A single number written in scientific notation (such as 2.35×10^{-3}) contains implicit accuracy information in the number of digits of the fractional part—in this case the three digits 2.35. A frequently used convention is to let the last displayed digit be incorrect by at most ± 1 unit. Unfortunately, no accuracy information exists in the floating-point representation used to store such numbers in computers. Using floating-point computer notation, when the number 2.35E-03 is entered, it is incorrectly stored as if it were much more accurate.

Unfortunately, two problems arise as a consequence:

- First, the actual input value uncertainty has no convenient way to be either represented or rigorously propagated through a floating-point computation.

- Second, most real numbers cannot even be represented as finite precision floating-point values.

Without intervals, validated arithmetic (that produces guaranteed bounds on correct results) has been almost unknown in numerical computing. To the exclusion of any concern for accuracy, computer science focus has been only on speed as measured by floating-point operations per second (FLOPS). Evidence of this fact is not difficult to find. For example, the Fortran language standard contains not a single word about accuracy of floating-point or even integer results. See the Fortran standards committee [235].

As critical decisions are increasingly based on unvalidated computing, the resulting risk becomes essentially unbounded. Clearly, there are growing requirements to solve ever-increasingly difficult nonlinear problems; to do so with guaranteed accuracy; and finally, to do so the first time. See [346].

9.3.2   Enter interval arithmetic

These requirements are logically satisfied by interval arithmetic. An interval is simply a range of numbers bounded by the interval's endpoints. For example, the range from 950 to 1050 is written as [950, 1050] and contains all the numbers between and including 950 and 1050. Hence, in planning a trip, assume the following: number of traveled miles will be bounded by the interval [950, 1050] miles; the number of miles traveled per gallon of gasoline is bounded by the interval [20, 23] miles; and the price of gasoline per gallon is bounded by the interval $[1.15, 2.00]. Performing arithmetic on the given intervals produces the interval $[47.50, 105.00] that must contain the set of all possible total costs of gasoline for the planned trip.

The width of any interval is a natural accuracy measure. Computing with intervals makes accuracy as visible as program execution time. A direct consequence of seeing numerical accuracy is the motivation to develop interval procedures and algorithms that quickly return ever narrower (more accurate) intervals.

The two common ways to improve numerical accuracy also reduce interval width:

- First, reduce the width of input values.

- Second, increase the number of interval data values used to compute interval bounds on a given parameter.

Although the first is obvious, the second is more subtle because working with intervals leads to new and unfamiliar ways to compute parameter bounds from fallible interval data.

For example, given n interval measurements X_i ($i = 1, \ldots, n$) of the same true value, say, t, the best way to compute a narrow interval bound T on t is *not* to compute the average value (or arithmetic mean) of the interval observations. Rather, the *intersection* of the interval observations is used. The logic for this is simple: Given that each and every observation X_i must contain t, so must their intersection; see [475]. If all the observations do not contain at least one common value, then their intersection is the empty interval. The beauty of this interval procedure is that the empty outcome is unambiguous *proof* that something is wrong: The assumed error in the observations might be too small, or because of uncontrolled factors in the measurement procedure, there might really be no single value t in the given observations. That is, the observation model (or theory) is wrong.

Another simplicity of this interval parameter estimation procedure is that it requires only interval observation error bounds. No assumption about statistical error distributions must be made. Nevertheless, if available in any of a variety of forms, statistical distributions also can be used rigorously in interval algorithms, even when computing complicated nonlinear expressions. See [31] and, for example, [187].

Three properties of intervals and interval arithmetic precisely link the fallible observations of real engineering and scientific observations to mathematics and floating-point numbers:

- Any contiguous set of real numbers (a continuum) is represented by a containing interval.

- The fundamental theorem of interval analysis guarantees that interval evaluation of any expression produces an interval bound on the expression's range over the expression's interval arguments.

- Intervals provide a convenient and mechanical way to represent and compute error bounds from fallible data.

With the use of *directed rounding*, the most important properties of infinite precision intervals are preserved in finite precision floating-point interval arithmetic. Directed rounding is commonly available on all computers supporting the IEEE 754 floating-point standard; see [215]. The *raison d'être* for directed rounding in the floating-point standard is to support rigorously computed interval bounds.

9.4 The Path to Intrinsic Compiler Support

When Moore published his first interval analysis book in 1966, no existing computing language supported operator overloading and user defined types. Most early interval programs were implemented using subroutine calls to perform each interval arithmetic operation or function call. As a consequence, only members of the interval research community were willing to spend the time and effort required to write experimental interval programs. Mostly these codes were used to produce the numerical results for interval analysis and algorithm demonstrations in journal articles and books.

In [500] Yohe describes the early efforts to provide compilers and precompilers support to remove the drudgery of writing subroutine calls. Pre-compilers did not improve runtime performance, which could be up to 300 times slower than the same precision floating-point arithmetic. Nevertheless, great strides were made by formalizing the mathematical foundations of finite interval analysis and elaborating possible syntax and semantics of language support for interval data types in Algol 60, Pascal, Fortran, C, and C++. A list of interval bibliographies is available on line; see [270].

The "dependence problem" of interval arithmetic (see below) caused unnecessarily wide results to be produced in early experiments with simple interval ports of linear algebra algorithms. The dependence problem and these early pessimistic results convinced many to abandon interval arithmetic as impractical. Interval arithmetic is now becoming mainstream computing technology because enough interval researchers remained undaunted by these early negative results.

Ada, C++, Fortran 90, and Fortran 95 provide a convenient way for users to implement support for user defined data types. The book *Fortran 90/95 Explained* [315] uses interval examples to illustrate how to implement user defined types and operator overloading.

In parallel, interval analysis developments were made, including the recognition that intervals can be used to compute bounds on the entire set of solutions to nonlinear problems; see [242]. It is arguable that the interval version of Newton's algorithm (discovered by Moore [318]) for finding the roots of nonlinear functions, and the interval global optimization algorithm (discovered by Hansen [192], developed primarily in [193], and extended in [191]) are two of the most important and uniquely interval algorithms. In addition, increasingly sophisticated interval algorithms continue to be developed, all with the goal of efficiently producing narrow interval bounds on the set of all possible outcomes. See [242] and [191]. Important practical examples include:

- Martin Berz' cosy infinity system for integrating ordinary differential equations in particle beam physics; see [32];

- Mark Stadtherr's award winning work minimizing the Gibbs free energy equation in Computational Chemistry; see [423].

Other successful interval applications are documented in [270]; other bibliographies are on the Internet.

Interval algorithm developments and practical interval applications continue to be made. Support for computing with intervals now exists in Mathematica [491], Maple [303], MATLAB [389], and MuPAD [183]. Support for interval graphics exists in GrafEq [457]. In spite of the increasing availability of interval support, published commercial applications have been rare. However, interval algorithms and interval products are quietly being used commercially even though not much has been said publicly about this fact. The reason is that intervals can be a competitive advantage within a given vertical market.

Until recently:

- Companies were reluctant to use fundamental computing technology that is not supported by major hardware and software manufacturers.

- C++ class and Fortran 95 module implementations made the interval software development process so difficult that commercial software developers were not eager to write interval-based products.

Then Sun Microsystems Inc. provided full intrinsic support for interval data types in Fortran 95. With the release of Forte™ Developer 6 Fortran 95 (now Sun™ ONE Studio Fortran 95 and hereafter in this chapter simply f95), all of the normal software development tools are now available that are required to write and support commercial interval programs. Intrinsic compiler support for interval data types is not yet available in the C, C++, and Java™ languages, and there remain opportunities to further improve support for intervals in f95. However, this first step will make it increasingly difficult for skeptics to sit on the sidelines while early adopters use intervals to establish competitive advantages.

In the remainder of this paper, different aspects of compiler support for intervals in f95 are described and justified. Section 9.4.1 contains an overview of the interval-specific features in f95 that developers both expect to see and frequently use. The goal is to provide insight into why these features have been included. User documentation and supporting technical white papers are available on line; see [431].

9.4.1 Interval-specific operators and intrinsic functions

Given defined arithmetic operations on bounded intervals, it is straightforward to overload the four basic arithmetic operators to implement interval versions of required standard Fortran intrinsic functions. Interval-specific operators and intrinsic functions also must be supplied in a complete implementation of interval data types.

9.4.1.1 Operators

Excluding division by intervals containing zero, interval arithmetic operations on bounded intervals have been defined by Moore. Refinements have been made, for example, with the integer power operation ($X**N$ in Fortran).

Integer powers. Evaluating the interval expression $X \times X$ does not always produce a sharp bound on the range of x^2. This is an example of an easily solved form of the *dependence problem of interval arithmetic*. The solution is to treat x^2 as a function of one variable, x, rather than as a function of two variables, x and y.

Multiplication can be thought of as a function of two variables:

$$f_\times (x, y) = xy. \tag{9.5}$$

To compute x^2 using points, one can simply evaluate

$$f_\times (x, x) = xx \tag{9.6a}$$

$$= x^2. \tag{9.6b}$$

For points and degenerate (zero width) intervals, expressions (9.6a) and (9.6b) are identical. However, interval arithmetic does not recognize when the same interval variable appears more than once, either in different interval arguments of a function or in operands of an arithmetic operation.

For example, if $X = [-1, 2]$ and $Y = [-1, 2]$, then $X \times Y = [-2, 4]$. However, the range of the function

$$f_{x^2}(x) = x^2 \tag{9.7}$$

over the interval $X = [-1, 2]$ is

$$f_{x^2}(X) = [0, 4]. \tag{9.8}$$

Computing $f_\times(X, X)$ in place of $f_{x^2}(X)$ with a nondegenerate interval argument is not wrong. The containment set (or cset for short) is contained in the interval result. However, answers will not always be as narrow as possible (or as sharp) when a nondegenerate interval variable appears more than once in an arithmetic expression. For example,

$$f_\times(X, X) = [-1, 2] \times [-1, 2] \tag{9.9a}$$
$$= [-2, 4]. \tag{9.9b}$$

To compute sharp bounds on integers and real powers, dependence can be explicitly taken into account by associating the Fortran $**$ operator with the functions

$$f_{x^n}(x, n) = x^n \tag{9.10a}$$

and

$$f_{x^y}(x, y) = \exp(y \ln x), \tag{9.10b}$$

respectively. For an interval argument, $X = [\underline{X}, \overline{X}]$, the following expression defines the required result for x^n:

$$f_{x^n}(X) = \begin{cases} \left[0, \left(\max\left(|\underline{X}|, |\overline{X}|\right)\right)^n\right] & \text{if } n \text{ is even and } 0 \in X, \\ \left[\min\left(\underline{X}^n, \overline{X}^n\right), \max\left(\underline{X}^n, \overline{X}^n\right)\right] & \text{otherwise.} \end{cases} \tag{9.11}$$

This example illustrates the important point that it is not always obvious how to compute sharp bounds on the range of interval expressions. Quality compiler support for interval data types automatically produces code to compute narrow bounds on the range of arbitrary expressions over any interval arguments. A compiler should construct the required executable code without requiring programmers to contort their algorithm's source code.

Order relations. Ordering finite real numbers is unambiguous. Similarly, the set of Fortran operators, $\{.\text{LT}., .\text{LE}., .\text{EQ}., .\text{NE}., .\text{GE}., .\text{GT}.\}$ or equivalently $\{<, <=, ==, /=, >=, >\}$, on REAL- and INTEGER-type variables is unambiguous. Likewise, a degenerate interval's order is unambiguous. However, because nondegenerate intervals are real number continua, their order is inherently ambiguous. For example, the two intervals $[1, 3]$ and $[2, 4]$ contain points that are simultaneously less than, equal to, and greater than points in the other. To resolve this ambiguity, three useful classes of interval-specific order relations are implemented in f95. Each is defined using Fortran order relations on interval endpoints. Coding INTERVAL-type relational tests using interval-specific operators increases readability and thereby reduces coding errors.

The three interval order relation classes are illustrated using the less-than relation:

1. $[a, b] < [c, d]$ is true if $b < c$.

2. $[a, b] < [c, d]$ is true if $a < d$.

3. $[a, b] < [c, d]$ is true if $a < c$ and $b < d$.

Associating an interpretation with each interval-specific relation class clarifies how to define the remaining interval-specific relations.

Certainly true relations. In the first case above, every element of the interval $[a, b]$ is less than every element of the interval $[c, d]$. Consequently, it is reasonable to say the interval $[a, b]$ is *certainly less* than the interval $[c, d]$. For each of the relations in the set $\{<, \leq, =, \neq, \geq, >\}$, there is a *certainly true* interval equivalent. The intervals $[a, b]$ and $[c, d]$ are certainly equal if $a = d$ and $b = c$, or equivalently, given $a \leq b$ and $c \leq d$, if $a = b = c = d$.

Possibly true relations. In the second case, there is at least one element of the interval $[a, b]$ that is less than one element of the interval $[c, d]$. Consequently, it is reasonable in this case to say that the interval $[a, b]$ is *possibly less* than the interval $[c, d]$. As with certainly true relations, each of the relations in the set $\{<, \leq, =, \neq, \geq, >\}$ has a *possibly true* equivalent. The intervals $[a, b]$ and $[c, d]$ are possibly equal if $a \leq d$ and $c \leq b$.

Set relations. In the third case, relations apply to the elements of the operand intervals as *sets*, in which case the following two conditions must both be true:

1. For every element $x \in [a, b]$, there exists an element $y \in [c, d]$ for which $x < y$.

2. For every element $y \in [c, d]$, there exists an element $x \in [a, b]$ for which $x < y$.

As with certainly true and possibly true relations, each of the relations in the following set $\{<, \leq, =, \neq, \geq, >\}$ has an equivalent *set* definition. The intervals $[a, b]$ and $[c, d]$ are set-equal if $a = c$ and $b = d$.

Convergence. When both interval relation operands are degenerate, the certainly, possibly, and set relations converge to the corresponding point operations. Interval relational operations on a pair of degenerate intervals are the same as the corresponding point relational operations on a pair of points. In this case the distinctions between certainly, possibly, and set operators vanish.

Naming order relations. Given the variety of possible interval order operations, how should they be named? An obvious convention that distinguishes among the three sets of operators is to introduce a three-letter mnemonic in which the first letter is an element of the set $\{C, P, S\}$ to represent the *certainly*, *possibly*, or *set* case, and the last two letters are the same as those in standard Fortran. Therefore, the certainly less-than relational operator is denoted .CLT..

The next question is which relations should be the default? Two intervals are normally treated as equal if they are equal as sets. Therefore, the default .EQ. and .NE. (or == and /=) operators in Fortran, when applied to INTERVAL data items, perform the .SEQ. and .SNE. operations. All other relational operations on INTERVAL data items explicitly use the three-letter specification to identify the type of operation. By making interval code explicit, both programmers and algorithm developers are encouraged in every situation to choose the most appropriate relational operator.

Negating interval relational operations.   When one or both interval operands is not degenerate, negating an interval expression is not the same as negating the operation. For example,

$$.NOT.(X.CLT.Y) \tag{9.12}$$

does *not* have the same truth value as

$$X.CGE.Y.$$

In fact, the expression in (9.12) has the same truth value as

$$X.PGE.Y.$$

In general, let op be used to denote an element of the set of Fortran relational operators {LT, LE, EQ, NE, GE, GT} and nop be used to denote the complement of the operator op. For example, if op is LT, nop is GE. Then the general rule is

$$X.Cop.Y = .NOT.(X.Pnop.Y) \tag{9.13a}$$

and

$$X.Pop.Y = .NOT.(X.Cnop.Y). \tag{9.13b}$$

This De Morgan-like rule can be used to construct exhaustive sets of relational tests. This is important to preclude an empty interval from leading to an unanticipated branch. Without the full complement of certainly and possibly relations, coding complicated relational expressions is more difficult to write and read, and more likely to lead to coding errors.

Implementation choices.   By simply changing data type declaration statements, meaningful interval algorithms generally cannot be constructed from existing point algorithms. In particular, this is true if the algorithms contain relational tests. In addition to the requirement to resolve relational test ambiguity, the logic of interval algorithms can be quite different from that of point algorithms. For example, an interval algorithm can *prove* where solutions are impossible. At algorithm termination, the remaining set of intervals (or boxes in *n*-dimensional Cartesian space) bounds all possible solutions. There is no point algorithm counterpart to this interval algorithm logic.

Interval-specific operators.   In addition to interval versions of standard Fortran operators, useful interval-specific, set-theoretic operators are implemented in f95. Each row in Table 9.1 contains the name of the operator, its mathematical notation, Fortran syntax, and result type. In this table, the Fortran variables X and Y have the INTERVAL type, while R has type REAL.

Table 9.1. *Set-theoretic interval operators.*

Name	Math. notation	Fortran	Result type
Interval hull	$X \underline{\cup} Y$ (1)	X.IH.Y	INTERVAL
Intersection	$X \cap Y$	X.IX.Y	INTERVAL
Disjoint	$X \cap Y = \emptyset$	X.DJ.Y	LOGICAL
Element	$r \in Y$	R.IN.Y	LOGICAL
Interior	$\underline{Y} < \underline{X}$ and $\overline{X} < \overline{Y}$	X.INT.Y	LOGICAL
Proper subset	$X \subset Y$	X.PSB.Y	LOGICAL
Proper superset	$X \supset Y$	X.PSP.Y	LOGICAL
Subset	$X \subseteq Y$	X.SB.Y	LOGICAL
Superset	$X \supseteq Y$	X.SP.Y	LOGICAL

Note: (1) The symbol $\underline{\cup}$ is used by some interval authors to denote the convex, or interval hull operator.

9.4.1.2 Intrinsic functions

As with operators, interval intrinsic functions can be grouped into interval versions of Fortran intrinsic functions and interval-specific forms. In the f95 compiler, all Fortran intrinsic functions have an interval counterpart if they either return a REAL type result or accept REAL type arguments. The type conversion intrinsic routine INTERVAL plays the same role for interval data types as the REAL and COMPLEX type conversion routines do for their respective data types.

When kind type parameter value (KTPV[38]) conversion is performed from an interval with one KTPV to another, containment is guaranteed, as it is with all interval operations and intrinsic functions. When the INTERVAL type conversion intrinsic function is used to convert two higher KTPV REAL values into a lower KTPV INTERVAL, argument's KTPVs are *first* converted and then the interval result is formed. This sequence follows standard Fortran type conversion practice.

Provided indeterminate forms do not arise, as in X**Y with X and Y both equal to zero, it is a simple matter to code the logic required to identify which argument endpoints to use when computing interval result endpoints. Either Fortran intrinsic functions are monotonic or monotonic subdomains are precisely known.

Care is taken with periodic trigonometric functions to perform correct large-angle reductions. As an illustrative example, for a degenerate interval angle A with a value of 1.0E50, the expression SIN(A) returns a valid interval result having a width of 1 or 2 ulps.[39]

Interval-specific intrinsic functions. Interval-specific intrinsic functions are provided to give access to interval endpoints and standard functions thereof. (See the first six entries in Table 9.2.) Because the empty interval is supported, an intrinsic function is

---

[38]Readers who are unfamiliar with the Fortran expression "kind type parameter value," KTPV can be read as "precision."

[39]An *ulp* is one unit in the last place of the mantissa of a floating-point number.

provided to test for an empty interval. An intrinsic function is also provided to compute the number of digits in a single-number-formatted interval. See the discussion of interval input/output in sections 9.4.1.3 and 9.4.2.3.

Table 9.2. *Interval-specific intrinsic functions.*

Name	Definition	Generic name	Result type
Infimum	$\inf([a, b]) = a$	INF	REAL
Supremum	$\sup([a, b]) = b$	SUP	REAL
Width	$w([a, b]) = b - a$	WID	REAL
Midpoint	see note (1)	MID	REAL
Magnitude	see note (2)	MAG	REAL
Mignitude	see note (3)	MIG	REAL
Empty interval test	see note (4)	ISEMPTY	LOGICAL
Number of digits	see note (5)	NDIGITS	INTEGER

Notes: (1) $\text{mid}([a, b]) = (a + b)/2$. A valid finite real value is returned for all real a and $b \in \text{HUGE} \times [-1, 1]$.

(2) $\text{mag}([a, b]) = \max(|x|)$ given $x \in [a, b]$
$= \max(|a|, |b|)$.

(3) $\text{mig}([a, b]) = \min(|x|)$ given $x \in [a, b]$
$= \begin{cases} \min(|a|, |b|), & \text{if } 0 \notin [a, b] \\ 0, & \text{otherwise.} \end{cases}$

(4) ISEMPTY returns true if argument interval is empty.

(5) NDIGITS returns the maximum number of digits using the Y edit descriptor.

9.4.1.3 Input/output

The syntax in Fortran modules is not sufficiently rich to support reading and writing interval data with the same power and flexibility provided by standard Fortran edit descriptors. In f95 all the edit descriptors that accept REAL data items also accept INTERVAL data. Square brackets are used to delimit intervals, so input and displayed values follow the accepted [inf,sup] form.

This concludes a general description of intrinsic compiler support of bounded finite interval data types. In the next section, enhancement opportunities are described.

9.4.2 Quality of implementation opportunities

The above description contains no surprises, because it includes the features most users expect in a competent, intrinsic, interval-data-type compiler implementation. However, a number of issues have been glossed over and a number of opportunities have not been seized to use inherent interval properties to good advantage. These difficulties and opportunities are now described, together with the resulting quality of implementation features that have been introduced to support intervals in f95.

9.4.2.1   Difficulties

As long as intervals are viewed as sets of real numbers, and interval operations are defined in terms of real arithmetic operations, interval arithmetic is constrained by the limitations of real analysis. For example, when undefined events are encountered, compilers treat them as an IEEE exception by halting, issuing a message, transferring control to a specified address, and/or returning a special value such as an IEEE default NaN. The following difficulties with arithmetic on points have been successfully overcome using interval innovations introduced in f95.

Singularities and indeterminate forms.   Division by zero is undefined. Therefore, division by an interval containing zero remains undefined. Similarly, indeterminate forms such as x^y when $x = y = 0$, and operations on infinite values including $\infty - \infty$, ∞/∞, and $0 \times \infty$, are undefined for points and therefore remain undefined for intervals.

Domain constraints.   When a point argument is outside a function's domain of definition, the result is undefined. Similarly, when an interval argument of an intrinsic or user defined function is partially or completely outside the function's domain of definition, interval results remain undefined. Therefore, in a real-based interval system $\sqrt{[-2, -1]}$ and $\sqrt{[-1, 1]}$ are both undefined.

The value of a literal constant.   In Fortran, the internal value of a literal constant is an approximation to the value represented by the literal constant's character string. Because there is no accuracy requirement in the Fortran standard, the internal value associated with a given literal constant cannot be known without performing runtime tests. It is therefore difficult to anticipate, for example, if the REAL literal constant 0.1 is less than or greater than $\frac{1}{10}$. As a consequence, it is difficult to know how to construct a one-ulp-width interval that contains a given real value, such as 0.1.

To ameliorate this difficulty, the concept of the *external value* of a literal constant is introduced. The notation ev (string) is used to denote the external *mathematical value* of a literal constant's character string. In any interval expression containing a literal constant, the constant's external value must be available to construct an internal, machine-representable interval that contains the constant's external value. The difficulty is that the concept of a literal constant's external value does not yet exist in the Fortran standard.

9.4.2.2   Opportunities

In addition to the above difficulties addressed in f95, a number of opportunities exist to use interval properties in ways that are impossible with points. In each case, the question is what syntax and semantics are required to achieve the desired results.

Closed interval systems.   The fact that intervals are *sets* of values rather than single *points* can be used to define events that are undefined in point systems. As a result, closed interval systems with respect to arithmetic operations can be constructed in which there are *no* undefined outcomes. The practical consequence for interval compiler support is that exceptional events are impossible.

Literal constants.   With the Fortran 95 standard, literal constants have a type and a KTPV, just like variables with the same type. As a consequence, when changing the KTPV of expressions, all the literal constants must be physically altered to reflect the changed KTPV. For example, in standard Fortran 95, the code fragment

```
REAL X
X = 0.1
```

must be changed to

```
DOUBLE PRECISION X
X = 0.1D0
```

or else the value of X will not be the DOUBLE PRECISION approximation of the number $\frac{1}{10}$.

Mixed-mode expressions.   Because the accuracy of interval results are self-evident in the width of computed intervals, interval programmers are naturally compelled to select algorithms that produce narrow interval results. Sometimes a change in precision is needed. To facilitate making KTPV changes, it is necessary to evaluate mixed-mode expressions containing interval variables of more than one KTPV, as well as interval and noninterval variables and literal constants.

Input/output.   Entering and reading interval data in the [inf, sup] format can be time consuming and error prone. A simple alternative facilitates convenient interval input/output.

In the next section, specific f95 Fortran extensions are described that:

- surmount the difficulties outlined in section 9.4.2.1, and

- realize the opportunities outlined in section 9.4.2.2.

9.4.2.3   Interval-specific features in f95

Inherent interval features are used to provide flexible, powerful, and easy-to-use interval compiler support. The result is a set of interval-specific innovations in the form of language extensions. No changes to noninterval data types are required. These innovations are briefly summarized below and more completely documented in the f95 and C++ interval documentation and technical white papers; see [431].

Closed interval systems.   There is one and only one requirement that any interval system must satisfy: The containment constraint of interval arithmetic must be satisfied. Speed, narrow width, and ease of use are all *quality of implementation* features. The containment constraint must never be violated. If it is, the ability to construct numerical proofs is lost.

As long as interval operations, functions, and expressions are defined in terms of finite real variables, undefined outcomes can be avoided by precluding singularities and indeterminate forms. This has been done using the IEEE exception mechanism described above.

Fortunately an exception-free alternative exists. To realize it, a broader set-based conception is needed for all possible values that an interval operation or expression evaluation must contain. This set is the result's *containment set* or *cset*. The cset of any operation or expression might or might not be an interval, but all the values in the cset must be enclosed in the result of any interval operation or expression evaluation.

The idea is to define csets of algebraically equivalent expressions so that they are identical even when only one of the expressions has a normally defined value. To do this in a consistent way requires that expression csets can be *sets* not just *points* and that expression csets can contain infinite values.

Two expressions are *algebraically equivalent* if they have the same value for all expression arguments in the intersection of their natural domains. The cset is the smallest set of values that always satisfies the containment constraint for all algebraically equivalent expressions. For example, consider the expressions

$$f(x) = \frac{x}{1 + x} \tag{9.14a}$$

and

$$g(x) = \frac{1}{1 + \frac{1}{x}}. \tag{9.14b}$$

The functions f and g are equal except when $x = -1$ because $f(x)$ and $g(x)$ are undefined; or when $x = 0$ because only $g(x)$ is undefined. Whenever the expressions f and g are both defined, they are identical and therefore algebraically equivalent.

For an expression, f, and the point, x_0, the cset is symbolically represented using the notation

$$\text{cset}(f, \{x_0\}). \tag{9.15}$$

The second argument in (9.15) is enclosed in braces because the cset is a mapping of sets to sets, in this case from the singleton set $\{x_0\}$ to the cset of f. Any expression's cset must be equal to the expression's value if it is defined.

The reason the expressions f and g in (9.14) are not everywhere identical is because argument values exist where f is defined and g is not. This is the reason their natural domains are not the same. Because csets need not be singleton sets (whereas real functions must be single-valued), it is possible for *cset equivalence* to hold when algebraically equivalent expressions do not have the same natural domain. Imposing cset equivalence for all argument values is the condition needed to define csets of expressions at any point. As a consequence, two positive results are achieved:

1. Sets are defined that an interval expression must contain, even when the original point expression is undefined.

2. Real and extended-real-system domain limitations are eliminated.

For example, in the present case cset equivalence requires that if functions f and g are to be cset equivalent then

$$\text{cset}(f, \{x_0\}) = \text{cset}(g, \{x_0\}) \tag{9.16}$$

for all values of x_0, including $-\infty$, -1, 0, and $+\infty$.

From this requirement, a conclusion can be made about the cset of the expression $h(x) = \frac{1}{x}$ at the point $x_0 = 0$. Because $\frac{1}{0}$ is undefined in the real number system, it is natural to conclude that the cset of h at the point $x_0 = 0$ is the empty set, $\emptyset$. However, this leads to the conclusion that the cset of g in (9.14b) at the point $x_0 = 0$ must also be empty. This contradicts the cset equivalence requirement that the csets of f and g are everywhere identical. The contradiction occurs because $f(0)$ is defined and equal to zero. Therefore $\text{cset}(f, \{0\}) = \{0\}$, but cset equivalence requires that $\text{cset}(g, \{0\}) = \text{cset}(f, \{0\})$. A consistent value for $\text{cset}(h, \{0\})$ is the set $\{-\infty, +\infty\} = \{-\infty\} \cup \{+\infty\}$. This result is also consistent with the csets of f and g both being the set $\{-\infty, +\infty\}$ if $x_0 = -1$.

The interval hull of an expression's cset is the narrowest interval result that can be returned for the enclosure of an expression evaluated at a point. The cset of an expression evaluated over an arbitrary set X_0 is simply the union of all possible csets as arguments range over their values. That is,

$$\text{cset}(f, \{X_0\}) = \bigcup_{x_0 \in \{X_0\}} \text{cset}(f, \{x_0\}). \tag{9.17}$$

Because intervals are sets, the cset of any expression over interval arguments is immediately defined by letting the set $\{X_0\}$ in (9.17) be an interval. Therefore, the containment constraint on the interval evaluation of an expression f when evaluated over an interval X is

$$f(X) \supseteq \text{hull}(\text{cset}(f, X)), \tag{9.18}$$

where $\text{hull}(S_1, \ldots, S_n)$ is the convex hull (or the narrowest closed interval) containing all the values in the set $\{S_1, \ldots, S_n\}$.

Extending this line of reasoning, it can be proved that the cset of any expression at any point inside its natural domain is simply the value of the expression. Strictly outside an expression's domain, the expression's cset is empty. On the boundary of the expression's natural domain, its cset is the expression's *closure*. The closure of an expression at a point is the union of all possible limiting sequences of the expression as its argument approaches the argument value in question. For example, with $x_j = \frac{1}{\pm j}$, $\lim_{j \to \infty} x_j = 0$, and with $h(x) = \frac{1}{x}$, then

$$\text{cset}(h, \{0\}) = \lim_{j \to \infty} \frac{1}{\pm x_j} \tag{9.19a}$$

$$= \lim_{j \to \infty} \pm j = \pm\infty. \tag{9.19b}$$

Note that in this case the cset is the set of two disjoint values, $-\infty$ and $+\infty$. Using the traditional notation $\overline{h}$ for the closure of the expression, h,

$$\overline{h}(\{0\}) = \{-\infty, +\infty\} \tag{9.20a}$$

$$= \text{cset}(h, \{0\}). \tag{9.20b}$$

This is a particular example of the cset closure identity, which is proved in [478].

A subtle point is that an expression's closure is not defined if the expression has an empty domain. This case is described in Chapter 4 of [191].

The csets for the arithmetic indeterminate forms are

$$\text{cset}\,(x - y, \{(+\infty, +\infty)\}) = [-\infty, +\infty], \tag{9.21a}$$

$$\text{cset}\,(x \times y, \{(0, +\infty)\}) = [-\infty, +\infty], \tag{9.21b}$$

$$\text{cset}\,(x \div y, \{(0, 0)\}) = [-\infty, +\infty], \tag{9.21c}$$

$$\text{cset}\,(x \div y, \{(+\infty, +\infty)\}) = [0, +\infty]. \tag{9.21d}$$

The cset closure identity extends to expressions of n variables, whether the expressions are single-valued functions with different natural domains or multivalued relations. The practical consequence for the implementation of compiler support of interval data types is that *without exception*, any interval expression's cset is a defined set of values that the interval result of evaluating the expression must contain. It is this fact that permits closed interval systems to be defined and implemented.

To simplify notation, the formally correct cset $(f, \{x_0\})$ notation can be replaced by $f(x_0)$, with the understanding that any symbolic expression or function represents the expression's or the function's cset. Hereafter, this convention is followed.

Context-dependent literal constants. Literal interval constants are represented with square brackets and a comma separating the infimum and supremum, for example, in [0.1, 0.2]. To represent a degenerate interval containing a particular value, the notation [0.1] is also accepted in f95. This eliminates the need to enter both the lower and upper bounds when they are equal.

Because the external value of a literal constant is self-evident, internal interval constants can be constructed with an appropriate KTPV provided by context from the expression in which the literal constant appears. For example, in the interval code fragment

```
INTERVAL(8) X
X = [0.1_4]
```

KIND(X) = 8 and KIND(0.1_4) = 4. If the literal constant [0.1_4] is interpreted as a KTPV-4 INTERVAL containing the number $1/10$, then the interval variable, X, will be set to this value, which is not as narrow as the interval [0.1_8]. Alternatively, if it is recognized that the external value of the literal constant [0.1_4] is exactly $1/10$, then the narrowest possible KTPV-8 interval containing this value can be constructed and assigned to the interval variable, X. The context of the expression in which the literal constant appears is used to determine the KTPV of the interval to which the external value of the literal constant is converted.

A significant convenience associated with this mechanism is that the KTPV of X can be changed and no expression in which X occurs needs to be touched. All the literal constants in these expressions will be adjusted accordingly when expression context changes. Indeed, no KTPVs are necessary when specifying interval literal constants.

Only when there is no expression context, as in the code fragment

```
PRINT *, [0.1],
```

is the KTPV of the literal interval constant used.

Widest-need expression evaluation.   f95 has two expression processing modes denoted by the command-line macros

```
-xia=strict, and
-xia=widestneed, or simply
-xia.
```

In -xia=strict mode, all the data items in any interval expression must be intervals with the same KTPV. Any deviation is a compile-time error that is flagged. "Strict" is the only available mode in the C++ class library.

Widest-need expression processing (see [101] and [476]) is used to guarantee that mixed-mode expressions involving interval and noninterval (REAL and/or INTEGER) data items satisfy the containment constraint of interval arithmetic. Widest-need expression processing promotes data items to the required type and highest KTPV in the expression *before* expression evaluation begins. In an interval context, the compiler scans each expression to determine if it contains any interval data items. In assignment statements, the left-hand side (or object of the assignment) is included in the scan for interval types. If any interval data items are found, the expression to be evaluated is an interval expression and all data items in it are promoted to intervals with the maximum KTPV found anywhere in the assignment statement, including the object of the assignment. Only then does expression evaluation begin. Widest-need expression processing permits interval and noninterval data items, including variables and literal constants, to be freely mixed in the same expression without violating the containment constraint of interval arithmetic.

Single-number input/output.   An inconvenient aspect of interval arithmetic is reading and interactively entering interval data. Scanning interval output to determine the accuracy of printed results is mind numbing and eye straining. Entering interval data is error prone when the infimum and supremum differ only in the last few of many digits.

To avoid this difficulty, a single-number interval format (see [475] and [397]) is supported in f95. In this format, the last decimal digit is used to construct an interval. Any single decimal number not contained in square brackets denotes an interval constructed by subtracting and adding one unit to the last decimal digit of the single number. For example,

```
0.123 = [0.122, 0.124].
```

Trailing zero digits are significant, for example, in

```
0.12300 = [0.12299, 0.12301].
```

To denote a degenerate interval, square brackets around a single number are used as described above in the case of literal interval constants. Thus

$$[0.123] = \frac{123}{1000}. \tag{9.22}$$

New, interval-specific format edit descriptors are introduced to support single-number input/output. Whenever a data item is input into a variable in an interval input list item, single-number processing is automatically available, regardless of the edit descriptor used. On output, the interval data display format can be controlled. The intrinsic function NDIGITS is used during program execution to identify the maximum number of digits needed to display the maximum possible accuracy of a given interval data item using a single-number edit descriptor.

9.5 Fortran Code Example

The following code example[40] illustrates how the above syntax and semantics are used to write a small program that implements the interval version of Newton's algorithm for computing roots of a given continuous nonlinear function of one variable. The interval algorithm is noteworthy because it has the same asymptotic quadratic convergence as the point version of Newton's method. In addition, the interval algorithm has none of the undesirable characteristics of the point method. In particular, the interval version converges at least as quickly as bisection and is guaranteed never to cycle. Even more importantly, the interval algorithm (within the limits of the floating-point precision employed) isolates and bounds *all* the roots of a continuous nonlinear function. The algorithm can be extended to systems of nonlinear equations. See [193] and [191]. It can also be extended to gracefully handle discontinuous functions.

```
SUBROUTINE Newton(init_X, root_eps, f_eps)
INTERVAL(8), INTENT(IN) :: init_X
REAL(8), INTENT(IN) :: f_eps, root_eps
REAL(8) mid_of_X
INTEGER, PARAMETER :: STACK_SIZE = 1000
INTERVAL(8) domain_stack(STACK_SIZE)
INTEGER stack_pointer
INTERVAL(8) cur_X, new_X, I_mid_of_X, I_deriv, I_val_f
stack_pointer = 1
domain_stack(stack_pointer) = init_X
MAIN_LOOP: DO WHILE (stack_pointer .NE. 0)
  cur_X = domain_stack(stack_pointer)
  stack_pointer = stack_pointer - 1
  DO
    I_val_f = f_interval(cur_X)
    IF (.NOT. (0.0 .IN. I_val_f)) CYCLE MAIN_LOOP
      IF (wid(cur_X) < root_eps .AND. mag(I_val_f) < f_eps) THEN
        CALL print_root(cur_X)
        CYCLE MAIN_LOOP
      ENDIF ! (wid(cur_X) < root_eps )
      mid_of_X = mid(cur_X)
      I_deriv = f_deriv(cur_X)
      IF (0.0 .IN. I_deriv) THEN
        IF (mid_of_X == inf(cur_X) .OR. mid_of_X == sup(cur_X)) &
  & CYCLE MAIN_LOOP
        stack_pointer = stack_pointer + 1
        IF (stack_pointer > STACK_SIZE) THEN
```

[40]Thanks for this program to Alexander Kulibaba, Alexander Semenov, and Ilya Vazhev of the Interval Compiler Team at UniPro in Novosibirsk, Siberia.

```
              PRINT *, "More than ", STACK_SIZE, "intervals required."
              PRINT *, "Increase PARAMETER STACK_SIZE in SUBROUTINE Newton."
              RETURN
            ENDIF
            domain_stack(stack_pointer) = INTERVAL(mid_of_X, sup(cur_X))
            cur_X = INTERVAL(inf(cur_X), mid_of_X)
            CYCLE
          ELSE   ! f' is bounded away from 0 => a Newton step
            I_mid_of_X = INTERVAL(mid_of_X)
            new_X = cur_X .IX. I_mid_of_X - f_interval(I_mid_of_X)/I_deriv
            IF (ISEMPTY(new_X)) THEN
              CYCLE MAIN_LOOP
            ELSEIF (cur_X == new_X) THEN
              CALL print_root(cur_X)
              CYCLE MAIN_LOOP
            ELSE
              cur_X = new_X
              CYCLE
            ENDIF
          ENDIF   ! (0.0 .IN. I_deriv)
    ENDDO
  ENDDO MAIN_LOOP
  CONTAINS
  INTERVAL(8) FUNCTION f_interval(x) !  interval function
  INTERVAL(8), INTENT(IN) :: x
  f_interval = exp(x) - x - 5.0
  END FUNCTION f_interval
  !
  INTERVAL(8) FUNCTION f_deriv(x) ! interval first derivative
  INTERVAL(8), INTENT(IN) :: x
  f_deriv = exp(x) - 1.0
  END FUNCTION f_deriv
  !
  END SUBROUTINE Newton
  !
  PROGRAM TEST_NEWTON
  INTERVAL(8) X_0
  REAL(8) f_eps, root_eps
  X_0 = [-100.0_8, 100.0_8]
  f_eps = 1.0E-5_8
  root_eps = 1.0E-5_8
  PRINT*, "Over the interval ", X_0, "use the interval "
  PRINT*, "Newton algorithm to find all roots of the nonlinear "
  PRINT*, "function f(X) = EXP(X) - X - 5.0."
  PRINT*, "Roots are printed using the [inf, sup] and single-number"
  PRINT*, "format in which root + [-1, +1]_uld contains the root."
  PRINT*
  CALL Newton(X_0, root_eps, f_eps)
  END PROGRAM TEST_NEWTON
  !
  SUBROUTINE print_root(X)
  INTERVAL(8), INTENT(IN) :: X
  WRITE(UNIT=6, FMT="(' root = ', VF40.15, ' or ', Y25.15)") X, X
  END SUBROUTINE print_root
```

Compiling this program with the command "f95 -xia" and running it produces the following output:

```
Over the interval  [-100.0,100.0] use the interval
Newton algorithm to find all roots of the nonlinear
function f(X) = EXP(X) - X - 5.0.
Roots are printed using the [inf, sup] and single-number
format in which root + [-1, +1]_uld contains the root.

root =   [-4.993216486979403,-4.993216048078400] or  -4.993216
root =   [ 1.936847403131665, 1.936847411893129] or   1.93684741
```

The code uses support for interval data types to implement the interval version of Newton's algorithm for isolating and tightly bounding all the roots of the nonlinear function of one variable

$$f(x) = e^x - x - 5. \tag{9.23}$$

The code on pages 191–193 can be modified easily to find all the roots of a user-supplied function.

9.6 Fortran Standard Implications

The interval-specific innovations that are implemented in f95 and briefly described above are designed to provide complete, reliable, and easy-to-use intrinsic compiler support for interval data types. To accomplish these goals, some deviations from the Fortran 95 and Fortran 2003 standards are necessary. For interval data types to become part of standard Fortran, these deviations must be addressed. There are two alternatives: If intervals are added as an intrinsic data type to Fortran, then the required extensions (or their equivalent) must be added to guarantee that the containment constraint of interval arithmetic is not violated. Alternatively, if interval support is only possible through Fortran modules, additional module features will be required to support the interval features users expect.

9.6.1 The Interval-specific alternative

If intrinsic interval data types are introduced, language simplicity can be achieved by permitting only strict expression processing. This forces programmers to bear the responsibility for all data type and KTPV conversions. Ease-of-use features, such as single-number input/output can also be eliminated to keep the standard small.

Mixed-mode and KTPV expressions require widest-need expression processing, which can be argued is permitted by the standard under the "mathematically equivalent" clause in the discussion of permitted Fortran expression processing optimizations. Intervals introduce a second optimization goal besides speed: narrow interval width.

The next challenge to compiler developers is to introduce compile-time algorithm changes that simultaneously increase runtime speed and reduce interval result width. Provided the containment constraint of interval arithmetic is not violated, there must be no language constraints imposed on permitted compiler optimizations to achieve runtime performance and narrow interval width. The need to perform symbolic expression-altering optimizations to achieve narrow interval width is a good reason why interval data type support is best made intrinsic.

9.6.2 The enriched module alternative

If interval modules (or class libraries) are to provide the features users require, a number of additions must be made to the existing Fortran module and C++ class infrastructures. These include

- edit-descriptor overloading and user defined, type-specific edit descriptors to permit single-number input/output;

- expression processing control as represented in widest-need expression processing and context-dependent literal constants;

- overloaded and user defined operator precedence;

- user defined variable attributes and associated functionality; and

- software development tool integration, as provided in debuggers and performance analysis tools.

These features and others under development are required to support commercial applications that employ user defined types. The existing, or somewhat enhanced, module functionality is sufficient to support many user defined types. However, core functionality—such as that provided by intervals—is best made intrinsic.

9.7 Conclusions

Intervals contain the features needed to cause a renaissance in scientific and technical high-performance computing. Consequently, Fortran is a natural language in which to write many foundation interval solvers and applications. With its enhanced object-oriented features, Fortran should be able to successfully compete with C++ in many numerical applications that have drifted away from Fortran. For example, numerically intense nonlinear interval solvers should remain Fortran's purview.

Intervals have attained the stature and success needed to justify them being an intrinsic data type in Fortran, because of the following:

- Rigorous error analysis is more often required when computers are used (as they increasingly are) to perform calculations for which correct answers are unknown.

- The processing power of computers makes it possible to solve nonlinear design and analysis problems using interval nonlinear solvers. See [111], for example.

- Closed interval systems have fundamental consequences for both real and interval analysis.

Sun f95 includes much of the necessary and sufficient syntax and semantics to support commercial interval applications. More is under development at Sun Microsystems Laboratories.

Chapter 10

Computer-assisted Proofs and Self-validating Methods

Siegfried M. Rump

10.1   Introduction

In this chapter[41] we discuss the possibility of computing validated answers to mathematical problems. Among such approaches are so-called computer-assisted proofs, exact computations, methods from computer algebra, and self-validating methods. We will discuss common aspects and differences of these methods, as well as their potential reliability. We present in detail some concepts for self-validating methods, and their mathematical background, as well as implementation details.

Self-validating methods will be introduced using INTLAB, a MATLAB toolbox entirely written in MATLAB. Due to the operator concept it is a convenient way to get acquainted with self-validating methods. Many examples in this chapter are given in executable INTLAB code. This toolbox is freely available from our homepage for noncommercial use. To date we have an estimated number of 3500 users in more than 40 countries.

We stress that this exposition will cover only a small part of the subject, some basic concepts of self-validating methods. Nevertheless, we hope to give some impression of this interesting and promising area.

10.2   Proofs and Computers

Since the invention of digital computers the question has arisen (again) whether computers can perform mathematical proofs. Put into that form the answer, in my opinion, is a simple "No!" since computers don't do anything without some person ordering them to do so. So a more appropriate formulation may be whether proofs may be performed with the aid of digital computers.

---

[41]Extended workout of the special lecture presented at the Annual Conference of Japan SIAM at Kyushu University, Fukuoka, October 7–9, 2001; an excerpt has been published in Bull. JSIAM, 2004.

IBM   Thomas J. Watson Research Center
             P.O. Box 218
             Yorktown Heights, New York 10598

$2^{19937}-1$ is a prime

Figure 10.1. *IBM prime letterhead.*

There are a number of famous examples where people claimed to have proven a theorem with the aid of digital computers. And people became proud of this so that it even found its way into letterheads and postmarks. For example, when you received a letter from IBM Thomas J. Watson Research Center in Yorktown Heights in the 1970's, the letterhead appeared as pictured in Figure 10.1. At that time this was the largest known Mersenne [312] prime, with some 600 decimals. Primality was proven in 1971 [456] by the Lucas–Lehmer test, and this fact even found its way into the Guiness book of records. A new era in the run for the largest explicitly known prime began with the Great Internet Mersenne Prime Search (GIMPS). In this mutual international effort $2^{6972593} - 1$, a number with more than two million decimal digits, was found and earned the discoverer Nayn Hajratwala some 50,000 U.S. dollars. The latest finding in 2004 is $2^{24036583} - 1$ with more than seven million digits.

Department of Mathematics

273 Altgeld Hall
1409 West Green Street
Urbana, IL 61801

FOUR COLORS

SUFFICE

Figure 10.2. *University of Illinois postmark.*

When receiving a letter from the University of Illinois at Urbana-Champaign in the late 1970's or early 1980's, next to the postage stamp you would see what is pictured in Figure 10.2 (thanks to Bhama Srinivasan for providing the original picture), crediting the celebrated effort of Kenneth Appel and Wolfgang Haken. They checked thousands of sample graphs using some two thousand hours of computing time to attack the Four Color Theorem. At the time there was (and still is) quite some discussion about whether their efforts really "proved" the theorem. There are significant differences between the first and the second example.

The first example, proving primality of a Mersenne number, uses solely long integer arithmetic. There are numerous implementations of such packages for algebraic computations. And, the Lucas–Lehmer test for $n = 19937$ takes less than a minute on today's laptops. Moreover, the implementation is very clear and straightforward, and the arithmetic programs have been tested innumerable times. So it seems not "likely" that there are errors in such programs.

In contrast, the attack of the Four Color Theorem consists of very many individual programs, seeking coloring patterns for individual graphs. The programming is by no means straightforward, and comparatively few people have looked at the programs. Once I asked Wolfgang Haken what would be his answer to the obvious question of whether the proof is valid. He explained, "Well, put it this way. Every error in our programming found so far has been repaired within 24 hours." We tend to agree with Paul Erdös, the late ever-traveling mathematician, who said [208], "I'm not an expert on the four color problem, but I assume the proof is true. However, it's not beautiful. I'd prefer to see a proof that gives insight into why four colors are sufficient." In fact, the proof by Appel and Haken seems ill suited for *Proofs from THE BOOK* [9]. There are newer approaches to proving the Four Color Theorem; see, for example, [384].

Before going on we collect some more examples of possibilities of proofs by computers. Tarski [437] proved his famous theorem that the elementary theory of real closed fields is decidable. Later Collins [99] developed his Quantifier elimination method, which drastically reduces the necessary computational time to "prove" a corresponding theorem. With this quantifier elimination method, questions from geometry can be reduced to equivalent, quantifier-free formulae. The input formula is a theorem if and only if it reduces to "1" or "always true."

Another famous example is Risch's algorithm [379, 173] for integration in finite terms. This algorithm "decides" whether some function consisting of basic arithmetic operations, roots, powers, and elementary standard functions can be integrated in finite terms, and if so, it calculates a closed formula for the integral. It is a decision algorithm, and the maximum computing time can be estimated in terms of the length of the input. The algorithm is available, for example, in the computer algebra system Maple. For the input

$$\int x e^{x^2} dx = \frac{1}{2} e^{x^2} + C,$$

the integral can also be easily calculated by standard methods. But that

$$\int e^{x^2} dx \quad \text{is not solvable}$$

is a nontrivial result: It *proves* that no finite combination of arithmetic operations, powers, or elementary standard functions can be found such that the derivative is equal to e^{x^2}. In fact, the algorithm does more by calculating that

$$\int e^{x^2} dx = -\frac{1}{2} \sqrt{-\pi} \cdot \operatorname{erf}(\sqrt{-1} \cdot x) + C$$

involving the error function, which cannot be expressed in finite terms.

Another recent example is the Kepler conjecture that the face-centered cubic packing is the densest packing of equally sized balls. This almost 400-year-old conjecture was solved by Hales in 1998 [188]. More examples can be found in [155].

So what is common and what are differences in the above examples? In other words,

What is a proof?

We do not want (and cannot) give a final answer to that question, but we want to offer some relevant thoughts. The traditional mathematical proof can be followed line by line with pencil and paper. And this is still the classical way mathematicians work. As mathematicians are human beings, they might draw false conclusions, and there are famous examples of that. Often such "false" approaches, originally intended to prove some specific problem, lead to other interesting and new insights. A typical and well-known example is Kummer's approach to prove Fermat's Last Theorem. Although it did not prove the theorem, it led to a deep and different understanding of the matter.

There are also examples of "theorems" that were accepted for years but proved later to be false. A nice example is the following.

NOT A THEOREM. *Let a C^1 function $f : \mathbb{R}^2 \to \mathbb{R}$ be given. For some given point x_0, assume that for every $y \in \mathbb{R}^2$ the projection $f_y : \mathbb{R} \to \mathbb{R}$ with $f_y(\lambda) := f(x_0 + \lambda y)$ has a minimum at $\lambda = 0$. Then f has a minimum at x_0.*

This was presented in beginners' courses in calculus some 100 years ago by saying the "proof" is obvious. With today's education we have seen too many counterexamples of similar "theorems" and would ask for a solid proof. In this case, Peano (cf. [430]) gave the nice counterexample $f(x_1, x_2) = (x_2^2 - 2px_1)(x_2^2 - 2qx_1)$ at the origin, where $p > q > 0$.

Moreover, a proof becomes a proof by human beings reading, understanding, and accepting the proof. If a proof becomes lengthy and difficult, naturally the number of mathematicians who really follow the ideas decreases. A famous example is the celebrated result by Feit and Thompson, who proved in 1963 that all nonabelian finite simple groups are of even order. They published this result in "Solvability of Groups of Odd Order," a 250-page paper that appeared in the *Pacific Journal of Mathematics*, 13 (1963), pp. 775–1029. Despite the importance of the paper several journals declined to publish it because of its length.

Of course, we do not question the correctness of the result. The point is that acceptance of a proof is also based on mutual trust: If trustworthy colleagues accept a proof, we also tend to accept it—a very reasonable point of view.

So what does it mean to "follow and to accept" a proof? Consider the following story. At the meeting of the American Mathematical Society in October 1903 in New York City, Frank N. Cole gave a quite unusual "talk." The story goes that when his talk was announced, Cole went to the blackboard and wrote the following two integers

$$761838257287 * 193707721$$

and multiplied them out manually. He then wrote

$$2^{67} - 1$$

on the board and worked it out manually. The results of the two computations were equal. Thunderous applause broke out. Cole sat down. He never spoke a word, and there were no questions. The account of this event appeared in a letter in the February 1983 issue of Scientific American. When asked later how long it took to find this factorization of the Mersenne number, Cole explained, "Three years, every Sunday."

Imagine if this happened today: how many of us would sit down and work out the multiplications by hand? I guess many would at least use a pocket calculator or use some computer algebra system—which can also be found on advanced pocket calculators today (such as mupad and derive). I also guess that many of us would have no difficulty accepting the use of such electronic equipment as part of the proof.

However, there are different levels of trust. I think it is fair to say that for the purpose of supporting a mathematical proof,

- the use of pocket calculators is widely accepted,
- the use of computer algebra systems is more or less accepted,
- but the use of floating-point arithmetic seems questionable to many mathematicians.

But is this fair? Common sense is sometimes biased by what we want to believe. For example, statistics tells us that the chance is higher one would be killed by a bee than by a shark. Similarly, pocket calculators look simple enough to be reliable because—which is of course true in a certain sense—the probability of an error may be considered to be proportional to the complexity of the system. But does this mean that pocket calculators, on the market for decades, are error-free?

We know that this is not true. Severe errors due to the limited length of the internal accumulator occur in many pocket calculators (see Figure 10.3): the standard 8-digit plus-minus-times-divide-square root pocket calculator with decimal point but *without* exponent, the one you may have found as an ad in your mail for some years, are still widely in use today.

Figure 10.3. *Pocket calculators with 8 decimal digits, no exponent.*

Calculate with any calculator of this kind

$$1\,000\,000 - 999\,999.99$$

Both numbers have 8 significant digits, so both can be stored in the calculator without any error. If the units are Dollars, the result is obviously 1 cent, whereas the calculator will give the result as 10 cents—a typical effect of the too short internal 8-digit accumulator: First the numbers are adjusted according to their decimal point such that digits of equal value can be added.

$$\begin{array}{r|l} 1\,000\,000 & \\ 999\,999.9 & 9 \\ \hline 0.1 & \end{array}$$

This implies that the subtrahend $999\,999.99$ has to be shifted one to the right. However, the internal accumulator is also only 8 decimal digits long, so that the final figure 9 vanishes. The result is a kind of catastrophic cancellation, but due to an inappropriate implementation of the arithmetic.

So if such simple machines can produce results with a relative error of 900 %, we might ask whether personal computers or mainframes can produce any reliable result at all. Many would answer this question with a simple "no" meaning that "results obtained by floating-point operations are per se not reliable." Not long ago numerical mathematics was considered "dirty." And many people believe(d) that floating-point computations, where almost every operation is afflicted with some error, may produce some useful approximations, but they are not suited for any kind of verification or guarantee.

The above example occurs not only in pocket calculators. For example, mainframes such as the Univac 1108 in use until the 1980's calculated

$$16777216 - 16777215 = 2.$$

The reason is again the short accumulator of length 24 bits, the same as the working precision, and $16777216 = 2^{24}$. A similar error occurred in the early 1960's in IBM S/360 mainframes, and we can thank Vel Kahan that the company changed the architecture to cure this. Even until very recently similarly poor implementations could be found in Cray supercomputers. This is the reason why sometimes the statement

$$a = 2 * a - a$$

can be found in programs. It "simulates" one bit less precision so that an accumulator of working precision has one additional bit compared to this reduced precision.

10.3   Arithmetical Issues

To discuss whether it is at all possible to produce correct or validated results on a digital computer, consider the following example. Let a real matrix A be given, and for simplicity assume that all entries A_{ij} are floating-point numbers. In other words, the matrix is exactly representable in the computer. Can we "prove" that the matrix A is nonsingular?

A typical aspect of self-validating methods is the mutual benefit of theoretical analysis and practical implementation. A possible theoretical approach goes as follows. Let R be an arbitrary real matrix, a preconditioner. If the spectral radius $\varrho(I - RA)$ is less than 1, then R and A are nonsingular because otherwise $C := I - RA$ would have an eigenvalue 1. By Perron–Frobenius theory we know that $\rho(C) \leq \rho(|C|)$, where $|C|$ denotes the nonnegative matrix consisting of entrywise absolute values $|C_{ij}|$. Moreover, a well-known theorem by Collatz [98] says that

$$|I - RA|x < x \qquad (10.1)$$

for an arbitrary entrywise positive vector x implies $\rho(|I - RA|) < 1$, and therefore $\rho(I - RA) < 1$ and R and A are nonsingular. In other words, if we can prove (10.1) for any positive vector x, for example, the vector consisting of all 1's, then we have proved A to be nonsingular. The result remains true without any further requirements on the matrix R. A good choice is an approximate inverse of A.

Now we aim to verify (10.1) in floating-point arithmetic. To do that we need further information about properties of floating-point arithmetic or, as trivial as it sounds, we need to know

How is the floating-point arithmetic in use defined?

Until the 1980's not much information about this was available from computer manufacturers. This was one reason for a mutual initiative to define the first standardization of floating-point arithmetic, the IEEE 754 binary standard in [215]. Among other things, this standard defines the maximum relative error of all floating-point operations to be less than or equal to the unit roundoff **u**. Moreover, the floating-point standard defines directed roundings, a rounding downward and a rounding upward.

Today the IEEE 754 standard of floating-point arithmetic is implemented in the large majority of all computers in use in scientific computation, from PCs to workstations to mainframes. Switching the rounding mode is frequently done by setting the processor into a specific rounding mode. For example, if the processor is switched to rounding downward, then *every* subsequent floating-point operation yields as the result the unique maximal floating-point number less than or equal to the exact result. This is quite a remarkable property, and it is a *mathematical* property we can build upon.

Denote by fl(*expression*) the value of an expression with all operations executed as floating-point operations. Moreover, let fl_∇(*expression*) and fl_Δ(*expression*) denote that the rounding mode has been switched to downward or upward, respectively (if the rounding symbol is omitted, we assume rounding to nearest). Then, we already obtain the mathematical statement

$$\text{for all } x, y \in \mathbf{F}: \quad \text{fl}_\nabla(x + y) = \text{fl}_\Delta(x + y) \quad \Leftrightarrow \quad x + y \in \mathbf{F}.$$

The (true, real) result of a floating-point operation is a (representable) floating-point number if and only if the floating-point results obtained by rounding downward and rounding upward are equal. This is also true for subtraction, multiplication, and division. It is also true for the square root:

$$\text{for all } x \in \mathbf{F}: \quad \text{fl}_\nabla(\sqrt{x}) = \text{fl}_\Delta(\sqrt{x}) \quad \Leftrightarrow \quad \sqrt{x} \in \mathbf{F}.$$

These results are also true in the presence of underflow; it is a *mathematically reliable statement*. At this point one may argue that this, as a mathematical statement, is true only as long as

- the implementation of floating-point arithmetic actually follows the definition by the IEEE 754 standard,

- the compiler, the operating system, and in fact all of the hardware and software involved are working correctly,

- no external distortions, such as very short power failures, radiation, and other nasty things occur.

This is absolutely true. In this sense we can never trust the result of any machine, and mathematical proofs with the aid of computers are not possible at all (however, human brains may also fail). On the other hand, the arithmetic of digital computers is tested very thoroughly every day, and a failure, at least due to one of the first two reasons, seems unlikely.

But there is more than a "likeliness argument," and we want to further explore this. Years ago I was working on a rigorous implementation of elementary standard functions, and I had an intensive discussion about the accuracy and reliability of the standard functions provided by some library. In a nutshell, I was asked why it is necessary at all to work on "reliable" standard functions when no example is known where the existing library produces an error greater than one unit in the last place.

But there is a fundamental difference between the accuracy of the floating-point arithmetic and the accuracy of standard functions in a library. The latter are implemented by very clever techniques such as continued fractions, table-based approaches, or Cordic algorithms. Everything is done to provide an accurate approximation of the result. But for most libraries there is no *rigorous* error estimate valid for *all* possible input arguments. And millions of nonfailing tests cannot *prove* that an algorithm never fails. In contrast, the implementation of floating-point algorithms according to the IEEE 754 standard is well understood, and the analysis shows that conclusions like (10.1) are valid for all possible input arguments.

So the mathematical specification of the algorithms for floating-point arithmetic can be correct and never-failing, but the implementation might not follow the specification. We assume in the following that the implementation of floating-point arithmetic follows its specification and therefore the IEEE 754 standard, and that the software and hardware in use are operating correctly. Then, we may ask again whether it is possible to validate results with the aid of digital computers.

For the above example, to validate (10.1) and therefore the nonsingularity of the matrix A this is simple. The only additional knowledge we need is that when x is a floating-point number, $|x|$ is a floating-point number as well. Then, for given R, A, and x, we calculate

$$
\begin{aligned}
C_2 &:= \mathrm{fl}_\nabla(R * A - I), \\
C_1 &:= \mathrm{fl}_\Delta(R * A - I), \\
C &:= \max(\mathrm{abs}(C_1), \mathrm{abs}(C_2)), \\
y &:= \mathrm{fl}_\Delta(C * x).
\end{aligned}
$$

By definition,

$$
\mathrm{fl}_\nabla(r_{ik} \cdot a_{kj}) \le r_{ik} \cdot a_{kj} \le \mathrm{fl}_\Delta(r_{ik} \cdot a_{kj}) \quad \text{for all } i, j, k,
$$

and therefore

$$
C_1 \le RA - I \le C_2,
$$

where the comparison is to be understood entrywise. This implies

$$|I - RA| \leq \max(|C_1|, |C_2|) = C,$$

where maximum, absolute value, and comparison are again to be understood component-wise. Combining this with (10.1) it follows that

$$y < x \quad \text{implies } A \text{ (and } R) \text{ are nonsingular.}$$

Note that the inequalities need not to be true when replacing $RA - I$ by $I - RA$. Also note that this approach needs two switches of the rounding mode and otherwise only floating-point operations; in particular, no branches are required. This means that matrix multiplications can be performed by BLAS routines [285, 124, 120, 122] and thus are very fast. So in a certain way the rounded operations create speed with rigor. In the following we want to discuss this in more detail, particularly the domain of applicability and the distinction from computer algebra methods.

10.4 Computer Algebra Versus Self-validating Methods

A major objective of computer algebra methods is to deliver not only correct answers but also exact answers. For example, it is standard to calculate in algebraic number fields [173]. Then, for instance, $\sqrt[3]{17} - \sqrt[5]{5}$ is not calculated by some numerical approximation within hundreds of digits of accuracy but as an element of a suitable algebraic extension of the field of rational numbers. Thus the operation is *exact*. This allows for the development of so-called decision algorithms: Given an inquiry as a yes/no problem, a decision algorithm will definitely answer this question in a finite computing time, where the latter can be estimated in terms of the length of the input data.

We already mentioned famous examples of decision algorithms, such as quantifier elimination and Risch's integration in finite terms. Another famous and well-known example for the power of computer algebra algorithms is Gröbner bases. For a given system of multivariate polynomial equations it can be decided whether these are solvable, and the number of solutions can be calculated as well as inclusion intervals for the roots. A major breakthrough was the development of constructive and fast algorithms [58, 59].

Computer algebra methods generally always compute exactly. There are exceptions in the sense that error bounds may be calculated, if this is sufficient. But in that case there is usually a fall-back algorithm if error bounds are not of sufficient quality.

Exact computations may take quite some computing time. In contrast, self-validating methods calculate in floating-point arithmetic. This means they are fast, with the possibility of failure in the sense that no answer can be given. As we will see, they can *never fail* by giving a false answer.

This is the reason why self-validating methods are applicable only to well-posed problems. For example, we can verify that a matrix is nonsingular, but in general it is not possible to verify that it is singular. If the answer to a problem can change for arbitrarily small changes of the input data, then the problem is ill-posed and the slightest rounding error may change the answer. But self-validating methods *intentionally use floating-point arithmetic*, so such problems are beyond their scope.

Similarly, it is possible to calculate an inclusion of a multiple eigenvalue [390] or of a multiple root of a polynomial [393]. However, it is not possible to verify that the eigenvalue or root is indeed multiple, that is, that the multiplicity is greater than one. The computation of error bounds for a multiple root is well-posed, whereas the fact that the multiplicity is greater than one is ill-posed: The fact may change for arbitrarily small perturbations of the input data. So we may say that one reason for the speed of self-validating methods is the inaccuracy (the rounding) of floating-point operations.

One example of self-validating methods is that equation (10.1) implies nonsingularity of the matrices A and R. This is in fact a mainstream of self-validating methods, that is,

to verify the assumptions of mathematical theorems with the aid of digital computers.

This implies validity of the assertions, as in the simple example the nonsingularity of matrices. Obviously, the only requirement for the arithmetic in use to verify (10.1) is the availability of true error bounds. Using directed roundings is one possibility, using exact arithmetic would be another, and there are more possibilities. Another possibility that is widely used is interval arithmetic. Interval operations have the advantage of easy formulation and implementation. However, interval arithmetic does not have the best reputation. We will come to that in a moment.

10.5   Interval Arithmetic

Closed intervals are one possibility for representing sets of numbers. They were already described in a little recognized but nevertheless very comprehensive paper by Sunaga [432]; see also [318]. For the moment we ignore rounding errors and representation on the computer but define the set $\mathbb{IR}$ of real intervals as usual by

$$A \in \mathbb{IR} \ :\Leftrightarrow \ A \neq \emptyset \quad \text{and} \quad A = [\underline{a}, \overline{a}] = \{x \in \mathbb{R} : \underline{a} \le x \le \overline{a}\}.$$

In the degenerate case $\underline{a} = \overline{a}$, the interval $[\underline{a}, \overline{a}]$ represents one real number $a = \underline{a} = \overline{a}$ and can be identified with it. This defines the natural embedding of $\mathbb{R}$ into $\mathbb{IR}$ using so-called *point intervals* $[a, a]$. The interval operations between real intervals are just the power set operations. One easily verifies for all $A = [\underline{a}, \overline{a}]$, $B = [\underline{b}, \overline{b}] \in \mathbb{IR}$ and $\circ \in \{+, -, \cdot, /\}$

$$
\begin{aligned}
\{a \circ b : a \in A, b \in B\} &= \bigcap \{C \in \mathbb{IR} : \ a \circ b \in C \text{ for all } a \in A, b \in B\} \\
&= [\,\min(a \circ b : \ a \in A, b \in B), \max(a \circ b : \ a \in A, b \in B)\,] \\
&= [\,\min(\underline{a} \circ \underline{b}, \underline{a} \circ \overline{b}, \overline{a} \circ \underline{b}, \overline{a} \circ \overline{b}), \max(\underline{a} \circ \underline{b}, \underline{a} \circ \overline{b}, \overline{a} \circ \underline{b}, \overline{a} \circ \overline{b})\,] \\
&=: A \circ B,
\end{aligned}
$$

where $0 \notin B$ in case of division. It is also evident that

$$
\begin{aligned}
A + B &= [\underline{a} + \underline{b}, \overline{a} + \overline{b}], \\
A - B &= [\underline{a} - \overline{b}, \overline{a} - \underline{b}].
\end{aligned}
$$

The quality of an interval may be measured by its diameter $d(A) = d([\underline{a}, \overline{a}]) = \overline{a} - \underline{a}$. One computes

$$d(A + B) = d(A) + d(B),$$

but also $d(A - B) = d([\underline{a} - \overline{b}, \overline{a} - \underline{b}]) = (\overline{a} - \underline{b}) - (\underline{a} - \overline{b}) = (\overline{a} - \underline{a}) + (\overline{b} - \underline{b})$, and therefore

$$d(A - B) = d(A) + d(B). \tag{10.2}$$

So the diameter of the sum *and of the difference* of two intervals is equal to the sum of the diameters. This is a major reason for overestimation, as we will discuss in more detail later.

Similarly, bounds for multiplication and division can be determined by some case distinctions depending on the operands being entirely positive, negative, or including zero, respectively. Interval vectors can be defined equivalently by

$$\begin{pmatrix} [\underline{x}_1, \overline{x}_1] \\ \dots \\ [\underline{x}_n, \overline{x}_n] \end{pmatrix} \in (\mathbb{IR})^n \quad \text{or} \quad X = [\underline{x}, \overline{x}] \in \mathbb{IR}^n,$$

where the latter uses the partial ordering of vectors by componentwise comparison. We proceed similarly for matrices and define operations among matrices, vectors, and scalars by replacing every operation in the usual definition by the corresponding interval operation. For example, $Y = AX$ for interval quantities $X, Y \in \mathbb{IR}^n$ and $A \in \mathbb{IR}^{n \times n}$ is defined by

$$Y := AX \quad \text{with} \quad Y_i := \sum_{k=1}^{n} A_{ik} X_k \quad \text{for } 1 \leq i \leq n, \tag{10.3}$$

where additions and multiplications are the corresponding (scalar) interval operations. Obviously,

$$\widetilde{y} = \widetilde{A}\widetilde{x} \in Y \quad \text{for all } \widetilde{A} \in A, \widetilde{x} \in X.$$

This is one incarnation of the fundamental underlying principle of the inclusion isotonicity for all interval operations:

Inclusion isotonicity: For all interval quantities A, B and all operations $\circ \in \{+, -, \cdot, /\}$ such that $\widetilde{a} \circ \widetilde{b}$ is well defined for $\widetilde{a} \in A, \widetilde{b} \in B$ there holds

$$\widetilde{a} \circ \widetilde{b} \in A \circ B \quad \text{for all } \widetilde{a} \in A, \widetilde{b} \in B. \tag{10.4}$$

Inclusion isotonicity, the central property of interval arithmetic

We mention that the definition of interval operations is the *best possible* with respect to inclusion isotonicity: Moving any of the bounds "inward" will violate (10.4). However, there is nevertheless some overestimation. Consider

$$A \cdot X := \begin{pmatrix} -1 & 2 \\ 1 & 2 \end{pmatrix} \begin{pmatrix} [1, 2] \\ [1, 3] \end{pmatrix} = \begin{pmatrix} [0, 5] \\ [3, 8] \end{pmatrix}.$$

This defines a linear transformation of a rectangle resulting in a parallelogram. The resulting interval vector is the best possible in the sense that both interval components $[0, 5]$ and $[3, 8]$ cannot be narrowed without violating inclusion isotonicity. It is easy to find (real) vectors out of X such that the bounds 0, 5, 3, and 8 of the resulting interval vector are met.

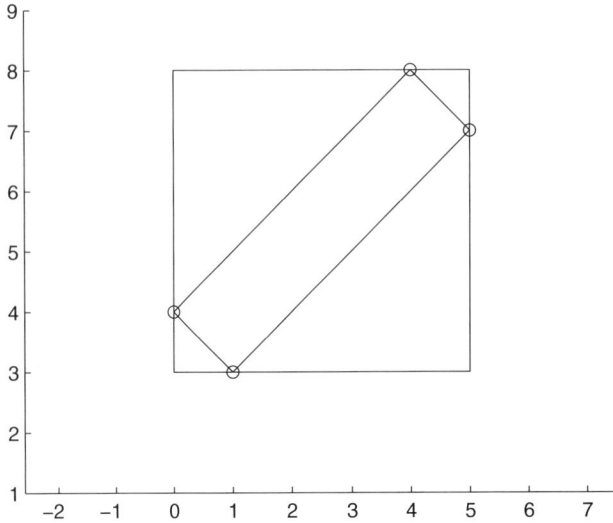

Figure 10.4. *Point matrix times interval vector.*

However, Figure 10.4 displays the true rectangle AX. Obviously no vector $x \in X$ can be found such that $A\widetilde{x} = (0, 3)^T$ for $\widetilde{x} \in X$. This illustrates a common pitfall of interval arithmetic: Given $A \in \mathbb{R}^{n \times n}$, $b \in \mathbb{R}^n$, and $X \in \mathbb{IR}^n$, and check $b \in AX$ to verify $A^{-1}b \in X$. This is an incorrect conclusion because

$$\text{for all } x \in X : \quad Ax \in AX$$

but not necessarily

$$y \in AX \quad \Rightarrow \quad \exists x \in X : \quad y = Ax.$$

These fundamentals of interval operations have been written down many times, and the interested reader is referred to [319], [340], or [11] and the literature cited therein for more details.

We briefly mention that complex interval arithmetic can be defined as well. In this case, for function theoretical reasons, it seems more appropriate to use discs, i.e., a midpoint-radius arithmetic (but rectangular arithmetic is also used). Define for $a \in \mathbb{C}, 0 \leq r \in \mathbb{R}$,

$$\langle a, r \rangle := \{z \in \mathbb{C} : |a - z| \leq r\}. \tag{10.5}$$

Then interval operations satisfying inclusion isotonicity have been defined in [159], for example,

$$\langle a, r \rangle \cdot \langle b, s \rangle := \langle ab, |a|s + r|b| + rs \rangle. \tag{10.6}$$

Corresponding complex interval vector and matrix operations are defined similarly as in (10.3).

10.6   Directed Roundings

The definitions thus far are for real bounds and exactly performed operations. For implementation on digital computers, special care must be taken since the result of a floating-point operation is, in general, not a floating-point number. These problems can be solved by using directed rounding. First, recall that the set $\mathbb{IF}$ of intervals with floating-point bounds is defined by

$$A \in \mathbb{IF} :\Leftrightarrow A \neq \emptyset \quad \text{and} \quad A = [\underline{a}, \overline{a}] = \{x \in \mathbb{R} : \underline{a} \leq x \leq \overline{a}\} \text{ for } \underline{a}, \overline{a} \in \mathbb{F}.$$

Note that the two floating-point bounds $\underline{a}$ and $\overline{a}$ represent the set of all *real* numbers between them. In the degenerate case $\underline{a} = \overline{a}$ this is one single floating-point number, and every floating-point number can be identified with this point interval. In other words, $\mathbb{F} \subseteq \mathbb{IF}$ with the natural embedding. When computing with intervals having floating-point endpoints the same definitions as above can be used except that the lower bound is computed by rounding downward, and the upper bound is computed by rounding upward. For example,

$$[\underline{a}, \overline{a}] + [\underline{b}, \overline{b}] = [\mathrm{fl}_\nabla(\underline{a} + \underline{b}), \mathrm{fl}_\triangle(\overline{a} + \overline{b})]$$

or

$$[\underline{a}, \overline{a}] - [\underline{b}, \overline{b}] = [\mathrm{fl}_\nabla(\underline{a} - \overline{b}), \mathrm{fl}_\triangle(\overline{a} - \underline{b})].$$

Other definitions follow the same lines. For example, definition (10.3) of $Y = AX$ does not change, but interval additions and multiplications are now performed with floating-point endpoints; i.e., the operations are executed with directed roundings. One may argue that this requires many switches of the rounding mode and may slow the computation significantly. This is indeed true, and we will discuss how to overcome this problem later.

Before continuing we mention that the interval arithmetical operations are implemented in a number of software packages. Most easy to use is INTLAB [389], a recent implementation as a MATLAB interval toolbox. A nice introduction to INTLAB and a tutorial can be found in [196]. INTLAB has a built-in new data type called `intval`, and due to operator overloading every operation between an `intval`-quantity and something else (for example, a real or complex number, or a real or complex interval) is recognized as an interval operation and executed with directed rounding. For example, an INTLAB implementation, i.e., executable code, of the above algorithm to verify nonsingularity of a matrix may be as in the program in Figure 10.5.

```
R = inv(A);
C = abss(eye(n)-R*intval(A));
x = ones(n,1);
setround(+1)
nonsingular = all( C*x < x )
```

Figure 10.5. *INTLAB program to check $|I - RA|x < x$ and therefore the nonsingularity of A.*

We want to stress that this is executable code in INTLAB. Given a square matrix A of dimension n, first an approximate inverse R is computed using pure floating-point arithmetic. Then, the multiplication `R*intval(A)` is performed in interval arithmetic since the type cast `intval(A)` transforms the matrix A to an interval matrix. The result is of type `intval`, so that the subtraction `eye(n)-R*intval(A)` is also an interval subtraction. For an interval matrix $\mathbf{C} \in \mathbb{IF}^{n \times n}$, the function `abss` is defined by

$$\mathrm{abss}(\mathbf{C}) := \max\{|\widetilde{C}| : \widetilde{C} \in \mathbf{C}\},$$

where the maximum is to be understood entrywise. So $\text{abss}\,(\mathbf{C}) \in \mathbf{F}^{n \times n}$ satisfies $|\tilde{C}| \leq \text{abss}\,(\mathbf{C})$ for all $\tilde{C} \in \mathbf{C}$, and this is the entrywise smallest matrix with this property. This implies

$$|I - RA| \leq \mathrm{C},$$

where C denotes the computed (floating-point) result. The vector x is defined to be a vector of ones, and `setround(+1)` switches the rounding mode to upward. So the product C*x of the nonnegative quantities C and x is an upper bound of the true value of the product. The assertion follows.

Note that the value `nonsingular=1` proves A to be nonsingular, whereas the value `nonsingular=0` means the algorithm failed to prove nonsingularity. Rather than giving a false answer the result is to be interpreted as "don't know." So this self-validating program may fail to prove nonsingularity (for very ill-conditioned matrices), but it never gives a false answer. In contrast, a computer algebra algorithm could always decide nonsingularity or singularity when computing in sufficiently long arithmetic or infinite precision.

At this point we note that almost every self-validating algorithm for point data can be transformed into a corresponding one accepting interval data. In the above case let an interval matrix $\mathrm{A} \in \mathbf{IF}^{n \times n}$ be given. It represents the set of all real matrices $\tilde{A}$ within the interval entries. The question is whether every matrix $\tilde{A}$ within A is nonsingular. Consider the algorithm in Figure 10.6.

```
R = inv(mid(A));
C = abss(eye(n)-R*intval(A));
x = ones(n,1);
setround(+1)
nonsingular = all( C*x < x )
```

Figure 10.6. *INTLAB program for checking nonsingularity of an interval matrix.*

The only difference between this and the program in Figure 10.5 is the first line. Here `mid(A)` denotes the mid-point matrix of A. We claim that the result `nonsingular=1` proves that every matrix $\tilde{A} \in \mathrm{A}$ is nonsingular. The *proof* of this fact is very simple and very typical for self-validating methods. Let $\tilde{A} \in \mathrm{A}$ be a fixed but arbitrary (real) matrix. Then, by the fundamental principle (10.4) of inclusion isotonicity,

$$I - R\tilde{A} \in I - R\mathrm{A} \text{ and therefore } |I - R\tilde{A}| \leq \mathrm{C},$$

and the assertion follows. The point is to take any fixed but arbitrary data out of the input data and apply inclusion isotonicity. What is true for interval data is true for every point data out of the interval data.

For interval rather than floating-point input data `intval` in the second line of the program in Figure 10.6 could be omitted. In the stated way the program works correctly for interval as well as for noninterval input matrices.

We note that the proof of nonsingularity of an interval matrix is nontrivial. In fact this is an NP-hard problem; see [365]. We also note that the present implementation is nothing else but to check $\|I - RA\|_\infty < 1$, which, of course, implies nonsingularity of R and A. If the vector `x=ones(n,1)` fails to prove nonsingularity, one may iterate x. This is a power iteration to approximate the Perron vector of C.

10.7 A Common Misconception About Interval Arithmetic

The arguments so far follow a simple but powerful pattern: If arithmetic operations are replaced by their corresponding interval operations, then the true result must be an element of the interval result. In our example we used this to prove $|I - RA|x < x$ and therefore the nonsingularity of the matrix A. This technique might be applied to any numerical algorithm, for example, to Gaussian elimination for a linear system $Ax = b$. After execution, the true result, the solution of the system of linear equations $Ax = b$ must be an element of the computed interval result, provided no pivot element contained zero, because otherwise the algorithm would come to a premature end.

This technique is called *naive interval arithmetic* and represents the most common *misuse* of interval arithmetic. For a general application this approach will most certainly fail. Note that the assertion, namely, that the final interval result contains the exact solution of the linear system, thereby also proving nonsingularity of the matrix in use, is true. However, this approach will most certainly come to a premature end due to a pivot interval containing zero. The reason is interval dependency, and we will explain the effects with a simple example.

Consider a linear system with lower triangular matrix, where all elements on and below the diagonal are equal to 1, and a right-hand side with all elements being equal to 1 except the first one, which is equal to 0.1. For $n = 4$ the linear system looks as follows:

$$\begin{pmatrix} 1 & & & \\ 1 & 1 & & \\ 1 & 1 & 1 & \\ 1 & 1 & 1 & 1 \end{pmatrix} \begin{pmatrix} x_1 \\ x_2 \\ x_3 \\ x_4 \end{pmatrix} = \begin{pmatrix} 0.1 \\ 1 \\ 1 \\ 1 \end{pmatrix}. \tag{10.7}$$

The real number 0.1 is not exactly representable in binary floating point, so to treat the original linear system it has to be replaced by some interval $[\underline{\beta}, \overline{\beta}]$ containing 0.1, where $\underline{\beta}$ and $\overline{\beta}$ are adjacent binary floating-point numbers. This is an optimal inclusion, the best one can do in finite precision. For simplicity of the following we change this interval to midpoint-radius notation $[\underline{\beta}, \overline{\beta}] = \alpha \pm \mathbf{u}$, where α is the midpoint of $[\underline{\beta}, \overline{\beta}]$ and $\mathbf{u}$ is the radius. Now we perform a forward substitution using interval operations, and we will do this theoretically without any further rounding, i.e., using real interval operations. Obviously,

$$\begin{aligned} X_1 &= \alpha \pm \mathbf{u}, \\ X_2 &= 1 - X_1 = 1 - \alpha \pm \mathbf{u}, \\ X_3 &= 1 - X_1 - X_2 = X_2 - X_2 = \pm 2\mathbf{u}, \\ X_4 &= 1 - X_1 - X_2 - X_3 = X_3 - X_3 = \pm 4\mathbf{u}. \end{aligned}$$

The point is that the interval subtraction $X_2 - X_2$ does not cancel to zero but is an interval with midpoint zero and doubled diameter. As we saw in equation (10.2), this is always the case.

So, from X_2 on, the diameter of every X_i doubles and the overestimation grows exponentially! Unfortunately, this is the typical behavior for this kind of naive interval approach. For the same reason it is most likely, even for small dimensions, that a pivot interval will contain zero at an early stage of naive interval Gaussian elimination—unless the matrix has special properties such as being an M-matrix.

In Table 10.1 we show some statistics obtained for randomly generated matrices, where all matrix elements are uniformly distributed within $[-1, 1]$. For matrix dimensions $n = 40 \ldots 70$ we generate 100 samples each and monitor the average and maximum condition number, the number of failures of naive interval Gaussian elimination, i.e., the number of cases where a pivot element contains zero, and, for the nonfailing cases, the average and maximum of the radius of U_{nn}.

Table 10.1. *Exponential growth of radii of forward substitution in equation (10.7) in naive interval arithmetic.*

	cond(A)			rad(U_{nn})	
n	average	maximum	failed	average	maximum
40	$4.5280 \cdot 10^2$	$9.7333 \cdot 10^3$	0	$3.5633 \cdot 10^{-4}$	$4.6208 \cdot 10^{-3}$
50	$8.9590 \cdot 10^2$	$4.5984 \cdot 10^4$	1	$7.1158 \cdot 10^{-1}$	$3.8725 \cdot 10^1$
60	$1.6132 \cdot 10^3$	$9.1094 \cdot 10^4$	98	$1.5774 \cdot 10^0$	$1.5603 \cdot 10^2$
70	$1.1159 \cdot 10^3$	$4.3883 \cdot 10^4$	100	-	-

The failure is not a question of the condition number of the matrix but of the *number of operations*. The failure is due to the fact that certain computations depend on previous computations. The previously computed results are already perturbed by some error, and this amplifies in the next computation and so forth. This effect can also be read off the radius of the diagonal elements U_{ii}. Figure 10.7 shows typical behavior for a random matrix of dimension $n = 50$ on a semilogarithmic scale.

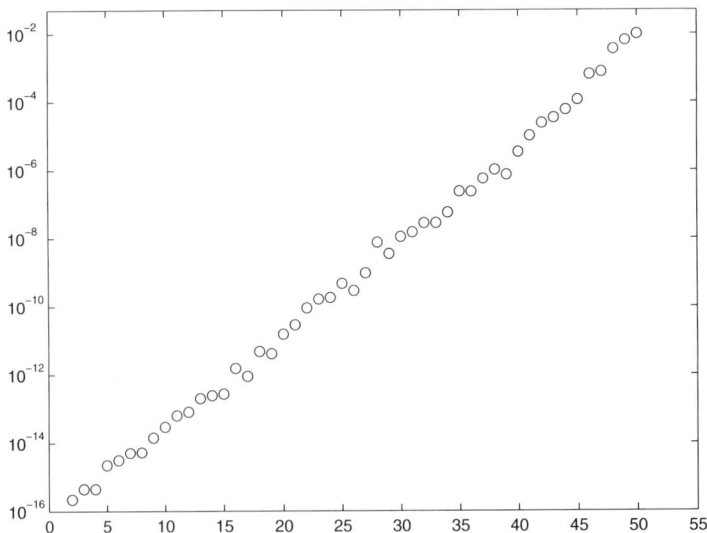

Figure 10.7. *Naive interval Gaussian elimination: Growth of* rad(U_{ii}).

These observations also give the key to the design of self-validating methods. First, using already computed data may cause amplification of interval diameters; therefore, one should try to use original data as much as possible. Second, the only way to decrease the radius of result intervals is to multiply them by a small factor (or divide by a large one). Adding and subtracting intervals add the radii. Therefore, one should try to have small factors multiplying interval quantities where possible.

Before continuing, two things should be mentioned. First, the application of interval methods is not restricted to linear problems and/or basic arithmetical operations. There are libraries for the standard elementary functions available [51, 267] for real and complex point and interval data. Also INTLAB provides rigorous interval standard functions for real and complex input data [391]. For any elementary standard function f and for any real or complex interval X, the computed result $f(X)$ is a superset of all $f(x)$ for $x \in X$. For monotone functions such as the exponential or logarithm this requires only rigorous standard functions for a point argument. For functions like sine some case distinctions are necessary. For the sine and other periodic functions an accurate argument reduction is also necessary [358] in order to maintain accuracy of the result for larger arguments. All this is implemented in INTLAB, which is fast and accurate even for very large arguments, following the methods presented in [391].

The second remark is that the naive interval approach may cause exponential over-estimation, as in naive interval Gaussian elimination, but it need not. Consider the following example which describes exactly how it happened to us. In global optimization there are a number of well-known test functions, among them the following example by Griewank:

$$g(x) = (x^2 + y^2)/4000 + \cos(x)\cos(y)/\sqrt{2} + 1. \tag{10.8}$$

The minimum of this function in the domain

$$-60 \le x \le 60 \quad \text{and} \quad -60 \le y \le 60$$

is sought. In order to obtain a first overview we plotted this function. Figure 10.8 from MATLAB displays 20 meshpoints in each coordinate direction.

At first sight one may wonder why it should be difficult to find the minimum of this (apparently convex) function. Calculating the minimum of the function values at the meshpoints yields 1.7119. By nature this is in fact an *upper bound* for the minimum. Interval evaluation is also very simple. The following

```
G = inline('(x^2+y^2)/4000+cos(x)*cos(y)/sqrt{2}+1')

>> X = infsup(-60,60); Y = X; G(X,Y)
```

is executable INTLAB code and yields

```
intval ans =
[    0.2928,    3.5072]
```

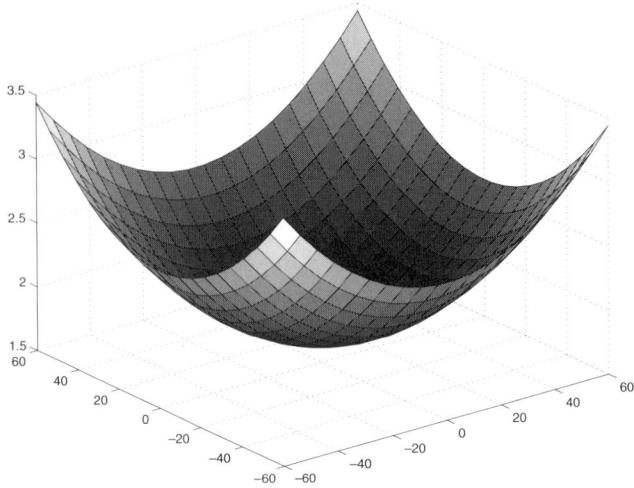

Figure 10.8. *Plot of the function in equation (10.8) with 20 meshpoints in x- and y-directions.*

Note that the left endpoint is a true lower bound of the true minimum of the function g within the domain under investigation. One may argue that some, though not much, overestimation took place. However, evaluating the same function with 50 meshpoints in each direction produces Figure 10.9.

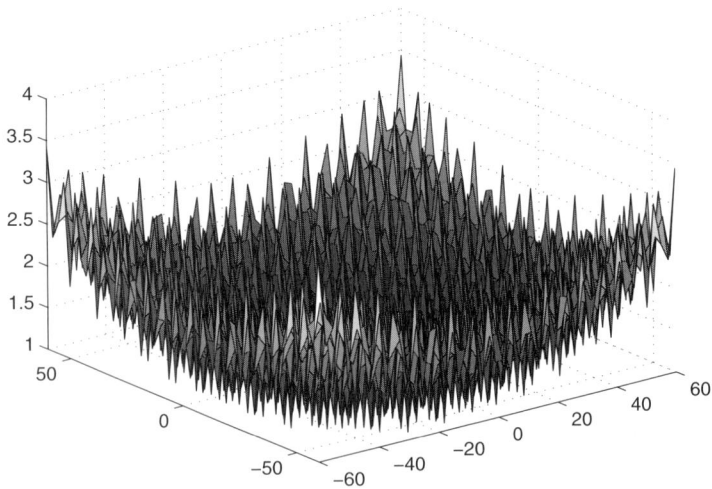

Figure 10.9. *Plot of the function in equation (10.8) with 50 meshpoints in x- and y-directions.*

This reveals more of the true nature of this nasty function and justifies its use as a test function for global optimization. The minimum of the 50^2 function values is 0.3901, again an *upper bound* for the true minimum. Evaluation at 2000 meshpoints in each direction, that is, a total of 4 million meshpoints, yields the upper bound 0.2957 for the true minimum, not too far from the valid lower bound 0.2928 obtained by naive interval evaluation.

Although sometimes affected by overestimation, naive interval evaluation provides a very powerful tool to estimate the range of a function over a domain. This estimation is valid and rigorous and is obtained in a very simple way without any further knowledge of the behavior of the function, a quite remarkable property.

This is why during the first steps of the development of verification algorithms people were a little overwhelmed by this powerful property. So sometimes interval methods were advocated to solve numerical problems per se in an easy and elegant way, with automatic verification of the correctness of the results. To be fair, we must say that up to that time, in the 1960's, computers and programming languages were in a fairly premature state. Compared to today's possibilities we readily have at hand, this is more like a horse pulled carriage compared to a sportscar. In particular, powerful interactive numerical programming environments like MATLAB were not widely available. So testing was not as easy as we have become accustomed to today at the push of the fingertip.

No wonder it took some time until others could try to verify the claims. Additionally, this was hindered by the fact that interval operations were available to few. And finally, computers were still slow. It could take a couple of minutes to solve a 100×100 linear system (cf. the enlightening Table 9.2 in [205]), not to mention how much additional time software simulation of interval operations would consume; and, of course, not everybody had access to the fastest computers.

But then people tried standard examples, such as naive interval Gaussian elimination, and had to assert that there is quite some overestimation. In fact, exponential overestimation is not only not rare but rather typical. No wonder interval advocates were measured by their own claims, and this remains the reason for divided reputation of interval analysis.

Naive interval arithmetic can also be regarded as an automated forward error analysis: The worst case of every single operation is estimated. For Gaussian elimination this has been shown in the famous paper [344]. The results were very pessimistic, as are those of naive interval arithmetic. This paper led for some time even to the conclusion that larger linear systems could not be solved reliably on digital computers because of accumulating rounding errors. Here, "large" could mean dimension 10; remember that, for example, in 1947 a 10×10 linear system was successfully solved on the Harvard Mark I in 45 minutes of computing time [37]. This was "fast" compared to the 4 hours for a problem of the same size on an IBM 602 in 1949 [466].

This kind of automated forward error analysis, i.e., naive interval analysis, estimates the worst case error of every simple operation, and it treats all operations as being independent. But rounding errors are not independent, and they are also by no means randomly distributed (cf. the enlightening talk by Kahan [249]). Fortunately we know today how to estimate the forward error very precisely, for example, in terms of the condition number.

However, interval analysis has developed since then, and the times of naive interval approaches are long over. In addition, despite overestimation, such an easy way to obtain a valid inclusion of the range of a function can be useful. Moreover, the overestimation in naive interval Gaussian elimination for matrices with larger dimension stems from using computed results over and over again. This is not the case when using other algorithms.

Let us again consider an example, the computation of the determinant of a matrix. One method is, of course, to use Gaussian elimination and to compute the product of the diagonal elements of the factor U. This approach may work for small dimensions but definitely not for larger ones. Another approach is given in the program in Figure 10.10, again an executable INTLAB program.

```
[L U P] = lu(A);
Linv = inv(L);
Uinv = inv(U);
B = Linv*intval(P*A)*Uinv;
B0 = B;
B0(1:n+1:n*n) = 0;
G = diag(B)' + midrad(0,abss(sum(B0)));
d = prod(G)/prod(intval(diag(Uinv)))/det(P)
```

Figure 10.10. *INTLAB program for the inclusion of the determinant of a matrix.*

Here `Linv` and `Uinv` are approximate inverses of the approximate LU-factors of A. Then `B` is an inclusion of `Linv*P*A*Uinv`, so the determinant of B is equal to the quantity $\pm$ `det(A)prod(diag(Uinv))`, with the plus or minus depending on the sign of the permutation matrix P. The next statements compute an inclusion of the product of the Gershgorin circles of B, which is an inclusion of the product of the eigenvalues of `LinvPAUinv`, which in turn is equal to the determinant. The final line then computes an inclusion of the determinant of A.

The point is (i) to use original data where possible, (ii) to use floating-point approximations where possible, and (iii) to design the algorithm in a way that potential overestimation is minimized. This is the fundamental difference between the naive approach and a self-validating method. Figure 10.11 shows the accuracy by means of the relative error of the inclusion of the determinant calculation by naive interval Gaussian elimination (depicted by "×") and by the above algorithm (i.e., Gershgorin applied to a preconditioned matrix, depicted by "∘" for dimensions 10 to 500).

All matrices were generated randomly with entries uniformly distributed in $[-1, 1]$. Since the determinant of such random matrices of larger dimension are likely to be out of the floating-point range, matrices are scaled by powers of 2 to avoid this. For example, the determinant of a matrix of dimension 500 will be calculated in double precision by the above algorithm to about 8 correct figures. The naive approach cannot handle matrices of dimension greater than 60.

The lesson is that what works well for numerical computations need not be a good method for interval approaches. We need individual methods for each given problem. Standard numerical methods may help (and they do), but usually something more is needed.

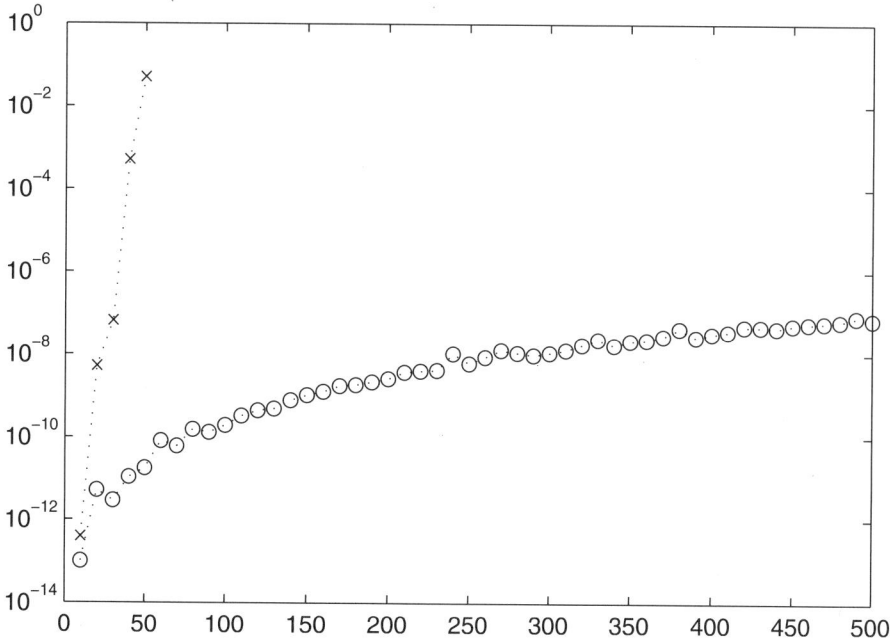

Figure 10.11. *Comparison of a naive interval algorithm and a self-validating method: Naive Gaussian elimination depicted by "×," Gershgorin for preconditioned matrix by "∘."*

10.8 Self-validating Methods and INTLAB

Consider a system of nonlinear equations given by a function $f : \mathbb{R}^n \to \mathbb{R}^n \in C^1$, for which we look for an inclusion of a zero $\widehat{x}$ near some approximation $\widetilde{x}$. A simplified Newton procedure transforms the function f into a function g with

$$g(x) := x - Rf(x)$$

for some preconditioner R. A standard choice for R is an approximate inverse of the Jacobian of f at $\widetilde{x}$. Suppose R is nonsingular and there is some interval vector $X \in \mathbb{IR}^n$ with

$$g(X) \subseteq X.$$

That means the continuous function g maps the nonempty, convex, and compact set X into itself, and Brouwer's fixed point theorem implies existence of a fixed point $\widehat{x}$ of g in X:

$$\exists\, \widehat{x} \in X : \; g(\widehat{x}) = \widehat{x}.$$

By definition this implies

$$R \cdot f(\widehat{x}) = 0 \quad \text{and therefore } f(\widehat{x}) = 0$$

because R was supposed to be nonsingular. In other words, the set X is proved to be an inclusion of a zero of f if we can verify that (i) R is nonsingular, and (ii) g maps X into itself. The first problem might be solved by the previously described method, and the second one by observing that

$$g(X) \subseteq X - R \cdot f(X).$$

This is a naive approach, and it definitely does not work. Although it is correct that $X - R \cdot f(X) \subseteq X$ implies $g(X) \subseteq X$ and therefore there exists a zero of f in X, the condition $X - R \cdot f(X) \subseteq X$ can be satisfied only if $R \cdot f(X) = 0$, which in turn is possible only if $f(X) \equiv 0$. The overall approach is good, but the point is that the condition $g(X) \subseteq X$ must be verified another way.

A convenient way to do this is by using a first-order Taylor expansion, i.e., the mean value theorem. To do this we need the differential of a function, and this can be conveniently calculated by automatic differentiation. We assume the reader is familiar with this technique; for an overview see [370] and [178]. The forward mode of automatic differentiation can easily be implemented in every programming language with an operator concept. In MATLAB version 5 and following versions there is a nice and easy-to-use operator concept available. Consider, for example, Broyden's test function [57]

$$\begin{aligned}
f_1(x, y) &= 0.5 \sin(xy) - \frac{y}{4\pi} - \frac{x}{2}, \\
f_2(x, y) &= \left(1 - \frac{1}{4\pi}\right) \cdot (e^{2x} - e) + e\frac{y}{\pi} - 2ex.
\end{aligned} \tag{10.9}$$

A MATLAB implementation of the function in equation (10.9) may use the inline concept:

```
>> f = inline('[ .5*sin(x*y) - y/(4*pi) - x/2 ; ...
    (1-1/(4*pi))*(exp(2*x)-exp(1)) + exp(1)*y/pi ...
    - 2*exp(1)*x ]')
```

Then the function value at $x = 0.5$ and $y = 3$ can be calculated by

```
>> f( [ .5 ; 3 ] )
ans =
      0.0100
     -0.1225
```

This is the screenshot from MATLAB. In INTLAB, we implemented automatic differentiation in forward mode. The corresponding call is

```
>> f( gradientinit( [ .5 ; 3 ] ) )
gradient value ans.x =
      0.0100
     -0.1225
gradient derivative(s) ans.dx =
     -0.3939    -0.0619
     -0.4326     0.8653
```

The computed result is an approximation of the Jacobian of f evaluated at $(x, y) = (0.5, 3)$. The remarkable property of interval arithmetic is the possibility of estimating the range of a function without any further knowledge of the function. In this example we may evaluate the range of Broyden's function for $x = 0.5$ and y varying within $[2.9, 3.1]$. The INTLAB call is

```
>> Z = [ .5 ; infsup(2.9,3.1) ]; f(Z)
intval ans =
    [    -0.0004,      0.0192]
    [    -0.2091,     -0.0359]
```

The result must be a superset of all function values $f(0.5, y)$ for $2.9 \le y \le 3.1$. In the same way we may calculate the range of function values and the range of partial derivatives:

```
>> f(gradientinit(Z))
intval gradient value ans.x =
    [    -0.0004,      0.0192]
    [    -0.2091,     -0.0359]
intval gradient derivative(s) ans.dx =
    [    -0.4699,     -0.3132] [    -0.0744,     -0.0494]
    [    -0.4327,     -0.4326] [     0.8652,      0.8653]
```

The mathematical assertion is that for every (x, y) within Z the values of the partial derivatives of f are included in the intervals shown. However, this correct mathematical assertion refers to the given function f and the given interval Z. Here things are a little tricky because of possible conversion errors, and we want to bring attention to this. When the user inputs the interval Z = infsup(2.9,3.1), the set of real numbers between the *real* numbers 2.9 and 3.1 is anticipated. Neither 2.9 nor 3.1 is exactly representable in floating point. So, to be on the safe side, the smallest interval with floating-point endpoints containing this real interval is the best choice. But the function infsup, which creates an interval of the given endpoints, requires floating-point input parameters. And the input data 2.9 and 3.1 are already converted to binary floating point when arriving at the function infsup.

This is a common problem in every programming language. In order to round the input data correctly, seemingly the only way is to specify it as a *string* and to perform the conversion in the correct way. The INTLAB input may be

```
Y = intval('[2.9,3.1]'); Z = [ .5 ; Y ];
```

Accidentally (or luckily?) the intervals Y and infsup(2.9,3.1) coincide. This solves the first problem that the input data are not exactly representable.

The second problem is that the original Broyden function contains the constant π. The MATLAB constant pi is the best double precision floating-point approximation to the transcendental number π, but, of course, is not equal to π. For floating-point evaluation of the function or the gradient value this is no problem; in fact, it is the best one can do. But for a valid estimation of the range, it is not enough.

The problem is a little delicate because for floating-point evaluation, i.e., floating-point arguments, we wish to use the floating-point approximation pi, whereas for range estimation we wish to use a valid inclusion of the transcendental number π. So the constant in the function depends on the type of the input argument. This is solved in INTLAB as in the program in Figure 10.12.

```
function y = f(x)
  y = x;
  cpi = typeadj( intval('3.14159265358979323') , typeof(x) );
  c1 = typeadj( 1 , typeof(x) );
  y(1) = .5*sin(x(1)*x(2)) - x(2)/(4*cpi) - x(1)/2;
  y(2) = (1-1/(4*cpi))*(exp(2*x(1))-exp(c1)) ...
              + exp(c1)*x(2)/cpi - 2*exp(c1)*x(1);
```

Figure 10.12. *INTLAB program of the function in equation (10.9) with special treatment of* π.

The function `typeof` determines whether x is of type `intval`. Then the function `typeadj` adjusts the output to the same type as the second input argument. If both arguments of `typeadj` are of type interval or not of type interval, nothing happens. Otherwise, the output either is the midpoint of the first argument or it is the point interval equal to the first argument. In that way either an approximation of π or an inclusion is used, depending on the type of the input argument x.

Note that the same is applied to the constant 1. Of course, 1 is exactly representable in floating point. But in the function, `exp(1)` is calculated. The operator concept adheres strictly to the type concept, which means that `exp(1)` computes a floating-point approximation to the transcendental number e, whereas `exp(intval(1))` calculates an inclusion.

Let us now turn to the calculation of bounds for the solution of systems of nonlinear equations. We mention only some characteristic points, as there are a number of well-written surveys (see, for example, [11, 392]). We need an estimation of the range $g(X)$. So first the function g is expanded at some $\widetilde{x}$, an approximate zero of f. Denote the convex union by $\cup$. Then for every x we have

$$g(x) = g(\widetilde{x}) + M \cdot (x - \widetilde{x}), \tag{10.10}$$

where $M_i = \frac{\partial g}{\partial x}(\zeta_i)$, $\zeta_i \in x \cup \widetilde{x}$. Note that the points ζ_i are determined individually within $x \cup \widetilde{x}$. Then, for every $x \in X$,

$$\begin{aligned} g(x) &= g(\widetilde{x}) + M \cdot (x - \widetilde{x}) \\ &= \widetilde{x} - R \cdot f(\widetilde{x}) + \{I - R \cdot M\}(x - \widetilde{x}) \\ &\subseteq \widetilde{x} - R \cdot f(\widetilde{x}) + \{I - R \cdot [M]\}(X - \widetilde{x}) \\ &=: K_f(\widetilde{x}, X) \qquad \text{Krawczyk operator.} \end{aligned} \tag{10.11}$$

In the proof most calculations are performed over $\mathbb{R}^n$; only the last step changes to intervals. The reason is that for interval calculations simple laws like distributivity or $X - X = 0$ do not hold. Moreover, an inclusion $[M]$ of the set of matrices M for which equation (10.10) is true is easily calculated by interval automatic differentiation evaluation of g at X. To complete the approach we need the nonsingularity of a preconditioning matrix R. This is established by Theorem 10.1.

Theorem 10.1. *Let* $f : \mathbb{R}^n \to \mathbb{R}^n \in C^1$, $\tilde{x} \in \mathbb{R}^n$, *and* $X \in \mathbb{IR}^n$ *be given. Suppose* $\tilde{x} \in X$ *and* $K_f(\tilde{x}, X) \subseteq \text{int}(X)$, *where the operator* K_f *is defined in equation (10.11). Then there exists one and only one* $\hat{x} \in X$ *with* $f(\hat{x}) = 0$.

Here $\text{int}(X)$ denotes the interior of X; the check whether the left-hand side is enclosed in the interior of the right-hand side means just replacing the "less than or equal" comparison by "less than." This is the principle of a self-validating method for systems of nonlinear equations [386]. Of course we need to discuss many details. For example, how to construct a suitable starting interval X and what to do if the inclusion condition $K_f(\tilde{x}, X) \subseteq \text{int}(X)$ is not satisfied. Such details are worked out in the routine `verifynlss` (cf. [387]) which is part of INTLAB. Figure 10.13 shows the executable code with input and output.

```
>> xs = [ .5 ; 3 ];  verifynlss(f,xs)
intval ans =
[     0.4999,  0.5001]
[     3.1415,  3.1416]

>> xs = [ 0 ; 0 ];  X = verifynlss(f,xs)
intval X =
[ -0.2606,  -0.2605]
[   0.6225,   0.6226]

>> format long; X
intval X =
[ -0.26059929002248,  -0.26059929002247]
[   0.62253089661391,   0.62253089661392]
```

Figure 10.13. *INTLAB results of* `verifynlss` *for Broyden's function (10.9).*

The number of displayed digits depends on the output format in MATLAB chosen by the user. The first inclusions look rather crude, but this is the best that can be done in short output format. Changing the format to long reveals the actual accuracy of the bounds.

We wrote specially designed routines for the output in INTLAB to ensure that the displayed answer is indeed correct. For example, the real number 0.1 is not exactly representable in binary floating point, and X=`intval('0.1')` calculates a valid inclusion of this real number. Displaying X in short format yields

```
>> X=intval('0.1')
intval X =
[     0.0999,      0.1001]
```

because this is the *best possible* answer using 5 decimal digits: The interval X must contain the real number 0.1, and because this is not a floating-point number, 0.1 *cannot* be a bound for X. Sometimes it may be tedious to count coinciding digits. For example,

```
>> X = midrad(2.718281828459045,1e-12)
intval X =
[   2.71828182845804,   2.71828182846005]
```

declares an interval of radius 10^{-12}, which is not immediately recognizable from the output. In that case one may switch to another output by

```
>> intvalinit('display_'); X
intval X =
    2.71828182846___
```

The rule is that subtracting one unit from the last displayed digit and adding one unit produces a correct inclusion of the result. In this way the accuracy is easily determined by looking at the number of displayed digits. Sometimes the format can describe vividly the convergence rate of an iteration. Consider, for example, the interval Newton iteration, displayed in Figure 10.14 with executable code and input and output.

```
>> f=inline('sqr(x)-2'), X=infsup(1,1.5);
   for i=1:4, y=f(gradientinit(X)); X=X.mid-y.x.mid/y.dx, end
f =
    Inline function:
    f(x) = sqr(x)-2
intval X =
   1.4_____
intval X =
   1.414_____
intval X =
   1.4142136_____
intval X =
   1.41421356237309
```

Figure 10.14. *INTLAB example of quadratic convergence.*

10.9   Implementation of Interval Arithmetic

The implementation of interval arithmetic may be performed along the lines of the definition of interval arithmetic for scalars, vectors, and matrices as in (10.3), and this is the way it was done for a long time. However, this may result in poor performance. When floating-point multiplication took significantly more computing time than floating-point addition, it was reasonable to compare the speed of algorithms by comparing the count of floating-point multiplications (the time for additions was comparatively negligible). Also, it was not too important whether an algorithm contained some branches.

This situation has changed completely. Today, many elementary operations, such as addition, subtraction, multiplication, division, and even a multiplication and an addition (multiply and add) require one cycle. This is also the reason why today multiplications and additions are counted equally. Both statements that Gaussian elimination requires $\frac{1}{3}n^3$ or $\frac{2}{3}n^3$ operations are correct, the first one 20 years ago, the other today.

By far more important, the actual execution time of today's algorithms depends on how the data are available: in registers, in cache, in memory, or possibly on external devices. Depending on data location the computing time may vary tremendously.

The various optimizing options in a compiler try to improve a given code as much as possible in that respect. But sometimes it is advisable to "help" the compiler to do a better job. A well-known example is the use of unrolled loops. The standard loop for the computation of a scalar product $x^T y$ is given in Figure 10.15.

```
s = 0;
for i=1:n
  s = s + x(i)*y(i);
end
```

Figure 10.15. *Dot product.*

An unrolled loop is given in Figure 10.16.

```
r = mod(n,4);
s = 0;
nmax = n-r-3;
for i=1:4:nmax
  s = s + x(i)*y(i) + x(i+1)*y(i+1) + x(i+2)*y(i+2) + x(i+3)*y(i+3);
end
for i=n-r+1:n
  s = s + x(i)*y(i);
end
```

Figure 10.16. *Dot product with unrolled loop.*

Here we use MATLAB notation to describe the approaches; of course, MATLAB execution time in this case would be mainly determined by the interpretation overhead. But executing the two versions in a compiled programming language reveals the difference. Here we used the C programming language and Gnu compiler [165]. The performance for non-optimized code without unrolled loops is normed to 1; i.e., a larger number indicates better performance. The difference is significant—more than a factor 4 from plain code to optimized unrolled code.

Table 10.2. *Relative performance without and with unrolled loops.*

	Without unrolled loop	With unrolled loop
opt. 0	1.0	1.6
opt. 2	3.0	4.4

This ansatz is well known and implemented in today's packages, such as the BLAS [285, 124, 122] and Atlas [482]. For higher operations the differences are even more significant. Consider, for example, matrix multiplication. A standard loop for multiplying two $n \times n$ matrices A, B is given in the program in Figure 10.17, where the elements of C are assumed to be initialized with zero.

Again, we use MATLAB notation to show the point. It is well known and often exploited that the loops can be interchanged. Depending on the sequence of execution of the i-, j-, and k-loops, the access to matrix elements is rowwise or columnwise in the inner loop, and the data in memory may or may not be available in cache or registers.

```
for i=1:n
  for j=1:n
    for k=1:n
      C(i,j) = C(i,j) + A(i,k)*B(k,j);
    end
  end
end
```

Figure 10.17. *ijk-loop for matrix multiplication.*

Table 10.3 shows computing times in MFLOPS for the different possibilities, again for the GNU C-compiler. The data are for 500×500 matrices.

Table 10.3. *Relative performance for different methods for matrix multiplication.*

	jki	kji	ikj	kij	ijk	jik
opt. 0	1.0	1.0	1.4	1.4	1.4	1.4
opt. 2	2.8	2.6	12.9	11.9	29.5	29.5
BLAS 3			47.6			

The BLAS3 [122] routines use, in addition, blocked routines again optimizing memory access. So from worst to best there is a factor of almost 50 in computing time.

So far all code was rather simple. Next, we will demonstrate the disastrous effects of branches in professionally written codes. Consider first matrix multiplication of two real $n \times n$ matrices, second LU decomposition of a real $n \times n$ matrix with partial pivoting, and third LU decomposition with complete pivoting. Counting operations $+, -, \cdot, /$ and if-statements as one flop, these routines require $2n^3 + \mathcal{O}(n^2)$, $\frac{2}{3}n^3 + \mathcal{O}(n^2)$, and $\frac{4}{3}n^3 + \mathcal{O}(n^2)$ operations, respectively. In fact, each of the mentioned operations is executed in one cycle; the if-statement, however, implies great consequences with respect to optimization of the code.

The three tasks are accomplished by the LAPACK routines DGEMM, DGETRF and DGETC2, respectively.[42] The first test is on a 933 MHz Mobile Pentium 3 CPU and executed using MKL, the Intel Math Kernel Library. Table 10.4 shows the performance in MFLOPS of the matrix multiplication routine DGEMM, of LU decomposition with partial pivoting DGETRF, and of LU decomposition with complete pivoting DGETC2, for different dimensions n.

Table 10.4 shows that matrix multiplication is executed at close to the peak performance, that matrix multiplication executes about 10% faster than Gaussian elimination with partial pivoting, and that complete pivoting decreases the performance by about a factor 10.

We executed the same example on a 2.53 GHz Pentium 4 CPU using the ATLAS routines. The results are shown in Table 10.5.

Here matrix multiplication is beyond peak performance due to multiply-and-add instructions, and is faster by 60% to 20% compared with Gaussian elimination with partial

---

[42]Thanks to Dr. Ogita from Waseda University, Tokyo, for performing the following computations.

Table 10.4. *Performance of LAPACK routines using Intel MKL.*

	Performance [MFLOPS]		
n	DGEMM	DGETRF	DGETC2
500	708	656	73
1000	746	672	68
2000	757	688	66
3000	757	707	64

Table 10.5. *Performance of ATLAS routines.*

	Performance [MFLOPS]		
n	DGEMM	DGETRF	DGETC2
500	2778	1725	215
1000	2970	2121	186
2000	3232	2525	151
3000	3249	2663	101

pivoting. The seeming decrease of relative performance of DGEMM is rather a more rapid increase of performance of DGETRF. This makes it even worse for Gaussian elimination with complete pivoting: In this case if-statements slow computation up to *a factor 30*.

For interval operations things are even worse. Consider an implementation of Theorem 10.1 for the inclusion of the set of solutions

$$\sum(\mathbf{A}, \mathbf{b}) := \{x \in \mathbb{R}^n : \exists A \in \mathbf{A} \,\exists b \in \mathbf{b} \quad \text{with } Ax = b\}$$

of a linear system with interval data $\mathbf{A} \in \mathbb{IR}^{n \times n}$ and $\mathbf{b} \in \mathbb{IR}^n$. The computation of the product $\mathbf{C} = R\mathbf{A}$, a point matrix times an interval matrix, takes the major part of the computing time. A standard loop is given in Figure 10.18.

```
for i=1:n
   for j=1:n
      for k=1:n
         C(i,j) = C(i,j) + R(i,k)*A(k,j);
      end
   end
end
```

Figure 10.18. *Top-down approach for point matrix times interval matrix.*

For better readability we typed the interval quantities in boldface. Note that both the addition and the multiplication in the inner loop are interval operations.

The multiplication of a point matrix and an interval matrix is implemented this way in many libraries. However, the inner loop is very costly in terms of computing time. Even in an optimal implementation it requires two changes of the rounding mode, and at least one if-statement concerning the sign of R(i,k). The if-statement, however, frequently empties the computation pipe and the contents of registers become unknown, so it jeopardizes any attempt to optimize this code.

In 1993, Knüppel found a simple way to improve this computation; it is published as BIAS [263, 264]. He interchanged the j- and the k-loops such that the element in the R(i,k) inner loop remains constant. Then the sign can be determined in the j-loop reducing the number of changes of rounding mode and the number of if-statements from n^3 to n^2. The BIAS code in Figure 10.19 illustrates his idea.

```
for i=1:n
   for k=1:n
      if R(i,k)>=0
         setround(-1)
         for j=1:n
            Cinf(i,j) = Cinf(i,j) + R(i,k)*Ainf(k,j);
         end
         setround(+1)
         for j=1:n
            Csup(i,j) = Csup(i,j) + R(i,k)*Asup(k,j);
         end
      else
         setround(-1)
         for j=1:n
            Cinf(i,j) = Cinf(i,j) + R(i,k)*Asup(k,j);
         end
         setround(+1)
         for j=1:n
            Csup(i,j) = Csup(i,j) + R(i,k)*Ainf(k,j);
         end
      end
   end
end
```

Figure 10.19. *Improved code for point matrix times interval matrix.*

Note that in the inner loops there is no changing of rounding mode and no if-statement. Computing times on a Convex SPP 200 for different matrix dimensions are given in Table 10.6. The decreasing performance for higher dimensions is due to cache misses since the BIAS routine was implemented as above, i.e., not blocked.

For the comparison of different interval libraries, Corliss [102] developed a test suite for basic arithmetic operations, vector and matrix operations, nonlinear problems, and others. Comparing BIAS (which is implemented in the C++ library PROFIL [265]) with other

Table 10.6. *Performance of algorithms in Figures 10.18 and 10.19 for point matrix times interval matrix.*

[MFLOPS]	$n = 100$	$n = 200$	$n = 500$	$n = 1000$
Traditional	6.4	6.4	3.5	3.5
BIAS	51	49	19	19

libraries shows a performance gain of a factor 2 to 30, depending on the application. This is basically due to better optimizable code.

The approach has some drawbacks. It does not carry over to the multiplication of two interval matrices, and it cannot be used for a MATLAB implementation. This is because the interpretation overhead would be tremendous. Table 10.7 shows the performance for a matrix product A*B implemented in MATLAB with the traditional 3 loops, with using a scalar product in the most inner loop, with outer products, and finally with the MATLAB command $A * B$ (using BLAS3 routines).

Table 10.7. *Relative performance of* MATLAB *matrix multiplication with interpretation overhead.*

Loops	3	2	1	$A * B$
MFLOPS	0.05	1.9	36	44

So the BIAS implementation would, besides other overheads, still be slower by more than an order of magnitude, only because of the interpretation overhead due to the use of loops.

Fortunately we developed another method for overcoming those problems. It uses solely BLAS3 routines, needs no branches, is applicable to the multiplication of two interval matrices, and is parallelizable by using parallel BLAS. The key is the midpoint-radius representation of intervals; see (10.5). An interval matrix $\mathbf{A} \in \mathbb{IR}^{n \times n}$ may be represented by

$$\mathbf{A} = [\underline{A}, \overline{A}] \quad \text{or} \quad \mathbf{A} = mA \pm rA \quad \text{with} \quad \underline{A}, \overline{A}, mA, rA \in \mathbb{R}^{n \times n}.$$

Here the $\pm$ is understood to be independent for each individual component. The radius matrix rA is nonnegative. In any case

$$\mathbf{A} = \{A \in \mathbb{R}^{n \times n} : \underline{A} \le A \le \overline{A}\} = \{A \in \mathbb{R}^{n \times n} : mA - rA \le A \le mA + rA\},$$

with comparison understood to be componentwise. Then, it is not difficult to see (cf. (10.6)) that

$$R \cdot \mathbf{A} = R \cdot mA \pm |R| \cdot rA = \{C \in R^{n \times n} : R \cdot mA - |R| \cdot rA \le C \le R \cdot mA + |R| \cdot rA\},$$

with the absolute value understood to be componentwise. The result is the best possible in the sense that none of the bounds on the result can be improved without violating inclusion isotonicity. This result, however, doesn't take rounding errors into account. In the world of floating-point operations we face two additional problems. First, the input matrix $\mathbf{A} = [\underline{A}, \overline{A}]$ has to be transformed into midpoint-radius form $mA \pm rA$, with floating-point matrices mA and rA such that $[\underline{A}, \overline{A}] \subseteq mA \pm rA$, and, second, the product $R \cdot mA$ is, in general, not exactly representable in floating point.

The first problem can be solved by an ingenious trick due to Oishi [353]. Consider the INTLAB code in Figure 10.20.

```
setround(+1)
mA = (Ainf+Asup)/2;
rA = mA-Ainf;
```

Figure 10.20. *INTLAB program to convert inf-sup to mid-rad representation.*

Given $\mathbf{A} = $ [Ainf, Asup], this code computes mA and rA such that

$$\mathbf{A} = [\texttt{Ainf}, \texttt{Asup}] \subseteq \{A \in \mathbb{R}^{n \times n} : \texttt{mA} - \texttt{rA} \le A \le \texttt{mA} + \texttt{rA}\}.$$

The second problem can be solved by computing the product $R * mA$ both in rounding downward and rounding upward. So the entire INTLAB code for point matrix times interval matrix is as in Figure 10.21.

```
setround(+1)
mA = (Ainf+Asup)/2;
rA = mA-Ainf;
rC = abs(R)*rA;
Csup = R*mA + rC;
setround(-1)
Cinf = R*mA - rC;
```

Figure 10.21. *INTLAB program for point matrix times interval matrix.*

This calculates an interval matrix $\mathbf{C} = $ [Cinf, Csup] with inclusion isotonicity

$$RA \in \mathbf{C} \quad \text{for all} \quad A \in \mathbf{A}.$$

The computational effort is basically three floating-point matrix multiplications, and those can be executed in BLAS or Atlas. The interpretation overhead is negligible. So the factor in computing time compared to one floating-point multiplication of matrices of the same size is almost exactly three, and that is what is observed in MATLAB/INTLAB. Note that the result is an interval matrix, so we cannot expect a factor less than two. Therefore, the result is almost optimal. Again, note that we are talking about the *actual computing time*, not about an operation count.

The concept is easily applied to the multiplication of two interval matrices. The program in Figure 10.22 is executable INTLAB code for $A * B$.

Note that only two switches of the rounding mode are necessary, and that in total only four matrix multiplications are needed. Only computing the mutual products of the bounds of A and B would require the same computing time—although this would not help much for the computation of $A * B$.

```
setround(+1)
mA = (Ainf+Asup)/2;
rA = mA-Ainf;
mB = (Binf+Bsup)/2;
rB = mB-Binf;
rC = abs(mA)*rB + rA*(abs(mB)+rB);
Csup = mA*mB + rC;
setround(-1)
Cinf = mA*mB - rC;
```

Figure 10.22. *INTLAB program for interval matrix times interval matrix.*

In MATLAB/INTLAB we observe exactly this factor four. In a compiled language, in this case C, the results on the Convex SPP 200 for the multiplication of two interval matrices are given in Table 10.8. Here, we can also use the parallel processors just by linking the parallel BLAS routines to our MidRad approach. The other approaches might be parallelized, but this would require a lot of programming. Note that there is almost no difference between the traditional and the BIAS approaches. The lower performance of the MidRad approach for $n = 500$ may be due to suboptimal utilization of the cache.

Table 10.8. *Performance of interval matrix times interval matrix.*

[MFLOPS]	$n = 100$	$n = 200$	$n = 500$	$n = 1000$
Traditional	4.7	4.6	2.8	2.8
BIAS	4.6	4.5	2.9	2.8
MidRad	91	94	76	99
MidRad 4 proc.	95	145	269	334

The implementation of complex interval arithmetic follows the same lines. Note that midpoint-radius arithmetic causes some overestimation compared to the infimum-supremum arithmetic. An example is

$$[3.14, 3.15] * [2.71, 2.72] = [8.5094, 8.5680],$$
$$(3.145 \pm 0.005) * (2.715 \pm 0.005) = 8.538675 \pm 0.029325 = [8.50935, 8.56800].$$

However, one can show that the overestimation is limited to a factor 1.5 in the worst case, and it is in general much smaller, as in the example above, depending on the relative accuracy of the input intervals. This is true for scalar, vector, and matrix operations, real and complex, and independent of the size of the numbers. Those results can be found with various other details in [387].

Sometimes it may be useful to calculate inner products with higher precision (and then to round the result to working precision). For example, in the residual iteration

$$x^{k+1} = x^k - A\backslash(Ax^k - b),$$

the residual $Ax^k - b$ is exposed to severe cancellation (we use MATLAB notation $A\backslash y$ to indicate the solution of a linear systems with matrix A and right-hand side y). It has been shown by Skeel [418] that a residual iteration with the residual calculated in *working precision* suffices to produce a *backward stable* result. However, for a small *forward error*, higher precision accumulation of dot products is necessary. This may be interesting in case of exactly given and exactly representable input data; otherwise the input error is amplified by the condition number and a highly accurate forward error does not make much sense. There are various algorithms available [40, 275, 289] as well as a discussion of hardware implementations [274]. A practical implementation by means of a coprocessor board is presented in [441, 442].

Recently, new and very fast summation and dot product routines have been developed in [351]. They use only double precision floating point addition, subtraction, and multiplication. Nevertheless they compute a result of an accuracy *as if* computed in quadruple or even higher precision. The reason is the extensive use of so-called error-free transformations. The algorithms do not contain a single branch so that the compiled code can be highly optimized. Therefore they are not only fast in terms of flop count but, more importantly, in terms of *measured computing time*. Apparently, these are the fastest dot product algorithms currently available, some 40 % faster than the corresponding XBLAS routines [289], while sharing similar error estimates.

Other design and implementation details of INTLAB can be found in [389]. For a tutorial and applications see [196]. INTLAB is comprised of

- real and complex interval scalars, vectors, and matrices,

- dense and sparse interval matrices,

- real and complex (interval) elementary functions,

- automatic differentiation (gradients and Hessians),

- automatic slopes,

- univariate and multivariate (interval) polynomials,

- a rudimentary (interval) long arithmetic.

Finally we mention that INTLAB is entirely written in MATLAB. All algorithms are designed to minimize interpretation overhead. Under Windows operating systems, they do not depend on assembly language routines since the switch of the rounding mode is provided by MATLAB (thanks to Cleve Moler). For other operating systems such a routine is provided, and this is the only non-MATLAB routine. For details see our home page [389].

10.10   Performance and Accuracy

Measuring computing time in MATLAB is a little unfair because of the interpretation overhead. However, with the fast implementation of interval arithmetic as described in the previous section there is, at least when solving linear systems, not much overhead. Notice that a pure flop count for a self-validating algorithm for linear systems along the lines of Theorem 10.1 needs $6n^3 + O(n^2)$ operations, with additions and multiplications counted separately. These are $2n^3$ operations to calculate the approximate inverse R and $4n^3$ operations to calculate the lower and upper bound of the inclusion of RA. So we may expect a factor 9 compared to the $\frac{2}{3}n^3 + O(n^2)$ floating-point operations for Gaussian elimination. Applying Theorem 10.2 to linear systems yields the computing times in Table 10.9, measured in INTLAB.

Table 10.9. *Measured computing time for linear system solver.*

INTLAB computing time ($n = 500$, 300 MHz Laptop)	
5 sec	for $A \backslash b$ (built-in solver)
27 sec	with verification as in Theorem 10.2
16 sec	verification by Oishi's method [353]

The first line in Table 10.9 refers to the built-in linear system solver in MATLAB 6.5, about the fastest we can get. The second line is the total computing time for the verification routine `verifylss` available in INTLAB, which is based on the methods described above. The last line is an improvement described in [353].

So the measured computing times of our self-validating methods are significantly better than can be expected. This is because the $2n^3$ floating-point operations for matrix multiplication do not take 6 times the time for $\frac{2}{3}n^3$ floating-point operations of Gaussian elimination due to better optimized code.

There is no question that one has to pay for an inclusion. However, the final result is verified to be correct, under any circumstances. If the matrix of the linear system is too ill-conditioned to be solved in the precision available, a corresponding error message is given rather than a false result.

It may happen that pure floating-point routines deliver false answers, i.e., severely wrong approximations are computed *without a corresponding error message*. A first, though not really fair, example is the following. Foster [146] describes a linear system arising from the integration of

$$\dot{x} = x - 1 \quad \text{with} \quad x(0) = x(T). \tag{10.12}$$

His example is in fact a little more general. He uses the trapezoidal rule to obtain a linear system, which he solves by MATLAB. This is an example derived from the work of [493] to show that there are other than constructed examples where partial pivoting may result in exponential growth of the pivot elements. Foster's paper contains the MATLAB code for the resulting linear system $Ax = b$. For $n = 70$ and $T = 40$, for example, the MATLAB solver $A \backslash b$ delivers the results in Table 10.10, where only the first five and last ten components of x are displayed.

But the true solution not only of the defining equation (10.12) and also of the generated linear system is $x_i \equiv 1$ for all components! This "approximation" is given *without any warning or error message*. This is *not* due to ill-conditioning of the system matrix but solely due to the exponential increase of the growth factor for partial pivoting. In fact, the condition number of the matrix in this example is about 30. The self-validating method `verifylss` of INTLAB computes an inclusion of 1 with relative error less than $2.2 \cdot 10^{-16}$ in all components.

Table 10.10. MATLAB *solution of a linear system derived from (10.12) for* $n = 70$ *and* $T = 40$.

```
>> x([1:5 61:70])
ans =
    1.00000000000000
    1.00000000000000
    1.00000000000000
    1.00000000000000
    1.00000000000000
          . . .
    1.40816326530612
    2.81632653061224
    4.22448979591837
    5.63265306122449
   11.26530612244898
   11.26530612244898
   22.53061224489796
                   0
                   0
    1.00000000000000
```

As mentioned before the comparison is not really fair. This is because obviously the MATLAB routine does not perform a single residual iteration. As has been shown by Skeel [418] this would yield a backward stable result, even if the residual iteration is performed in working precision. The verification does perform iteration steps before starting the inclusion step. In that sense the comparison is not quite fair. Nevertheless the result computed by MATLAB is grossly wrong and delivered without any warning.

When solving systems of nonlinear equations it is much easier to find examples where the computed approximation is afflicted with severe errors but is delivered without an error message. We will return to such examples later.

10.11   Uncertain Parameters

Next we discuss nonlinear systems with uncertain parameters. This is at the heart of interval extensions and self-validating methods. Consider a function

$$f : \mathbb{R}^{k \times n} \to \mathbb{R}^n, \qquad f(\widetilde{p}, \widetilde{x}) \approx 0,$$

and assume the parameter p varies within a certain interval P. We wish to calculate an inclusion X such that *for all* $p \in P$ there exists some $x \in X$ with $f(p, x) = 0$. This is surprisingly simple by the following theorem.

Suppose an interval extension $F(P, X)$, $F : \mathbb{IR}^{k \times n} \to \mathbb{IR}^n$ of f is given such that for $P \in \mathbb{IR}^k$, $X \in \mathbb{IR}^n$ and for all $p \in P, x \in X$ it holds that $f(p, x) \in F(P, X)$. Furthermore, define

$$L_F(P, \widetilde{x}, X) := -R \cdot F(P, \widetilde{x}) + \{I - RM\}X,$$

where M is computed by automatic differentiation applied to F at P and X. Then the following is true [386].

Theorem 10.2. *Let* $f : \mathbb{R}^{k \times n} \to \mathbb{R}^n \in C^1$, $P \in \mathbb{IR}^n$, *and* $\widetilde{x} \in \mathbb{R}^n$ *be given. Suppose* $\widetilde{x} \in X$ *and* $L_F(P, \widetilde{x}, X) \subseteq \text{int}(X)$. *Then for all* $\widehat{p} \in P$ *there exists one and only one* $\widehat{x} = \widehat{x}(\widehat{p}) \in \widetilde{x} + X$ *with* $f(\widehat{p}, \widehat{x}) = 0$.

The proof is trivial: just consider *some fixed but arbitrary* $p \in P$, and apply Theorem 10.1 to $f(p, \widetilde{x} + x)$. Using this approach for given values of a parameter also gives a clue to the sensitivity of the zeros with respect to this parameter. Replacing, for example, the constant `pi` in Broyden's function by

```
>> Pi = midrad( 3.141592653589793, 1e-15 )
```

yields the result in Table 10.11.

Table 10.11. *INTLAB example of* `verifynlss` *for Broyden's function (10.9) with uncertain parameters.*

```
>> xs = [ .6 ; 3 ];   verifynlss(f,xs)
intval ans =
[ 0.49999999999740,  0.50000000000260]
[ 3.14159265357934,  3.14159265360025]

>> xs = [ 0 ; 0 ];   y = verifynlss(f,xs)
intval ans =
[ -0.26059929002903, -0.26059929001592]
[  0.62253089659741,  0.62253089663041]
```

Obviously, both zeros do not react very sensitively to changes in that parameter. Note that we used a formulation of the inclusion theorem, where the interval X includes the difference of the approximation $\widetilde{x}$ rather than the solution itself. This turns out [387] to produce inclusions of better quality than the original operator K_f in Theorem 10.1.

So far the application has been restricted to continuously differentiable functions. This allows us to use automatic differentiation and also ensures the uniqueness of the computed zero within the computed bounds. It also implies that it is impossible to calculate an inclusion of a multiple zero. For a real root of even multiplicity of a univariate function this is clear because an arbitrarily small perturbation can move the roots into the complex plane. But also for odd multiplicities greater than one this approach does not allow us to calculate an inclusion. We mention that inclusion of multiple zeros of continuous but not necessarily differentiable functions is possible using slopes (see [269] and improvements described in [388]).

We return to parameterized problems with data varying within some tolerances. The aim is to investigate whether the amount of overestimation can be estimated. Consider the following simple model problem.

$$A = \begin{pmatrix} [-0.5796, -0.5771] & [\ 0.2469, \ 0.2581] \\ [\ 0.2469, \ 0.2581] & [-0.4370, -0.4365] \end{pmatrix},$$

$$b = \begin{pmatrix} 0.5731 \\ -0.4910 \end{pmatrix}. \tag{10.13}$$

An inclusion of the set of all solutions

$$\sum(A, b) := \{x \in \mathbb{R}^2 : \tilde{A}x = \tilde{b}, \tilde{A} \in A, \tilde{b} \in b\} \tag{10.14}$$

may be computed by Theorem 10.3, much along the lines of the previous discussion.

Theorem 10.3. *Let $A \in \mathbb{I}M_n(\mathbb{R})$, $b \in \mathbb{IR}^n$, $R \in M_n(\mathbb{R})$, $X \in \mathbb{IR}^n$ be given and suppose*

$$R(b - A\tilde{x}) + (I - RA)X \subseteq \text{int}(X).$$

Then for all $\tilde{A} \in A$ and for all $\tilde{b} \in b$, $\tilde{A}$ and R are nonsingular and $\tilde{A}^{-1}\tilde{b} \in \tilde{x} + X$.

Theorem 10.3 is a direct consequence of Theorem 10.1 applied to $Ax = A\tilde{x} - b$. The definition and solution of our model problem in INTLAB is Table 10.12. A plot of the inclusion interval X is given in Figure 10.23.

Table 10.12. *INTLAB example of* `verifylss` *for a linear system with uncertain data.*

```
>> A = infsup( [-0.5796 0.2469 ; 0.2469 -0.4370 ] , ...
               [-0.5771 0.2581 ; 0.2581 -0.4365 ] );
        b =   [ 0.5731 ; -0.4910 ];
>> X = verifylss(A,b)
  intval X =
[    -0.6862,    -0.6517]
[     0.7182,     0.7567]
```

First remember that this result includes the proof that all matrices $\tilde{A} \in A$ are nonsingular, and this is, in general, an NP-hard problem. But, we may ask how much the interval X overestimates the true solution set $\sum(A, b)$. The latter is known to be convex in every orthant.[43] Indeed a so-called *inner* inclusion can be calculated by Theorem 10.4 [388], which is based on ideas developed in [339].

Theorem 10.4. *Let $A \in \mathbb{IR}^{n \times n}$, $b \in \mathbb{IR}^n$, $\tilde{x} \in \mathbb{R}^n$, $R \in \mathbb{R}^{n \times n}$, $X \in \mathbb{IR}^n$ be given and define*

$$Z := R(b - A\tilde{x}) \quad and \quad \Delta := \{I - RA\} \cdot X.$$

---

[43]Orthant is the generalization of quadrant (2D) and octant (3D) to higher dimensions.

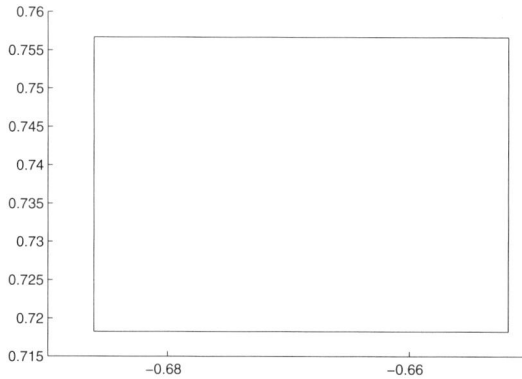

Figure 10.23. *Inclusion as computed by* `verifylss` *for the example in Table 10.12.*

Let the solution set $\sum(A, b)$ be defined as in (10.14) and assume

$$Z + \Delta \subseteq \text{int}(X).$$

Then

$$\sum(A, b) \subseteq \widetilde{x} + Z + \Delta,$$

or, in coordinate notation, for all $x \in \sum(A, b)$ and all $i \in \{1, \ldots, n\}$,

$$\widetilde{x}_i + \inf Z_i + \inf \Delta_i \leq x_i \leq \widetilde{x}_i + \sup Z_i + \sup \Delta_i.$$

Furthermore, for all $i \in \{1, \ldots, n\}$ there exist $\underline{x}, \overline{x} \in \sum(A, b)$, with

$$\underline{x}_i \leq \widetilde{x}_i + \inf Z_i + \sup \Delta_i \quad and \quad \widetilde{x}_i + \sup Z_i + \inf \Delta_i \leq \overline{x}_i.$$

Theorem 10.4 estimates every component of the solution set from the outside *and the inside*. For our model problem, the inner rectangle has the property that the projection to every coordinate is an inner inclusion of the corresponding projection of the true solution set $\sum(A, b)$. The outer and inner inclusions together with the true solution set (the parallelogram) are displayed in Figure 10.24.

Of course, this approach has its limits. When widening the interval components of the linear system, the inner inclusion becomes smaller and smaller, and finally vanishes (which means nothing can be said about the quality of the outer inclusion), and, when further widening the input intervals, the inclusion will fail at a certain point. This happens, in general, *before* a singular matrix enters the input intervals. This is to be expected because the self-validating algorithm for an $n \times n$ linear system requires some $O(n^3)$ operations, whereas, as has been mentioned before, the problem of determining whether an interval matrix contains a singular matrix is NP-hard [365].

The model problem above looks pretty simple. However, a nontrivial problem has been solved: the determination of the maximum variation of the individual components of

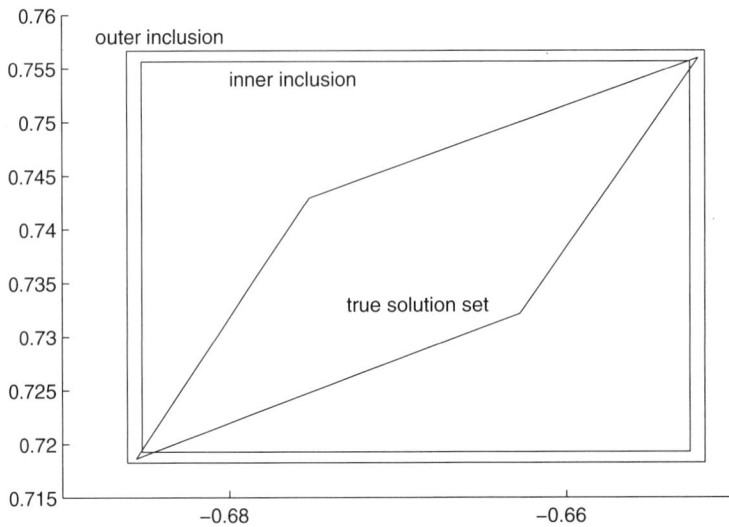

Figure 10.24. *Inner and outer inclusions and true solution set for the linear system with tolerances in Table 10.12.*

a linear system when varying the input data within a certain range, and the computation of an upper bound *and a lower bound* for this variation. Using traditional numerical methods such as Monte Carlo to determine similar information may be difficult.

In order to demonstrate this, consider an interval matrix A and interval right-hand side b, for which we wish to estimate $\sum(A, b)$. A Monte Carlo approach may be like in the program of Figure 10.25.

$$
\begin{aligned}
&\text{for} \quad i = 1 : K \\
&\qquad \text{choose } \widetilde{A} \in A \\
&\qquad \text{choose } \widetilde{b} \in b \\
&\qquad \text{compute } \widetilde{x} = \widetilde{A} \backslash \widetilde{b} \\
&\qquad x_{\min} = \min(x_{\min}, \widetilde{x}) \\
&\qquad x_{\max} = \max(x_{\max}, \widetilde{x}) \\
&\text{end}
\end{aligned}
$$

Figure 10.25. *Monte Carlo approach to estimate the solution set of a parameterized linear system.*

Consider a linear system with randomly generated matrix $\widetilde{A}$ and right-hand side $\widetilde{b}$, both with entries within $[-1, 1]$. Then an interval matrix A and interval right-hand side b are defined by perturbing each component of $\widetilde{A}$ and $\widetilde{b}$ with a relative error 10^{-4}, respectively. The Monte Carlo approach is improved by choosing $\widetilde{A}$ and $\widetilde{b}$ only on the boundary of A and b, respectively, in order to achieve a best possible (i.e., as wide as possible) result. For

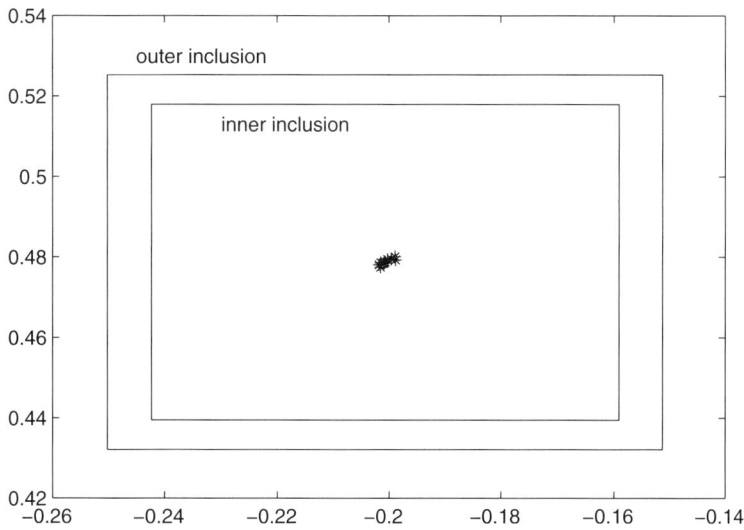

Figure 10.26. *Result of Monte Carlo approach as in the program in Figure 10.25 for* 100×100 *random linear system with tolerances, projection of 1st and 2nd component of solution.*

$K = 100$ samples the projection of the first and second components of the result is shown in Figure 10.26.

Figure 10.26 shows the variation achieved by the Monte Carlo method (the black cloud of asterisks) and the outer and inner inclusions computed by the self-validating method based on Theorem 10.4. The computing times on our 300 MHz laptop are as follows.

| Self-validating method | 0.39 sec, |
| Monte Carlo method | 11.9   sec. |

Note that 100 samples have been used for a 100×100 linear system. These results are typical. Although the computed inclusions are almost sharp, they are usually achieved only for a very few choices of input data.

This good news is shadowed by the bad news that the self-validating method assumes the input data vary *independently* within the tolerances. This assumption is frequently not fulfilled. For example, the restriction of variation to symmetric matrices may shrink the size of the solution set significantly. However, this and other linear dependencies between the input data can be handled by self-validating methods. The following shows a plot of example (10.13) with symmetric matrices; see [237, 387].

The plot in Figure 10.27 shows the previous unsymmetric solution set (big parallelogram) as well as the true symmetric solution set (in bold). The latter can be calculated exactly using methods described in [10]. Moreover, the outer and inner inclusions for the symmetric solution set are displayed. In the same way, Toeplitz, Hankel, tridiagonal symmetric, and other linear structures can be handled [387]. However, the Monte Carlo

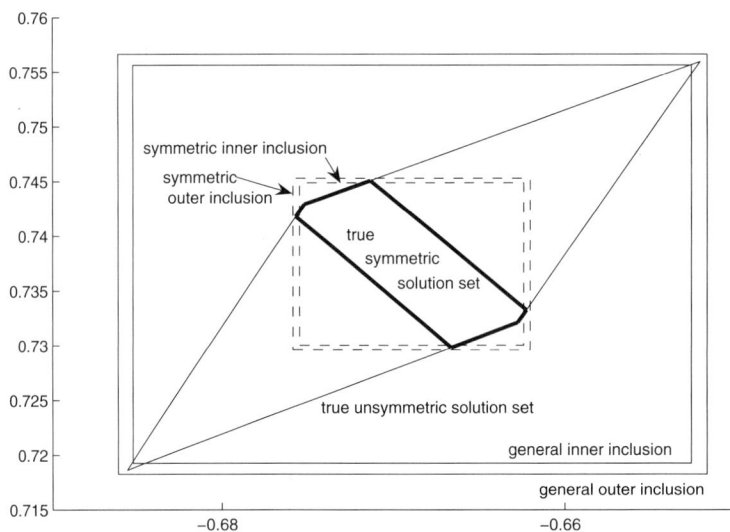

Figure 10.27. *Inner and outer inclusions of symmetric solution set for the example in Table 10.12.*

approach easily allows almost arbitrary dependencies between the input data, for which no self-validating method is known.

We mention that there are self-validating algorithms for sparse systems of linear and nonlinear equations [387]. Of course, they do not use an approximate inverse as in Theorem 10.1 but are based on a lower bound of the smallest singular value of the system matrix or the Jacobian matrix, respectively. Figure 10.28 shows a matrix from the Harwell/Boeing test suite [128]. It has 3948 unknowns and comes from a static analysis in structural engineering of some offshore platform. Computing times for this example for the MATLAB built-in sparse linear system solver and INTLAB routine `verifylss` are given in Table 10.13.

Table 10.13. *Computing time without and with verification.*

	Time [sec]
MATLAB	2.5
`verifylss`	6.3

So verification is still slower by a factor of 3, which is partly due to interpretation overhead in MATLAB. However, verified linear system solvers are still based on factorizations. For matrices with large fill-in these methods are not applicable. In particular, practically no self-validating methods based on iterative approaches are known.

As stated earlier, a numerical method may deliver a poor approximate answer without warning. Problems may occur when using this information for further computations. Consider, for example, the matrix in Table 10.14.

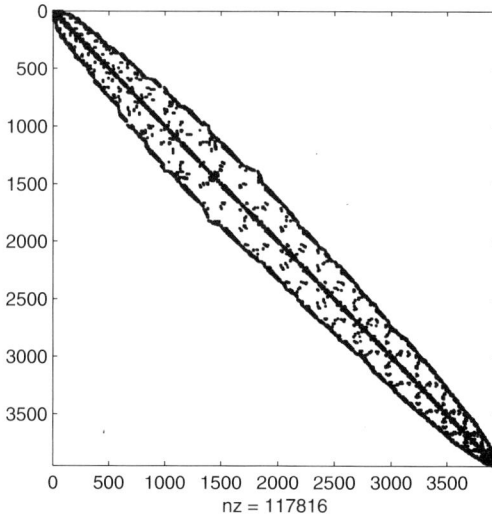

Figure 10.28. *Nonzero elements of the matrix from Harwell/Boeing BCSSTK15.*

Table 10.14. *Matrix with ill-conditioned eigenvalues.*

```
A  =
     170     122     -52    -317    -247     265      86
     -38     -28      13      71      56     -59     -21
     -90     -64      27     167     130    -140     -46
      61      42     -16    -111     -85      94      31
      -7      -4       1      11       8     -10      -5
     -26     -19       9      49      39     -41     -14
     -51     -37      16      96      75     -80     -25
```

The question is "What are the eigenvalues of that matrix?" When entering this matrix into MATLAB, the approximations in Figure 10.29 depicted by the plus signs are computed without warning or error message. When computing the eigenvalues of A^T, the approximate "eigenvalues" depicted by the circles are computed, again without warning or error message. Notice the scale of the plot: the approximations of eigenvalues of A and A^T differ by about 0.005. The reason for the inaccuracy is that this matrix has a multiple (7-fold) eigenvalue zero of geometric multiplicity 1. This implies a sensitivity of $\sqrt[7]{\epsilon_M} \approx 0.006$ for changes of the input data of order ϵ_M, the machine precision $2^{-52} \approx 2.2 \cdot 10^{-16}$.

The circle is a verified inclusion of all eigenvalues of the matrix. It has been computed by the methods described in [390] for the inclusion of multiple eigenvalues and the corresponding invariant subspace. In view of the previous discussion the circle gives reasonable information about the sensitivity of the eigenvalues. It is a little pessimistic, but it is correct information. Taking only the approximations (depicted by the plus signs or the circles) one

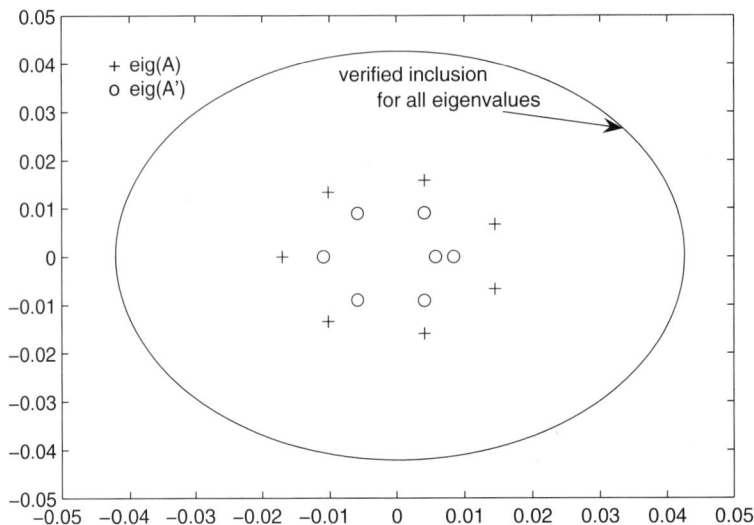

Figure 10.29. *Approximation of eigenvalues of the matrix in Table 10.14 computed by* MATLAB.

might be led to the conclusion that these are accurate approximations to the eigenvalues of the matrix—neglecting their sensitivity.

Another interesting point is *testing*. In our experience, testing self-validating algorithms is different from testing traditional numerical algorithms. Consider an algorithm for solving systems of linear equations. A standard test suite would randomly generate some matrices of different condition numbers. Then, for given solution vector $\widehat{x}$, one would calculate $b := A\widehat{x}$ and test for the difference of the computed approximation $\widetilde{x}$ and $\widehat{x}$.

However, in general the product $A\widehat{x}$ would be perturbed by rounding errors, such that $\widehat{x}$ would *not* be the solution of the linear system $Ax = b$. Accordingly, the test suite could only check for

$$\|\widehat{x} - \widetilde{x}\|/\|\widetilde{x}\| \leq \varphi \cdot \text{eps} \cdot \text{cond}(A) \qquad (10.15)$$

with a moderate factor φ. Such a test suite would not be suitable for testing a self-validating algorithm because the solution of the given linear system $Ax = b$ is not known. In contrast, one would make sure that the product $A\widehat{x} = b$ is exactly representable in floating point (and is computed exactly). One way to achieve this is to round A (and $\widehat{x}$) such that only a few (leading) digits of all entries are nonzero. Then, for a computed inclusion X, one can test for $\widetilde{x} \in X$—a more stringent test than (10.15).

Another, even more stringent, test for robustness and accuracy is the following. Suppose we have a model problem, and the exact solution is π. Moreover, suppose a self-validating method produces the result

[3.141592653589792,   3.141592653589793].

Each of the bounds would be an *approximation* of superb quality, and any numerical algorithm delivering one of the two bounds as final result would pass any test with flying colors.

But a self-validating algorithm delivering these bounds *would fail*, because the transcendental number π is not enclosed in the above interval! Such tests are powerful for detecting erroneous implementations of self-validating methods.

10.12   Conclusion

We have tried to show that self-validating methods may be used to compute true and verified bounds for the solution of certain problems. There would be much more to say to that, and many more examples could be given. Because of the limited space we could in particular show only some small examples and applications. But self-validating methods have been applied to a variety of larger problems with tens of thousands of unknowns, particularly in connection with computer-assisted proofs.

Examples of those include

- verification of the existence of the Lorenz attractor [455],

- the verification of the existence of chaos [343],

- the double-bubble conjecture [199],

- verification of the instability for the Orr–Sommerfeld equations with a Blasius profile [278],

- dynamics of the Jouanolou foliation [63],

- solution of the heat convection problem [335],

- verified bounds for the Feigenbaum constant [133],

- existence of an eigenvalue below the essential spectrum of the Sturm–Liouville problem [56],

- eigenfrequencies of a turbine (Kulisch et al., unpublished),

- SPICE program for circuit analysis (Rump, unpublished),

- extreme currents in Lake Constance (Rump, unpublished),

- forest planning [236].

A more detailed description of some of these can be found in [155]. Also, self-validating methods have been designed for various other areas of numerical mathematics. They include

- global optimization [52, 86, 171, 179, 182, 238, 239, 240, 241, 265, 320, 341, 374, 375, 461],

- *all* the zeros of a nonlinear system in a box [182, 265, 375, 396, 461, 498],

- least squares problems [268, 302, 386],

- sparse linear and nonlinear problems [387],

- ordinary differential equation initial value and boundary value problems [294, 337],

- partial differential equations [25, 334, 335, 362, 363, 364].

Most recently, efforts were started to design self-validating methods which require in total *the same* computing time as a traditional numerical algorithm; see [353].

We started with the question "What is a proof?" As mentioned earlier, we did not intend to (and cannot) give an answer to that. However, we have shown why using self-validating methods, executed in floating-point arithmetic, can be considered as a serious way to ascertain the validity of mathematical assertions. Self-validating methods are by no means intended to replace a mathematical proof, but they may assist. A lot has been done, but there is much more to do; see, for example, [342].

As a final remark we want to stress that self-validating methods are also not designed to replace traditional numerical methods. This fact is quite obvious as (i) most self-validating methods rely on a good numerical approximation to start a verification, and (ii) in direct comparison an interval computation must include the floating-point result. This applies to the direct solution of numerical problems such as systems of nonlinear equations or partial differential equations. However, self-validating methods do more: They verify existence and possibly uniqueness of a solution within computed bounds. This is outside the scope of traditional numerical algorithms.

A different regime is global optimization methods, where sophisticated inclusions of the range of functions may be used to discard certain boxes by proving that they cannot contain a global minimum. This is a very promising area with recent and quite interesting results.

The MATLAB toolbox INTLAB is a simple way to get acquainted with self-validating methods and to solve problems. It is freely available from our homepage for noncommercial use. Every routine comes with a header explaining input, output, and behavior of the routines. To date we have an estimated number of 3500 users in more than 40 countries.

In conclusion, we want to say that self-validating methods are an option; they are a possibility to verify the validity of a result, when necessary. In that sense they deserve their space in the realm of computational mathematics.

Chapter 11

Hardware-assisted Algorithms

Craig C. Douglas and Hans Petter Langtangen

11.1 Introduction

Computers are complex electrical devices with many hardware components. As more functionality moves from separate chips onto a single chip, it is easy to forget (or never learn) how to exploit hardware functionality that can greatly speed up common numerical methods.

Just as carefully programming for vector operations made codes run very quickly on old Cray vector supercomputers, carefully programming for data locality and reuse makes codes today run very quickly on cache memory-based CPUs. In this chapter, we will discuss techniques that can make implementations of common numerical algorithms much more cache aware. As a result, the cache aware implementations will run faster than standard implementations.

Cache experts used to believe that portable, cache aware algorithms were a myth. Folklore said that only by using every last detail of the CPU and its memory hierarchy could a fast, cache aware algorithm be designed.

Users who maintain a collection of portable cache aware algorithms in their code portfolios have suddenly discovered their codes' performance are very high on a wide variety of platforms, from laptops and PCs to supercomputers, though with the caveat that not the last bit of performance is achieved on any system—*just good enough performance*.

There are several good references about how caches are designed and should be used:

- [356] is updated often, and any edition is encyclopedic about processor design.

- The book [190] is small, provides clear details, and has historically interesting anecdotes.

- [167] provides a simple introduction to memory caches and programming tricks to make use of them in scientific codes.

241

- The online tutorial [127] is updated once or twice a year and provides a much more in-depth description of how to use caches for iterative methods related to solving partial differential equations (PDEs).

11.2   A Teaser

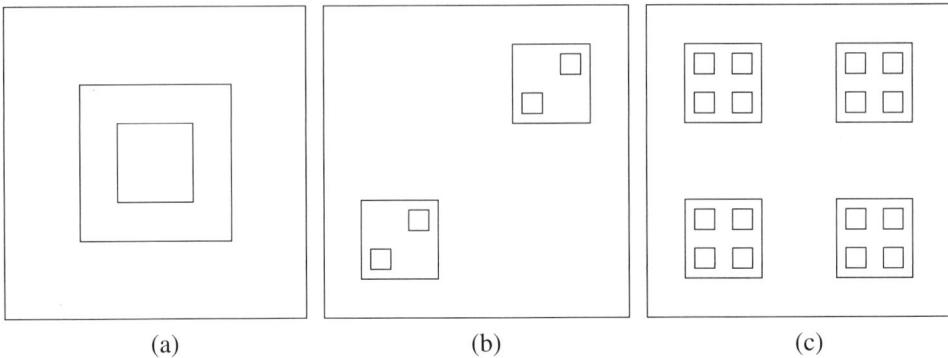

Figure 11.1. *Refinement patterns:* (a) *One refinement per patch.* (b) *Two refinements per patch.* (c) *Four refinements per patch.*

Consider an adaptive mesh refined multigrid solver on structured grids (e.g., [443]), such as the three examples in Figure 11.1. Each refinement reduces the mesh spacing by a factor of two inside the patches. So in the One case (Figure 11.1(a)), the outermost patch has mesh spacing h, the first refined patch has spacing $h/2$, and the next, or innermost, patch has spacing $h/4$. A similar procedure is used in the Two and Four cases.

We applied a simple variable coefficient, second order, variable coefficient elliptic boundary value problem on the unit square to the three example meshes in Figure 11.1. Table 11.1 contains typical speedups for the three examples in Figure 11.1 as well as for full grid refinement. The speedups reported were using an HP workstation (Itanium^2, McKinley type) with a 2.2 megabyte L2 cache and a typical Pentium IV laptop with a 512 kilobyte L2 cache. We tested a number of other architectures and found similar speedups.

Table 11.1. *Speedups using a cache aware multigrid algorithm on adaptively refined structured grids.*

Non–Cache Aware(2,2) versus CAMG(0,4)		
Refinements	Itanium^2 (McKinley)	Pentium IV
Full	2.6902	2.2830
One	4.1683	3.4504
Two	5.1062	4.1290
Four	5.0812	4.0294

How do we get such great speedups? We cheat. We do not get the exact same solution numerically, but one that has the same error in some appropriate error norm. This is both a plus (speed) and a minus (reliability). There are other methods for getting bitwise compatibility between the standard implementations and cache aware ones. We will discuss bitwise compatible algorithms later in Section 11.9.

11.3 Processor and Memory Subsystem Organization

A CPU performs the numerical and logical calculations when a program is executed. Today, almost all CPUs are some form of microprocessor.

The data for the CPU is stored in the main memory. When the CPU requires data that it does not already have, it makes a request to memory. Memory chips run at almost the same speed as a decade ago while CPUs are orders of magnitude faster. Unfortunately, current CPUs perform numerical operations far faster than memory can deliver data, which leads to fast CPUs being idle most of the time.

While the performance of a program used to be evaluated based on the number of floating-point operations, now it should be measured by the number of cache misses or the cost of getting data. The floating-point operations are virtually free in a program that has a large quantity of cache misses.

Many hardware and software strategies exist to reduce the time that a CPU is waiting for data. The standard hardware strategy is to divide computer memory into a hierarchy of different levels with the CPU linked directly to the highest level. These layers are referred to as the cache or the memory subsystem [190, 356].

The cache memory subsystem is fast, expensive memory that replicates a subset of data from main memory. It is usually made from static rather than dynamic RAM and has a very fast cycle time. The purpose of the cache is to provide data to the CPU faster than the main memory can. The CPU should be less idle when cached data is used.

Caches are motivated by two principles of locality in time and space:

- The principle of temporal locality states that data required by the CPU now will also be necessary again in the near future.

- The principle of spatial locality states that if specific data is required now, its neighboring data will be referenced soon.

The cache is itself a hierarchy of levels, called L1, L2, ..., each with a different size and speed. One to three levels of cache is typical. The L1 cache is smaller and 2–6 times faster than the L2 cache. The L2 cache in turn is smaller than main memory but is 10–40 times faster than main memory. Other cache levels continue this trend.

The smallest block of data moved in and out of a cache is a *cache line*. A cache line holds data which is stored contiguously in the main memory. A typical cache line is 32–256 bytes in length, with 32 being most common. A cache line is the smallest unit of data transfer between the memory units and the CPU.

If the data that the CPU requests is in a cache, it is called a *cache hit*. Otherwise it is a *cache miss* and data must be copied from a lower level (i.e., a slower level) of memory into a cache. The *hit rate* is the ratio of cache hits to total memory requests. The *miss rate* is one minus the hit rate.

We clearly want to maximize the number of cache hits since cache is faster than main memory in fulfilling the CPU's memory requests. In designing algorithms to maximize cache hits, we must first decide which cache to optimize for. For a database or Web server, L1 caches of only 8–16 KiB are useful. For a coupled PDE solver in three dimensions, a 6 MiB cache is interesting, but one of 256 KiB is not.

Caches on any level may be unified or split:

- Unified caches mix both computer instructions and data.

- Split caches are two separate caches with instructions in one and data in the other.

Split caches are superior to unified ones since the hit ratio tends to be much better for instructions than in unified caches and conflicts are reduced. Unified caches exhibit evil behavior and are best left out of a computer.

Programmers think of memory as a linear space with addressing beginning at zero. Actually, memory is set of physical memory pages that are neither contiguous nor linear. A translation scheme is used from virtual memory addresses to physical memory addresses using hardware. The logic in most cache systems uses the physical addresses of the pages, not the virtual addresses used by the programs, to determine where in cache memory chunks should be copied. Since running a program twice usually means that it is loaded into different physical memory pages, the cache effects are rarely exactly reproducible and, in fact, exhibit a nondeterministic behavior.

In order to service CPU requests efficiently the memory subsystem must be able to determine whether requested data is present in a cache and where in the cache that data resides. This must be done extremely quickly, which limits the methods that can be implemented severely to ones that are less than optimal in strategy.

The original method is a *direct mapped* cache. The location in the cache is determined using the remainder of the (physical) main memory address divided by the cache size:

$$\text{cache address} = (\text{main memory address}) \bmod (\text{size of cache}).$$

Unfortunately, multiple addresses in the main memory map to the same cache line.

Hence, there is only one location in the cache that a given main memory address can occupy. Traditionally, the number of lines, N, in the cache is always a power of two, so that the remainder operation is equivalent to taking the last $\log_2(N)$ bits of the main memory address. The set bits are the last bits of the main memory address corresponding to the cache address. The tag bits are the remaining bits of the main memory address. The set bits of a request determine where in the cache to look, and the tag bits determine whether a match occurs.

Another hardware cache technique is *n-way set associativity*, which maps memory to n "ways," or segments, inside a cache. A given memory address could be placed in any of the n segments of the cache. (A direct mapped cache corresponds to a 1-way set associative cache.) A policy for deciding in which "way" a piece of data should be stored is required for set associative caches. There are three common algorithms for choosing in which "way" a cache line should be placed:

- least recently used (LRU),

- least frequently used (LFU), and

- random replacement.

These are called replacement policies since when a cache line is placed into the cache it replaces a cache line that is already there.

Accessing memory on a memory chip is determined by passing an address through a small collection of AND, OR, and XOR gates. A cache can be considerably more complex since it must have logic to copy or replace a collection of memory locations from the main memory, all of which takes time.

LRU caches track how long ago cache lines were referenced. LFU caches track how often cache lines have been referenced. For many PDE algorithms, LRU caches tend to provide the best performance. However, both of these algorithms are expensive to implement in hardware.

The random replacement policy is very popular with computer architects since it is relatively inexpensive and studies show that it is almost equivalent to LRU (see [190] and its references). The examples picked for the study were clearly well chosen since this strategy is horrible for problems involving the solution of PDEs.

11.4 Cache Conflicts and Trashing

Suppose that three n-vectors A, B, and C each map to the same cache locations. Then each reference to $A(i)$, $B(i)$, or $C(i)$ causes the same cache line to be used. The cache line is constantly emptied and refilled causing *cache thrashing*. Hence, in terms of the memory latency time L, the cost of running the code fragment is at least nL for the code fragment

    1: **for** $i = 1, n$ **do**
    2:     $C(i) = A(i) + \alpha * B(i)$
    3: **end for**

There are two simple fixes for this example.

1. The vectors can be padded by a small multiple of the cache line length (common padding sizes are 128 or 256 bytes independent of whether better padding sizes might exist). This is hardly portable, however, since the correct size of a padding is very machine dependent.

2. The data structure is changed to combine A, B, and C into a single array, e.g., r. Then the code fragment becomes

       1: **for** $i = 1, n$ **do**
       2:     $r(3, i) = r(1, i) + r(2, i)$
       3: **end for**

The second fix assumes that the vector elements are in adjacent memory locations. This reduces the number of cache misses by approximately a factor of three on any of the cache designs discussed, and it is highly portable.

11.5 Prefetching

Bringing data into cache before it is needed, and while the memory to cache lines are free, is known as *prefetching*. This technique reduces the effect of memory latency.

Cache lines longer than one word are one example of prefetching. When data is brought into cache, surrounding data accompanies it. For data exhibiting spatial locality, the surrounding data has been prefetched. Hence, prefetching satisfies CPU requests at the speed of cache instead of slower memory.

Prefetching is particularly effective within loops. For example, consider the following code fragment:

```
1: (intervening code)
2: for i = 1, n do
3:     A(i) = A(i) + β * B(i)
4:     (more intervening code)
5:     D(i) = D(i) + γ * C(i)
6:     (yet more intervening code)
7: end for
```

Assume that the intervening code depends on data already in the cache. On iteration i it may be possible to bring $A(i + 1)$, $B(i + 1)$, $C(i + 1)$, and $D(i + 1)$ into the cache before the CPU needs them by means of explicit prefetch instructions.

```
 1: PREFETCH A(1), B(1), and β
 2: (intervening code)
 3: for i = 1, n do
 4:     A(i) = A(i) + β * B(i)
 5:     PREFETCH C(i) and D(i)
 6:     (more intervening code)
 7:     C(i) = C(i) + γ * D(i)
 8:     PREFETCH A(i + 1) and B(i + 1)
 9:     (yet more intervening code)
10: end for
```

Prefetching is, unfortunately, highly machine dependent and therefore not portable. It can be accomplished with compiler flags, programmer intervention, or hardware.

11.6   Pipelining and Loop Unrolling

Breaking complex calculations into simpler steps is referred to as *pipelining* and is often used in combination with prefetching. A common analogy to pipelining is an assembly line. The result of one simple calculation is passed onto the next simple calculation, which is passed on until the final result is assembled. This does not speed up a single calculation, but it can speed up the same calculation repeated many times.

Pipelining can be implemented either by hardware (as in many RISC processors) or by software. In the latter case, loops are unrolled and complex calculations are broken into very simple steps. Pipelining also helps hide memory latency since calculations occur at the same time as data is fetched from the main memory.

Consider the following code fragment illustrating a scalar multiply and add (*daxpy*) with two n-vectors A and B:

```
1: for i = 1, n do
2:     A(i) = A(i) + γ * B(i)
3: end for
```

Provided that the CPU supports pipelining (i.e., it has several independent arithmetic units), a good compiler can generate good, pipelined code. In executing such code, one arithmetic unit performs the scalar multiply while the other unit performs an addition. Once the pipeline has been filled, a *daxpy* operation is completed at each cycle. Hence, the time to complete the operation is the time to load the pipeline plus n times the basic operations time. The programmer can provide a hint to the compiler by breaking the *daxpy* into two simpler operations:

1: **for** $i = 1, n$ **do**
2:     $t = \gamma * B(i)$
3:       $A(i) = A(i) + t$
4: **end for**

Most compilers are capable of automatically recognizing and generating optimal machine code for a *daxpy* loop. However, it is quite easy to fool a compiler with code that is similar, but not close enough to a *daxpy*. Then it is common for a programmer to do a better job of loop unrolling by hand than the compiler provides automatically. This leads to nonportable constructs like

1: **for** $i = 1, n, 4$ **do**
2:     $A(i) = A(i) + \gamma * B(i)$
3:     $A(i + 1) = A(i + 1) + \gamma * B(i + 1)$
4:     $A(i + 2) = A(i + 2) + \gamma * B(i + 2)$
5:     $A(i + 3) = A(i + 3) + \gamma * B(i + 3)$
6: **end for**

It is nonportable since on some systems, unrolling by 4 is suboptimal.

This type of hand optimization is quite dangerous to long term performance unless it is isolated to modules that are automatically generated through some other process. The ATLAS project [482] is an example of automatically generating the Basic Linear Algebra Subroutines (BLAS) using a series of tests to determine good enough or optimal loop unrolling.

11.7   Padding and Data Reorganization

Padding has already been mentioned as one method for avoiding cache thrashing. An array is lengthened by adding a small number of extra elements, usually the amount in one cache line. This forces arrays that originally thrashed the cache to map to different cache addresses.

Stride-1 access to arrays enhances spatial locality, since bringing one array element into cache also brings in neighboring array elements that are on the same cache line.

Data reorganization has a serious impact on performance. Most programmers assume that this technique is too intrusive. However, when possible, it usually is an inexpensive way to speed up codes.

Suppose a matrix M has only nd nonzero diagonals and can be stored as an array $A(nd, n)$. If an n-vector f is always used in loops involving A, then it frequently makes sense to add f into A as either the first or the last column. Hence, the array is redefined as $A(nd + 1, n)$.

Another example is accessing memory in a sparse matrix that is stored using a row (or column) compressed storage scheme. Normally, three vectors are used to access a nonzero. There is a vector with indices into the other vectors that represent the beginning of where a row is stored. One of the other vectors has the column index and the last vector has the actual nonzero value of the matrix.

One way to think of this process is that the first vector provides an index into the other vectors for 1×1 blocks of nonzeros. For many applications, storing small ($r \times c$) blocks makes more sense. Even a 1×2 or 1×3 can make up to a 50 % reduction in the time to compute a sparse matrix-vector multiplication.

11.8   Loop Fusion

Loops can be combined and/or blocked by reordering data access so that the number of memory accesses is minimized. The reordering depends on both the data and cache sizes. The benefit is that data is reused (many times) in the cache.

The simplest form of loop fusion is to combine two related loops, e.g.,

```
1: for i = 1, n do
2:     A(i) = A(i) + B(i)
3: end for
4: for i = 1, n do
5:     C(i) = C(i) − A(i)
6: end for
```

into one loop:

```
1: for i = 1, n do
2:     A(i) = A(i) + B(i)
3:     C(i) = C(i) − A(i)
4: end for
```

The initial version with two loops required $4n$ memory references while the fused, single loop requires only $3n$ memory references.

Matrix-matrix multiplication is a common example [125]. It is blocked to enhance performance in commercial vendors' libraries. The ATLAS project [482] relies extensively on blocking to tune the Basic Linear Algebra Subroutines (BLAS) automatically.

The standard form of matrix-matrix multiplication is the following:

```
1: for i = 1, n do
2:     for j = 1, n do
3:         for k = 1, n do
4:             C(i, j) = A(i, k) ∗ B(k, j)
5:         end for
6:     end for
7: end for
```

A cache aware, blocked form has twice as many loops and requires tuning to pick the blocking parameter s correctly for a given machine, but data only passes through the cache once. We here[44] use the notation $1, n, s$ to mean running from 1 to n with an increment of s.

```
 1: for i = 1, n, s do
 2:    for j = 1, n, s do
 3:       for k = 1, n, s do
 4:          for l = i, i + s - 1 do
 5:             for m = j, j + s - 1 do
 6:                for p = k, k + s - 1 do
 7:                   C(l, m) = A(l, p) * B(p, m)
 8:                end for
 9:             end for
10:          end for
11:       end for
12:    end for
13: end for
```

Combining loop fusion with loop unrolling leads to very efficient implementations. Some software libraries (typically provided and tuned by a computer vendor) can reach 90% of the peak performance of a CPU for (dense) matrix-matrix multiplication.

11.9 Bitwise Compatibility

Using cache algorithms can be both intrusive to programming styles and can cause the results to change subtly, and therefore appear at first like bugs in the code. By implementing a mathematical algorithm in such a way that the arithmetic is performed exactly in the same order as a standard implementation, bitwise compatibility can be maintained and debugging the cache aware program becomes far easier.

If u is the result using a standard implementation and u_{ca} is the result using a cache aware implementation, then

$$\|u - u_{ca}\| = 0$$

in order for bitwise compatibility to exist. If the norm is nonzero, one of the implementations is incorrect and does not satisfy the mathematical algorithm.

A good summary of techniques for solving elliptic PDEs on either structured or unstructured meshes in a bitwise compatible manner is in [126].

Consider once again the structured meshes from Section 11.2. If the smoother inside the multigrid algorithm is k iterations of the naturally ordered Gauss–Seidel algorithm, then we can adapt the algorithm to be completely cache aware in a bitwise compatible manner rather easily. For a two-dimensional tensor product mesh, define Update(i) to be a Gauss–Seidel update for the entire row i of the mesh. For a five- or nine-point discretization of the PDE, doing

```
Update(i), Update(i-1),..., Update(i-k+1), k>0,
```

---

[44]If the third parameter is omitted it gets the default value 1. For simplicity we assume that $n = s \times v$ for some integer v.

leads to all i rows being updated in a bitwise compatible manner. (We ignore here for simplicity how updates in the last k rows are completed.)

If k rows fit in the cache, then the data is only moved through the cache once (in theory). A standard implementation brings data through cache k. If the Gauss–Seidel implementation is fused with a final residual calculation, then data passes through cache once versus $k + 1$ times. This leads, in theory, to significant speedups.

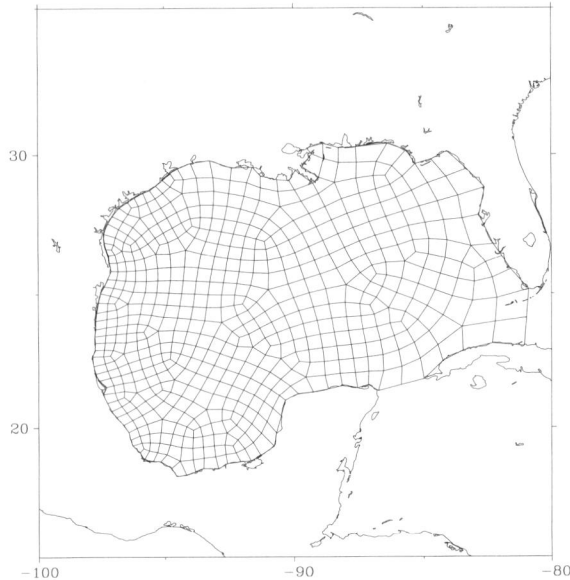

Figure 11.2. *An unstructured grid.*

For unstructured meshes, a similar method can be developed [209]. Consider the mesh in Figure 11.2. The mesh can be decomposed into cache blocks using standard domain decomposition and load-balancing algorithms used to solve PDEs on parallel computers. By measuring the distance from a cache boundary, an update ordering can be constructed using simple graph theory and bitwise compatibility can be established for Gauss–Seidel or similar algorithms.

11.10   Useful Tools

There are several tools that are quite useful in identifying *hotspots* inside of codes that warrant attention for substituting reliable cache aware implementations. These tools use hardware registers to collect statistics, are not intrusive, and provide accurate performance information.

- Valgrind [405] is particularly simple and provides information about cache activity, including the number of cache misses. It is a library that is linked to a code and just works. It does not work on parallel systems using MPI, however.

- PAPI [325] is similar to the Silicon Graphics hardware measuring tool perfmon, but runs on many platforms. It provides an interface to CPUs' hardware statistical counters in order to see how the cache memory is utilized.

- HPCToolkit [147] is by far the most comprehensive tool and runs on many different platforms, including single and multiple processor cases. Many measures can be used, not just cache misses. This tool allows a user to see how small changes in a routine can have different effects on different platforms.

There are several other, vendor-specific tools.

An underlying piece of logic for creating the HPCToolkit is the following: *Using the 90-10 rule (90% of the run time is in 10% of a code), finding where cache aware methods are useful is difficult if a 500,000 line code is the object of attention since dealing with a 50,000 line hotspot is beyond most people's capability to work with simultaneously.*

Finally, while improving code performance while maintaining the same results is important, accurately and unobtrusively measuring the performance is also still somewhat of an art.

Chapter 12

Issues in Accurate and Reliable Use of Parallel Computing in Numerical Programs

William D. Gropp

12.1 Introduction

Parallel computing, as used in technical computing, is fundamentally about achieving higher performance than is possible with a uniprocessor. The unique issues for accurate and reliable computing are thus directly related to this desire for performance. This chapter briefly covers the major types of parallel computers, the programming models used with them, and issues in the choice and implementation of algorithms.

12.2 Special Features of Parallel Computers

The fundamental feature of parallel computation is multiple *threads of control*. That is, a parallel computer can execute more than one operation at a time. The most common parallel computers today can execute different instructions on different data; these are called multiple instruction multiple data (MIMD) computers. Another type executes the same operation on different data (same instruction multiple data, or SIMD). While some of the issues discussed in this chapter apply to SIMD computers, many are the result of the ability of different processors within MIMD systems to execute different instructions at the same time. The discussion focuses on MIMD parallel computers.

Parallel computers can also be distinguished by the way they provide access to data. A computer that provides hardware support for a common address space accessible by all processors is said to provide *shared memory*. The most common systems are *symmetric multiprocessors* (SMPs), where symmetric here means that all processors are equal; that is, no processor is designated as the "operating system" processor. The other major type of parallel computer does not provide support for a common address space and instead consists of essentially separate computers (often called nodes), each with its own memory space, and an interconnection network that allows data to be communicated between the nodes.

These machines are said to be *distributed-memory* parallel computers. Most of the largest parallel computers are distributed-memory computers.

12.2.1   The major programming models

The two most common programming models are distinguished by how they treat the memory of each processor being used by a single parallel program. In the *shared-memory* programming model, all of the memory is available to every thread of control. In the *distributed-memory* (or *shared-nothing*) programming model, only the memory of the process is available to that process (and a parallel program is made up of many processes). The most common instances of the shared-memory model are threads and compiler-directed parallelism through interfaces, such as OpenMP [354]. The most common distributed-memory model is the message-passing model, specifically using the Message Passing Interface (MPI) [313, 314].

Another important programming model is the *bulk synchronous parallel* (BSP) model [308, 35]. This model emphasizes organizing a parallel computation around "supersteps" during which each processor can act on local data and initiate communications with other processors. At the end of the superstep a barrier synchronization is performed. One of the most common implementations of this model, the Oxford BSP library [207], provides remote memory operations (also known as put/get programming). Aspects of the BSP model were incorporated into version 2 of the MPI standard.

We note that the programming model and the hardware model are separate. For example, one can use the message-passing programming model on shared-memory parallel computers. In all cases, the programming models address two issues: *communication* of data between two (or more) threads and *coordination* of the exchange of data.

Hybrids of these programming models are also common; many parallel systems are built from a collection or cluster of SMPs, where shared memory is used within each SMP and message passing is used between SMPs. This more complex model shares the issues and features of both and will not be discussed further.

For a more comprehensive discussion of parallel computer hardware, see [121, Chapter 2] or [107].

12.2.2   Overview

This chapter is divided into two main sections. Section 12.3 discusses the impact of parallel computing on the choice of numerical algorithms. Because the cost of coordinating separate parallel threads of execution is not zero, just counting floating-point operations is often not an effective way to choose among numerically stable algorithms for a parallel computer. Section 12.3 describes a simple, yet effective time-complexity model for parallel computations and provides an example of its use in understanding methods for orthogonalizing a collection of vectors that are distributed across a parallel computer.

Section 12.4 discusses the implementation issues, with emphasis on the hazards and pitfalls that are unique to parallel programs. This section provides only an introduction to some of the issues in writing correct parallel programs but it does cover the most important sources of problems. The chapter closes with recommendations for developing accurate and correct parallel programs.

12.3 Impact on the Choice of Algorithm

The costs of communicating data between processes or coordinating access to shared data strongly influence the choice of algorithms for parallel computers. This section illustrates some of the pitfalls in emphasizing performance over good numerical properties.

12.3.1 Consequences of latency

The cost of communicating data between processes in the distributed-memory, or message-passing, model is often modeled as

$$T = s + rn, \tag{12.1}$$

where s is the latency (or startup cost), r the inverse of the bandwidth (or rate), and n the number of words. Typical numbers are $s = 10 - 50$ microseconds and $r = 10^{-7}$ seconds/word. The factors that contribute to the latency include the time to access main memory (itself relatively slow) and any software overheads. (A more detailed model, called logP, separates the overhead from the latency [106].) For completeness in what follows, let f be the time for a floating-point operation. When conducting performance studies, it is often valuable to consider the quantities s/f and r/f so as to make the terms relative to the speed of floating-point computation.

The cost of communicating and coordinating data in a shared-memory model is more complex to model because of the interaction with the memory system hardware. However, the cost of memory-atomic operations such as locks, which are often necessary to coordinate the activities of two threads, is also on the order of a microsecond. With modern processors running at speeds of over 2 GHz (2×10^9 cycles/second), a microsecond corresponds to roughly 2,000 floating-point operations. Because of this relatively high cost, algorithms for parallel processors often trade more local computation for fewer communication or coordination steps.

Orthogonalization of vectors. A common operation in many numerical algorithms is adding a vector $\vec{u}$ to a set of orthonormal vectors $\vec{v}_i$, $i = 1, \ldots, n$, to form a new vector, $\vec{v}_{n+1}$, that is orthonormal to the original set. In exact arithmetic, the new vector $\vec{v}_{n+1}$ is given by

$$\vec{v}' = \vec{u} - \sum_{i=1}^{n} \vec{v}_i (\vec{u} \circ \vec{v}_i),$$

$$\vec{v}_{n+1} = \frac{\vec{v}'}{\|\vec{v}'\|_2}.$$

This is the Gramm–Schmidt process. Note that the individual inner products are independent; thus they can be computed with a single parallel reduction operation (over a vector with n entries). Because reduction operations, particularly on systems with many processors, are relatively expensive, this is an attractive formulation. Using the performance model in equation (12.1), and assuming that the vectors are of length (dimension) m, one can compute the cost of this approach on a parallel distributed-memory computer with p

processors as roughly

$$T_{gs} = (s + rn) \log p + (s + r) \log p + nmf/p$$
$$= (2s + r(n + 1)) \log p + nmf/p.$$

The cost of this algorithm, for large m, scales as m/p, with a term, due to the inner products, that grows as $\log p$.

Unfortunately, the classical Gramm–Schmidt algorithm is well known to be unstable in floating-point arithmetic (see, e.g., [170]). Numerical analysis texts often recommend the *modified Gramm–Schmidt* method[45]:

$$\vec{v}_0' \leftarrow u$$
$$\text{for } i = 1, \ldots, n \ \{$$
$$\vec{v}_{i+1}' \leftarrow \vec{v}_i' - (\vec{v}_i' \circ \vec{v}_i)$$
$$\vec{v}_{i+1}' = \frac{\vec{v}_{i+1}'}{\|\vec{v}_{i+1}'\|_2}$$
$$\}$$
$$\vec{v}_{n+1} = \vec{v}_{n+1}'.$$

While this is numerically superior to the unmodified form, the cost on a parallel computer is much greater because of the need to compute each inner product separately, since the ith step relies on the results of step $i - 1$. The cost of the modified Gramm–Schmidt method on a parallel computer can be modeled as

$$T_{mgs} = (n + 1)(s + r) \log p + nmf/p.$$

On message-passing platforms, s is of the order of 10 μsec, or roughly 20,000 floating-point operations. (Even on shared-memory platforms, s is on the order of 1 μsec if remote memory is involved, or roughly the same time as for 2,000 floating-point operations.)

An important lesson from this discussion is that the performance goals of parallel computing can conflict with good numerical behavior. Further, for a programmer unskilled in numerical analysis, the transformation from the poorly performing modified Gramm–Schmidt to the much faster unmodified Gramm–Schmidt will be an obvious one. In addition, parallel performance tools are likely to draw the attention of the programmer to this part of the computation.

The situation isn't lost, however. Versions of Gramm–Schmidt that iterate on the unmodified version can often be used. These have time complexity

$$T_I = k((2s + r(n + 1)) \log p) + knmf/p, \tag{12.2}$$

where k iterations are taken. This algorithm would be chosen only on a parallel computer because the floating-point cost is larger than that of either original Gramm–Schmidt algorithm. In the parallel case, however, it combines adequate numerical properties with good parallel performance. In the final analysis, one must balance the numerical properties of an

---

[45]Other methods could be used that have even better stability properties; the same analysis used here may be used to evaluate the performance of those methods on parallel computers.

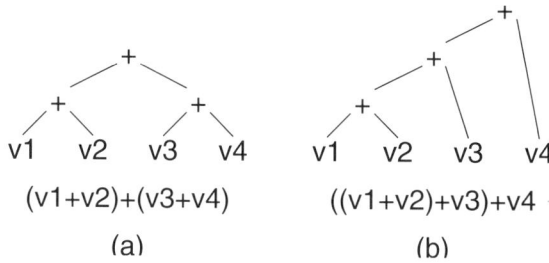

$$(v1+v2)+(v3+v4) \qquad ((v1+v2)+v3)+v4$$

(a)   (b)

Figure 12.1. *Two orderings for summing 4 values. Shown in* (a) *is the ordering typically used by parallel algorithms. Shown in* (b) *is the natural "do loop" ordering.*

algorithm with the performance properties, just as partial rather than complete pivoting is usually considered adequate for the solution of linear systems of equations on uniprocessors. For example, in the GMRES method, classical Gramm–Schmidt is often considered sufficient, particularly when only modest accuracy is required.

12.3.2   Consequences of blocking

Another algorithmic technique that is used in parallel computing is blocking. Blocking is a problem decomposition technique that divides a problem into smaller blocks, which may be better able to take advantage of the computer. Examples of blocking include algorithms for dense matrix-matrix multiply that reduce the problem into one of multiplying subblocks of the matrix. Just as blocking can make better use of memory systems on uniprocessors (e.g., BLAS3 [122]), blocking in parallel computers can make better use of the communication interconnect by reducing the number of separate communication events. In the case of a shared-memory system, it may also reduce the number of locks or other techniques used to avoid race conditions (described in section 12.4.1). However, blocked algorithms, because they perform operations in a different order from that of unblocked algorithms, have different numerical properties. This effect of ordering operations is most easily seen in the simple operation of a parallel dot product.

   Dot products.   When discussing the orthogonalization example, we assumed the existence of a fast parallel dot product routine. Such routines exist, but they rely on associating the arithmetic so that the values are added together in a tree-like fashion. This is not the same order of operations that would normally be used on a single processor. Figure 12.1 shows two possible orderings for adding the results from four processors. Note that a careful numerical routine may choose an order for the summation that depends on the magnitude of the values.

   One result is that many parallel programs lack *bitwise reproducibility*. That is, because efficient parallel execution may require reassociating floating-point operations, the exact values computed may depend on the number of threads of execution. Hence, validating a parallel program is more difficult because one of the most common validation approaches is to require bitwise identical results whenever a program is modified. Addressing the issue of validating a parallel computation against a nonparallel (uniprocessor) computation is difficult, and it is further complicated by implementation issues specific to parallel computers.

12.4   Implementation Issues

Parallel computing provides new ways to write incorrect programs. These are a result of the tension between performance and correctness. That is, most programming models for parallel computers have made a deliberate choice to present opportunities for performance at the cost of a greater chance for programmer error. This section details a few of the most common programming errors for both shared-memory and message-passing programming models.

12.4.1   Races

One of the most dangerous and common errors in shared-memory parallel programs is a *race condition*. This occurs in parts of the code where a race between two or more threads of execution determines the behavior of the program. If the "wrong" thread wins the race, then the program behaves erroneously. To see how easy it is to introduce a race condition, consider the following OpenMP program:

```
integer n
n = 0
!$omp parallel shared(n)
n = n + 1
!$omp end parallel
```

The intent of this program is to count the number of threads used in the parallel region.[46] Variations on this program are commonly used in programming texts to introduce parallel programming using threads. Unfortunately, this program has a race condition. The statement n = n + 1 is not executed atomically (that is, without possibility of interruption) on any modern processor. Instead, it is split into a sequence of instructions, such as the following, presented here in a generic assembly language:

```
load  n, r1
add   #1, r1
store r1, n
```

In other words, this loads the value n into a register, adds one to that value, and stores the result back into the memory location n. A possible execution sequence with two threads is as follows (comments on the execution are to the right of the exclamation point, and time proceeds down the page):

---

[46]There are easier ways to perform this particular operation in OpenMP; this example was picked because it is easy to explain and similar code is common in real applications.

Thread 0	Thread 1
load n, r1 ! r1 has value 0	
	load n, r1 ! r1 also has value 0
add #1, r1 ! r1 had value 1	
	add #1, r1 ! r1 has value 1
store r1, n ! n now has value 1	
	store r1, n ! n gets value 1 again

Each thread is executing on its own processor with its own set of registers. After this sequence, the program will have counted one rather than two threads.

The consequences of races are made more serious by the fact that in many codes, the races are almost always "won" as the programmer expects. Thus, codes with races will often work and pass tests, even though the possibility of losing the race (and thus returning an incorrect result) remains. Validating such codes is very difficult; races are in fact a common source of error in complex programs such as operating systems.

Avoiding such race conditions is difficult. One approach was suggested by Lamport [279]. In his *sequential consistency* model, the processor must execute the program as if the lines of the program are executed by the different processors in some interleaved (but not interchanged) order. With the interpretation of "line" as "line of the program in the programming language," sequential consistency will avoid the race illustrated above. Unfortunately, the performance consequences of sequential consistency are severe, leading computer science researchers to define various weaker consistency models and for most programming languages to provide no guarantees at all. Most processors provide a way to guarantee atomic execution of some operations. However, this always comes with a performance cost. As a result, programming models such as OpenMP do not provide atomic execution (and hence sequential consistency) by default. In fact, no major programming model provides sequential consistency; all major parallel programming models *allow* the programmer to explicitly enforce sequential consistency, but none ensures sequential consistency.

12.4.2 Out-of-order execution

In writing algorithms with the shared-memory model, one often has to ensure that data on one thread is not accessed by any other thread until some condition is satisfied. For this purpose *locks* are often used. The following shows a simple example of two threads controlling access to shared data with a lock:

Thread 0	Thread 1
lock	(wait for data to be available)
update array	
unlock	
	lock
	access array
	unlock

Unfortunately, locks are often quite expensive to execute. Programmers are often tempted to use a simple flag variable to mediate access to the data, as shown in the following:

Thread 0	Thread 1
flag=0	
update array	do while(flag .eq. 0)
flag=1	
	access array
	flag = 0

However, this code may not execute correctly. The reason is there is no guarantee that either the compiler or the processor will preserve the order of the operations to what appears to be (within a single thread) independent statements. Either the compiler or the CPU may thus move the assignment flag=1 before the array update is complete (a very aggressive optimizing compiler may move the assignment flag=1 *before* the update to avoid what the compiler sees as an unnecessary store of zero to the storage location flag). In general, even within a single thread, the order of operations is not guaranteed. Special assembly language instructions can be used to force the processor to complete memory operations before proceeding, but these must usually be inserted explicitly by the programmer.[47]

If the array update is part of a time integration, then this bug will introduce a Δt error into the calculation. This is one of the worst possible bugs, because it reduces the accuracy of the computation rather than providing a clear indication of trouble.

In addition to these correctness issues, there exist many issues related to performance that are specific to shared-memory parallel programs. One important case is called *false sharing*. This occurs when a parallel program has two separate memory locations on the same cache line. Even though each item is accessed only by a single thread, the fact that the two items share a cache line can cause serious performance problems. For the programmer, the situation is made more difficult by the fact that most programming languages try to insulate the programmer from details of the hardware, thus making it more likely that performance problems will occur.

The issues described so far have pertained to a shared-memory programming model. The message-passing model has its own share of issues.

12.4.3 Message buffering

Many message-passing programs are immune to race conditions because message passing combines data transfer and notification into a single routine and because there is no direct access to the memory of another process. However, message-passing programs are susceptible to resource limits. Consider the following simple program in which each process sends n words to the other:

```
Process 0                      Process 1
dest = 1;                      dest = 0;
Send( buf, n, dest );          Send( buf, n, dest );
Recv( rbuf, n, dest );         Recv( rbuf, n, dest );
```

This is an example of an *unsafe* program. It is unsafe because it depends on the underlying system to *buffer* the message data (the array buf on both processes in this example) so that the Send operations can complete. At some size n, there cannot be

---

[47]C programmers may use volatile to avoid some but not all of these problems.

enough space available, and the processes will wait forever (*deadlock*). In some ways, the limit on the size of n under which a program will complete is the analogue of machine precision—it is a number that reflects a reality of computing, a number that we wish was infinite but is all too finite.

The real risk in message passing comes from using buffered send operations in unsafe ways. The program may operate correctly for some inputs but deadlock for others. There are several ways to avoid this problem.

- Use a synchronous send instead of a regular send. In MPI terms, use `MPI_Ssend` instead of `MPI_Send`. This ensures that the program is independent of buffering, that is, that unsafe programs will deadlock for all input, not just some. This approach simplifies validation of the program.

- Use explicit buffer spaces, and manage them carefully. In MPI terms, use `MPI_Buffer_attach` and the `MPI_Bsend` routine.

- Avoid point-to-point operations entirely, and use collective operations such as broadcast and reduce.

- Use nonblocking send operations; in MPI terms, these are the family of routines that include `MPI_Isend` and `MPI_Send_init`.

All of these approaches have drawbacks. Their major advantage is that they make the code's dependence on buffering explicit rather than relying on the implicit buffering within the message-passing system.

12.4.4   Nonblocking and asynchronous operations

A common technique for working around high-latency operations is to split the operation into separate initiation and completion operations. This is commonly used with I/O operations; many programmers have used nonblocking I/O calls to hide the relatively slow performance of file read and write operations. The same approach can be used to hide the latency of communication between processes. For example, in MPI, a message can be sent by using a two-step process:

```
MPI_Request request;
MPI_Isend( buf, n, MPI_INT, dest, tag, comm, &request );
... other operations and program steps
MPI_Wait( &request, MPI_STATUS_IGNORE );
```

This sequence sends n integers from the calling process to the process dest and allows the code to perform other operations without waiting for the data to be transfered until the call to `MPI_Wait`. Because MPI (and most other approaches to message passing) uses libraries rather than introducing a new parallel language, there is no way to enforce this requirement or to confirm that the user has not violated it. As a result, this approach is not without its dangers [195]. In particular, the user must not change (or even access) the elements of buf until after the `MPI_Wait` completes.

Unfortunately, programming languages provide little direct support for nonblocking operations, and hence the programmer must exercise care when using these operations.

Programming languages such as Fortran can make such approaches (for asynchronous I/O as well as for parallel computing) quite hazardous, because a Fortran compiler may not preserve the data array after the call that initiates the operation (`MPI_Isend` above) returns. A particular example in Fortran is array sections; the compiler may not preserve these, even in simple cases, after the call returns. See [314, Section 10.2.2] for a discussion of this problem in the context of MPI and Fortran. Another example is variable scope. Particularly in C and C++, many variables are local to the routine in which they are used; their space is reused once the routine exits (the variables are usually allocated on a stack that is shared by all routines within the same thread). A nonblocking operation should ensure that a variable remains allocated (also called "in scope") until the nonblocking operation completes.

12.4.5   Hardware errors

Because parallel computers are often used for the most challenging problems, another source of problems is the low, but not zero, probability of an error in the computer hardware. This has sometimes led to problems with long-running simulations, particularly with high-performance interconnect networks. For example, an interconnect that has an error rate of 1 in 10^{12} bits sent and a data rate of 100 MB/sec will have an error roughly every 20 minutes (per link!). In the past, the role of error rates in the interconnect has not always been recognized, leading to unexpected errors in the computation. Since most parallel programming models, both libraries and languages, specify error-free behavior of the hardware, hardware and system software implementors work together to provide an error-free system. Unfortunately, not all parallel systems have properly addressed these issues, and often the application developer must check that internode communications are reliable.

12.4.6   Heterogeneous parallel systems

A *heterogeneous parallel system* is one in which the processing elements are not all the same. They may have different data representations or ranges. For example, some processors may have 32-bit integers stored with the most significant byte first, whereas others may have 64-bit integers with the least significant byte first. Such systems introduce additional complexity because many algorithms assume that given the exact same input data, the same floating-point operations will produce, bit for bit, the same output data. For example, in some cases, a parallel algorithm will distribute the same (small) problem and then have each processor compute a result rather than try to parallelize a small problem; this approach is sometimes used in multigrid and domain decomposition methods for solving the coarse-grid problem.

On a heterogeneous system, such an approach may not be valid, depending on how the results are used. Additional issues concern the different handling of the less specified parts of the IEEE 754 floating-point specification, such as the exact meaning of the bits in a NaN (not a number). These issues must be considered when contemplating the use of heterogeneous systems.

12.5   Conclusions and Recommendations

Algorithms for parallel computers must often trade additional floating-point operations against communication. Moreover, providing adequate parallelism may require using different algorithms. These algorithms must be chosen carefully because it is all too easy to use numerically unstable algorithms for common operations.

Writing correct parallel programs is also difficult. There is really no substitute for disciplined coding practices, particularly for shared-memory programs. One approach is to carefully annotate all accesses to shared or nonlocal data; these annotations may be processed by program development tools to identify potential race conditions. Some tools along these lines have been developed (e.g., [136]), but much more needs to be done. In particular, an approach is needed that allows an algorithm with no race conditions to be expressed in a way that provably cannot introduce a race condition.

For message-passing codes, no code should rely on system buffering for correct operation. In MPI terms, any program should still work if all uses of `MPI_Send` are replaced with `MPI_Ssend` (the synchronous send). Fortunately, it is easy to test this by using the MPI profiling interface.

Moreover, the recommendations must depend on the scale of the parallelism, that is, the number of processing elements. If the number is relatively small (on the order of four to eight), then parallelism should be considered cautiously. The reason is that with the rapid increase in computing power (typically doubling every 18 months), improving performance by a factor of four is like waiting three years for a faster computer. This does not mean that parallelism at this scale should not be used—only that it should be used with care and without going to extreme lengths to get better performance. For example, such applications should use robust synchronization mechanisms in a shared-memory code rather than relying on write-ordering and flags, as described in section 12.4.2.

At much greater scales, particularly in the tens of thousands of processors, distributed-memory computers programmed with message-passing dominate. Applications at this scale both are more sensitive to performance scaling and are unlikely to be replaced by a non-parallel application in the forseeable future. These codes should exploit modern software engineering practices to isolate the parallel implementation into a small number of well-tested library routines. Their algorithms should be carefully chosen for the scale at which they will operate, and attention must be paid to the effects of ordering of operations and decompositions based on the layout of the parallel computer's memory.

With proper care, parallel computers can be used effectively for numeric computation. One approach is to isolate within a numerical library most of the issues described in this chapter. Additional challenges in creating numerical libraries for high-performance computing systems are discussed in [181].

Acknowledgment

This work was supported by the Mathematical, Information, and Computational Sciences Division subprogram of the Office of Advanced Scientific Computing Research, Office of Science, U.S. Department of Energy, under Contract W-31-109-ENG-38.

Chapter 13

Software-reliability Engineering of Numerical Systems

Mladen A. Vouk

13.1 Introduction

Software-reliability engineering (SRE) stems from the needs of software users. The day-to-day operation of our society is increasingly more dependent on software-based systems and tolerance of *failures* of such systems is decreasing [468]. Numerical software holds one of the central positions in this context. Because of the high stakes involved, it is essential that the software be accurate, reliable, and robust. Software engineering is not only expected to help deliver a software product of required functionality on time and within cost; it is also expected to help satisfy certain quality criteria. The most prominent one is *reliability*. SRE is the "applied science of predicting, measuring, and managing the reliability of software-based systems to maximize customer satisfaction" [330, 298, 409, 329].

Numerical software has many characteristics of a general software system coupled with issues very specific to numerical algorithms, their stability, their implementation in software, and the computational framework they run on. Hence, many software engineering techniques that apply to software in general apply to numerical software as well, but there are also special issues.

This work is based in part on the prior SRE work of the author [471, 307, 246]. Section 13.2 provides general information about the nature of SRE and how it relates to software processes including factors such as testing, cost, and benefits. This is followed by an overview of the SRE terminology (Section 13.3) and modeling issues (Section 13.4). Finally, SRE practice is addressed both in the general context (Section 13.5), and in the context of numerical software (Section 13.6). We discuss specifics of SRE activities required during different software life-cycle phases, including an example of how to generate SRE-based test-cases automatically, and we address result verification and fault-tolerance (Section 13.7) issues related to numerical software.

13.2   About SRE

SRE is the focus of practical technology transfer efforts in many organizations with advanced software processes. For example, SRE is an accepted "best practice" for one of the major developers of telecommunications software (AT&T, Lucent). It is practiced also in many other software development areas, including aerospace industry and network-based education [409, 329]. This increased interest in SRE is driven, at least in part, by the expectation that adoption of adequate SRE technology will increase the competitiveness of an organization or a project. There is mounting evidence that this is the case. The benefits include more precise satisfaction of customer needs, better resource and schedule control, and increased productivity.

Examples of organizations that are using, experimenting with, or researching SRE are Alcatel, AT&T, Cisco, Lucent, Hewlett-Packard, Hitachi, IBM Corp., Jet Propulsion Laboratories, MITRE Corp., Motorola, NASA, NCR Corp., Nortel, Telcordia, U.S. Air Force, U.S. Navy, U.S. Army, and Toshiba [327]. Although direct economic information is usually difficult to obtain for proprietary reasons, studies show that the cost-benefit ratio of using SRE techniques can be six or more [134]. In one case, SRE has been credited with reducing the incidence of customer-reported problems, and maintenance costs, by a factor of 10. In addition, in the system-test interval the number of software-related problems was reduced by a factor of two, and in the product introduction interval by 30 percent. The same system showed no serious service outages within the first two years after its release, and considerably increased customer satisfaction. Its sales were increased by a factor of 10, but only part of this is attributed to the increased quality [2, 328].

It is estimated that routine application of SRE does not add more than several percent to the overall cost of a project [327]. For example, a project involving 40 to 100 persons may require preproject activities totaling about one to two person-weeks, definition of the operational profile(s) may require one to three person-months, and routine collection and analysis of project failure and effort data may cost between one half to one person-day per week.

However, introduction of SRE into an organization will be a strong function of the (software process) maturity of that organization. Startup costs may include deployment of an automated failure, fault, and effort collection system, calibration of existing and development of organization-specific reliability models and tools, staff training, modification of the organizational culture, and modifications in the employed software processes. SRE introduction periods can range from six months to several years, again depending on the maturity of the organization and the available resources.

It is recommended that SRE be implemented incrementally. The starting point should be the activities needed to establish a baseline and learn about the product, about customer expectations, and about the constraints that the organizational business model imposes on its software production [366]. The initial effort includes collection of basic failure data, monitoring of reliability growth during system tests, field trials and software operation, and the initial formulation of operational profiles. This should be followed by the development of detailed operational profiles, detailed classification of system failures and faults, and development of business-based reliability objectives. More advanced stages involve continuous tracking of customer satisfaction, trade-off studies, quantitative evaluation of software process capabilities with respect to reliability, and proactive process control.

13.3   Basic Terms

Software-reliability engineering (SRE) is the quantitative study of the operational behavior of software-based systems with respect to user requirements [330]. It includes

1. software reliability measurement (assessment) and estimation (prediction);

2. effects of product and development process metrics and factors (activities) on operational software behavior;

3. application of this knowledge in specifying and guiding software development, testing, acquisition, use, and maintenance.

Reliability is the *probability* that a system, or a system component, will deliver its intended functionality and quality for a specified period of *"time,"* and under specified conditions, given that the system was functioning properly at the start of this *"time"* period. For example, this may be the probability that a real-time system will give specified functional and timing performance for the duration of a ten hour mission when used in the way and for the purpose intended. Since software reliability will depend on how software is used, software usage information is an important part of reliability evaluation. This includes information on the environment in which software is used as well as the information on the actual frequency of usage of different functions (or operations, or features) that the system offers. The usage information is quantified through *operational profiles.*

"Time" is execution exposure that software receives through usage. Experience indicates that often the best metric is the actual CPU execution time. However, it is possible, and sometimes necessary, to reformulate measurements, and *reliability models,* in terms of other exposure metrics, such as calendar-time, clock-time, number of executed test cases (or runs), fraction of planned test cases executed, inservicetime, customer transactions, or structural coverage. In considering which "time" to use, it is necessary to weigh factors such as availability of data for computation of a particular metric, error-sensitivity of the metric, availability of appropriate reliability models, etc. An argument in favor of using CPU time, or clock-time, instead of, for example, structural software coverage, is that often engineers have a better physical grasp of time, and, in order to combine hardware and software reliabilities, the time approach may be essential. On the other hand, it may make more sense to use "printed pages" as the exposure metric when dealing with reliability of printers.

When a system in operation does not deliver its intended functionality and quality, it is said to fail. A **failure** is an *observed* departure of the external result of software operation from software requirements or user expectations [218, 219, 220]. Failures can be caused by hardware or software faults (defects), or by how-to-use errors. What is defined as a failure is critical. A failure can manifest as a complete stoppage of a software-based service, as a measurable degradation of the service, or as a user-perceived flaw. For example, when a software application crashes, failure is obvious. When a numerical application delivers a subtly incorrect result it may be less obvious, particularly if the final manifestation is the result of an accumulation of smaller incorrect results. When a software system delivers its response time that is more than required (e.g., 1 second instead of 100 ms) this may also be a failure for some users. Similarly, if a software system fails to provide adequate security (e.g., has a security flaw that can be exploited after a certain number of tries), this is also a failure, and so on. Appropriate definition of what constitutes a failure allows use of SRE methodologies in a wide range of situations. Natural associated metrics are mean-time-to-failure, mean-time-between-failures, and mean-time-to-recover. These and other metrics are discussed further later in this text.

A **fault** (or defect, or bug) is a defective, missing, or extra instruction, or a set of *related* instructions that is the cause of one or more actual or potential failures. Inherent faults are the faults that are associated with a software product as originally written, or modified. Faults that are introduced through fault correction, or design changes, form a separate class of modification faults. An associated measure is **fault density**—for example, the number of faults per thousand lines of executable source code. Faults are the results of (human) **errors**, or mistakes. For example, an error in writing a programming language branching statement, such as an if-statement condition, will result in a physical defect in the code, or fault, that will on execution of that statement transfer control to the wrong branch. If, on execution, such a program does not produce the desired results, for example, display a particular picture, it is said to fail and a failure has been observed.

How-to-use errors. Failures can be caused by software faults, functional lacks in software, or user errors (for example, lack of user knowledge). It is important to understand that failures and how-to-use errors, and their frequency, tend to relate very strongly to *customer satisfaction* and perception of the product quality. On the other hand, faults are more *developer oriented* since they tend to be translated into the amount of effort that may be needed to repair and maintain the system.

The **severity** of a failure or fault is the impact it has on the operation of a software-based system. Severity is usually closely related to the threat the problem poses in functional (service), economic (cost) terms, or in the case of critical failures, to human life. Examples of a service impact classification are critical, major, and minor failure. Severity of failures (or faults) is sometimes used to subset the operational failure data, and thus make decisions regarding failures of a particular severity, or to weight the data used in reliability and availability calculations.

The **operational profile** is a set of relative frequencies (or probabilities) of occurrence of disjoint software operations during its operational use. A detailed discussion of operational profile issues can be found in [331, 328, 329]. A software-based system may have one or more operational profiles. Operational profiles are used to select **test cases** and direct development, testing, and maintenance efforts toward the most frequently used or most risky components. Construction of an operational profile is preceded by definition of a **customer** profile, a **user** profile, a system **mode** profile, and a **functional** profile. The usual participants in this iterative process are system engineers, high-level designers, test planners, product planners, and marketers. The process starts during the requirements phase and continues until the system testing starts. **Profiles** are constructed by creating detailed hierarchical lists of customers, users, modes, functions, and operations that the software needs to provide under each set of conditions. For each item it is necessary to estimate the probability of its occurrence (and possibly **risk** information) and thus provide a quantitative description of the profile. If usage is available as a rate (e.g., transactions per hour) it needs to be converted into probability. In discussing profiles, it is often helpful to use tables and graphs and annotate them with usage and criticality information.

13.4   Metrics and Models

A significant set of SRE activities are concerned with measurement and prediction of software reliability and availability. This includes modeling of software failure behavior and modeling of the process that develops and removes faults. A number of metrics and models are available for that purpose [329, 298, 331, 218, 219, 301, 495, 8]. This section examines the basic ideas.

13.4.1   Reliability

We distinguish two situations. In one situation, detected problems are further pursued, and fault identification and correction or operational avoidance takes place—for example, during software development, system and field testing, and active field maintenance. In the other situation, no fault removal takes place—for example, between successive releases of a product. In the first case we would expect the product to improve over time, and we talk about **reliability growth**.

The quality of software, and in particular its reliability, can be measured in a number of ways. A metric that is commonly used to describe software reliability is *failure intensity*. **Failure intensity** is defined as the number of failures experienced per unit "time" period. Sometimes the term **failure rate** is used instead. An interesting associated measure is the mean-time-to-failure. Often **mean-time-to-failure** is well approximated by the inverse of the failure intensity or failure rate. Failure intensity can be computed for all experienced failures, for all unique failures, or for some specified category of failures of a given type or severity. Failure intensity is a good measure for reflecting the user perspective of software quality. When reliability growth is being experienced, failure intensity will decrease over time and mean-time-to-failure will grow longer.

When there is no repair, it may be possible to describe the reliability of a software-based system using **constant** failure intensity, λ, and a very simple exponential relationship,

$$R(\tau) \sim e^{-\lambda\tau}, \tag{13.1}$$

where $R(\tau)$ is the reliability of the system, and τ is the duration of the mission. For example, suppose that the system is used under *representative and unchanging* conditions, and the faults causing any reported failures are not being removed. Let the number of failures observed over 10,000 hours of operation be 7. Then, failure intensity is about $\widehat{\lambda} = 7/10000 = 0.0007$ failures per hour, and the corresponding mean-time-to-failure is about $1/\lambda = 1428$ hours. From equation (13.1), and given that the system operates correctly at time $\tau = 0$ hours, the probability that the system will **not** fail during a 10 hour mission is about $R(10) = e^{-0.0007*10} = 0.993$.

Where software **reliability growth** is present, failure intensity, $\lambda(\tau)$, becomes a decreasing function of time τ during which software is exposed to testing and usage under **representative** (operational) conditions. There is a large number of software reliability models that address this situation [298]. But, before any modeling is undertaken, it is a good idea to confirm the presence of the growth using **trend** tests [331, 251]. All models have some advantages and some disadvantages. It is extremely important that an appropriate model be chosen on a case by case basis by a qualified person [331, 55, 298].

Two typical models are the basic execution time (BET) model [168, 331] and the logarithmic-Poisson execution time (LPET) model [331]. Both models assume that the testing uses operational profiles and that every detected failure is immediately and perfectly repaired.[48] The **BET** failure intensity $\lambda(\tau)$ with exposure time τ is

$$\lambda(\tau) = \lambda_0 e^{-\frac{\lambda_0}{\nu_0}\tau}, \tag{13.2}$$

where λ_0 is the initial intensity and ν_0 is the total expected number of failures (faults). It is interesting to note that the model becomes linear if we express intensity as a function of cumulative failures

$$\lambda(\tau) = \lambda(\mu) = \lambda_0 \left(1 - \frac{\mu}{\nu_0} \right), \tag{13.3}$$

where $\mu(\tau)$ is the mean number of failures experienced by time τ, or the **mean value function**, i.e.,

$$\mu(\tau) = \nu_0 \left(1 - e^{-\frac{\lambda_0}{\nu_0}\tau} \right). \tag{13.4}$$

On the other hand, the **LPET** failure intensity $\lambda(\tau)$ with exposure time τ is

$$\lambda(\tau) = \frac{\lambda_0}{\lambda_0 \theta \tau + 1}, \tag{13.5}$$

where λ_0 is the initial intensity and θ is called the failure intensity decay parameter since

$$\lambda(\tau) = \lambda(\mu) = \lambda_0 e^{-\theta\mu} \tag{13.6}$$

and $\mu(\tau)$ is the mean number of failures experienced by time τ, i.e.,

$$\mu(\tau) = \frac{1}{\theta} \ln (\lambda_0 \theta \tau + 1). \tag{13.7}$$

The BET model represents a class of **finite-failure** models for which the mean value function tends toward a level asymptote as exposure time grows, while the LPET model is a representative of a class of models called **infinite-failure** models since it allows an unlimited number of failures. Of course, both classes of models can be, and are being, used to describe software fault removal processes that may involve only a finite number of actual faults [247].

Given failure intensity data, it is possible to estimate model parameters. Estimates can be made in many ways. Two common methods are **maximum likelihood** and **least squares** [331]. It is very important to understand that there are two distinct ways of using a model. One is to provide a **description** of historical (already available) data. The other is to **predict** future reliability measures and events during actual testing or operation, such as "when will the intensity reach a target value," or "when can I stop testing." Predictions are more interesting from a practical standpoint but also more dangerous. Brocklehurst and Littlewood note that no single model can be universally recommended, and accuracy of reliability measures produced by a model can vary greatly. However, there are advanced

---

[48]There are some other assumptions that have to be satisfied; see [331]. Also, there are model variants that operate with different assumptions, such as delayed and less than perfect fault repair [298].

statistical techniques, such as **u-plots** and the **prequential likelihood ratio**, that can alleviate the accuracy problem to some extent [55, 298].

Once a model has been selected and its parameters estimated, it is possible to compute quantities such as the total number of faults in the code, future failure intensity, and, given a target intensity, how much longer the testing needs to go on. For instance, suppose that it was determined that the BET model is appropriate. Then it follows from equations (13.2)–(13.4) that the number of additional failures, $\Delta\mu$, that must be experienced to achieve failure intensity objective λ_F is

$$\Delta\mu = \frac{\nu_0}{\lambda_0}(\lambda_P - \lambda_F), \tag{13.8}$$

where λ_P is the present failure intensity. Similarly, the additional execution time, $\Delta\tau$, required to reach the failure intensity objective is

$$\Delta\tau = \frac{\nu_0}{\lambda_0}\ln\frac{\lambda_P}{\lambda_F}. \tag{13.9}$$

For example, assume that it is estimated that there are a total of $\nu_0 = 120$ faults in the code, that $\lambda_0 = 15$ failures per CPU hour, that $\lambda_P = 2.55$ failures per CPU hour, and the objective is to achieve 0.0005 failures per CPU hour. Then, $\Delta\mu = \frac{120}{15}(2.55 - 0.0005) \sim 21$ failures, and $\Delta\tau = \frac{120}{15}\ln\frac{2.55}{0.0005} \sim 68.3$ CPU hours. If it is known what effort expenditure is required to detect a failure and identify and correct the corresponding fault, and how much cost is associated with exposure time, it is possible to construct economic models that relate the testing not only to the resultant quality, but also to the expended effort (cost) [331, 134, 496].

The estimates given in the above example are known as **point estimates** since they involve only the "most likely" or the "best" value. However, in practice, it is *extremely* important to compute confidence bounds for any estimated parameters and derived quantities in order to see how much one can rely on the obtained figures [331]. This involves computation of probable errors (variances) for both the model parameters and the derived quantities. Instead of presenting the projections as single values we need to present them as an appropriate **interval** (e.g., 70 %, 90 %, or 95 % confidence interval). For example, instead of saying that 21 failures are expected to occur before we reach the target intensity, we might use the 90 % interval, say, from 17 to 25 failures, or [17, 25]. It is essential that a person selecting models and making reliability predictions is appropriately trained in both software (reliability) engineering and statistics.

Since a large fraction of the variability in the estimates usually derives from the variability in the collected data, accurate and comprehensive data collection is of ultimate importance. For example, data collection should include the times of successive failures (alternatively, intervals between failures may be collected, or the number of failures experienced during an interval of testing—grouped data—may be recorded), information about each corrected fault, information about the parts of the code and product modules affected by the changes, and information about the expended effort.

It is recommended that both the data collection and the model estimation be automated and tool-based. Examples of reliability oriented data sets and tools can be found on the CD-ROM that comes with the *Handbook of Software Reliability Engineering* [298].

Examples of tools that can aid in software reliability estimation are SMERFS [140, 298] and RelTools [330] on Unix, CASRE on DOS and Windows [300, 298], and SoRel on Macintosh computers [252, 298]. Example of a tool that can help in test-case development, and that we discuss further later in this tutorial, is PairTest [286, 436].

Figure 13.1 illustrates maximum likelihood fits for BET and LPET models to a well-known system test data set called T1 [331]. The plot is of the natural logarithm of failure intensity versus execution time. It is also quite common to plot failure intensity against cumulative failures to see if the relationship given in equation (13.3) holds. While graphs can be used to screen the data for trends, statistical tests must be used to actually select a model [331, 55]. In this case the tests show that the LPET model fits somewhat better than the BET model. However, in a different project the BET, or some other model, may be better than the LPET model. Figure 13.2 shows the cumulative failure distribution obtained from the data and the models.

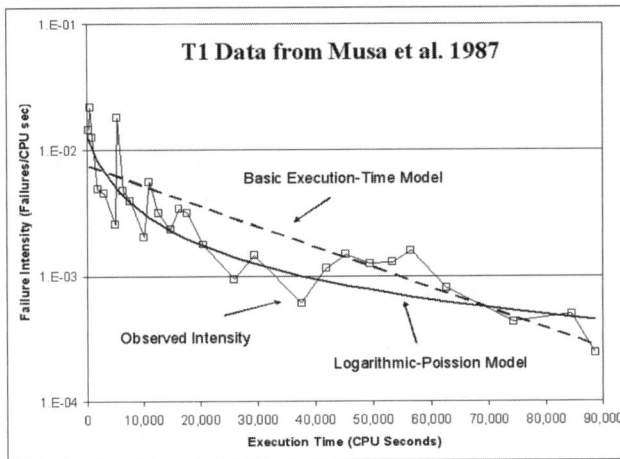

Figure 13.1. *Empirical and modeled failure intensity.*

SRE models tend to assume exposure (testing) based on an operational profile. Since this assumption is usually violated during early software testing phases (for example, during unit testing and integration testing), assessment and control of software quality growth during nonoperational testing stages is difficult and open to interpretation. In an organization that constructs its final deliverable software out of a number of components that evolve in parallel, an added problem can be the variability of the quality across these components.

Another confounding factor can be the (necessary) discontinuities that different testing strategies introduce within one testing phase, or between adjacent testing phases. For instance, unit testing concentrates on the functionality and coverage of the structures within a software unit, and integration testing concentrates on the coverage of the interfaces, functions, and links that involve two or more software units. It is not unusual to observe an apparent failure-intensity decay (reliability growth) during one of the phases, followed by an upsurge in the failure intensity in the next phase (due to different types of faults and failures). This oscillatory effect can make reliability growth modeling difficult, although

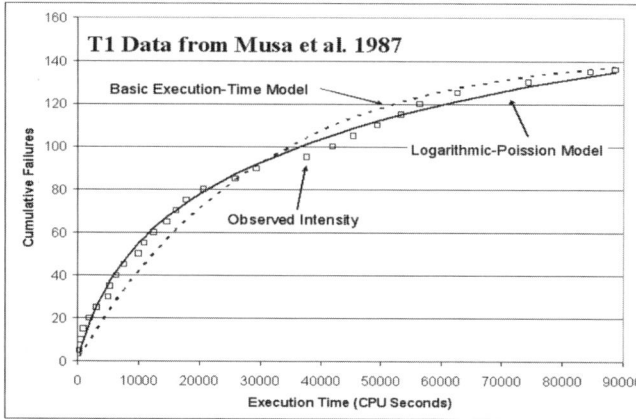

Figure 13.2. *Observed and modeled cumulative failures.*

several different approaches for handling this problem have been suggested (e.g., [331, 300, 298]).

A large class of models that can be useful in the context of early testing phases, and nonoperational testing in general, are the so-called **S-shaped** models that describe failure intensity that has a mode or a peak [497, 352, 331, 496]. These models derive their name from the S-like shape of their cumulative failure distributions. Figures 13.3 and 13.4 illustrate use of a Weibull-type model [331] during unit and integration testing phases of a telecommunications software product [474, 298].

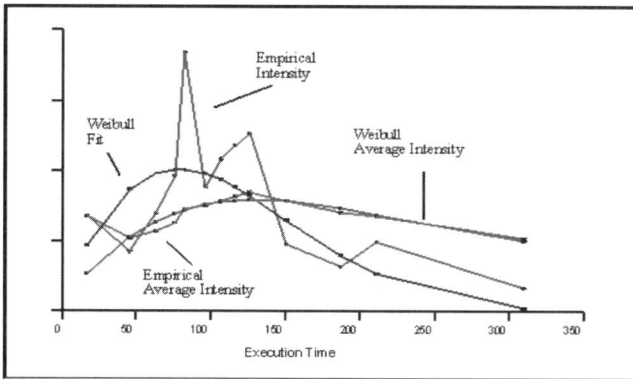

Figure 13.3. *Empirical and modeled intensity profiles obtained during an early testing phase. Exposure is the cumulative test case execution time "t." Average intensity at time "t" is the total number of failures experienced by "t" divided by the total execution time.*

The need to recognize software problems early, so that appropriate corrections (process feedback) can be undertaken within a single software release frame, is obvious. How to

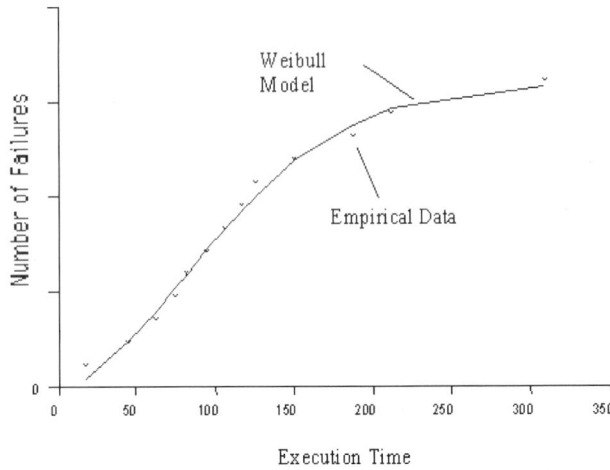

Figure 13.4. *Empirical and modeled failures obtained during an early testing phase.*

achieve this is less clear. In general, it is necessary to link the symptoms observed during the early testing phases with the effects observed in the later phases, such as, identification of components that may be problem-prone in the early operational phase. Several authors have published models that attempt to relate some early software metrics, such as, the size of the code, Halstead length, or cyclomatic number, to the failure proneness of a program [258, 326, 53]. A more process-oriented approach is discussed in [474, 298]. The highly correlated nature of the early software verification and testing events may require the use of a more sophisticated, time-series, approach [416].

13.4.2 Availability

Another important practical measure for software quality is *availability*. For example, the typical unavailability target for telecommunications network elements is about 3 minutes of downtime per year. **Availability** is the probability that a system, or a system component, will be available to start a mission at a specified "time" [149]. **Unavailability** is the opposite, the probability that a system or a system component will **not** be available to start a mission at a specified "time." The concept of (un)availability is closely connected to the notion of repairable failures.

Recovery from failures can be expressed through recovery or **repair rate**, ρ, that is, the number of repaired failures per unit time. For example, software failures may result in a computer system outages that, on the average, last 10 minutes each before the system is again available to its users; i.e., the mean-time-to-repair is about 10 minutes. The estimated repair, or recovery, rate for the system is then 1/10 failures per minute. System availability can be expressed in several ways. For example, **instantaneous availability** is the probability that the system will be available at any random time t during its life. **Average availability** is the proportion of time, in a specified interval $[0, T]$ that the system is available for use [394].

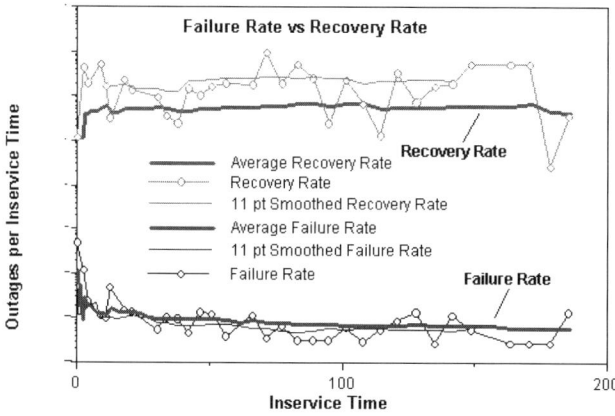

Figure 13.5. *Field recovery and failure rates for a telecommunications product.*

We can estimate average software availability in the period $[0, T]$ as

$$\widehat{A_c}(T) = \frac{\text{Total time software operated correctly in the given period}}{T}. \qquad (13.10)$$

Associated with average availability are average failure $\widehat{\lambda_c}(T)$ and recovery rate $\widehat{\rho_c}(T)$ estimates

$$\widehat{\lambda_c}(T) = \frac{\text{Total number of failures in period } T}{\text{Total time system was operational during period } T}, \qquad (13.11)$$

$$\widehat{\rho_c}(T) = \frac{\text{Total number of failures in period } T}{\text{Total time system was under repair or recovery during period } T}. \qquad (13.12)$$

If the period T is long enough, the average availability approaches **steady state availability**, A_{ss}, which, given some simplifying assumptions, can be described by the following relationship [449, 412]:

$$A_{ss} = \frac{\rho}{\lambda + \rho}. \qquad (13.13)$$

We see that two measures which directly influence the availability of a system are its failure rate (or **outage** rate as failure rate is sometimes called) and its field repair rate (or software recovery rate). Figure 13.5 shows failure and recovery rates observed during operational use of a telecommunications product [105]. Apart from the censored[49] "raw" data, two other representations are shown. In one, the data are smoothed using an

---

[49]Zero valued data points are not shown in order to allow the use of logarithmic scale on the ordinate.

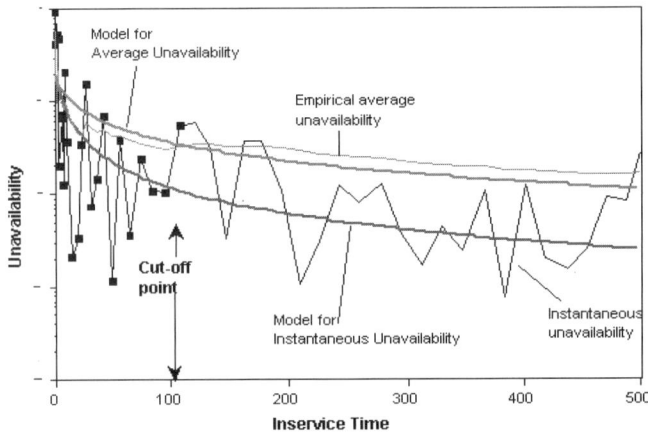

Figure 13.6. *Unavailability fit using LPET and constant repair rate with data* **up to** *"cut-off point" only.*

11-point symmetrical moving average. In the other, we show cumulative average of the data. Note that immediately after the product release date, there is considerable variation in the failure rate. This is the **transient** region. Later the failure rate reduces and stabilizes. In a system which improves with field usage we would expect a decreasing function for failure rate with **inservice-time**[50] (implying fault or problem reduction and reliability growth).

The field failure rate is usually connected to both the operational usage profile and the process of problem resolution and correction. The recovery rate depends on the operational usage profile, the type of problem encountered, and the field response to that problem (i.e., the duration of outages in this case). It is not unusual for a recovery rate to be 3 to 4 orders of magnitude larger (faster) than the failure rate.

In practice, reliability and availability models would be used to predict future unavailability of a system. Of course, only the data up to the point from which the prediction is being made would be available. The prediction would differ from the true value depending on how well the model describes the system. We illustrate this in Figure 13.6. It shows the empirical unavailability data and fits for two simple models. The fits are based on the average recovery rate observed at the "cut-off point," and the LPET failure fit to the points from the beginning of the release's operational phase up to the "cut-off point." The figure shows that, in this case, both models appear to predict future system behavior well. The models are described in [105]. Other models are available (e.g., [281]).

The point to note is that a relatively simple model can have quite reasonable predictive properties for a system that has a known history (through multiple releases) and is maintained in a stable environment.

---

[50]The total time the software-based system was in service, that is, either operating correctly or going through a repair or recovery episodes, at all sites that have the software installed.

13.5 General Practice

13.5.1 Verification and validation

It is not feasible to practice SRE without a sound and solid *software verification and validation* plan, process, and activities throughout the software life-cycle. An example of such a plan can be found in the IEEE software engineering standards [216]. SRE implies use of modern fault-avoidance, fault-identification, fault-elimination, and fault-tolerance technology. SRE extends that technology through quantification and matching with the business model. This includes construction and quantification of software usage profiles and specification of a balance between software reliability and other constraints. SRE practices require collection and analysis of data on software product and process quality, estimation and tracking of reliability, guidance of software development processes in terms of resources and "when-to-stop" testing information, and monitoring of software field reliability. SRE tracking and analysis are used to improve organizational software development and maintenance processes and maximize customer satisfaction. The following paragraphs provide an overview of the principal SRE activities during a typical [368] software lifecycle.

The IEEE verification and validation (V&V) standard suggests that following V&V tasks be conducted during a **software requirements specification and analysis** phase: (i) software requirements traceability analysis, (ii) software requirements evaluation, (iii) software requirements interface analysis, (iv) system test plan generation, and (v) software acceptance test plan generation. SRE augments these activities by requiring that the developers, in conjunction with the customers (users) need to (a) explicitly define and categorize software **failure modes**, (b) determine **reliability needs** of the customer and analyze the economic trade-offs (schedule versus quality versus cost), (c) determine software usage profile(s), and (d) set **reliability targets** for the product.

Identification and classification of software **failure modes** and their severity will depend on the application, customers, and maintenance needs. For example, the U.S. Federal Communications Commission requires service disruptions, such as loss of telephone service, that exceed 30 minutes and affect more than 50,000 customers to be reported to FCC within 30 minutes of its occurrence [141]. In this context, a telephone switch failure may be classified, in descending order of severity, as (1) FCC-reportable, (2) complete system outage of less than 30 minutes or affecting less than 50,000 customer lines, (3) loss of one or more principal functionalities or services, (4) loss of functionality that allows use of back-up or workaround options, or (5) minor inconvenience or inefficiency.

In order to diagnose the **root causes** of failures it is important to gather failure data. A failure that caused a complete system outage may be further subclassified by its identified, or hypothesized, cause into hardware-caused, software-caused, procedural (e.g., the system operator made a mistake and accidentally shut the system down), or unknown. Within each subclass it is possible to have additional categories. For example, if system availability (or repair time) is important, it may be advantageous to classify failures by their duration (e.g., less than 2 minutes, 2 to less than 5 minutes, 5 to less than 10 minutes, 10 to less than 30 minutes, 30 or more minutes). When dealing with communications software, or time-critical numerical computations, the delay classification could involve categories such as acceptable delay, marginal delay, and unacceptable delay, and failures may cluster in the unacceptable delay category.

In the case of numerical software, cause classification should include issues specific to such software—for example, specific algorithm design problems, roundoff error propagation problems, arithmetic exception handling, memory handling, and communication and data transfer delays (in the case of distributed software, such as cluster software).

The **reliability target** is established by considering the needs of customers as well as the limitations of the software engineering technology, capabilities of the developers, and other constraints such as the organizational **business model**, development costs, and schedules. Usually, separate objectives are set for each software failure category. For example, Bellcore has established generic requirements for performance evaluation of telecommunications systems [26]. The Bellcore target for a network switching element (e.g., a telephone exchange) is about 3 minutes of downtime per year and a complete outage failure is recognized if the service is down for over 30 seconds. Of course, this is not just a reliability requirement but also an availability requirement. In fact, it specifies average *unavailability* for the system of about $3/(60*24*365) = 0.00000571$. To compute the reliability target it is necessary to also establish a target value for system repair. For instance, under a simplifying assumption that the system has actually stabilized in its steady state, we can use the relationship (13.13) to set a possible reliability target. Let the average system repair rate be $\rho = 0.3$ failures per minute. Then substituting required availability $1 - 0.00000571 = 0.99999429$ and known repair rate into (13.13) and solving for the average system failure rate, we find that it should not exceed 0.00000171 failures per minute. Practice shows that this is a reasonable and achievable target for telecommunication software.

The IEEE standard also suggests that the following tasks be conducted during software **design, coding, unit testing, and integration testing** phases: (i) design and code traceability analysis, (ii) evaluations of software designs, code and documentation, (iii) software interface analysis, (iv) generation of test plans for software components and for their integration, and (v) design, generation and execution of test cases. SRE augments these activities by requiring software developers to (a) finalize functional and define **operational profiles**, (b) evaluate reliability of software components that are **reused**, (c) explicitly **allocate reliability** among software components and engineer the product to meet reliability objectives, (d) use **resource and schedule** models to guide development workload according to functional profiles, and (e) track and manage **fault introduction and removal** processes.

An important activity in the design phase is **allocation of reliability** objectives to subsystems and components in such a way that the total system reliability objective is achieved. The allocation approach should be iterative and it should include consideration of alternative solutions. The "balance" one is looking for is between the overall system reliability and the development schedule and effort (cost). Available options include inclusion of good exception handling capabilities and use of different fault-tolerance techniques [359, 297] combined with systems and software risk analysis and management [38].

Use of **inspections** and **reviews** is highly recommended in all phases of the software development process [216]. They provide a means of **tracking and managing** faults during the stages where the software is not in executable form, as well as in the stages where it is. A rule-of-thumb metric is the number of major faults per person-hour spent on preparation and conduct of inspections. If this metric is in the range 3 to 7, the inspection process as well as the software process is probably under control; otherwise, some corrective action is needed. More details can be found in [216, 92]. Once executable software is available tracking and management can be supplemented using reliability models and reliability control charts.

Evaluation of the reliability of **legacy code** and of any **acquired or reused code**, using operational profiles appropriate for the current application, is also recommended to ensure that the reliability of the "inherited" code is still acceptable. A special form of control charts may be used to monitor progress and decide on whether to accept or reject the components [331].

13.5.2 Operational profile

A crucial activity is definition of **operational profiles** and associated test cases. The process involves definition of customer, user, and system-mode profiles, followed by the definition of functional and operational profile(s). For example, a customer is a person, a group, or an institution that acquires the system. Table 13.1 illustrates a hypothetical customer profile for telephone switch software. We show two categories of customers and the associated probability that the customer will use the product. The probability information could come from actual measurements, or it could be gleaned from sales data.

Table 13.1. *Hypothetical telephone switch.*

Customer group	Probability
Local carrier	0.7
Intercity carrier	0.3

The next step is to identify the users. A user is a person, a group, or an institution that employs the system. Users are identified within each customer category. For example, see Table 13.2.

Table 13.2. *User breakdown of the profile.*

User group	Local (0.7)		Intercity (0.3)		Total
	within	total	within	total	
Households	0.6	0.42	0.2	0.06	0.48
Businesses	0.3	0.21	0.6	0.18	0.39
Emergency services	0.05	0.035	0.001	0.0003	0.0353
Other	0.05	0.035	0.199	0.0597	0.0947

For instance, the above table shows that *within* the local carrier category 60 % of the users are households, 30 % businesses, 5% emergency services, and 5 % other users. The contribution that local households make to the total traffic is 42 % ($0.7*0.6 = 0.42$), the contribution that intercity household calls make to the total traffic is 6 %, and the household user class as a whole accounts for 48 % of the total switch usage. The system can be used in several modes. A system mode is a set of functions or operations that are grouped for convenience in analyzing execution behavior [330]. The system can switch among modes, and two or more modes can be active at any one time. The procedure is to determine the operational profile for each system mode. Modes can be defined on the basis of user groups, environment (e.g., overload versus normal, high-noise versus low-noise), criticality, user experience, platform, and how the user employs system operations to accomplish system functions. For example, see Table 13.3.

Table 13.3. *Mode decomposition.*

Mode		Probability
Voice (personal)	0.4374	*0.42*0.9+0.06*0.99*
Voice (business)	0.273	*0.39*0.7*
Data	0.1596	*0.42*0.1+0.06*0.01+0.3*0.39*
Emergency	0.0353	*0.0353*
System administration	0.02841	*0.0947*0.3*
Maintenance	0.06629	*0.0947*0.7*

In Table 13.3 we assume that 99 % of intercity and 90 % of local household traffic is voice, while only 70 % of business traffic is voice for both customer categories. Furthermore, we assume that system administration accounts for 30 % and maintenance for 70 % of the "other" user category, while the rest of the traffic is data. Then, to obtain the functional profile it is now necessary to break each system mode into user-oriented functions needed for its operations and associated probabilities (e.g., features plus the environment). A function may represent one or more tasks, operations, parameters, or environmental variables (e.g., platform, operating system). The list of functions should be kept relatively short (e.g., from about 50 to several hundred). It should be noted that the functions will tend to evolve during system development and the profiling process is an iterative one.

The final two steps are the definition of an operational profile through explicit listing of operations and generation of test cases. The operations are the ones that are tested. Their profile will determine verification and validation resources, test cases, and the order of their execution. The operations need to be associated with actual software commands and input states. These commands and *input states* are then sampled in accordance with the associated probabilities to generate test cases. Particular attention should be paid to the generation of test cases that address critical and special issues.

Operational profiles should be updated on a regular basis since they can change over time, and the number of operations that are being tested should be limited. Probability may not be the only criterion for choosing the profile elements. Cost of failure (severity, importance) of the operations plays a role. In fact, separate profiles should be generated for each category of criticality (typically four separated by at least an order of magnitude in effects) [330].

13.5.3 Testing

Input space for a program is the set of discrete **input states** that can occur during the operation of the program. The number of dimensions of the input space is equal to the sum of the dimensions of the input variables. An *input* variable is any data item that exists external to a program and is *used* by the program, while an *output* variable is any data item that exists external to the program and is *set* by the program [331]. Note that in addition to the usual program parameters, externally initiated interrupts are also considered as input variables. Intermediate data items are neither input nor output variables.

13.5.3.1   Generation of test cases

In principle, one would use the operational profile of a product to identify the most important **scenarios** for the system, the corresponding operations, and the associated input states and thus develop test cases. Operational-profile–based testing is quite well behaved and, when executed correctly, allows dynamic evaluation of software reliability growth based on "classical" reliability growth metrics and models and use of these metrics and models to guide the process [331, 329].

Unfortunately, in reality things may not be so straightforward. The challenges of modern "market-driven" software development practices, such as the use of various types of incentives to influence workers to reduce time to market and overall development cost, seem to favor a resource constrained approach which is different from the "traditional" software engineering approaches [366]. In this case, the testing process is often analogous to a "sampling without replacement" of a finite (and sometimes very limited) number of **pre-determined** input states, data and other structures, functions, and environments [381, 382]. The principal motive is to verify required product functions (operations) to an **acceptable** level, but at the same time minimize the re-execution of already tested functions (operations). This is different from strategies that advocate testing of product functions according to the relative frequencies of their usage in the field, or according to their operational profile discussed in the previous subsection [329]. These testing strategies tend to allow for much more re-execution of previously tested functions and the process is closer to a "sampling with (some) replacement" of a specified set of functions.

In an "ideal" situation the test suite may consist only of test cases that are capable of detecting all faults, and defect removal is instantaneous and perfect. In "best" cases sampling without replacement, the one that usually operates in resource constrained situations, requires fewer test steps to reach a desired level of "defects remaining" than methods that reuse test steps (or cases) or recover already tested constructs, such as those based on operational profiles. However, in practice, it may turn out that test cases constructed using operational profiles may be more efficient and more comprehensive than those constructed using some nonideal coverage-based strategy. If not executed properly, testing based on sampling without replacement will yield poorer results.

For instance, when there are deviations from the "ideal" sampling without replacement, as is usually the case in practice, a number of defects may remain uncovered by the end of the testing phase. Figure 13.7 illustrates the differences.

"Unguided" constrained testing illustrates a failed attempt to cut the resources to about 20 % of the resources that might be needed for a complete operational-profile–based test of a product. The selection of the test cases suite was inadequate, and although the testing is completed within the required resource constraints, it detects only a small fraction of the latent faults (defects). In the field, this product will be a constant emitter of problems and its maintenance will probably cost many times the resources "saved" during the testing phases. **"Traditional" testing** illustrates ideal testing based on operational profile that

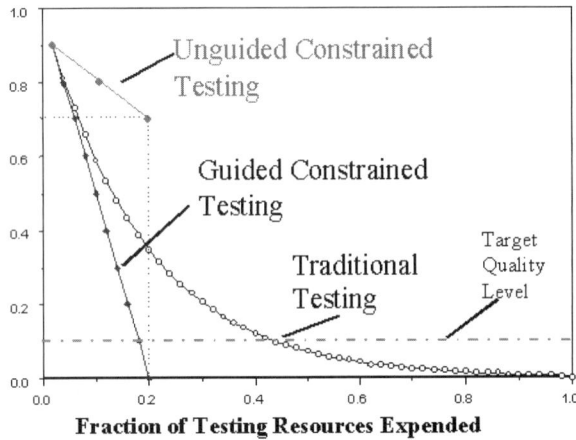

Figure 13.7. *Fraction of shipped defects (y-axis) for two "ideal" testing strategies based on sampling with and without replacement, and a "nonideal" testing under schedule and resource constraints.*

detects all faults present in the software but takes up more resources. Finally, **"guided" constrained testing** illustrates an ideal situation where every test case reveals a fault and no resources or time is wasted.

A good way to develop "guided" test cases is to start with a test suite based on the operational profile and trim the test cases in a manner that preserves coverage of important parameters and coverage measures. One such approach is discussed by Musa in his book [329]. Another one is to use pairwise test case generation systems [95, 96, 94, 286]. Of course, there are many other possible approaches, and many of the associated issues are still research topics.

13.5.3.2   Pairwise testing

Pairwise testing is a specification-based testing strategy which requires, in principle, that every combination of valid values of any two input parameters of a system be covered by at least one test case. Empirical results show that pairwise testing is practical and effective for various types of software systems [95, 96, 94]. According to Lei and Tai the pairwise testing steps are as follows [286, 436]:

"For each input parameter, specify a number of valid input values. If a parameter has a large number of valid values, choose representative and boundary values. The first value of each parameter must be a representative value of the parameter."

"Specify a number of relations for input parameters, where a relation is a set of two or more related input parameters. An input parameter may be in two or more relations. If an input parameter does not appear in any relation, it is called a non-interacting parameter. For each relation, constraints can be provided to specify prohibited combinations of values of some parameters in the relation. Each constraint is defined as a set of values for distinct parameters."

"Generate a test set for the system to satisfy the following requirements: (i) For each relation, every allowed combination of values of any two parameters in the relation is covered by at least one test, (ii) For each non-interacting parameter, every value of the parameter is covered by at least one test, (iii) Each test does not satisfy any constraint for any relation, and (iv) The first test contains the first value of each parameter."

For example, a system was found to have parameters A, B, and C as the most important parameters according to the operational profile studies (it could also be that it only has these three parameters at the level of abstraction at which the testing is being conducted; these parameters could be numerical or not). Let the most important (e.g., most frequent, or highest risk, or all) values (or equivalence classes) for the parameters be A1, . . . ,C2, i.e., as in Table 13.4.

Table 13.4. *Illustration of parameter values.*

A	B	C
A1	B1	C1
A2	B2	C2
A3	B3	

Then, we will need $3 \times 3 \times 2 = 18$ test cases if all three parameters are related (interacting) and we wish to cover all combinations of the parameters. On the other hand, pairwise testing strategy requires only nine tests to cover all PAIRS of combinations at least once. Table 13.5 illustrates this.

Table 13.5. *Pairwise test cases.*

A	B	C
A1	B1	C1
A1	B2	C2
A1	B3	C1
A2	B1	C2
A2	B2	C1
A2	B3	C2
A3	B1	C1
A3	B2	C2
A3	B3	C1

One can, of course, add constraints and further reduce the number of test cases. For example, if combination (A3, B3) is forbidden, the last test case could be deleted without affecting the coverage of (A3,C1) and (B3,C1), since they are covered by (A3,B1,C1) and (A1,B3,C1), respectively. As the number of parameters grows, the number of test cases required by the pairwise testing strategy grows linearly with the number of parameters rather than exponentially as it does with strategies which execute all combinations of the parameters [436].

Pairwise testing can be used for different levels of specification-based testing, including module testing, integration testing, and system testing. It is also useful for specification-based regression testing. Different levels of testing for a system have different sets of input parameters. The number of tests generated for pairwise testing of a program unit depends upon the number of input parameters, the number of values chosen for each input parameter, the number of relations, and the number of parameters in each relation.

PairTest is a software tool that generates a test set satisfying the pairwise testing strategy for a system [286]. The major features of PairTest include the following:

"PairTest supports the generation of pair-wise test sets for systems with or without existing test sets and for systems modified due to changes of input parameters and/or values.

PairTest provides information for planning the effort of testing and the order of applying test cases.

PairTest provide a graphical user interface (GUI) to make the tool easy to use.

PairTest is written in Java and thus can run on different platforms."

The PairTest tool was developed by Dr. K. C. Tai and his students Ho-Yen Chang and Yu Lei at North Carolina State University [286]; see the website `http://renoir.csc.ncsu.edu/SRE/Tools/`. Another such tool is AETG [94]. PairTest uses a somewhat different test case generation algorithm than does AETG.

13.5.4   Software process control

The importance of continuous software reliability evaluation is in establishing quality conditions which can be used for software process control. In the **system** and **field testing** phases standard activities include (i) execution of system and field acceptance tests, (ii) checkout of the installation configurations, and (iii) validation of software functionality and quality. In the **operation and maintenance** phases the essential SRE elements are (a) continuous monitoring and evaluation of software field reliability, (b) estimation of product support staffing needs, and (c) software process improvement.

SRE augments all these activities by requiring software developers and maintainers to (a) finalize and use operational profiles, (b) actively track the development, testing and maintenance process with respect to quality, (c) use reliability growth models to monitor and validate software reliability and availability, and (d) use reliability-based test stopping criteria to control the testing process and product patching and release schedules.

Ideally, the reaction to SRE information would be quick, and correction, if any, would be applied already within the life-cycle phase in which the information is collected. However, in reality, introduction of an appropriate feedback loop into the software process, and the latency of the reaction, will depend on the accuracy of the feedback models, as well as on the software engineering capabilities of the organization. For instance, it is unlikely that organizations below the third maturity level on the SEI Capability Maturity Model scale [357] would have processes that could react to the feedback information in less than one software release cycle. Reliable latency of less than one phase is probably not realistic for organizations below level 4. This needs to taken into account when the level and the economics of SRE implementation are considered.

13.6   Numerical Software

Numerical software has a number of special aspects because it deals with one of the elementary "features" of modern computing systems—their inherent inability to represent floating-point numbers exactly without special treatment.

There are essentially three ways of ensuring that a numerical software product operates correctly, and in an expected manner.

1. By appropriate specification, **design,** implementation. This is by **fault avoidance**. Especially in the areas related to the numerical properties of the solution, the platform on which it operates, and its interfaces to other numerical software and the platform hardware.

2. By **analytical** compensation for specification, design, and implementation errors through verification, validation, and testing efforts. This is **fault elimination**.

3. Through **runtime** compensation for any residual problems, through out-of-specification changes in the operational environment, user errors, etc. This is called **fault tolerance**. There are two steps in this process: (a) anomaly **detection**, and (b) **handling** of the anomaly. The preferred way would be through seamless dynamic recovery, but recognition of the problem accompanied with an instructive error message may be acceptable in many instances. There are three basic modes in which recovery can be effected: (a) exception handling, (b) check-pointing, and (c) through diversity-based mechanisms.

In this section we visit some of the basic techniques for anomaly detection, result verification, and recovery (fault tolerance) in numerical, scientific, and engineering applications. In combination with sound numerical methods and algorithms, these software engineering techniques can provide high assurance that numerical software meets specifications.

13.6.1   Acceptance testing

The most basic approach to result verification is self-checking through an (internal) *acceptance test*. An acceptance test is a programmer-provided software- or application-specific error detection mechanism which provides a check on the results of software execution. An acceptance test can be as complex and as costly to develop as the modules it is intended to accept, or it can be very simple. For example, an acceptance test might consist of numerical bounds only, or it may be a statistical test to determine acceptability of deviations of the results from a norm, or it could be another version of the program itself. For instance, it is much easier to develop software which determines if a list is sorted than it is to develop software which performs the sorting. An acceptance test normally uses only the data that are also available to the program at runtime.

Implicit relationships and specifications are often good acceptance tests. An example is the following implicit specification of the square root function [139], SQRT, which can serve as an acceptance test:

```
for (0 ≤ x ≤ y)        (ABS((SQRT(x)*SQRT(x)) − x) < E)  (13.14)
```

where E is the permissible error size, and x and y are real numbers. If E is computed for the actual code generated for the SQRT program on a particular platform (machine accuracy), then the above can serve as a full self-checking (acceptance) test. If E is known only to the programmer (or tester), and at runtime the program does not have access to machine specifications and/or the information about the allowable error propagation within the program, then the test is either partial, or cannot be executed by the program at general runtime at all.

Another option, in the above example, is to access precomputed tables of square root values. This is known as **table-driven answer verification**. Of course, in comparing the computed and the tabulated answers we must use accuracy/significance/tolerance levels commensurate with both the accuracy of the tables and the accuracy of the computation.

Acceptance tests that are specifically tailored to an algorithm are sometimes called *algorithmic* [1, 213]. For example, provision of checksums for rows and columns of a matrix can facilitate detection of problems and recovery [210].

13.6.2   External consistency checking

An *external consistency check* is an extended error detection mechanism. It may be used to judge the correctness of the results of program execution, but only with some outside intervention. In contrast to runtime production acceptance testing, it is a way of providing an "oracle" for off-line and development testing of the software, and for runtime **exception handling**. In situations where the exact answer is difficult to compute beforehand, it may the most cost-effective way of validating components of a software-based system, or of checking on runtime results.

A consistency check may use *all* information, including information that may not be available to the program in operation, but which may be available to an outside agent. An example are watchdog processes that monitor the execution of software-based systems and use information that may not be available to software, such as timing, to detect and resolve problems [459, 213]. Another example is periodic entry (manual or automatic) of location coordinates to a navigation system. Yet another example is an exception signal raised by the computer hardware or operating system when floating-point or integer overflow and divide-by-zero are detected. The interrupt, or exception, signal that abnormal events occurring in computer systems generate represents a particularly useful and prevalent resource for external consistency checking. Often, these signals can be detected and trapped in software and the exceptions can be handled to provide a form of failure tolerance.

For example, many modern programming languages[51] allow trapping of floating-point exceptions, divide-by-zero exceptions, or IEEE arithmetic signals (such as NANs[52]) [217, 215] and subsequent invocation of appropriate exception handlers that can provide an alternative computation, or other action, and thus shield the users from this type of runtime errors. A good example of applied exception handling in Fortran is work by Hull, Fairgrieve, and Tang [214].

Consistency checking may include comparisons against exact results, but more often it involves use of knowledge about the exact nature of the input data and conditions, combined with the knowledge of the transformation (relationship) between the input data and the output data. The consistency relationship must be sufficient to assert correctness.

For example, suppose that navigational software of an aircraft samples accelerometer readings and from that computes its estimate of the aircraft acceleration [131]. Let an

---

[51]For example, UNIX signals can be trapped in C (e.g., see standard "man" pages for "signal(3)" system calls).

[52]Not-a-Number, used to describe exception events that are not numbers [215, 217].

acceleration vector estimate, $\widehat{x}$, be given by the least squares approximation

$$\widehat{x} = [C^T C]^{-1} C^T y. \tag{13.15}$$

The matrix C is the transformation matrix from the instrument frame to the navigation frame of reference, C^T is its transpose, "-1" denotes matrix inverse, and the sensor measurements are related to the true acceleration vector x by

$$y = Cx + \widetilde{y}, \tag{13.16}$$

where $\widetilde{y}$ is the sensor inaccuracy caused by noise, misalignment, and quantization. Then,

$$C^T C(\widehat{x} - x) = C^T \widehat{y} \tag{13.17}$$

is a criterion to assert correctness for acceleration estimates. Note that x and $\widehat{y}$ are not normally available to the navigation software. However, if we supply all information, including that pertaining to the environment, we can control x and $\widehat{y}$ and detect problems with algorithms without having advance knowledge of the "correct" answer. This can provide "oracle" capabilities during the off-line testing of fault-tolerant software when the environment is completely under control. Of course, such a test cannot be employed during operational use of software unless an accurate environment status is provided independently.

In contrast, hardware and operating system **exceptions,** such as overflow and underflow, **can and should** be handled at runtime. Appropriate exception handling algorithms should be part of any software system that strives to provide a measure of failure tolerance.

13.6.3 Automatic verification of numerical precision (error propagation control)

A rather special set of techniques for dynamic detection and control of numerical failures is **automatic verification of numerical precision.** This type of verification treats errors resulting from algorithmic micromemory, that is, error propagation within a numerical algorithm, and possibly numerical algorithm instability.

A solution to the problem discussed here is based on accurate interval arithmetic [276, 277, 5]. The essence of the problem is that verification of a numerical algorithm does not guarantee in any way its numerical correctness unless its numerical properties are explicitly verified.

Floating-point arithmetic is a very fast and very commonly used approach to scientific and engineering calculations. As a rule, *individual* floating-point operations made available in modern computers are maximally accurate, and yet it is quite possible for the reliability of numerical software to be abysmally poor because a series of consecutive floating-point operations delivers completely wrong results due to rounding errors and because large numbers swamp small ones. To illustrate the issue we consider the following example due to [277, 5].

Let x and y be two vectors with 6 components, $\mathbf{x} = (10^{20}, 1223, 10^{24}, 10^{18}, 3, -10^{21})$, and $\mathbf{y} = (10^{30}, 2, -10^{26}, 10^{22}, 2111, 10^{19})$. The scalar product of these two vectors is defined as

$$\mathbf{x} * \mathbf{y} = \sum_{i=1}^{6} x_i\, y_i. \qquad (13.18)$$

The correct answer is 8779. However, implementation of this expression on practically every platform available today will return zero unless special precautions are taken. The reason is the rounding coupled with the large difference in the order of magnitude of the summands. This happens despite the fact that each individual number can be quite comfortably represented within the floating-point format of all platforms.

A much more basic, but similar problem, is exemplified by a well-known spreadsheet software when used to compute such a basic quantity as standard deviation. For example, my copy of the spreadsheet happily produces data in Table 13.6. It is obvious that the right-hand column calculation, using exactly the same built-in function as in the middle column—the standard deviation function—is in gross error. The problem itself, error propagation in combination with the use of a one-step (bad) instead of a multistep (good) algorithm for computation of standard deviation, is well known.[53] It is described well in the literature, and one can only speculate as to why a less than adequate algorithm appears to be implemented in this widely used spreadsheet. However, a bigger, related, and more frightening problem is an apparent frequent lack of awareness of this and similar problems with numerical software on the part of the users of such software, many of whom ought to know better.[54]

Table 13.6. *Example of standard deviation computation.*

	Number	**Number**
Value	0.1000000	10000000.1000000
Value	0.1000000	10000000.1000000
Value	0.1000000	10000000.1000000
Value	0.2000000	10000000.2000000
Value	0.2000000	10000000.2000000
Value	0.2000000	10000000.2000000
Value	0.4000000	10000000.4000000
Value	0.4000000	10000000.4000000
Value	0.4000000	10000000.4000000
Standard deviation	0.1322876	0.0000000
Average	0.2333333	10000000.2333333

It is possible to construct more subtle and more complex examples which show that simple numerical algorithms, such as Newton's method, can become very unstable if ordinary floating-point arithmetic is used without explicit error propagation control [277]. The arithmetic error propagation problem can become very acute in applications such as simulation and mathematical modeling, and it is exacerbated by modern high-speed computers.

---

[53]E.g., $s^2 = \frac{1}{n(n-1)}\left(n\sum_{i=1}^{n} x_i{}^2 - \left(\sum_{i=1}^{n} x_i\right)^2\right)$ versus $\bar{x} = \sum_{i=1}^{n} \frac{x_i}{n}$ and $s^2 = \sum_{i=1}^{n} \frac{(x_i - \bar{x})^2}{n-1}$.

[54]For example, few years ago a line manager in a high-technology company seriously considered using this spreadsheet for calculations related to development of real-life satellite-based communication networks.

The solution proposed by Kulisch et al. [276, 261, 260, 277, 5] relies on the computation of the optimal dot product using fixed point accumulation to *guarantee* maximal computational accuracy [276], on interval arithmetic (which implies certain rounding rules) to compute accurate upper and lower bounds on the result and on automatic differentiation methods [179]. If the computed result cannot be verified to be correct (for example, the computed bounds are too large), then the user can be given the option of providing alternatives to the algorithms and methods, or the option of changing to higher precision arithmetic followed by reverification of results and a decision regarding the acceptability of the results. This approach dynamically tolerates and controls this type of failure. Anyone involved with design of critical systems that use numerical software is strongly advised to consult relevant literature (e.g., [5, 64, 179]).

13.6.4   Redundancy-based techniques

The technique of using redundant software modules to verify result correctness and protect against residual software faults was inherited from hardware. Hardware failures are usually random (e.g., due component aging). Therefore identical back-up units, or redundant spare units, with automatic replacement of failed components at runtime, is a sensible approach, e.g., [449, 450, 338, 415]. However, replication of a software version to provide back-up redundancy has limited effectiveness since software faults are almost exclusively design and implementation related and therefore would also be replicated. The net effect would be that excitation of a replicated fault would result in a simultaneous failure of all versions and there would be no fault tolerance. This does not include timing or "transient" faults which often occur because of complex hardware/software/operating system interaction. Such failures, called "Heisenbugs" by Gray [176], can rarely be duplicated or diagnosed. A common solution is to re-execute the software in the hope that the transient disturbance is over. This is discussed more later in the section concerned with **fault tolerance and recovery** approaches.

Diversity. A solution proposed specifically for software was to have independent manufacturers produce functionally equivalent software components[55] [373, 21]. It was conjectured that different manufacturers would use different algorithms and implementation details, and that the residual faults from one independent software manufacturer would be different from those made by another, and therefore when one version failed, its back-up or spare would *not* fail for the same input data and conditions and would become the primary module, or at least could force a signal of the disagreement. The goal is to make the modules as "diverse" as possible. *The philosophy is to enhance the probability that the modules fail on* disjoint *subsets of the input space, and thus have at any time at least one correctly functioning software component.*

Specifications used in this process may themselves be diverse as long as final functional equivalency of the products is preserved. The specification indicates certain critical outputs which must be presented for an adjudication program to determine if the system is operating correctly. Each developer creates a software module or version which implements the specification and provides the outputs indicated by the specification.

---

[55]We shall use the terms "component(s)," "alternate(s)," "version(s)," "variants," and "module(s)" interchangeably.

Redundancy requires the ability to judge acceptability of the outputs of several modules either by direct evaluation or by comparison. The algorithm which compares or evaluates outputs is called an *adjudicator*. Such a program can be very simple or very complex depending on the application and therefore can also be a source of errors. An adjudication program uses the multiple outputs to determine which, if any, are correct or safe to pass on to the next phase of the processing. There are several techniques which have been proposed for implementation of the adjudication process. They may include voting, selection of the median value, and acceptance testing, as well as more complex decision making. Of course, in all situations problems arise if failures are coincidental, correlated, or similar.

13.6.4.1   Correlated failures and faults

We use the terms "coincident," "correlated," and "dependent" failures (faults) with the following meaning. When two or more functionally equivalent software components fail on the *same* input case we say that a *coincident* failure has occurred. Failure of k components raises a *k-way* coincident failure. The fault(s) that cause a k-way failure we shall call *k-way fault(s)*. When two or more versions give the same incorrect response (to a given tolerance) we say that an *identical-and-wrong* (IAW) answer was obtained. If the measured probability of the coincident failures is significantly different from what would be expected by random chance, usually based on the measured failure probabilities of the participating components, then we say that the observed coincident failures are *correlated*. Note that two events can be correlated because they *directly depend* on each other, or because they both depend on some other, but same, event(s) (*indirect dependence*), or both. Let Pr{ } denote probability. Then

$$\text{Pr}\{\text{version(i) fails} \mid \text{version(j) fails}\} \neq \text{Pr}\{\text{version(i) fails}\} \qquad (13.19)$$

means that the conditional probability that version "i" fails given that version "j" has failed is different from the probability that version "i", considered on its own, fails on the same inputs. If this relationship is true, we do **not** have failure **independence** [449, 450].

We shall say that several components contain the *same* or *similar* fault and possibly *common-cause* fault if the fault's nature, and the variables and function(s) it affects, are the same for all the involved components. The result (answer) of execution of such faults may be identical (IAW to within tolerance), or may be different. It is also possible that different faults result in a coincident failure by chance, giving either different answers or IAW answers.

Possible failure events are illustrated in Figure 13.8. The Venn diagram shown in the figure[56] represents the overlaps in the failure space of three functionally equivalent software units (or a 3-*tuple* of variants). Unshaded areas are regions where one of the three components (programs: P_1, P_2, P_3) fails for an input. Lightly shaded areas show the regions where two out of three components fail coincidentally, while the darkly shaded area in the middle is the region where all three components fail coincidentally. Of special interest are regions therein marked in black which represent events where components produce IAW responses.

---

[56]The diagram is not drawn to scale.

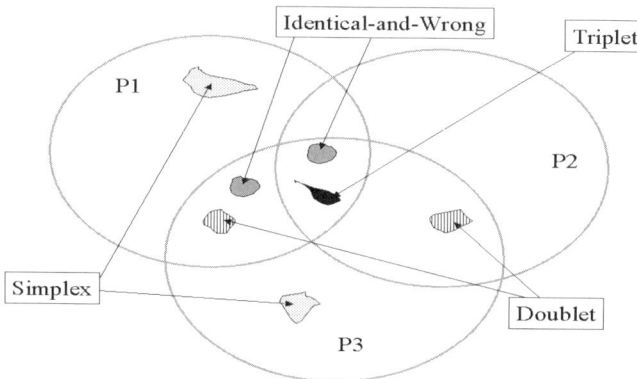

Figure 13.8. *Illustration of failure space for three functionally equivalent programs.*

13.6.4.2 Adjudication by voting

A common adjudication algorithm is voting. There are many variants of voting algorithms, e.g., [295, 306, 473, 161, 297]. A voter compares results from two or more functionally equivalent software components and decides which, if any, of the answers provided by these components is correct.

Majority voting. In an m-out-of-N fault-tolerant software system the number of versions is N (an N-tuple), and m is the *agreement number*, or the number of matching outputs which the adjudication algorithm (such as voting) requires for system success [132, 449, 450, 415]. The value of N is rarely larger than 3. In general, in *majority voting*, $m = \text{Ceiling}(\frac{N+1}{2})$.

2-out-of-N voting. Scott, Gault, and McAllister [402] showed that, if the output space is large, and true statistical independence of variant failures can be assumed, there is no need to choose m larger than 2 regardless of the size of N. We use the term *2-out-of-N voting* for the case where the agreement number is $m = 2$.

There is obviously a distinct difference between *agreement* and *correctness*. For example, a majority voter assumes that if a majority of the module outputs (e.g., numerical results) agree then the majority output must be the "correct" output. This, however, can lead to fallacious results, particularly in the extreme case when the number of possible module outputs is very small. For example, suppose that the output of each module is a single variable which assumes the values of either 0 or 1. This means that all incorrect outputs automatically agree and it is very likely if modules have any faults there may be a majority of IAW outputs. The behavior is similar to coincident and correlated failures.

In general, there will be multiple output variables, each one assuming a number of values. The total number of allowed combinations of output variables and their values defines the number "ρ" of program output states, or the cardinality of the output space. If there are multiple correct outputs then a simple voter is useless. Hence, when voting, we could assume that there is only one correct output for each input. From this it follows that, given output cardinality of ρ, we have one correct output state, and $\rho - 1$ error states. Whether this is justifiable or not should be part of the software design analysis when adjudication is used in any form.

In that context, midvalue select (or simple **median voting**) is an interesting and simple adjudication alternative whereby the median of all (numerical) output values is selected as the correct answer. The philosophy behind the approach is that, in addition to being fast, the algorithm can handle multiple correct answers (and for small samples is less biased than averaging, or mean value voting), and it is likely to pick a value which is at least in the correct range. This technique has been applied successfully in aerospace applications.

A generalization of majority voting is *consensus voting* described in McAllister et al. [306, 307]. The consensus voting strategy is particularly effective in small output spaces because it automatically adjusts the voting to the changes in the effective output space cardinality.

13.6.4.3   Tolerance

Closely related to voting is the issue of tolerance to which comparisons are made. Let TOL be the comparison tolerance, and consider an N-tuple of versions. The following two mutually exclusive events *do not depend* on whether the answers are correct or not.

1. All N components agree on an answer. In this case we have an "AGREEMENT" event.

2. There is at least one disagreement among the $_NC_2$ comparisons of alternate outputs, where $_NC_2$ denotes the number of combinations of N objects taken two at a time (2-tuples). We will call this case a "CONFLICT" event. All 2-tuples need to be evaluated because agreement may not be transitive, that is, $|a - b| \leq$ TOL and $|b - c| \leq$ TOL does not always imply that $|a - c| \leq$ TOL (see Figure 13.9).

It is very important to realize that use of an inappropriate tolerance value, TOL, may either completely mask failure events (that is, too large a tolerance will always return AGREEMENT events) or cause an avalanche of CONFLICT events (the tolerance is too small and therefore many answer pairs fail the tolerance test). Assume that we have an "oracle," so that we can tell the correctness of an answer.[57] The following mutually exclusive events *depend* on the knowledge of the correctness of the output, or agreement with the correct answer:

1. All N components agree with the *correct* (call it "golden") answer. Then a "NO_FAILURE" event occurs.

2. One or more of the versions disagree with the *correct* answer. Then a "FAILURE" event occurs.

The following events are examples of subevents of the FAILURE event:

1. The majority of the versions disagree with the correct answer. We then say that a "MAJORITY_FAILURE" event has occurred. All but one of the versions disagree with the correct answer.

2. Exactly k of the $N (1 \leq k \leq N)$ components disagree with the *correct* answer. This is a "k_FAILURE" event.

---

[57]For example, an "oracle" can take the form of an *external consistency check*.

3. All the components disagree with the correct answer. Then an "$N\_FAILURE$" event has occurred. If outputs are also identical, then comparisons will fail to signal an error.

It is possible to define other states such as the majority of components agreeing with the correct answer, two or more disagreeing, and exactly k agreeing. Combinations of the above "elementary" events produce the following mutually exclusive and collectively exhaustive multiversion comparison events:

1. An **ALL_"CORRECT"** event: a NO_FAILURE occurs with an AGREEMENT.

2. A **"FALSE_ALARM"** event: a NO_FAILURE occurs with a CONFLICT. Comparison signals an error when one is not present which may or may not lead to a failure of the adjudication algorithm. Recall that agreement is not transitive, so FALSE_ALARM events are not inconsistent.

3. A **"DETECTED_FAILURE"** event: a FAILURE occurs together with a CONFLICT. Comparison correctly detects a failure (fault).

4. A **"UN_DETECTED_FAILURE"** event: a FAILURE event occurs simultaneously with an AGREEMENT. This is the most significant event. A potential failure exists but is not detected by comparison.

Consider again Figure 13.8 which shows responses from a hypothetical three version system. A simplex failure (1_FAILURE) occurs when only one of the three versions fails (unshaded regions). A doublet failure (2-tuple, or 2_FAILURE) occurs when two components fail coincidentally (light shading). A triplet failure, or 3-tuple failure ($N\_FAILURE$, $N = 3$), occurs when all three components fail coincidentally (dark shading). If the probability that any of the *shaded* areas exceed or do not achieve the probability of overlap expected by random chance, then the assumption of independence is violated [449, 450]. That is,

$$\Pr\{p_i \text{ fails } \textbf{and } p_j \text{ fails}\} \neq \Pr\{p_i \text{ fails}\} \Pr\{p_j \text{ fails}\} \qquad (i \neq j) \qquad (13.20)$$

or

$$\begin{aligned} \Pr\{p_1 \text{ fails } \textbf{and } p_2 \text{ fails } \textbf{and } p_3 \text{ fails}\} \\ \neq \Pr\{p_1 \text{ fails}\} \Pr\{p_2 \text{ fails}\} \Pr\{p_3 \text{ fails}\}, \end{aligned} \qquad (13.21)$$

where p_i is the ith software variant.

The most undesirable state of the system, UN_DETECTED_FAILURE, occurs when the responses from three coincidentally failing versions are identical, in which case mutual comparison of these answers does not signal that a failure has occurred.

Figure 13.9 provides an illustration of the events that may result from comparison to tolerance TOL of floating-point outputs a, b, and c, from hypothetical programs P_1, P_2, and P_3, respectively. Excessively small tolerances may produce an excessive incidence of FALSE_ALARM events which may increase testing costs [470], while in operation this may result in degraded system operation, or even a critical system failure. The issue is discussed in more detail in [307].

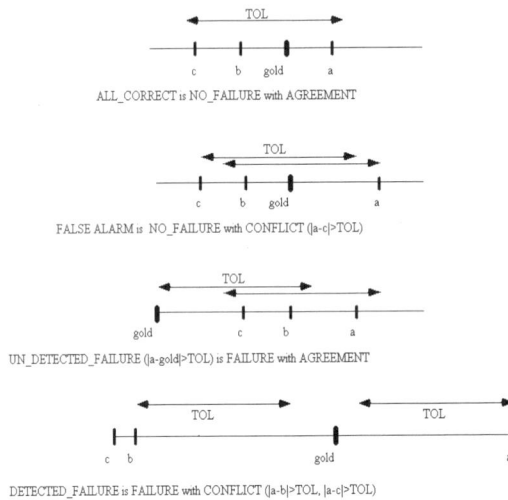

Figure 13.9. *Illustration of comparison events.*

13.7   Basic Fault-tolerance Techniques

A principal way of introducing **fault tolerance** into a system is to provide a method to dynamically determine if the system is behaving as it should, that is, an internal or external result verification, checking, or "oracle" capability. If unexpected and unwanted behavior (result) is detected, a fault-tolerant system then needs to provide a means of recovery or continuation of operation (preferably seamless from the perspective of the user). There are two basic ways of doing that: through partial, or complete, system state recovery and restart techniques, and through forward recovery techniques. There is also the issue of **safety**, e.g., [287].

It is important to understand that one can have a very **safe** system that has very little fault tolerance in it. It is also possible to have a system that is highly fault tolerant, but when it fails (rarely, one hopes), it can fail in an unsafe way. Hence, fault tolerance and safety are not synonymous. Safety is concerned with failures (of any nature) that lead to failures that can result in unacceptable harm to the user; fault tolerance is primarily concerned with runtime prevention of failures in any shape and form (including prevention of safety-critical failures). When safety is defined properly and adequately in the system specifications, then a well-designed fault-tolerant system will also be a safe one. A fault-tolerant and safe system will both minimize overall failures and make sure that when a failure occurs it is a safe failure.

This section is intended only as a brief introduction into the world of fault-tolerant software-based systems, including systems based on numerical software. For details, the reader is directed to key topic references such as [297] and [221].

13.7.1   Check-pointing and exception handling

A number of re-execution based methods exist (e.g., [297]). They include approaches that periodically store known good states (and data) of the system and then roll back the system to the closest check-pointed state if a problem is detected. Another set of methods is concerned with trapping anomalies, transients, and exceptions and then handling these events in a graceful manner. Often recovery in both approaches includes partial or full re-execution of the system software. If the recovery is **reactive**, i.e., it occurs as the result of, and when, an immediate threat to system is detected, it may be disruptive.

The related term is **software aging**. It basically means that the state of a software system degrades with time [211]. Frequent causes of degradation are exhaustion of operating system or application resources (such as memory leaks), data corruption, unreleased file-locks, and numerical error accumulation. Eventually, software aging may lead to system performance degradation, transient failures, and/or complete system stoppage. For example, popular and widely used software, such as the Web browser *Netscape,* is known to suffer from serious memory leaks. Often, the only solution to this problem is to stop the application and restart it. This problem is particularly pronounced in systems low on swap space. Software aging has also been observed in specialized software used in high-availability and safety-critical applications.

To counteract this phenomenon, a **proactive** approach of failure and fault management, called **software rejuvenation**, has been investigated by a number of researchers, e.g., [211, 434, 451]. It essentially involves detection of (anomalous) system parameter and variable patterns (fingerprints) and their correlation with undesirable system events (or failures), i.e., detection of a growing $\lambda(\tau)$. This is followed by occasional preventive, and well-controlled, stoppage of the system, cleaning of its internal states, and system restart. This process removes the accumulated errors and frees up operating system and other resources, thus preventing in a proactive manner the unplanned and potentially expensive system outages due to software aging. Since the preventive action can be done at optimal times, for example, when the load on the system is low and noncritical, it reduces the cost of system downtime compared to reactive recovery from failure. Thus, software rejuvenation is a cost-effective technique for dealing with software faults that include protection not only against hard failures but against performance degradation as well. Of course, its use has to be judged against the need for continuity of services and similar factors.

13.7.2 Recovery through redundancy

Forward error recovery methods tend to be less disruptive from the end-user viewpoint. They detect an erroneous internal state of the system (that might lead to a failure), and try to mask it, or on-the-fly transparently recover from it without resorting to stoppage of the system or excessive delays. Traditionally, they are used in information fault-tolerance contexts—error coding being one example, e.g., [290, 103]. Two common fault-tolerant software schemes that fall into the same general forward recovery class are the N-version programming [21, 20] and the Recovery Block [373]. Both schemes are based on software component redundancy and the assumption that coincident failures of components are rare, and when they do occur, responses are sufficiently dissimilar so that the mechanism for deciding answer correctness is not ambiguous.

Fault-tolerant software mechanisms based on redundancy are particularly well suited for parallel processing environments where concurrent execution of redundant components may drastically improve sometimes prohibitive costs associated with their serial execution [473, 27, 280]. The issue of fault tolerance will gain importance as computational, storage, and application "Grids" become more prevalent [163]. Some hybrid techniques, such as Consensus Recovery Block [401, 402], checkpoints [21], Community Error Recovery [454, 453], NVersion Programming variants [280, 435], and some partial fault-tolerance approaches are also available [203, 428, 316].

In this context, it is important to understand that redundancy in software, like in hardware, can take many forms. It may take the form of functionally equivalent software solutions, but it can also take other forms. For example, use of redundant links in linked lists is one form of fault tolerance that can help combat partial loss of list items [439].

13.7.2.1 Recovery blocks

One of the earliest fault-tolerant software schemes which used the multiversion software approach is the **Recovery Block** (RB) [373, 114]. The adjudication module is an *acceptance test* (AT). The output of the first module is tested for acceptability. If the acceptance test determines that the output of the first module is not acceptable it restores, recovers, or "rolls back" the state of the system before the first or primary module is executed. It then allows the second module to execute and evaluates its output, etc. If all modules execute and none produce acceptable outputs, then the system fails.

A problem with this strategy in a uniprocessor environment is the sequential nature of the execution of the versions [280, 28]. In a distributed and/or multiprocessor environment, the modules and the acceptance tests can be executed in parallel. Distributed recovery block is discussed in detail in [259, 297]. Another potential problem is finding a simple, and highly reliable, acceptance test which does not involve the development of an additional software version.

The form of an acceptance test depends on the application. There may be a different acceptance test for each module but in practice only one is usually used. An extreme case of an acceptance test is another complete module, and the acceptance test would then consist of a comparison of a given module output with the one computed by the acceptance test. This would be equivalent to a staged 2-version programming scheme (see the following section) where one of the outputs in each stage is always from the same version (the acceptance test).

13.7.2.2 N-version programming

N-version programming (NVP) [21, 91, 20] proposes parallel execution of N independently developed functionally equivalent versions with adjudication of their outputs by a voter. N-version programming or multiversion programming (MVP) is a software generalization of the N-modular-redundancy (NMR) approach used in hardware fault tolerance [338]. The N versions produce outputs to the adjudicator, which in this case is a *voter*. The voter accepts all N outputs as inputs and uses these to determine the correct, or best, output if one exists. There is usually no need to interrupt the service while the voting takes place. We note that the approach can also be used to help during testing to debug the versions. This method, called back-to-back testing, is discussed further in [307].

Simple majority voting–based N-version fault-tolerant software has been investigated by a number of researchers, both theoretically [21, 180, 132, 402, 113, 293, 469, 250, 297], and experimentally [403, 404, 34, 262, 411, 131, 299, 129, 474]. A reasonable alternative to majority voting could be to use consensus voting as described earlier. Another simple variation is **median voting**. There are also variants of the above architecture for distributed systems. One such variant is the **N-self-checking programming** (NSCP) outlined below.

13.7.3   Advanced techniques

There are ways to combine the simple techniques to create hybrid techniques. Studies of more advanced models such as consensus recovery block [27, 402, 113, 403, 404], consensus voting [306], or acceptance voting [27, 19] are less frequent and mostly theoretical in nature.

13.7.3.1   Consensus recovery block

In [401] and [402] a hybrid system called consensus recovery block (CRB) was suggested which combines NVP and RB in that order. If NVP fails the system reverts to RB (using the same modules, the same module results can be used, or modules may be rerun if a transient failure is suspected). Only in the case that both NVP and RB both fail does the system fail. CRB was originally proposed to treat the case of multiple correct outputs since appropriate acceptance testing can avoid that issue.

13.7.3.2   Acceptance voting

The "converse" of the CRB hybrid scheme, which we call acceptance voting (AV), was proposed in [19, 157, 28]. As in NVP, all modules can execute in parallel. The output of each module is then presented to an acceptance test. If the acceptance test accepts the output it is then passed to a voter.

The voter sees only those outputs which have been passed by the acceptance test. This implies that the voter may not process the same number of outputs at each invocation and hence the voting algorithm must be dynamic. The system fails if no outputs are submitted to the voter. If only one output is submitted, the voter must assume it to be correct and therefore passes it to the next stage. Only if two or more outputs agree can the voter be used to make a decision. We then apply dynamic majority voting (DMV) or dynamic consensus voting (DCV). The difference between DMV and MV is that even if a small number of results are passed to the voter, dynamic voting will try to find the majority among them. The concept is similar for DCV and CV. Both Athavale [19] and Belli and Jedrzejowicz [27] have limited their analytical work to DMV.

13.7.3.3   N self-checking programming

A variant of the N-version programming with recovery, that is, N self-checking programming, is used in the Airbus A310 system [280, 129]. In NSCP N modules are executed in pairs (for an even N) [280]. The outputs from the modules can be compared, or can be assessed for correctness in some other manner. Let us assume that comparison is used. Then, the outputs of each pair are tested and if they do not agree with each other, the response of the pair is discarded. If the outputs of both pairs agree then these outputs are compared again. Failure occurs if both pairs disagree or if the pairs agree but produce different outputs.

13.7.4   Reliability and performance

Although existing fault-tolerant software (FTS) techniques can achieve a significant improvement over non–fault-tolerant software, they sometimes may not be sufficient for ensuring adequate reliability of critical systems and at the same time conform with the prevailing business model, required timing and performance, and other constraints.

For example, experiments show that incidence of correlated failures of FTS system components may not be negligible in the context of current software development and testing techniques, and this may result in a disaster [403, 472, 132, 262, 256, 255]. Furthermore, comparison tolerance issues [54] can also result in unexpected behavior unless they are properly handled. This has led some researchers to question the validity of execution-time software fault tolerance using the multiversion approach [262, 54]. Hence, it is important to avoid, detect, and eliminate these errors as early as possible in the FTS life-cycle and develop FTS mechanisms that can adequately cope with any remaining faults.

Modeling different FTS mechanisms gives insight into their behavior and allows quantification of their relative merits. Detailed FTS design, and reliability and performance analysis of fault-tolerant software systems, is beyond the scope of this tutorial. Interested readers are directed to the bibliography and the references in key references such as [280, 297, 287, 298, 221].

13.8   Summary

The day-to-day operation of our society is increasingly more dependent on software-based systems, and tolerance of *failures* of such systems is decreasing. Numerical software holds one of the central positions in this context. Because of the high stakes involved, it is essential that the software be accurate, reliable, and robust. Numerical software has many characteristics of a general software system coupled with issues very specific to numerical algorithms, their stability, their implementation in software, and the computational framework they run on. Hence, many software engineering techniques that apply to software in general apply to numerical software as well.

In this paper we have first provided general information about the nature of software reliability engineering (SRE) and how it relates to software process, including factors such as testing, cost, and benefits. This was followed by an overview of the SRE terminology and modeling issues. Finally, SRE practice was addressed in both the general context and in the context of numerical software, as well as in the context of fault tolerance. We have discussed specifics of SRE activities required during different software life-cycle phases, including an example of how to generate SRE-based test cases automatically. We have also illustrated issues that may arise in numerical software. Many other numerical issues exist, some very algorithm and application specific. We know enough today about the general software engineering technologies, as well as about the construction and implementation of sound numerical algorithms, that we can make numerical software meet its specifications on time and within cost, provided a reasonable and realistic business model is employed.

Certainly, verification, validation, and testing of numerical software should be formalized. If diversity, or some other verification property, is relied upon, developers should strive to provide evidence that this property is present and preserved. It is also important to explicitly show that appropriate and stable numerical algorithms have been implemented. With a process that includes good specifications, realistic reliability, availability, and performance parameters, careful inspection and testing of specifications, designs, and code, correct and fault-tolerant numerical software becomes a viable option for increasing reliability of a numerical software-based system.

More information, and access to SRE tools, can be obtained from the following site: `http://renoir.csc.ncsu.edu/SRE/Tools/`.

Bibliography

[1] J. A. ABRAHAM, G. METZE, R. K. IYER, AND J. H. PATEL, *The evolution of fault-tolerant computing at the University of Illinois*, in Dependable Computing and Fault-Tolerant Systems, A. Avizienis, H. Kopetz, and J.C. Laprie, eds., vol. 1, Springer-Verlag, Wien and New York, 1987, pp. 271–311.

[2] S. R. ABRAMSON, *Customer satisfaction-based product development*, in Proc. Intl. Switching Symp., vol. 2, Inst. Electronics, Information, Communications Engineers, Yokohama, Japan, 1992, pp. 65–69.

[3] F. S. ACTON, *Numerical Methods that Usually Work*, Harper & Row, New York, 1970.

[4] F. S. ACTON, *REAL Computing Made REAL, Preventing Errors in Scientific and Engineering Calculations*, Princeton University Press, Princeton, New Jersey, 1996.

[5] E. ADAMS AND U. KULISCH, *Scientific Computing with Automatic Result Verification*, Academic Press, New York, 1993. See also the references therein.

[6] W. R. ADRION, M. A. BRANSTAD, AND J. C. CHERNIAVSKY, *Validation, verification, and testing of computer software*, ACM Comput. Surv., 14 (1982), pp. 159–192.

[7] AIAA, *Guide for the verification and validation of computational fluid dynamics simulations*, Tech. Report AIAA-G-077-1998, American Institute for Aeronautics and Astronautics, 1998.

[8] AIAA/ANSI, *Recommended practice for software reliability*, Tech. Report ANSI/ AIAA, R-103-1992, American Institute of Aeronautics and Astronautics, 1993.

[9] M. AIGNER AND G. M. ZIEGLER, *Proofs from THE BOOK*, Springer-Verlag, Berlin, Heidelberg, 1998.

[10] G. ALEFELD, V. KREINOVICH, AND G. MAYER, *On the shape of the symmetric, persymmetric, and skew-symmetric solution set*, SIAM J. Matrix Anal. Appl., 18(3) (1997), pp. 693–705.

[11] G. ALEFELD AND G. MAYER, *Interval analysis: Theory and applications*, J. Comput. Appl. Math., 121 (2000), pp. 421–464.

301

[12] E. ANDERSON, Z. BAI, C. H. BISCHOF, S. BLACKFORD, J. DEMMEL, J. J. DONGARRA, J. DU CROZ, A. GREENBAUM, S. HAMMARLING, A. MCKENNEY, AND D. C. SORENSEN, *LAPACK Users' Guide*, Software Environ. Tools 9. 3rd ed., SIAM, Philadelphia, 1999. http://www.netlib.org/lapack/lug/.

[13] ANSI, *American National Standard for Information Systems – Programming Language – C, ANSI X3.159-1989*, ANSI, 1989.

[14] J. APPLEYARD, *Comparing Fortran compilers*, Fortran Forum, 20 (2001), pp. 6–10. See also the Fortran pages of http://www.polyhedron.com/.

[15] E. ARGE, A. M. BRUASET, P. B. CALVIN, J. F. KANNEY, H. P. LANGTANGEN, AND C. T. MILLER, *On the efficiency of C++ in scientific computing*, in Mathematical Models and Software Tools in Industrial Mathematics, M. Dæhlen and A. Tveito, eds., Birkhäuser, Basel, 1997, pp. 91–118.

[16] M. ARIOLI, I. S. DUFF, AND D. RUIZ, *Stopping criteria for iterative solvers*, SIAM J. Matrix Anal. Appl., 13(1) (1992), pp. 138–144.

[17] ARUP, *Summary report on the millennium bridge*, 2003. http://www.arup.com/MillenniumBridge.

[18] ASSOCIATED PRESS, *Software disasters are often people problems*, October 2004. http://www.msnbc.msn.com/id/6174622/.

[19] A. ATHAVALE, *Performance evaluation of hybrid voting schemes*, Tech. Report, M.S. Thesis, North Carolina State University, Department of Computer Science, December 1989.

[20] A. AVIZIENIS, *The N-version approach to fault-tolerant software*, IEEE Transactions on Software Engineering, SE-11 (1985), pp. 1491–1501.

[21] A. AVIZIENIS AND L. CHEN, *On the implementation of N-version programming for software fault-tolerance during program execution*, in Proc. COMPSAC 77, 1977, pp. 149–155.

[22] JOHN C. BAEZ, *The octonions*, Bull. Amer. Math. Soc., 39 (2002), pp. 145–205. http://math.ucr.edu/home/baez/Octonions/octonions.html.

[23] R. BARRETT, M. BERRY, T. CHAN, J. DEMMEL, J. DONATO, J. DONGARRA, V. EIJKHOUT, R. POZO, C. ROMINE, AND H. VAN DER VORST, *Templates for the Solution of Linear Systems: Building Blocks for Iterative Methods*, SIAM, Philadelphia, 1994.

[24] BBC, *The Millennium bridge*, 2000. http://news.bbc.co.uk/hi/english/static/in_depth/uk/2000/millennium_bridge/default.stm.

[25] H. BEHNKE, U. MERTINS, M. PLUM, AND CH. WIENERS, *Eigenvalue inclusions via domain decomposition*, in Proc. Roy. Soc. London, A 456 (2000), pp. 2717–2730.

[26] BELLCORE, *Reliability and quality measurements for telecommunications systems (RQMS)*, 1990. TR-TSY-000929, Issue 1, June 1990.

[27] F. BELLI AND P. JEDRZEJOWICZ, *Fault-tolerant programs and their reliability*, IEEE Trans. Rel., 29 (1990), pp. 184–192.

[28] ——, *Comparative analysis of concurrent fault-tolerance techniques for real-time applications*, in Proc. Intl. Symposium on Software Reliability Engineering, Austin, TX, 1991, pp. 202–209.

[29] M. BENNANI, T. BRACONNIER, AND J.-C. DUNYACH, *Solving large-scale nonnormal eigenproblems in the aeronautical industry using parallel BLAS*, in High-Performance Computing and Networking, W. Gentzsch and U. Harms, eds., vol. 796, Springer-Verlag, New York, 1994, pp. 72–77.

[30] K. BERKUN, *London firms reportedly offer amnesty to "hacker thieves,"* The Risks Digest, 8 (1989). `http://catless.ncl.ac.uk/Risks/8.85.html#subj3.1`.

[31] D. BERLEANT AND V. KREINOVICH, *Intervals and probability distributions.* `http://class.ee.iastate.edu/berleant/home/ServeInfo/Interval/intprob.html`, 2003.

[32] M. BERZ AND K. MAKINO, *Cosy infinity beam theory and dynamical systems group.* `http://cosy.pa.msu.edu/`.

[33] D. BINDEL, J. DEMMEL, W. KAHAN, AND O. MARQUES, *On computing Givens rotations reliably and efficiently*, ACM Trans. Math. Software, 28 (2002), pp. 206–238.

[34] P. G. BISHOP, D. G. ESP, M. BARNES, P. HUMPHREYS, G. DAHL, AND J. LAHTI, *PODS– a project on diverse software*, IEEE Trans. Soft. Eng., SE-12 (1986), pp. 929–940.

[35] R. H. BISSELING, *Parallel Scientific Computation: A Structured Approach Using BSP and MPI*, Oxford University Press, Oxford, UK, 2004.

[36] L. S. BLACKFORD, A. CLEARY, J. DEMMEL, I. DHILLON, J. J. DONGARRA, S. HAMMARLING, A. PETITET, H. REN, K. STANLEY, AND R. C. WHALEY. *Practical experience in the numerical dangers of heterogeneous computing.* ACM Trans. Math. Software, 23 (1997), pp. 133–147.

[37] R. M. BLOCH, *Mark I calculator*, in Proc. of a Symposium on Large-Scale Digital Calculating Machinery, vol. 16 of The Annals of the Computation Laboratory of Harvard University, Harvard University Press, Cambridge, MA, 1948, pp. 23–30. Reprinted, with a new introduction by William Aspray, Volume 7 in the Charles Babbage Institute Reprint Series for the History of Computing, MIT Press, Cambridge, MA, USA, 1985.

[38] B. W. BOEHM, *Tutorial: Software Risk Management*, IEEE Computer Society, Los Alamitos, CA, 1989.

[39] B. W. BOEHM, J. R. BROWN, H. KASPAR, M. LIPOW, G. J. MACLEOD, AND M. J. MERRITT, *Characteristics of software quality*, Tech. Report TRW-SS-73-09, TRW Systems Group, December 1973.

[40] G. BOHLENDER, *Genaue Summation von Gleitkommazahlen*, Computing, Suppl.1 (1977), pp. 21–32.

[41] R. F. BOISVERT, J. MOREIRA, M. PHILIPPSEN, AND R. POZO, *Java and numerical computing*, Computing in Science and Engineering, 3 (2001), pp. 18–24.

[42] R. F. BOISVERT, R. POZO, K. REMINGTON, R. BARRETT, AND J. DONGARRA, *The Matrix Market, a Web repository for test matrix data*, in The Quality of Numerical Software: Assessment and Enhancement, Ronald F. Boisvert, ed., Chapman & Hall, London, 1997.

[43] BOOST C++ LIBRARIES, *Boost C++ libraries Web site.* http://www.boost.org/libs/libraries.htm.

[44] F. BORNEMANN, D. LAURIE, S. WAGON, AND J. WALDVOGEL, *The SIAM 100-Digit Challenge: A Study in High-Accuracy Numerical Computing*, SIAM, Philadelphia, 2004. http://www.ec-securehost.com/SIAM/ot86.html.

[45] G. E. P. BOX, W. G. HUNTER, AND S. J. HUNTER, *Statistics for Experimenters*, John Wiley & Sons, New York, 1978.

[46] T. BRACONNIER, *Sur le calcul de valeurs propres en précision finie*, Ph.D. Dissertation, Université H. Poincaré, Nancy, May 1994. TH/PA/94/24, CERFACS.

[47] T. BRACONNIER, F. CHATELIN, AND J.-C. DUNYACH, *Highly nonnormal eigenvalue problems in the aeronautical industry*, Japan J. Ind. Appl. Math., 12 (1995), pp. 123–136.

[48] R. W. BRANKIN AND I. GLADWELL, *Algorithm 771:* `rksuite_90`: *Fortran 90 software for ordinary differential equation initial-value problems*, ACM Trans. Math. Software, 23 (1997), pp. 402–415.

[49] R. W. BRANKIN, I. GLADWELL, AND L. F. SHAMPINE, *RKSUITE: A suite of Runge-Kutta codes for the initial value problem for ODEs*, Softreport 92-S1, Mathematics Department, Southern Methodist University, Dallas, TX, 1992.

[50] ———, *RKSUITE: A suite of explicit Runge-Kutta codes*, in Contributions to Numerical Mathematics, R. P. Agarwal, ed., World Scientific, River Edge, NJ, 1993, pp. 41–53.

[51] K. D. BRAUNE, *Hochgenaue Standardfunktionen für reelle und komplexe Punkte und Intervalle in beliebigen Gleitpunktrastern*, dissertation, Universität Karlsruhe, 1987.

[52] R. P. BRENT, *Algorithms for Minimization without Derivatives*, Prentice–Hall, Englewood Cliffs, NJ, 1973.

[53] L. C. BRIAND, W. M. THOMAS, AND C. J. HETSMANSKI, *Modeling and managing risk early in software development*, in Proc. 15th ICSE, 1993, pp. 55–65.

[54] S. S. BRILLIANT, J. C. KNIGHT, AND N. G. LEVESON, *The consistent comparison problem in N-version software*, ACM SIGSOFT Software Engineering Notes, 12 (1987), pp. 29–34.

[55] S. BROCKLEHURST AND B. LITTLEWOOD, *New ways to get accurate reliability measures*, IEEE Software, (1992), pp. 34–42.

[56] B. M. BROWN, D. K. R. MCCORMACK, AND A. ZETTL, *On the existence of an eigenvalue below the essential spectrum*, Proc. Roy. Soc. London, 455 (1999), pp. 2229–2234.

[57] C. G. BROYDEN, *A new method of solving nonlinear simultaneous equations*, Comput. J., 12 (1969), pp. 94–99.

[58] B. BUCHBERGER, *Ein Algorithmus zum Auffinden der Basiselemente des Restklassenringes nach einem nulldimensionalen Polynomideal*, Ph.D. Thesis, Universität Insbruck, 1965.

[59] ——, *Gröbner bases: An algorithmic method in polynomial ideal theory*, in Recent Trends in Multidimensional System Theory, N.K. Bose, ed., Reidel, Boston, 1985.

[60] J. M. BULL, L. A. SMITH, L. POTTAGE, AND R. FREEMAN, *Benchmarking Java against C and Fortran for scientific applications*, in Proceedings of the 2001 Java Grande/ISCOPE Conference, ACM, New York, 2001, pp. 97–105.

[61] C++ THREADS, *C++ Threads Web site*. http://threads.sourceforge.net.

[62] CALGO, *Collected Algorithms of the ACM*. http://www.acm.org/calgo.

[63] C. CAMACHO AND L. H. DE FIGUEIREDO, *The dynamics of the Jouanolou foliation on the complex projective 2-space*, Ergodic Theory and Dynamical Systems, 21 (2001), pp. 757–766. ftp://ftp.tecgraf.puc-rio.br/pub/lhf/doc/etds.ps.gz.

[64] W. C. CARTER, *Architectural considerations for detecting run-time errors in programs*, in Proc. 13th Int Symp. On Fault-Tolerant Computing (FTCS-13), Milano, Italy, IEEE Computer Society, Los Alamitos, CA, 1983, pp. 249–256.

[65] B. CHABAT, *Introduction à l'Analyse Complexe, Tome 1*, Mir, Moscow, Russia, 1990.

[66] G. J. CHAITIN, *Exploring Randomness*, Springer-Verlag, Singapore, 2001.

[67] F. CHAITIN-CHATELIN, *Is nonnormality a serious computational difficulty in practice?*, in Quality of Numerical Software, R. Boisvert, ed., Chapman and Hall, London, 1997, pp. 300–314.

[68] ——, *About singularities in Inexact Computing*, Technical Report TR/PA/ 02/106, CERFACS, Toulouse, France, 2002.

[69] ——, *The Arnoldi method in the light of Homotopic Deviation theory*, Technical Report TR/PA/03/15, CERFACS, Toulouse, France, 2003.

[70] ——, *Computing beyond Analyticity. Matrix algorithms in Inexact and Uncertain Computing*, Technical Report TR/PA/03/110, CERFACS, Toulouse, France, 2003.

[71] ——, *Elements of Hypercomputations on $\mathbb{R}$ and $\mathbb{Z}_2$ with the Dickson-Albert inductive process*, Technical Report TR/PA/03/34, CERFACS, Toulouse, France, 2003.

[72] ——, *On a recursive hierarchy for Numbers algorithmically emerging from processing binary sequences*, Technical Report TR/PA/03/08, CERFACS, Toulouse, France, 2003.

[73] ——, *The dynamics of matrix coupling with an application to Krylov methods*, Technical Report TR/PA/04/29, CERFACS, Toulouse, France, 2004.

[74] F. CHAITIN-CHATELIN, S. DALLAKYAN, AND V. FRAYSSÉ, *An overview of Carrier Phase Differential GPS*, Contract Report IR/PA/99/50, CERFACS, 1999.

[75] F. CHAITIN-CHATELIN AND V. FRAYSSÉ, *Lectures on Finite Precision Computations*, Software Environ. Tools 1. SIAM, Philadelphia, 1996. http://www.ec-securehost.com/SIAM/SE01.html#SE01.

[76] F. CHAITIN-CHATELIN, V. FRAYSSÉ, AND S. GRATTON, *Fiabilité des calculs en précision finie: Principes et mise en œuvre*, Contract Report FR/PA/97/55, CERFACS, 1997.

[77] F. CHAITIN-CHATELIN AND S. GRATTON, *Convergence of successive iteration methods in finite precision under high nonnormality*, BIT, 36 (1996), pp. 455–469.

[78] ——, *Etude de la non convergence de Gauss-Newton*, Contract Report IR/PA/97/14, CERFACS, 1997.

[79] F. CHAITIN-CHATELIN, A. HARRABI, AND A. ILAHI, *About Hölder condition numbers and the stratification diagram for defective eigenvalues*, in 1999 International Symposium on Computational Science, 54, North–Holland, Amsterdam, 2000, pp. 397–402.

[80] F. CHAITIN-CHATELIN AND T. MEŠKAUSKAS, *Inner-outer iterations for mode solver in structural mechanics application to Code Aster*, Contract Report FR/PA/02/06, CERFACS, Toulouse, France, 2002.

[81] F. CHAITIN-CHATELIN, T. MEŠKAUSKAS, AND A. N. ZAOUI, *Hypercomplex division in the presence of zero divisors on $\mathbb{R}$ and $\mathbb{Z}_2$*, Technical Report TR/PA/02/29, CERFACS, Toulouse, France, 2002.

[82] F. CHAITIN-CHATELIN AND E. TRAVIESAS, *PRECISE, a toolbox for assessing the quality of numerical methods and software*, Tech. Report TR/PA/00/12, CERFACS, Toulouse, France, 2000. Special session on Recommender systems (N. Ramakrishnan organizer), 16th IMACS World Congress, Lausanne, Switzerland, 2000.

[83] F. CHAITIN-CHATELIN AND E. TRAVIESAS, *Homotopic perturbation—unfolding the field of singularities of a matrix by a complex parameter: A global geometric approach*, Technical Report TR/PA/01/84, CERFACS, Toulouse, France, 2001.

[84] F. CHAITIN-CHATELIN AND M. VAN GIJZEN, *Homotopic Deviation theory with an application to Computational Acoustics*, Technical Report TR/PA/04/05, CERFACS, Toulouse, France, 2004.

[85] T. F. CHAN, G. H. GOLUB, AND R. J. LEVEQUE, *Algorithms for computing the sample variance: Analysis and recommendations*, The American Statistician, 37 (1983), pp. 242–247.

[86] C. CHARALAMBOUS AND J. W. BANDLER, *Non-linear Minimax Optimization as a Sequence of Least pth Optimization with Finite Values of p*, J. Comput. System Sci., 7 (1976), pp. 377–391.

[87] F. CHATELIN, *Spectral Approximation of Linear Operators*, Academic Press, New York, 1983.

[88] ———, *Valeurs propres de matrices*, Masson, Paris, 1988.

[89] ———, *Les ordinateurs calculent faux et c'est tant mieux*, Juin 1991. *Journées Observatoire de Paris*.

[90] ———, *Eigenvalues of Matrices*, Wiley, Chichester, U.K., 1993. Enlarged translation of the French publication [88] with Masson.

[91] L. CHEN AND A. AVIZIENIS, *N-version programming: A fault-tolerance approach to reliability of software operation*, in Proc. FTCS 8, Toulouse, France, 1978, pp. 3–9.

[92] D. A. CHRISTENSON, S. T. HUANG, AND A. J. LAMPEREZ, *Statistical quality control applied to code inspections*, IEEE J. on Selected Areas in Communications, 8 (1990), pp. 196–200.

[93] E. M. CLARKE AND J. M. WING, *Formal methods: State of the art and future directions*, ACM Computing Surveys, 28 (1996), pp. 626–643.

[94] D. M. COHEN, S. R. DALAL, M. L. FREDMAN, AND G. C. PATTON, *The AETG system: An approach to testing based on combinatorial design*, IEEE Trans. Soft. Eng., 23 (1997), pp. 437–444.

[95] D. M. COHEN, S. R. DALAL, A. KAJLA, AND G. C. PATTON, *The automatic efficient test generator (AETG) system*, in Proc. IEEE Int. Symp. Software Reliability Engineering, 1994, pp. 303–309.

[96] D. M. COHEN, S. R. DALAL, J. PARELIUS, AND G. C. PATTON, *Combinatorial design approach to test generation*, IEEE Software, (1996), pp. 83–88.

[97] M. COHEN, *Information technology – Programming languages – Fortran – Enhanced data type facilities*, ISO/IEC 15581:2001, 2001.

[98] L. COLLATZ, *Einschließungssatz für die charakteristischen Zahlen von Matrizen*, Math. Z., 48 (1942), pp. 221–226.

[99]   G. E. COLLINS, *Quantifier elimination for real closed fields by cylindrical algebraic decompositon*, in Automata Theory and Formal Languages, B.F. Caviness, ed., Lecture Notes in Comput. Sci. 33, Springer-Verlag, Berlin, 1975, pp. 134–183.

[100] R. COOLS, *Approximating integrals, estimating errors and giving the wrong solution for deceptively easy problems*, 2003. MATLAB program as a zip-file, http://www.cs.kuleuven.be/~ronald/perfprofiles/scripts.zip.

[101] R. P. CORBETT, *Enhanced arithmetic for Fortran*, SIGPLAN Notices, 17 (1982), pp. 41–48.

[102] G. F. CORLISS, *Comparing software packages for interval arithmetic*. Preprint presented at SCAN'93, Vienna, 1993.

[103] D. J. COSTELLO, J. HAGENAUER, H. IMAI, AND S.B. WICKER, *Applications of error-control coding*, IEEE Trans. Inform. Theory, 44 (1998), pp. 2531–2560.

[104] M. G. COX, M. P. DAINTON, AND P. M. HARRIS, *Testing spreadsheets and other packages used in metrology: Testing functions for the calculation of standard deviation*, NPL Report CMSC 07/00, Centre for Mathematics and Scientific Computing, National Physical Laboratory, Teddington, Middlesex, U.K., 2000.

[105] R. CRAMP, M. A. VOUK, AND W. JONES, *On operational availability of a large software-based telecommunications system*, in Proc. Third Intl. Symposium on Software Reliability Engineering, IEEE Computer Society, Los Alamitos, CA, 1992, pp. 358–366.

[106] D. E. CULLER, R. M. KARP, D. A. PATTERSON, A. SAHAY, K. E. SCHAUSER, E. SANTOS, R. SUBRAMONIAN, AND T. VON EICKEN, *LogP: Towards a realistic model of parallel computation*, ACM SIGPLAN Notices, 28 (1993), pp. 1–12.

[107] D. E. CULLER, J. P. SINGH, AND A. GUPTA, *Parallel Computer Architecture: A Hardware/Software Approach*, Morgan Kaufmann, San Francisco, 1999.

[108] G. DAHLQUIST AND Å. BJÖRCK, *Numerical methods*, Prentice–Hall, Englewood Cliffs, NJ, 1980. Second heavily expanded edition *Numerical Mathematics and Scientific Computation* to be published in three volumes by SIAM, Philadelphia. The first edition reprinted by Dover, 2003.

[109] S. R. DALAL AND C. L. MALLOWS, *Factor-covering designs in testing software*, Technometrics, 40 (1998), pp. 234–243.

[110] B. K. DANIELS AND M. HUGHES, *A literature survey of computer software reliability*, Tech. Report NCSR R16, National Centre of Systems Reliability, UKAEA, Wigshaw Lane, Culcheth, Warrington, U.K., 1979.

[111] DARPA, *High Productivity Computer Systems*. http://www.highproductivity.org/.

[112] R. DAVIES, *Newmat C++ matrix library*. http://www.robertnz.net/nm_intro.htm.

[113] A. K. DEB, *Stochastic Modelling for Execution Time and Reliability of Fault-Tolerant Programs Using Recovery Block and N-Version Schemes*, Ph.D. Thesis, Syracuse University, 1988.

[114] A. K. DEB AND A. L. GOEL, *Model for execution time behavior of a recovery block*, in Proc. COMPSAC 86, 1986, pp. 497–502.

[115] B. DEVOLDER, J. GLIMM, J. W. GROVE, Y. KANG, Y. LEE, K. PAO, D. H. SHARP, AND K. YE, *Uncertainty quantification for multiscale simulations*, Journal of Fluids Engineering, 124 (2002), pp. 29–41.

[116] C. F. DIETRICH, *Uncertainty, Calibration and Probability: The Statistics of Scientific and Industrial Measurement*, 2nd ed., Adam Hilger, Bristol, England, 1991.

[117] DIFFPACK SOFTWARE PACKAGE, *Diffpack software package Web site.* http://www.diffpack.com.

[118] D. S. DODSON, *Corrigendum: Remark on "Algorithm 539: Basic Linear Algebra Subroutines for Fortran usage,"* ACM Trans. Math. Software, 9 (1983), p. 140.

[119] D. S. DODSON AND R. G. GRIMES, *Remark on "Algorithm 539: Basic Linear Algebra Subprograms for Fortran usage,"* ACM Trans. Math. Software, 8 (1982), pp. 403–404.

[120] J. J. DONGARRA, J. J. DU CROZ, S. J. HAMMARLING, AND R. J. HANSON, *Algorithm 656. An extended set of Fortran basic linear algebra subprograms: Model implementation and test programs*, ACM Trans. Math. Software, 14 (1988), pp. 18–32.

[121] J. DONGARRA, I. FOSTER, G. FOX, W. GROPP, K. KENNEDY, AND L. TORCZON, eds., *The Sourcebook of Parallel Computing*, Morgan Kaufmann, San Francisco, 2002.

[122] J. J. DONGARRA, J. DU CROZ, I. S. DUFF, AND S. HAMMARLING, *A set of Level 3 Basic Linear Algebra Subprograms*, ACM Trans. Math. Software, 16 (1990), pp. 1–28. (Article on pp. 1–17, Algorithm 679 on pp. 18–28.)

[123] J. J. DONGARRA, J. DU CROZ, S. HAMMARLING, AND R. J. HANSON, *Corrigenda: "An extended set of FORTRAN Basic Linear Algebra Subprograms,"* ACM Trans. Math. Software, 14 (1988), p. 399.

[124] ———, *An extended set of FORTRAN Basic Linear Algebra Subprograms*, ACM Trans. Math. Software, 14 (1988), pp. 1–32, 399. (Algorithm 656. See also [123].)

[125] C. C. DOUGLAS, M. HEROUX, G. SLISHMAN, AND R. M. SMITH, *GEMMW: A portable level 3 BLAS Winograd variant of Strassen's matrix–matrix multiply algorithm*, J. Comput. Phys., 110 (1994), pp. 1–10.

[126] C. C. DOUGLAS, J. HU, W. KARL, M. KOWARSCHIK, U. RUEDE, AND C. WEISS, *Cache optimization for structured and unstructured grid multigrid*, Electron. Trans. Numer. Anal., 10 (2000), pp. 25–40.

[127] C. C. DOUGLAS, J. HU, M. KOWARSCHIK, AND U. RUEDE, *Very high performance cache based techniques for solving iterative methods.* `http://www.mgnet.org/~douglas/ml-dddas.html`.

[128] I. S. DUFF, R. G. GRIMES, AND J. G. LEWIS, *User's guide for Harwell-Boeing sparse matrix test problems collection*, Tech. Report RAL-92-086, Computing and Information Systems Department, Rutherford Appleton Laboratory, Didcot, U.K., 1992.

[129] J. B. DUGAN AND R. VAN BUREN, *Reliability evaluation of fly-by-wire computer systems*, J. Systems and Safety, (1993), pp. 109–124.

[130] P. S. DWYER, *Computation with approximate numbers*, in Linear Computations, P. S. Dwyer, ed., Wiley, New York, 1951, pp. 11–34.

[131] D. E. ECKHARDT, A. K. CAGLAYAN, J. P. J. KELLY, J. C. KNIGHT, L. D. LEE, D. F. MCALLISTER, AND M.A. VOUK, *An experimental evaluation of software redundancy as a strategy for improving reliability*, IEEE Trans. Soft. Eng., 17 (1991), pp. 692–702.

[132] D. E. ECKHARDT AND L. D. LEE, *A theoretical basis for the analysis of multiversion software subject to coincident errors*, IEEE Trans. Soft. Eng., SE-11 (1985), pp. 1511–1517.

[133] J.-P. ECKMANN AND P. WITTWER, *Computer Methods and Borel Summability Applied to Feigenbaum's Equation*, Lecture Notes in Phys. 227. Springer-Verlag, Berlin, Heidelberg, New York, Tokyo, 1985.

[134] W. EHRLICH, B. PRASANNA, J. SAMPFEL, AND J. WU, *Determining the cost of stop-test decisions*, IEEE Software, 10 (1993), pp. 33–42.

[135] M. EMBREE AND N. TREFETHEN, *Pseudospectra gateway.* `http://web.comlab.ox.ac.uk/projects/pseudospectra/`.

[136] D. ENGLER, B. CHELF, A. CHOU, AND S. HALLEM, *Checking system rules using system-specific, programmer-written compiler extensions*, in Proceedings of the Fourth Symposium on Operating Systems Design and Implementation (OSDI 2000), San Diego, Berkeley, 2000. `http://www.usenix.org/publications/library/proceedings/osdi2000/engler.html`.

[137] W. H. ENRIGHT, K. R. JACKSON, S. P. NØRSETT, AND P. G. THOMSEN, *Interpolants for Runge-Kutta formulas*, ACM Trans. Math. Software, 12 (1986), pp. 193–218.

[138] F2PY SOFTWARE PACKAGE, *F2PY – Fortran to Python interface generator.* `http://cens.ioc.ee/projects/f2py2e`.

[139] R. FAIRLEY, *Software Engineering Concepts*, McGraw–Hill, New York, 1985.

[140] W. H. FARR, *Statistical modeling and estimation of reliability functions for software (SMERFS)—library access guide*, Tech. Report TR84-371 (Rev.1), Naval Surface Warfare Center, Dahlgren VA, 1988. Also SMERFS User's Guide, TR84-373 (Rev.1).

[141] FCC, *Notification by common carriers of service disruptions*, Tech. Report 47 CFR Part 63, Federal Register, Vol. 57 (44), March 5, Federal Communications Commission, 1992.

[142] C. A. FLOUDAS, *Handbook of Test Problems for Local and Global Optimization*, Kluwer Academic Publishers, Dordrecht, 1999.

[143] G. E. FORSYTHE, *What is a satisfactory quadratic equation solver*, in Constructive Aspects of the Fundamental Theorem of Algebra. B. Dejon and P. Henrici, eds., Wiley, New York, 1969, pp. 53–61.

[144] ——, *Pitfalls in computation, or why a math book isn't enough*, Amer. Math. Monthly, 9 (1970), pp. 931–995.

[145] L. D. FOSDICK AND L. J. OSTERWEIL, *Data flow analysis in software reliability*, ACM Computing Surveys, 8 (1976), pp. 305–330.

[146] L. V. FOSTER, *Gaussian elimination with partial pivoting can fail in practice*, SIAM J. Matrix Anal. Appl., 15 (1994), pp. 1354–1362.

[147] R. FOWLER, *HPCToolkit*. http://www.hipersoft.rice.edu/hpctoolkit.

[148] L. FOX, *How to get meaningless answers in scientific computation (and what to do about it)*, IMA Bulletin, 7 (1971), pp. 296–302.

[149] E. G. FRANKEL, *Systems Reliability and Risk Analysis*, Kluwer Academic Publishers, Dordrecht, 1988.

[150] V. FRAYSSÉ, L. GIRAUD, AND V. TOUMAZOU, *Parallel computation of spectral portraits on the Meiko CS2*, in High-Performance Computing and Networking, H. Liddell, A. Colbrook, B. Hertzberger, and P. Sloot, eds., Lecture Notes in Comput. Sci. 1067, Springer-Verlag, New York, 1996, pp. 312–318.

[151] V. FRAYSSÉ AND S. GRATTON, *Moindres carrés pour l'orbitographie - Etude de stabilité - Partie II*, Contract Report FR/PA/95/28, CERFACS, 1995.

[152] V. FRAYSSÉ, S. GRATTON, AND V. TOUMAZOU, *Structured backward error and condition number for linear systems of the type $A^*Ax = b$*, BIT, 40 (2000), pp. 74–83.

[153] V. FRAYSSÉ, M. GUEURY, F. NICOUD, AND V. TOUMAZOU, *Spectral portraits for matrix pencils: A physical application*, Tech. Report TR/PA/96/19, CERFACS, 1996.

[154] V. FRAYSSÉ AND G. W. STEWART, *References on the Vancouver Stock Exchange*, 2000. (1) The Wall Street Journal, November 8, 1983, p. 37. (2) The Toronto Star, November 19, 1983. (3) B.D. McCullough and H.D. Vinod, The Numerical Reliability of Econometric Software, Journal of Economic Literature, Vol XXXVII (June 1999), pp. 633–665. http://www.aeaweb.org/journal/contents/june1999.html#AN0494689.

[155] A. FROMMER, *Proving Conjectures by Use of Interval Arithmetic*, in Perspectives on enclosure methods. SCAN 2000, GAMM-IMACS international symposium on scientific computing, computer arithmetic and validated numerics, Univ. Karlsruhe, Germany, 2000. U. Kulisch et al., ed., Springer, Wien, 2001.

[156] W. A. FULLER, *Measurement Error Models*, John Wiley & Sons, New York, 1987.

[157] R. E. GANTENBEIN, S. Y. SHIN, AND J. R. COWLES, *Evaluation of combined approaches to distributed software-based fault tolerance*, in Pacific Rim International Symposium on Fault Tolerant Systems, 1991, pp. 70–75.

[158] GAO, *GAO Report, Patriot Missile Defense—software problem led to system failure at Dhahran, Saudi Arabia*, Tech. Report B-247094, United States General Accounting Office, February 1992. `http://www.fas.org/spp/starwars/gao/im92026.htm`.

[159] I. GARGANTINI AND P. HENRICI, *Circular arithmetic and the determination of polynomial zeros*, Numer. Math., 18 (1972), pp. 305–320.

[160] F. GASPERONI AND G. DISMUKES, *Multilanguage programming on the JVM*, in The Ada 95 Benefits, Proceedings of the Sig'Ada Conference, 2000.

[161] J. GERSTING, R. L. NIST, D. R. ROBERTS, AND R. L. VAN VALKENBURG, *A comparison of voting algorithms for n-version programming*, in Proc. 24th Ann. Hawaii Intl. Conf. on System Sciences, vol. II, 1991, pp. 253–262. Reprinted in *Fault-Tolerant Software Systems: Techniques and Applications*, Hoang Pham, ed., IEEE Computer Society, Los Alamitos, CA, 1992, pp. 62–71.

[162] D. GERT, *Euro page: Conversion arithmetics*. Webpage no longer available but a similar page is `http://ta.twi.tudelft.nl/nw/users/vuik/wi211/disasters.html#euro`. Background information is available in European Central Bank, *Fixed euro conversion rates*. `http://www.ecb.int/bc/intro/html/index.en.html#fix`, 2001.

[163] GGF, *Global Grid Forum*. `http://www.gridforum.org/` and references and links therein. Also available as `http://www.ggf.org/`.

[164] W. GIVENS, *Numerical computation of the characteristic values of a real symmetric matrix*, Technical Report ORNL-1574, Oak Ridge National Laboratory, Oak Ridge, TN, 1954.

[165] GNU, *GNU Compiler Collection*. `http://gcc.gnu.org/`.

[166] S. GODET-THOBIE, *Eigenvalues of large highly nonnormal matrices (Valeurs propres de matrices hautement non normales en grande dimension)*, Ph.D. Dissertation, Université Paris IX Dauphine, 1992.

[167] S. GOEDECKER AND A. HOISIE, *Performance Optimization of Numerically Intensive Codes*, Software Environ. Tools 12, SIAM, Philadelphia, 2001.

[168] A. L. GOEL AND K. OKUMOTO, *Time-dependent error-detection rate model for software reliability and other performance measures*, IEEE Trans. Reliability, R-28 (1979), pp. 206–211.

[169] G. H. GOLUB, *Numerical methods for solving linear least squares problems*, Numer. Math., 7 (1965), pp. 206–216.

[170] G. H. GOLUB AND C. F. VAN LOAN, *Matrix Computations*, 3rd ed. Johns Hopkins Studies in the Mathematical Sciences, The Johns Hopkins University Press, Baltimore, MD, 1996.

[171] R. E. GOMORY, *Outline of an algorithm for integer solution to linear programs.*, Bull. Amer. Math. Soc., 64 (1958), pp. 275–278.

[172] J. GOSLING, B. JOY, G. STEELE, AND G. BRACHA, *The Java Language Specification*, 2nd ed. Addison–Wesley, Reading, MA, 2000.

[173] J. GRABMEIER, E. KALTOFEN, AND V. WEISPFENNIG, *Computer Algebra Handbook*, Springer-Verlag, New York, 2003.

[174] S. GRATTON, *On the condition number of linear least squares problems in a weighted Frobenius norm*, BIT, 36 (1996), pp. 523–530.

[175] ———, *Outils théoriques d'analyse du calcul à précision finie*, Ph.D. Dissertation, Institut National Polytechnique de Toulouse, 1998. TH/PA/98/30, CERFACS.

[176] J. GRAY, *A census of tandem system availability between 1985 and 1990*, IEEE Trans. Reliability, 39 (1990), pp. 409–418.

[177] D. GRIES, *Science of Programming*, Springer-Verlag, Berlin, 1984.

[178] A. GRIEWANK, *Evaluating Derivatives: Principles and Techniques of Algorithmic Differentiation*, Frontiers Appl. Math., 19. SIAM, Philadelphia, 2000.

[179] A. GRIEWANK AND G. F. CORLISS, eds., *Automatic Differentiation of Algorithms: Theory, Implementation, and Application*, SIAM, Philadelphia, 1991.

[180] A. GRNAROV, J. ARLAT, AND A. AVIZIENIS, *On the performance of software fault-tolerance strategies*, in Proc. FTCS 10, 1980, pp. 251–253.

[181] W. GROPP, *Exploiting existing software in libraries: Successes, failures, and reasons why*, in Object Oriented Methods for Interoperable Scientific and Engineering Computing, Michael Henderson, Christopher Anderson, and Stephen L. Lyons, eds., Proc. Appl. Math. 99, SIAM, Philadelphia, 1999, pp. 21–29.

[182] S. J. GROTZINGER, *Supports and Convex Envelopes*, Math. Programming, 31 (1985), pp. 339–347.

[183] MuPAD RESEARCH GROUP, *Interval arithmetic*. http://research.mupad.de/doc30+M554e9f5985d.html, 2003.

[184] J. A. GUNNELS, F. G. GUSTAVSON, G. M. HENRY, AND R. A. VAN DE GEIJN, *FLAME: Formal Linear Algebra Methods Environment*, ACM Trans. Math. Software, 27 (2001), pp. 422–455. http://www.cs.utexas.edu/users/flame/.

[185] E. GÜNTHNER AND M. PHILIPPSEN, *Complex numbers for Java*, Concurrency: Practice and Experience, 23 (2000), pp. 477–491.

[186] E. HAIRER AND G. WANNER, *Solving Ordinary Differential Equations II. Stiff and Differential-Algebraic Problems*, Springer Series in Comput. Mathematics 14, Springer-Verlag, New York, 1996.

[187] J. G. HAJAGOS, *Modeling uncertainty in population biology: How the model is written does matter*. http://www.stat.lanl.gov/SAMO2004/abstracts/pdf_files/Abs_046%20J_Hajagos.pdf, 2003.

[188] T. C. HALES, *Cannonballs and honeycombs*, Notices of the AMS, 47 (2000), pp. 440–449.

[189] R. HAMMER, M. HOCKS, U. KULISCH, AND D. RATZ, *C++ Toolbox for Verified Computing: Basic Numerical Problems*, Springer-Verlag, Berlin, 1995.

[190] J. HANDY, *The Cache Memory Book*, Academic Press, New York, 1998.

[191] E. HANSEN AND G. W. WALSTER, *Global Optimization Using Interval Analysis*, Marcel Dekker, New York, 2003.

[192] E. R. HANSEN, *Global optimization using interval analysis—the one dimensional case*, J. Optim. Theory Appl., 29 (1979), pp. 331–334.

[193] E. R. HANSEN, *Global Optimization Using Interval Analysis*, Marcel Dekker, New York, 1992.

[194] ———, *Publications related to early interval work of R. E. Moore*, 2001. http://interval.louisiana.edu/Moores_early_papers/bibliography.html.

[195] P. B. HANSEN, *An evaluation of the Message-Passing Interface*, ACM SIGPLAN Notices, 33 (1998), pp. 65–72.

[196] G. HARGREAVES, *Interval Analysis in MATLAB*, master's thesis, University of Manchester, 2002.

[197] J. HARRISON, *Formal verification of floating point trigonometric functions*, in Proceedings of the 3rd International Conference on Formal Methods in Computer-Aided Design (FMCAD), Warren A. Hunt and Steven D. Johnson, eds., 1954, Springer-Verlag, New York, 2000, pp. 217–233.

[198] ———, *Formal verification of square root algorithms*, Formal Methods in System Design, 22 (2003), pp. 143–153.

[199] J. HASS, M. HUTCHINGS, AND R. SCHLAfly, *The Double Bubble Conjecture*, Elec. Res. Announcement of the Am. Math. Soc., 1(3) (1995), pp. 98–102.

[200] L. HATTON, *Safer C: Developing Software for High-Integrity and Safety-Critical Systems*, McGraw–Hill, New York, 1995. `http://www.oakcomp.co.uk/TP_Books.html`.

[201] ———, *The T-experiments: Errors in scientific software*, in Quality of Numerical Software: Assessment and Enhancement, Proceedings of the IFIP TC 2/WG 2.5 Working Conference in Oxford, England, 8–12 July 1996, R. F. Boisvert, ed., Chapman & Hall, London, New York, 1997, pp. 12–31.

[202] A. M. HAYASHI, *Rough sailing for smart ships*, Scientific American, 1998.

[203] H. HECHT, *Fault tolerant software*, IEEE Trans. Reliability, R-28 (1979), pp. 227–232.

[204] D. J. HIGHAM AND N. J. HIGHAM, *MATLAB Guide*, 2nd ed., SIAM, Philadelphia, 2005. `http://www.ec-securehost.com/SIAM/ot92.html#OT92`.

[205] N. J. HIGHAM, *Accuracy and Stability of Numerical Algorithms*, 2nd ed., SIAM, Philadelphia, 2002. `http://www.ec-securehost.com/SIAM/ot80.html#ot80`.

[206] N. J. HIGHAM, *Can you "count" on your computer?* Public lecture for Science Week 1998, `http://www.ma.man.ac.uk/~higham/talks/`.

[207] J. M. D. HILL, B. McCOLL, D. C. STEFANESCU, M. W. GOUDREAU, K. LANG, S. B. RAO, T. SUEL, T. TSANTILAS, AND R. H. BISSELING, *BSPlib: The BSP programming library*, Parallel Computing, 24 (1998), pp. 1947–1980.

[208] P. HOFFMAN, *The Man Who Loved Only Numbers*, Hyperion, New York, 1998.

[209] J. J. HU, *Cache Based Multigrid on Unstructured Grids in Two and Three Dimensions*, Ph.D. Thesis, Department of Mathematics, University of Kentucky, Lexington, KY, 2000.

[210] K.-H. HUANG AND J. A. ABRAHAM, *Algorithms-based fault-tolerance for matrix operations*, IEEE Trans. Computers, C-33 (1984), pp. 518–528.

[211] Y. HUANG, C. KINTALA, N. KOLETTIS, AND N. D. FULTON, *Software rejuvenation: Analysis, module and applications*, in Twenty-Fifth International Symposium on Fault-Tolerant Computing, IEEE Computer Society, Los Alamitos, CA, 1995, pp. 381–390.

[212] T. HUCKLE, *Collection of Software Bugs*, 2002. `http://www5.in.tum.de/~huckle/bugse.html`.

[213] J. HUDAK, B. SUH, D. SIEWIOREK, AND Z. SEGALL, *Evaluation and comparison of fault-tolerant software techniques*, IEEE Trans. Reliability, 42 (1993), pp. 190–204.

[214] T. E. HULL, T. F. FAIRGRIEVE, AND P. T. P. TANG, *Implementing complex elementary functions using exception handling*, ACM Trans. Math. Software, 20 (1994).

[215] IEEE, *ANSI/IEEE standard 754-1985*, 1985. Standard for Binary Floating-Point Arithmetic, usually called IEEE 754, officially now IEC 60559.

[216] ——, *IEEE standard 1012-1986*, 1986. Software Verification and Validation Plans.

[217] ——, *ANSI/IEEE standard 854-1987*, 1987. Standard for Radix-Independent Floating-Point Arithmetic, usually called IEEE 854.

[218] IEEE, *IEEE standard 982.1-1988*, 1988. Dictionary of Measures to Produce Reliable Software.

[219] ——, *IEEE standard 982.2-1988*, 1988. IEEE Guide for the Use of IEEE Standard Dictionary of Measures to Produce Reliable Software.

[220] IEEE, *IEEE standard 610.12-1990*, 1990. Glossary of Software Engineering Terminology.

[221] IEEE, *Special issue on fault-tolerance*. IEEE Software Magazine, July/August 2001.

[222] A. ILAHI, *Validation du calcul sur ordinateur: Application de la théorie des singularités algébriques*, Ph.D. Dissertation, Université Toulouse I, June 1998. TH/PA/98/31, CERFACS.

[223] INTERMETRICS, *Ada 95 rationale*, tech. report, Intermetrics, 1995.

[224] E. ISAACSON AND H. B. KELLER, *Analysis of Numerical Methods*, Wiley, New York, 1966. (Reprinted with corrections and new Preface by Dover Publications, New York, 1994.)

[225] D. ISBELL, *Mars polar lander, Mars climate orbiter failure*, Tech. Report 99–134, NASA, 1999. http://mars.jpl.nasa.gov/msp98/news/mco991110.html.

[226] ISO, *Binary floating-point arithmetic for microprocessor systems*, 1989. IEC 559:1989, also known as IEC 60559 and IEEE 754.

[227] ——, *Information technology—programming languages—Ada semantic interface specification (asis)*, 1989. ISO/IEC 15291:1999.

[228] ——, *ISO/IEC 8652:1995 Information technology—Programming languages—Ada*, 1995.

[229] ——, *ISO/IEC 1539-1:1997 Information technology—Programming languages—Fortran—Part 1: Base language*, 1997. see also ISO/IEC 1539-2:2000 (*Part 2: Varying length character*), 1539-3:1999 (*Part 3: Conditional compilation*), TR 15580:2001 (*Floating-point exception handling*), and TR 15581:2001 (*Enhanced data type facilities*).

[230] ——, *Generic packages of real and complex vector and matrix type declarations and basic operations for Ada*, 1998. ISO/IEC 13813:1998, being revised.

[231] ——, *ISO/IEC 9899—Programming Language—C*, ISO, CH-1211 Genève 20, Switzerland, 1999.

[232] ——, *Guide for the use of the Ada programming language in high integrity systems*, 2000. ISO/IEC TR 15942:2000.

[233] ——, *ISO/IEC 14882—Programming Language—C++*, ISO, CH-1211 Genève 20, Switzerland, 2003.

[234] ——, *ISO/IEC 18015—Technical Report on C++ Performance*, ISO, CH-1211 Genève 20, Switzerland, 2003.

[235] J3, *Fortran Standards Technical Committee.* http://www.j3-Fortran.org/.

[236] C. JANSSON, *Zur linearen Optimierung mit unscharfen Daten*, dissertation, Universität Kaiserslautern, 1985.

[237] ——, *Interval linear systems with symmetric matrices, skew-symmetric matrices, and dependencies in the right hand side*, Computing, 46 (1991), pp. 265–274.

[238] ——, *Convex-concave extensions*, BIT, 40 (2000), pp. 291–313. http://www.ti3.tu-harburg.de/paper/jansson/extension.ps.

[239] ——, *Quasiconvex relaxations based on interval arithmetic*, Linear Algebra Appl., 324 (2001), pp. 27–53. http://www.ti3.tu-harburg.de/paper/jansson/quasiconvex.ps.

[240] C. JANSSON AND O. KNÜPPEL, *A Global Minimization Method: The Multidimensional Case*, Tech. Report 92.1, Forschungsschwerpunkt Informations- und Kommunikationstechnik, TU Hamburg-Harburg, 1992.

[241] ——, *A branch-and-bound algorithm for bound constrained optimization problems without derivatives*, J. Glob. Optim., 7(3) (1995), pp. 297–331.

[242] L. JAULIN, M. KEIFFER, O. DIDRIT, AND E. WALTER, *Applied Interval Analysis, with Examples in Parameter and State Estimation, Robust Control and Robotics*, Springer-Verlag, New York, 2001. http://www.springer.de/cgi-bin/search_book.pl?isbn=1-85233-219-0. Book review in SIAM Rev., 44(4):736–739, 2002.

[243] JAVA GRANDE FORUM, *Web site.* http://www.javagrande.org/.

[244] JAVA GRANDE FORUM NUMERICS WORKING GROUP, *Web site.* http://math.nist.gov/javanumerics/.

[245] G. JOHNSON, *At Los Alamos, two visions of supercomputing*, The New York Times, 2002. http://query.nytimes.com/gst/abstract.html?res=F70D16FA3D5A0C768EDDAF0894DA404482.

[246] W. JONES AND M. A. VOUK, *Software reliability field data analysis*, in Handbook of Software Reliability Engineering. M. Lyu, ed., McGraw–Hill, New York, 1996, pp. 439–489.

[247] W. D. JONES AND D. GREGORY, *Infinite failure models for a finite world: A simulation of the fault discovery process*, in Proceedings of the Fourth International Symposium on Software Reliability Engineering, 1993, pp. 284–293.

[248] W. KAHAN, *A survey of error analysis*, in Proc. IFIP Congress, Ljubljana, Information Processing 71, North–Holland, Amsterdam, 1972, pp. 1214–1239.

[249] ———, *The Improbability of PROBALISTIC ERROR ANALYSIS for Numerical Computations*. Talk given at the UCB Statistics Colloquium, 1996.

[250] K. KANOUN, M. KAANICHE, C. BEOUNES, J.-C. LAPRIE, AND J. ARLAT, *Reliability growth of fault-tolerant software*, IEEE Trans. Reliability, 42 (1993), pp. 205–219.

[251] K. KANOUN, M. KAANICHE, AND J.-C. LAPRIE, *Experience in software reliability: From data collection to quantitative evaluation*, in Proc. Fourth Intl. Symposium on Software Reliability Engineering, Denver, Colorado, 1993, pp. 234–245.

[252] K. KANOUN, M. KAANICHE, J.-C. LAPRIE, AND S. METGE, *SoRel: A tool for Software Reliability analysis and evaluation from statistical failure data*, in Proc. 23rd IEEE intl. Symp. on Fault-Tolerant Computing, Toulouse, France, 1993, pp. 654–659.

[253] G. E. KARNIADAKIS AND R. M. KIRBY, *Parallel Scientific Computing in C++ and MPI : A Seamless Approach to Parallel Algorithms*, Cambridge University Press, Cambridge, U.K., 2002.

[254] I. H. KAZI, H. H. CHEN, B. STANLEY, AND D. J. LILJA, *Techniques for obtaining high performance in Java programs*, ACM Computing Surveys (CSUR), 32 (2000), pp. 213–240.

[255] J. KELLY, D. ECKHARDT, A. CAGLAYAN, J. KNIGHT, D. MCALLISTER, AND M. VOUK, *A large scale second generation experiment in multi-version software: Description and early results*, in Proc. 18th Ann. Intl. Symp. on Fault-Tolerant Computing (FTCS-18), Tokyo, Japan, 1988, pp. 9–14.

[256] J. P. J. KELLY, A. AVIZIENIS, B. T. ULERY, B. J. SWAIN, R. T. LYU, A. T. TAI, AND K. S. TSO, *Multiversion software development*, in Proc. IFAC Workshop SAFECOMP'86, Sarlat, France, 1986, pp. 43–49.

[257] B. W. KERNIGHAN AND D. M. RITCHIE, *The C Programming Language*, Prentice–Hall, Englewood Cliffs, NJ, 1978.

[258] T. M. KHOSHGOFTAAR AND J. C. MUNSON, *Predicting software development errors using software complexity metrics*, IEEE J. Selected Areas in Communications, 8 (1990), pp. 253–261.

[259] K. H. KIM AND H. O. WELCH, *Distributed execution of recovery blocks: An approach for uniform treatment of hardware and software faults in real-time applications*, IEEE Trans. Computers, 38 (1989), pp. 626–636.

[260] R. KLATTE, U. KULISCH, CH. LAWO, M. RAUCH, AND A. WIETHOFF, *C-XSC— Language Description with Examples*, Springer-Verlag, New York, 1992.

[261] R. KLATTE, U. KULISCH, M. NEAGA, D. RATZ, AND CH. ULLRICH, *PASCAl-XSC— Language Description with Examples*, Springer-Verlag, New York, 1991.

[262] J. C. KNIGHT AND N. G. LEVESON, *An experimental evaluation of the assumption of independence in multiversion programming*, IEEE Trans. Soft. Eng., SE-12 (1986), pp. 96–109.

[263] O. KNÜPPEL, *BIAS—Basic Interval Arithmetic Subroutines*, Tech. Report 93.3, Forschungsschwerpunkt Informations- und Kommunikationstechnik, Inst. f. Informatik III, TU Hamburg-Harburg, 1993.

[264] ——, *PROFIL—Programmer's Runtime Optimized Fast Interval Library*, Tech. Report 93.4, Forschungsschwerpunkt Informations- und Kommunikationstechnik, TUHH, 1993.

[265] ——, *PROFIL / BIAS—a fast interval library.*, Computing, 53 (1994), pp. 277–287.

[266] L. KNÜSEL, *On the accuracy of statistical distributions in Microsoft Excel 97*, Comput. Statist. Data Anal., 26 (1998), pp. 375–377.

[267] W. KRÄMER, *Inverse Standardfunktionen für reelle und komplexe Intervallargumente mit a priori Fehlerabschätzung für beliebige Datenformate*, dissertation, Universität Karlsruhe, 1987.

[268] R. KRAWCZYK, *Newton-Algorithmen zur Bestimmung von Nullstellen mit Fehlerschranken*, Computing, 4 (1969), pp. 187–201.

[269] R. KRAWCZYK AND A. NEUMAIER, *Interval slopes for rational functions and associated centered forms*, SIAM J. Numer. Anal., 22 (1985), pp. 604–616.

[270] V. KREINOVICH, D. J. BERLEANT, AND M. KOSHELEV, *Applications of interval computations.* http://www.cs.utep.edu/interval-comp/appl.html.

[271] ——, *Bibliographies on interval and related methods.* http://www.cs.utep.edu/interval-comp/bibl.html.

[272] U. KULISCH, *A New Vector Arithmetic Coprocessor Chip for the PC*, October 1995. Presented at the IFIP WG 2.5 workshop in Kyoto, Japan. http://www.nsc.liu.se/~boein/ifip/kyoto/workshop-info/proceedings/kulisch/kulisch1.html (navigate with the next/up at the far bottom).

[273] ——, *Advanced arithmetic for the digital computer—interval arithmetic revisited*, in Perspectives on Enclosure Methods, U. Kulisch, R. Lohner, and A. Facius, eds., Springer-Verlag, Vienna, 2001, Also available as http://webserver.iam.uni-karlsruhe.de/documents/kulisch/advarith.ps.gz.

[274] U. KULISCH, *Advanced Arithmetic for the Digital Computer—Design of Arithmetic Units*, Springer-Verlag, New York, 2002.

[275] U. KULISCH AND W. L. MIRANKER, *Arithmetic operations in interval spaces*, Computing, Suppl., 2 (1980), pp. 51–67.

[276] U. KULISCH AND W. L. MIRANKER, *Computer Arithmetic in Theory and Practice*, Academic Press, New York, 1981 (and references therein).

[277] U. KULISCH AND L. B. RALL, *Numerics with Automatic Result Verification*. Preprint, 1993.

[278] J. LAHMANN AND M. PLUM, *A computer-assisted instability proof for the Orr-Sommerfeld equation with Blasius profile*, ZAMM Z. Angew Math. Mech., 84 (2004), pp. 188–204.

[279] L. LAMPORT, *How to make a multiprocessor computer that correctly executes multiprocess programs*, IEEE Trans. Computers, C-28 (1979), pp. 690–691.

[280] J. C. LAPRIE, J. ARLAT, AND K. KANOUN C. BÉOUNES, *Definition and analysis of hardware- and software-fault-tolerant architectures*, IEEE Computer, 23 (1990), pp. 39–51. Reprinted in Fault-Tolerant Software Systems: Techniques and Applications, Hoang Pham, editor, IEEE Computer Society, Los Alamitos, CA, 1992, pp. 5–17.

[281] J. C. LAPRIE, K. KANOUN, C. BEOUNES, AND M. KAANICHE, *The KAT (Knowledge-Action-Transformation) approach to the modeling and evaluation of reliability and availability growth*, IEEE Trans. Software Engineering, 18 (1991), pp. 701–714.

[282] C. L. LAWSON, R. J. HANSON, D. KINCAID, AND F. T. KROGH, *Basic linear algebra subprograms for FORTRAN usage*, ACM Trans. Math. Soft., 5 (1979), pp. 308–323.

[283] C. L. LAWSON AND R. J. HANSON, *Solving Least Squares Problems*, Prentice–Hall, Englewood Cliffs, NJ, 1974. (Republished as [284].)

[284] ——, *Solving Least Squares Problems*, Classics Appl. Math., 15, SIAM, Philadelphia, 1995. (Revised version of [283].)

[285] C. L. LAWSON, R. J. HANSON, D. KINCAID, AND F. T. KROGH, *Basic linear algebra subprograms for FORTRAN usage*, ACM Trans. Math. Software, 5 (1979), pp. 308–323. (Algorithm 539. See also [119] and [118].)

[286] Y. LEI AND K. C. TAI, *In-parameter-order: A test generation strategy for pairwise testing*, in Proc. 3rd IEEE High-Assurance Systems Engineering Symposium, 1998, pp. 254–261.

[287] N. LEVENSON, *Software System Safety and Computers*, Addison–Wesley, Reading, MA, 1995.

[288] P. LÉVY, *L'addition des variables aléatoires définies sur une circonférence*, Bull. Soc. Math. France, 67 (1939), pp. 1–41.

[289] X. LI, J. DEMMEL, D. BAILEY, G. HENRY, Y. HIDA, J. ISKANDAR, W. KAHAN, S. KANG, A. KAPUR, M. MARTIN, B. THOMPSON, T. TUNG, AND D. YOO, *Design, implementation and testing of extended and mixed precision BLAS*, ACM Trans. Math. Software, 28 (2002), pp. 152–205. http://crd.lbl.gov/~xiaoye/XBLAS/.

[290] S. LIN AND D. J. COSTELLO, *Error Control Coding—Fundamentals and Applications*, Prentice–Hall, Englewood Cliffs, NJ, 1983.

[291] T. LINDHOLM AND F. YELLIN, *The Java Virtual Machine Specification*, 2nd edition. Addison–Wesley, Reading, MA, 1999.

[292] J. L. LIONS, *Ariane 501—presentation of inquiry board report*, tech. report, ESA, Paris, 1996. http://www.esa.int/export/esaCP/Pr_33_1996_p_EN.html.

[293] B. LITTLEWOOD AND D. R. MILLER, *Conceptual modeling of coincident failures in multiversion software*, IEEE Trans. Soft. Eng., 15 (1989), pp. 1596–1614.

[294] R. LOHNER, *Einschließung der Lösung gewöhnlicher Anfangs- und Randwertaufgaben und Anordnungen*, Ph.D. Thesis, University of Karlsruhe, 1988.

[295] P. R. LORCZAK, A. K. CAGLAYAN, AND D. E. ECKHARDT, *A theoretical investigation of generalized voters for redundant systems*, in Proc. 19th Ann. Intl. Symp. on Fault-Tolerant Computing (FTCS-19), Chicago, IL, 1989, pp. 444–451.

[296] J. N. LYNESS, *When not to use an automatic quadrature routine*, SIAM Rev., 25 (1983), pp. 63–87.

[297] M. R. LYU, *Software Fault Tolerance*. Trends-in-Software Book Series, Wiley, Chichester, U.K., 1995.

[298] ——, *Handbook of Software Reliability Engineering*, McGraw–Hill, New York, 1996.

[299] M. R. LYU AND Y. HE, *Improving the N-version programming process through the evolution of design paradigm*, IEEE Trans. Reliability, 42 (1993), pp. 179–189.

[300] M. R. LYU AND A. NIKORA, *Applying reliability models more effectively*, IEEE Software, (1992), pp. 43–45.

[301] Y. K. MALAIYA, *Software Reliability Models: Theoretical Developments, Evaluation and Application*, IEEE Computer Society, Los Alamitos, CA, 1991.

[302] T. A. MANTEUFFEL, *An interval analysis approach to rank determination in linear least squares problems*, SIAM J. Sci. Statist. Comput., 2 (1981), pp. 335–348.

[303] MAPLESOFT, *Interval arithmetic*. http://www.mapleapps.com/powertools/interval/Interval.shtml, 2004.

[304] R. S. MARTIN AND J. H. WILKINSON, *Similarity reduction of a general matrix to Hessenberg form*, Numer. Math., 12 (1968), pp. 349–368. (See also [490, pp. 339–358].)

[305] THE MATHWORKS, *MATLAB 6.0*, The MathWorks, Inc., Natick, MA, 2000.
      http://www.mathworks.com/.

[306] D. F. MCALLISTER, C. E. SUN, AND M. A. VOUK, *Reliability of voting in fault-tolerant
      software systems for small output spaces*, IEEE Trans. Reliability, 39 (1990), pp. 524–
      534.

[307] D. F. MCALLISTER AND M. A. VOUK, *Software fault-tolerance engineering*. In M. Lyu,
      editor, Handbook of Software Reliability Engineering, McGraw–Hill, New York,
      1996, pp. 567–614.

[308] W. F. MCCOLL, *BSP programming*, in Proc. DIMACS Workshop on Specification
      of Parallel Algorithms, G. Blelloch, M. Chandy, and S. Jagannathan, eds., Prince-
      ton, 1994. AMS, Providence, RI, 1994. http://www.comlab.ox.ac.uk/
      oucl/users/bill.mccoll/p6.ps.Z.

[309] R. A. MCCOY AND V. TOUMAZOU, *PRECISE User's Guide—Version 1.0*, Tech. Rep.
      TR/PA/97/38, CERFACS, 1997.

[310] B. D. MCCULLOUGH AND B. WILSON, *On the accuracy of statistical procedures in
      Microsoft Excel 97*, Comput. Statist. Data Anal., 31 (1999), pp. 27–37.

[311] ——, *On the accuracy of statistical procedures in Microsoft Excel 2000 and Ex-
      cel XP*, Comput. Statist. Data Anal., 40 (2002), pp. 713–721.

[312] MERSENNE. http://primes.utm.edu/top20/page.php?id=4.

[313] MESSAGE PASSING INTERFACE FORUM, *MPI: A message passing interface standard*,
      International Journal of Supercomputer Applications, 8 (1994), pp. 159–416.

[314] ——, *MPI2: A message passing interface standard*, High Performance Computing
      Applications, 12 (1998), pp. 1–299.

[315] M. METCALF AND J. K. REID, *Fortran 90/95 Explained*, 2nd ed. Oxford University
      Press, Oxford, U.K., 1999. New version *Fortran 95/2003 Explained* published June
      2004.

[316] A. MILI, *An Introduction to Program Fault-Tolerance—A Structured Programming
      Approach*, Prentice–Hall, London, 1990.

[317] D. MONTGOMERY, *Design and Analysis of Experiments*, Wiley, New York, 2001.

[318] R. E. MOORE, *Interval Analysis*, Prentice–Hall, Englewood Cliffs, NJ, 1966.

[319] ——, *Methods and Applications of Interval Analysis*, SIAM Stud. Appl. Math. 2.
      SIAM, Philadelphia, 1979.

[320] R. E. MOORE, E. HANSEN, AND A. LECLERC, *Rigorous methods for global opti-
      mization*, in Recent Advances in Global Optimization, Princeton Series in Computer
      Science, Princeton University Press, Princeton, NJ, 1992, pp. 321–342.

[321] R. E. MOORE, *The dawning*, Reliable Computing, 5 (1999), pp. 423–424.

[322] J. E. MOREIRA, S. P. MIDKIFF, AND M. GUPTA, *From flop to megaflops: Java for technical computing*, ACM Transactions on Programming Languages and Systems (TOPLAS), 22 (2000), pp. 265–295.

[323] ——, *A comparison of three approaches to language, compiler, and library support for multidimensional arrays in Java*, in Proceedings of the 2001 Java Grande/ISCOPE Conference, ACM, New York, 2001, pp. 116–125.

[324] J. MORO, J. V. BURKE, AND M. L. OVERTON, *On the Lidskii–Vishik–Lyusternik perturbation theory for eigenvalues of matrices with arbitrary Jordan structure*, SIAM J. Matrix Anal. Appl., 18 (1997), pp. 793–817. http://epubs.siam.org/sam-bin/dbq/article/29466.

[325] P. J. MUCCI, *PAPI, Performance Application Programming Interface*. http://icl.cs.utk.edu/papi/.

[326] J. C. MUNSON AND T. M. KHOSHGOFTAAR, *The detection of fault-prone programs*, IEEE Trans. Software Engineering, 18 (1992), pp. 423–433.

[327] J. D. MUSA, *Software Reliability Engineering Web site*. http://members.aol.com/JohnDMusa/index.htm. http://members.aol.com/JohnDMusa/ARTweb.htm.

[328] ——, *Operational profiles in software-reliability engineering*, IEEE Software, 10 (1993), pp. 14–32.

[329] ——, *Software Reliability Engineering*, McGraw–Hill, New York, 1998.

[330] J. D. MUSA AND W. W. EVERETT, *Software-Reliability Engineering: Technology for the 1990s*, IEEE Software, 7 (1990), pp. 36–43.

[331] J. D. MUSA, A. IANNINO, AND K. OKUMOTO, *Software Reliability: Measurement, Prediction, Application*, McGraw–Hill, New York, 1987.

[332] NAG, *The NAG Library*. NAG Ltd. http://www.nag.com/numeric/numerical_libraries.asp http://www.nag.co.uk/numeric/numerical_libraries.asp.

[333] ——, *The NAG Fortran Library Manual, Mark 21*, The Numerical Algorithms Group Ltd., Oxford, U.K., 2004. http://www.nag.com/numeric/fl/manual/html/FLlibrarymanual.asp http://www.nag.co.uk/numeric/fl/manual/html/FLlibrarymanual.asp.

[334] M. R. NAKAO, *A numerical approach to the proof of existence of solutions for elliptic problems*, Japan J. Appl. Math., 5 (1988), pp. 313–332.

[335] M. T. NAKAO, Y. WATANABE, N. YAMAMOTO, AND T. NISHIDA, *Some computer assisted proofs for solutions of the heat convection problems*, Reliable Computing, 9 (2003), pp. 359–372.

[336] R. E. NANCE AND J. D. ARTHUR, *Managing Software Quality, A Measurement Framework for Assessment and Prediction*, Springer-Verlag, Heidelberg, 2002.

[337] N. S. NEDIALKOV AND K. R. JACKSON, *ODE software that computes guaranteed bounds on the solution*, in Advances in Software Tools for Scientic Computing, H.P. Langtangen, A.M. Bruaset, and E. Quak, eds., Springer-Verlag, New York, 2000, pp. 197–224.

[338] V. P. NELSON AND B. D. CARROLL, *Tutorial: Fault-Tolerant Computing*, 1987.

[339] A. NEUMAIER, *Rigorous sensitivity analysis for parameter-dependent systems of equations*, J. Math. Anal. Appl. 144, 1989, pp. 16–25.

[340] ——, *Interval Methods for Systems of Equations*, Encyclopedia of Mathematics and its Applications 37, Cambridge University Press, Cambridge, U.K., 1990.

[341] ——, *NOP—a compact input format for nonlinear optimization problems*, in Developments in Global Optimization. I. M. Bomze et al., eds., Proceedings of the 3rd Workshop, Szeged, Hungary, 1995. Kluwer Academic Publishers, Dordrecht, The Netherlands, 1997, pp. 1–18.

[342] ——, *Grand challenges and scientific standards in interval analysis*, Reliable Computing, 8 (2002), pp. 313–320.

[343] A. NEUMAIER AND T. RAGE, *Rigorous chaos verification in discrete dynamical systems*, Phys. D, 67 (1993), pp. 327–346.

[344] J. VON NEUMANN AND H. H. GOLDSTINE, *Numerical inverting of matrices of high order*, Bull. Amer. Math. Soc., 53 (1947), pp. 1021–1099.

[345] NEW SCIENTIST, *Bad vibrations, how could the designers of a revolutionary bridge miss something so obvious?* New Scientist Magazine, 2000.

[346] NIST, *NIST Physics Laboratory, The NIST Reference on Constants, Units, and Uncertainty.* http://physics.nist.gov/cuu/index.html.

[347] NUMERICAL COMPUTING RESOURCES, *Web site.* http://www.indiana.edu/~rac/hpc/numerics.html.

[348] NUMERICAL PYTHON SOFTWARE PACKAGE, *Web site.* http://sourceforge.net/projects/numpy.

[349] W. L. OBERKAMPF AND T. G. TRUCANO, *Validation methodology in computational fluid dynamics*, in Fluids 2000, Reston, VA, 2000, pp. 1–34. American Institute of Aeronautics and Astronautics, AIAA 2000-2549, invited paper.

[350] OBJECT-ORIENTED NUMERICS, *Scientific Computing in Object-Oriented Languages.* http://www.oonumerics.org/.

[351] T. OGITA, S. M. RUMP, AND S. OISHI, *Accurate sum and dot product*, SIAM J. Sci. Comput., 26 (2005), pp. 1955–1988.

[352] M. OHBA, *Software reliability analysis models*, IBM J. of Res. and Development, 28 (1984), pp. 428–443.

[353] S. OISHI AND S. M. RUMP, *Fast verification of solutions of matrix equations*, Numer. Math., 90 (2002), pp. 755–773.

[354] OPENMP, *OpenMP Fortran Application Program Interface, Version 2.0.* http://www.openmp.org/drupal/mp-documents/fspec20.pdf, November 2000.

[355] M. L. OVERTON, *Numerical Computing with IEEE Floating Point Arithmetic*, SIAM, Philadelphia, 2001.

[356] D. A. PATTERSON AND J. L. HENNESSY, *Computer Architecture: A Quantative Approach*, Morgan–Kaufmann, San Mateo, CA, 1996.

[357] M. C. PAULK, B. CURTIS, M. B. CHRISSIS, AND C. V. WEBER, *Capability maturity model, version* 1.1, IEEE Software, (1993), pp. 18–27.

[358] M. PAYNE AND R. HANEK, *Radian reduction for trigonometric functions*, SIGNUM Newsletter, 18 (1983), pp. 19–24.

[359] H. PHAM (Editor). *Fault-tolerant software systems: Techniques and applications*, IEEE Computer Society, Los Alamitos, CA, 1992.

[360] G. PHIPPS, *Comparing observed bug and productivity rates for Java and C++*, Software—Practice and Experience, 29 (1999), pp. 345–358.

[361] R. PIESSENS, E. DE DONCKER-KAPENGA, C. W. ÜBERHUBER, AND D. K. KAHANER, *QUADPACK—A Subroutine Package for Automatic Integration*, Springer-Verlag, Berlin, 1983.

[362] M. PLUM, *Computer assisted existence proofs for two point boundary value problems*, Computing, 46 (1991), pp. 19–34.

[363] ———, *Computer-assisted enclosure methods for elliptic differential equations*, Linear Algebra Appl., 324 (2001), pp. 147–187.

[364] M. PLUM AND C. WIENERS, *New solutions of the Gelfand problem*, J. Math. Anal. Appl., 269 (2002), pp. 588–606.

[365] S. POLJAK AND J. ROHN, *Radius of Nonsingularity*, no. 88-117, Universitas Carolina Pragensis, 1988.

[366] T. POTOK AND M. VOUK, *The effects of the business model on the object-oriented software development productivity*, IBM Systems Journal, 36 (1997), pp. 140–161.

[367] W. H. PRESS, S. A. TEUKOLSKY, W. T. VERTTERLING, AND B. P. FLANNERY, *Numerical Recipes in C*, 2nd ed. Cambridge University Press, Cambridge, U.K., 1992. Also available on the web from http://www.numerical-recipes.com/nronline_switcher.html.

[368] R. S. PRESSMAN, *Software Engineering: A Practitioner's Approach*, 5th ed. McGraw–Hill, New York, 2000.

[369] PYTHON PROGRAMMING LANGUAGE, *Python programming language Web site*. `http://www.python.org`.

[370] L. B. RALL, *Automatic Differentiation: Techniques and Applications*, Lecture Notes in Computer Science, 120, Springer-Verlag, Berlin, 1981.

[371] N. RAMAKRISHNAN AND C. J. RIBBENS, *Mining and visualizing recommendation spaces for PDE solvers: The continuous attributes case,* in Computational Science, Mathematics and Software, R. Boisvert and E. Houstis (eds.), Purdue University Press, West Lafayette, IN, 2002, pp. 171–196.

[372] N. RAMAKRISHNAN, J. R. RICE, AND E. N. HOUSTIS, *GAUSS: An online algorithm recommender system for one-dimensional numerical quadrature*, Adv. Engr. Software, 23 (2002), pp. 27–36.

[373] B. RANDELL, *System structure for software fault-tolerance*, IEEE Trans. Software Eng., SE-1 (1975), pp. 220–232.

[374] H. RATSCHEK AND J. ROKNE, *Computer Methods for the Range of Functions*, Halsted Press, New York, 1984.

[375] ——, *New Computer Methods for Global Optimization*, John Wiley & Sons, New York, 1988.

[376] J. REID, *Information technology—programming languages—Fortran—Floating-point exception handling*, ISO/IEC 15580:2001, 2001.

[377] J. R. RICE AND R. F. BOISVERT, *Solving Elliptic Equations Using ELLPACK*, Springer-Verlag, New York, 1985.

[378] C. RILEY, S. CHATTERJEE, AND R. BISWAS, *High-performance Java codes for computational fluid dynamics*, in Proceedings of the 2001 Java Grande/ISCOPE Conference, ACM, New York, 2001, pp. 143–152.

[379] R. H. RISCH, *The problem of integration in finite terms*, Trans. Amer. Math. Soc., 139 (1969), pp. 167–189.

[380] D. M. RITCHIE, *The development of the C language*, in History of Programming Languages-II, ACM, New York, 1993, pp. 201–208. Also available on line from `http://cm.bell-labs.com/cm/cs/who/dmr/chist.html`.

[381] A. RIVERS, *Software Reliability Modeling During Non-Operational Testing*, Ph.D. Thesis, North Carolina State University, 1998.

[382] A. T. RIVERS AND M. A. VOUK, *Resource-constrained non-operational testing of software*, in Proceedings ISSRE 98, 9th International Symposium on Software Reliability Engineering, Paderborn, Germany, IEEE Computer Society, Los Alamitos, CA, 1998, pp. 154–163.

[383] P. J. ROACHE, *Verification and Validation in Computational Science and Engineering*, Hermosa Publishers, Albuquerque, NM, 1998. http://kumo.swcp.com/hermosa/html/books.html#VVCSE.

[384] N. ROBERTSON, D. P. SANDERS, P. D. SEYMOUR, AND R. THOMAS, *A new proof of the four colour theorem*, Electron. Res. Announc. Amer. Math. Soc., 2 (1996), pp. 17–25.

[385] RTI, *The Economic Impacts of Inadequate Infrastructure for Software Testing*, Tech. Report RTI Project Number 7007.011, RTI; Health, Social and Economics Research, Research Triangle Park, NC, 2002. http://www.nist.gov/director/prog-ofc/report02-3.pdf.

[386] S. M. RUMP, *Solving algebraic problems with high accuracy. Habilitationsschrift*, in A New Approach to Scientific Computation, U.W. Kulisch and W.L. Miranker, eds., Academic Press, New York, 1983, pp. 51–120.

[387] ——, *Verification methods for dense and sparse systems of equations*, in Topics in Validated Computations—Studies in Computational Mathematics, J. Herzberger, ed., Elsevier, Amsterdam, 1994, pp. 63–136.

[388] ——, *Expansion and estimation of the range of nonlinear functions*, Math. Comp., 65 (1996), pp. 1503–1512.

[389] ——, *INTLAB—INTerval LABoratory*, in Developments in Reliable Computing, Tibor Csendes, ed., Kluwer Academic Publishers, Dordrecht, The Netherlands, 1999, pp. 77–104. http://www.ti3.tu-harburg.de/~rump/intlab/.

[390] ——, *Computational error bounds for multiple or nearly multiple eigenvalues*, Linear Algebra Appl., 324 (2001), pp. 209–226.

[391] ——, *Rigorous and portable standard functions*, BIT, 41 (2001), pp. 540–562.

[392] ——, *Self-validating methods*, Linear Algebra Appl., 324 (2001), pp. 3–13.

[393] ——, *Ten methods to bound multiple roots of polynomials*, J. Comput. Appl. Math., 156 (2003), pp. 403–432.

[394] G. H. SANDLER, *Systems Reliability Engineering*, Prentice–Hall, Englewood Cliffs, NJ, 1963.

[395] A. SARD, *The measure of the critical values of differentiable maps*, Bull. AMS, 48 (1942), pp. 883–896.

[396] C. A. SCHNEPPER AND M. A. STADTHERR, *Application of a parallel interval Newton/generalized bisection algorithm to equation-based chemical process flowsheeting*, Interval Computations, 4 (1993), pp. 40–64.

[397] M. SCHULTE, V. ZELOV, G. W. WALSTER, AND D. CHIRIAEV, *Single-number interval I/O*, in Developments in Reliable Computing, T. Csendes, ed., Kluwer Academic Publishers, Dordrecht, The Netherlands, 1999, pp. 141–148.

[398] SCIENTIfiCPYTHON SOFTWARE PACKAGE, *ScientificPython software package Web site.*
`http://starship.python.net/crew/hinsen.`

[399] SCIMARK, *The Scimark benchmark for scientific and numerical computing.*
`http://math.nist.gov/scimark/.`

[400] SCIPY SOFTWARE PACKAGE, *SciPy—Scientific tools for Python.* `http://www.`
`scipy.org.`

[401] R. K. SCOTT, J. W. GAULT, AND D. F. MCALLISTER, *The consensus recovery block*,
in Proc. The Total Systems Reliability Symposium, IEEE, Gaithersburg, MD, 1983,
pp. 74–85.

[402] ——, *Fault-tolerant reliability modeling*, IEEE Trans. Soft. Eng., SE-13 (1987),
pp. 582–592.

[403] R. K. SCOTT, J. W. GAULT, D. F. MCALLISTER, AND J. WIGGS, *Experimental validation
of six fault-tolerant software reliability models*, in IEEE FTCS 14, 1984.

[404] ——, *Investigating version dependence in fault-tolerant software*, 1984. AGARD
361, pp. 21.1–21.10.

[405] J. SEWARD, *Valgrind, a system for debugging and profiling x86-Linux programs.*
`http://valgrind.kde.org/.`

[406] L. F. SHAMPINE AND I. GLADWELL, *The next generation of Runge-Kutta codes*, in
Computational Ordinary Differential Equations, Cash J. R. and I. Gladwell, eds.,
Inst. Math. Appl. Conf. Ser. New Ser. 39, Oxford University Press, New York, 1992,
pp. 145–164.

[407] L. F. SHAMPINE, I. GLADWELL, AND S. THOMPSON, *Solving ODEs with MATLAB*,
Cambridge University Press, Cambridge, U.K., 2003.

[408] L. F. SHAMPINE AND M. W. REICHELT, *The MATLAB ODE suite*, SIAM J. Sci. Comput., 18 (1997), pp. 1–22.

[409] F. T. SHELDON, *Software reliability engineering case studies*, in 8th Intl. Symposium
on Software Reliability Engineering, IEEE Computer Society, Los Alamitos, CA,
1997.

[410] T. SHEPARD, M. LAMB, AND D. KELLEY, *More testing should be taught*, Communications of the ACM, 44 (2001), pp. 103–108. `http://portal.acm.org/`
`citation.cfm?id=376180` (requires a subscription).

[411] T. J. SHIMEALL AND N. G. LEVESON, *An empirical comparison of software fault-tolerance and fault elimination*, in 2nd Workshop on Software Testing, Verification and Analysis, Banff, 1988, IEEE Computer Society, Los Alamitos, CA, 1988,
pp. 180–187.

[412] M. L. SHOOMAN, *Software Engineering*, McGraw–Hill, New York, 1983.

[413] SIAM, *Inquiry board traces Ariane 5 failure to overflow error*, SIAM News, 29 (1996), pp. 1, 12, 13. `http://www.siam.org/siamnews/general/ariane.htm`.

[414] J. SIEK AND A. LUMSDAINE, *A modern framework for portable high-performance numerical linear algebra*, in Advances in Software Tools for Scientific Computing, E. Arge, A. M. Bruaset, and H. P. Langtangen, eds., Springer-Verlag, New York, 1999.

[415] D. P. SIEWIOREK AND R. S. SWARZ, *Reliable Computer Systems—Design and Evaluation*, Digital Press, Bedford, MA, 1992.

[416] N. D. SINGPURWALLA AND R. SOYER, *Nonhomogenous auto-regressive process for tracking (software) reliability growth, and their Bayesian analysis*, J. of the Royal Statistical Society, B 54 (1992), pp. 145–156.

[417] SINTEF, *SLEIPNER A GBS Loss, Reports 1–17*, tech. report, SINTEF, 1998. Available from SINTEF, Biblioteket, PB 124, Blindern, NO-0314 Oslo, Norway. A popular summary is available at `http://www.ima.umn.edu/~arnold/disasters/sleipner.html`.

[418] R. SKEEL, *Iterative refinement implies numerical stability for Gaussian elimination*, Math. Comp., 35 (1980), pp. 817–832.

[419] R. SKEEL, *Roundoff error cripples Patriot missile*, SIAM News, 25 (1992), p. 11. `http://www.siam.org/siamnews/general/patriot.htm`.

[420] G. SLABODKIN, *Software glitches leave navy smart ship dead in the water*, Government Computer News, (1998). `http://www.gcn.com/archives/gcn/1998/july13/cov2.htm`.

[421] R. L. SMITH, *Algorithm 116: Complex division*, Communications of the ACM, 5 (1962), p. 435.

[422] D. SPINELLIS, *The decay and failures of Web references*, Communications of the ACM, 46 (2003), pp. 71–77. `http://portal.acm.org/citation.cfm?id=602422` (requires a subscription).

[423] M. A. STADTHERR, *Computing in Chemical Engineering Award for Work Using Intervals*. `http://www.cs.utep.edu/interval-comp/chem98.html`.

[424] D. E. STEVENSON, *A critical look at quality in large-scale simulations*, IEEE Computing in Science & Engineering, 1 (1999), pp. 53–63. `http://csdl.computer.org/comp/mags/cs/1999/03/c3toc.htm` (full text requires a subscription).

[425] G. W. STEWART, *A note on complex division*, ACM Trans. Math. Software, 11 (1985), pp. 238–241.

[426] ——, *Matrix Algorithms: Basic Decompositions*, SIAM, Philadelphia, 1998.

[427] G. W. STEWART AND J. SUN, *Matrix Perturbation Theory*, Academic Press, London, 1990.

[428] L. STRIGINI AND A. AVIZIENIS, *Software fault-tolerance and design diversity: Past experience and future evolution*, in Proc. IFAC SAFECOMP '85, Como, Italy, 1985, pp. 167–172.

[429] B. STROUSTRUP, *The C++ Programming Language*, 3rd ed., Addison–Wesley, Reading, MA, 1997.

[430] K. STRUBECKER, *Einführung in die höhere Mathematik, Band IV: Grundzüge der linearen Algebra*, Oldenbourg Verlag, München, 1984.

[431] SUN, *Forte™ Developer 7: Fortran and C++ Interval Arithmetic Programming Reference*. http://docs.sun.com/db/doc/816-2462, http://docs.sun.com/db/doc/816-2465 *Sun C++ Interval Arithmetic Programming Reference*. http://docs.sun.com/db/doc/806-7998 *Sun Fortran 95 Interval Arithmetic Programming Reference*. http://docs.sun.com/db/doc/806-7994.

[432] T. SUNAGA, *Theory of an interval algebra and its application to numerical analysis*, RAAG Memoirs, 2 (1958), pp. 29–46.

[433] SWIG SOFTWARE PACKAGE, http://www.swig.org. (*SWIG is a software development tool that connects programs written in C and C++*.)

[434] A. T. TAI, L. ALKALAI, AND S. N. CHAU, *On-board preventive maintenance: A design-oriented analytic study for long-life applications*, Performance Evaluation, 35 (1999), pp. 215–232.

[435] A. T. TAI, J. F. MEYER, AND A. AVIZIENIS, *Performability enhancement of fault-tolerant software*, IEEE Trans. Reliability, 42 (1993), pp. 227–237.

[436] K. C. TAI AND Y. LIE, *A test generation strategy for pairwise testing*, IEEE Trans. Software Eng., 28(1) (2002), pp. 109–111.

[437] A. TARSKI, *A Decision Method for Elementary Algebra and Geometry*, RAND Corp., Santa Monica, CA, 1948.

[438] A. TARSKI, *La complétude de l'algèbre et la géométrie élémentaires*, In *Logique, sémantique, métamathématique*, Mémoires écrits entre 1923 et 1944, Armand Colin, Paris, 2 (1974), pp. 203–242.

[439] D. J. TAYLOR, D. E. MORGAN, AND J. P. BLACK, *Redundancy in data structures: Improving software fault-tolerance*, IEEE Trans. Software Eng., SE-6 (1980), pp. 585–594.

[440] M. TELLES AND Y. HSIEH, *The Science of Debugging*, Coriolis, Scottsdale, AZ, 2001.

[441] T. TEUFEL, *Genauer und trotzdem schneller - Ein neuer Coprozessor für hochgenaue Matrix- und Vektoroperationen*, Elektronik, Heft 26 (1994).

[442] ——, *A novel VLSI vector arithmetic coprocessor for advanced DSP applications*, in Proceedings of ICSPAT '96, volume 2, Boston, MA, 1996, pp. 1894–1898.

[443] D. T. THORNE, *Multigrid with Cache Optimizations on Adaptive Mesh Refinement Hierarchies*, Ph.D. Thesis, Department of Computer Science, University of Kentucky, Lexington, KY, 2003.

[444] TNT SOFTWARE PACKAGE, *Template Numerical Toolkit, An Interface for Scientific Computing in C++*. `http://math.nist.gov/tnt/`.

[445] V. TOUMAZOU, *Portraits spectraux de matrices: Un outil d'analyse de la stabilité*, Ph.D. Dissertation, Université H. Poincaré, Nancy, 1996. TH/PA/96/46, CERFACS.

[446] N. TREFETHEN, *The $100, 100-Digit Challenge*, SIAM News, 35(6) (2002).

[447] ——, *A Hundred-dollar, Hundred-digit Challenge*, SIAM News, 35(1) (2002).

[448] TRILINOS SOFTWARE PROJECT, *Trilinos software project web site*. `http://software.sandia.gov/trilinos`.

[449] K. S. TRIVEDI, *Probability & Statistics with Reliability, Queuing, and Computer Science Applications*, Prentice–Hall, Englewood Cliffs, NJ, 1982.

[450] ——, *Probability and Statistics with Reliability, Queueing and Computer Science Applications*, 2nd ed. John Wiley & Sons, New York, 2001.

[451] K. S. TRIVEDI, K. VAIDYANATHAN, AND K. GOSEVA-POPSTOJANOVA, *Modeling and analysis of software aging and rejuvenation*, in Proceedings of the 33rd Annual Simulation Symposium (SS 2000), IEEE Computer Society, Los Alamitos, CA, 2000, pp. 270–279.

[452] T. TRUCANO AND D. POST, *Guest editors' introduction: Verification and validation in computational science and engineering*, Computing in Science and Engineering, 6 (2004), pp. 8–9.

[453] K. S. TSO AND A. AVIZIENIS, *Community error recovery in N-version software: A design study with experimentation*, in Proc. IEEE 17th International Symposium on Fault-Tolerant Computing, Pittsburgh, PA, 1987, pp. 127–133.

[454] K. S. TSO, A. AVIZIENIS, AND J. P. J. KELLY, *Error recovery in multi-version software*, in Proc. IFAC SAFECOMP '86, Sarlat, France, 1986, pp. 35–41.

[455] W. TUCKER, *The Lorenz attractor exists*, C. R. Acad. Sci., Paris, Sér. I Math., 328 (1999), pp. 1197–1202.

[456] B. TUCKERMAN, *The 24th Mersenne Prime*, in Proc. Natl. Acad. Sci., USA, 68 (1971), pp. 2319–2320.

[457] J. TUPPER, *GrafEq*. `http://www.peda.com/grafeq/`.

[458] A. M. TURING, *Rounding-off errors in matrix processes*, Q. J. Mech. Appl. Math., 1 (1948), pp. 287–308.

[459] S. UPADHYAYA AND K. SALUJA, *A watchdog processor based general rollback technique with multiple retries*, IEEE Trans. Software Eng., SE-12 (1986), pp. 87–95.

[460] US-CERT, *Technical Cyber Security Alert TA04-041A, Multiple Vulnerabilities in Microsoft ASN.1 Library*, 2004. February 10. `http://www.us-cert.gov/cas/techalerts/TA04-041A.html`.

[461] P. VAN HENTENRYCK, P. MICHEL, AND Y. DEVILLE, *Numerica: A Modelling Language for Global Optimization*, MIT Press, Cambridge, MA, 1997.

[462] VAULTS OF PARNASSUS, *Web site with Python resources.* `http://www.vex.net/parnassus`.

[463] T. L. VELDHUIZEN, *Blitz++: The library that thinks it is a compiler*, in Advances in Software Tools for Scientific Computing, E. Arge, A. M. Bruaset, and H. P. Langtangen, eds., Springer-Verlag, New York, 1999, pp. 57–88.

[464] T. L. VELDHUIZEN AND M. E. JERNIGAN, *Will C++ be faster than Fortran?* in Scientific Computing in Object-Oriented Parallel Environments, Y. Ishikawa, R. R. Oldehoeft, J. V. W. Reynders, and M. Tholburn, eds., Lecture Notes in Comput. Sci., Springer-Verlag, New York, 1997, pp. 49–56.

[465] B. VENNERS, *A Conversation with Guido van Rossum*, Artima.com, (2002). `http://www.artima.com/intv`.

[466] F. M. VERZUH, *The solution of simultaneous linear equations with the aid of the 602 calculated punch*, M.T.A.C., 3 (1949), pp. 453–462.

[467] J. VIGNES, *A stochastic arithmetic for reliable scientific computation*, Math. Comput. Simulation, 35 (1993), pp. 233–261.

[468] J. VOAS, K. KANOUN, J. DUGAN, L. HATTON, AND M. VOUK, *Fault-tolerance—roundtable*, IEEE Software, 18 (2001), pp. 54–47.

[469] U. VOGES, *Software Diversity in Computerized Control Systems*, Dependable Computing and Fault-Tolerant Systems 2, A. Avizienis, H. Kopetz, and J. C. Laprie, eds., Springer-Verlag, Wien, New York, 1987.

[470] M. A. VOUK, *On engineering of fault-tolerant software*, in 10th International Symposium "Computer at the University," Cavtat, Croatia, 1988.

[471] ———, *Software reliability engineering*, 1998. A tutorial presented at the 1998, 1999, and 2000 Annual Reliability and Maintainability Symposiums, Anaheim, CA, January 1998; Washington, DC, January 1999; Los Angeles, January 2000.

[472] M. A. VOUK, D. F. MCALLISTER, AND K. C. TAI, *Identification of correlated failures of fault-tolerant software systems*, in Proc. IEEE COMPSAC '85, Chicago, IL, 1985, pp. 437–444.

[473] M. A. VOUK, A. PARADKAR, AND D. MCALLISTER, *Modeling execution time of multi-stage Nversion faulttolerant software*, in Proc. IEEE COMPSAC '90, 1990, pp. 505–511. Reprinted in Fault-Tolerant Software Systems: Techniques and Applications, Hoang Pham, eds. IEEE Computer Society, Los Alamitos, CA, 1992, pp. 55–61.

[474] M. A. VOUK AND K. C. TAI, *Some issues in multi-phase software reliability modeling*, in Proc. IBM CASCON '93, Toronto, ON, Canada, October 1993, pp. 513–523.

[475] G. W. WALSTER, *Philosophy and practicalities of interval arithmetic*, in Reliability in Computing, R. E. Moore, ed., Academic Press, San Diego, 1988, pp. 309–323.

[476] ———, *Widest-need expression processing*. http://wwws.sun.com/software/sundev/whitepapers/widest-need.pdf, 1999.

[477] ———, *Implementing the "simple" closed interval system*. http://wwws.sun.com/software/sundev/whitepapers/closed.pdf, 2000.

[478] G. W. WALSTER, E. R. HANSEN, AND J. D. PRYCE, *Extended real intervals and the topological closure of extended real relations*. http://wwws.sun.com/software/sundev/whitepapers/extended-real.pdf, 2000.

[479] M. WARMUS, *Calculus of approximations*, Bulletin de L'Academie Polonaise des Sciences, IV (1956), pp. 253–259.

[480] ———, *Approximations and inequalities in the calculus of approximations. Classification of approximate numbers*, Bulletin de L'Academie Polonaise des Sciences, IX (1961), pp. 241–245.

[481] D. WEBER-WULFF, *Rounding error changes parliament makeup*, The Risks Digest, 13 (1992). http://catless.ncl.ac.uk/Risks/13.37.html#subj4.

[482] R. C. WHALEY, A. PETITET, AND J. J. DONGARRA, *Automated empirical optimization of software and the ATLAS project*, Parallel Comput., 27 (2001), pp. 3–25.

[483] J. H. WILKINSON, *Error analysis of floating point computation*, Numer. Math., 2 (1960), pp. 219–340.

[484] J. H. WILKINSON, *Error analysis of direct methods of matrix inversion*, J. ACM, 8 (1961), pp. 281–330.

[485] ———, *Rounding Errors in Algebraic Processes*, Notes on Applied Science, 32, HMSO, London, 1963. (Also published by Prentice–Hall, Englewood Cliffs, NJ, 1964, translated into Polish as Bledy Zaokraglen w Procesach Algebraicznych by PWW, Warsaw, Poland, 1967, and translated into German as Rundungsfehler by Springer-Verlag, Berlin, Germany, 1969. Reprinted by Dover, New York, 1994.)

[486] ———, *The Algebraic Eigenvalue Problem*, Oxford University Press, Oxford, U.K., 1965. (Also translated into Russian by Nauka, Russian Academy of Sciences, 1970.)

[487] ——, *The perfidious polynomial*, in Studies in Numerical Analysis, Volume 24, G. H. Golub, ed., The Mathematical Association of America, Washington, DC, 1984, pp. 1–28. (Awarded the Chauvenet Prize of the Mathematical Association of America.)

[488] ——, *The state of the art in error analysis*, NAG Newsletter, 2/85 (1985), pp. 5–28. (Invited lecture for the NAG 1984 Annual General Meeting.)

[489] ——, *Error analysis revisited*, IMA Bulletin, 22 (1986), pp. 192–200. (Invited lecture at Lancaster University in honor of C. W. Clenshaw, 1985.)

[490] J. H. WILKINSON AND C. REINSCH, eds., *Handbook for Automatic Computation, Vol. 2, Linear Algebra*, Springer-Verlag, Berlin, Germany, 1971.

[491] S. WOLFRAM, *The Mathematica Book, Fifth Edition*, Wolfram Media, Champaign, IL, 2003. http://www.wolfram.com/.

[492] A. WRIGHT, *On Sapphire and Type-Safe Languages*, Communications of the ACM, 46 (2003), p. 120. http://portal.acm.org/citation.cfm?id=641237 (requires a subscription).

[493] S. J. WRIGHT, *A collection of problems for which Gaussian elimination with partial pivoting is unstable*, SIAM J. Sci. Comput., 14(1) (1993), pp. 231–238.

[494] P. WU, S. MIDKIFF, J. MOREIRA, AND M. GUPTA, *Efficient support for complex numbers in Java*, in Proceedings of the ACM 1999 Conference on Java Grande, ACM, New York, 1999, pp. 109–118.

[495] M. XIE, *Software Reliability Modeling*, World Scientific, Singapore, 1991.

[496] S. YAMADA, J. HISHITANI, AND S. OSAKI, *Software-reliability growth with Weibull test-effort: A model and application*, IEEE Trans. Reliability, R-42 (1993), pp. 100–106.

[497] S. YAMADA, M. OHBA, AND S. OSAKI, *S-shaped reliability growth modeling for software error detection*, IEEE Trans. Reliability, R-32 (1983), pp. 475–478.

[498] K. YAMAMURA, *An algorithm for representing nonseparable functions by separable functions*, IEICE Trans. Fundamentals, E79-A (1996), pp. 1051–1059.

[499] D. YANG, *C++ and Object Oriented Numeric Computing for Scientists and Engineers*, Springer-Verlag, New York, 2001.

[500] J. M. YOHE, *Interval analysis comes of age*, SIAM News, 13 (1980), p. 1, 8.

[501] R. C. YOUNG, *The algebra of multi-valued quantities*, Mathematische Annalen, 104 (1931), pp. 260–290.

[502] P. E. ZADUNAISKY, *On the estimation of errors propagated in the numerical integration of ordinary differential equations*, Numer. Math., 27 (1976), pp. 21–39.

Index

absolute error, 21, 36, 73, 114, 115
accuracy, accurate, 3, 7, 9–11, 13, 14, 17,
        21–23, 31, 35–37, 40–42, 48,
        49, 54–56, 70, 71, 73–75, 82,
        84, 96, 98, 99, 101, 108, 110,
        111, 123, 125, 126, 128, 130,
        133–135, 140, 158, 175, 176,
        185, 186, 190, 191, 202–204,
        211, 214, 219, 220, 227, 228,
        237, 238, 250, 251, 253, 254,
        257, 260, 265, 270, 271, 284–
        287, 289, 298
Ada, 125–128, 131–136, 138, 153, 178
Algol, 178
APL, 145

backward compatible, 20, 165
backward error, 60–63, 71, 74, 75, 88, 89,
        97–99, 101, 105, 106
backward stable, 63, 65, 66, 95, 228, 230
Bayesian inference, 32
benchmark, 27, 31, 158–161

C, 125, 126, 128, 133, 135–150, 152–
        154, 156, 158, 159, 161–171,
        178, 179, 221, 260, 262, 286
C++, 126, 136, 138, 140, 142–150, 153–
        155, 159, 162–171, 173, 178,
        179, 186, 190, 194, 262
C#, 166
Cobol, 135
code verification, 15–17, 24, 26, 27, 30
compiler, 9, 24, 25, 46, 126, 128, 131–
        133, 135, 136, 138–149, 156,
        157, 159, 163, 173, 177–180,
        183–186, 189–191, 193, 202,

        221, 222, 246, 247, 254, 260,
        262
component testing, 25
convergence rate, 29, 220
convergence testing, 29
convergent, 5, 14, 15, 23, 28–30, 82, 85,
        87, 91, 99, 181, 191, 220
CPU, central processing unit, 28, 170,
        171, 222, 241–244, 246, 247,
        249, 260, 267, 271

design of experiments, 25, 31
divergence portrait, 100
dynamic code analysis, 24

error, 4, 5, 10, 11, 17–19, 24–27, 29, 30,
        32, 36–38, 40, 42, 43, 45, 96,
        126, 130, 133, 137–139, 141,
        143–146, 151, 154, 155, 161,
        165, 167, 174–177, 180, 182,
        186, 190, 196, 197, 199, 200,
        202, 210, 229, 230, 237, 238,
        242, 259, 260, 262, 267, 268,
        271, 285–287, 290, 291, 293,
        295, 298
    absolute, 21, 36, 37, 73, 114, 115
    backward, 60–63, 71, 74, 75, 88, 89,
        97–99, 101, 105, 106, 108
    bound, 69–73, 75, 89, 95, 97, 102,
        132, 177, 203, 204
    control, 110
    conversion, 10, 19, 217
    estimate, 30, 32, 38, 40, 42, 202
    forward, 60, 62, 63, 71, 75, 89, 99,
        213, 295
    function, 197
    global, 109, 111, 112, 115, 116, 118

335